MIRRORS OF THE MIND

Ronald J. Manheimer

MIRRORS OF THE MIND

Reflecting on Philosophers' Autobiographies

JORVIK
PRESS

ISBN-10: 0988412284
ISBN-13: 978-0-9884122-8-6

Library of Congress Catalog No: 2014947062

Cover design: Keith Carlson

First edition

Jorvik Press
PMB 424, 5331 SW Macadam Ave., Ste. 258,
Portland OR 97239
JorvikPress.com

ABOUT THE AUTHOR

Ronald J. Manheimer holds a PhD from the History of Consciousness interdisciplinary graduate program of the University of California at Santa Cruz, where his dissertation on the Danish philosopher and theologian, Søren Kierkegaard, led to publication by the University of California Press of his book, *Kierkegaard as Educator* (1977). In 2003, an award-winning Korean translation of this book appeared with a new introduction by the author.

Manheimer has taught at UC Santa Cruz, San Diego State University, The Evergreen State College (Olympia, Washington), Wayne State University (Detroit), the Smithsonian, and the University of North Carolina at Asheville, where until his retirement in 2009 he held a joint appointment as Research Associate Professor of Philosophy and executive director of the NC Center for Creative Retirement.

In his *A Map to the End of Time: Wayfarings with Friends and Philosophers* (Norton, 1999), Manheimer demonstrates the fruitfulness of combining dual interests in philosophy and narrative studies. This work has been translated into Chinese and Korean.

Manheimer has taught courses on philosophers' autobiographies at both the university and adult education levels.

ACKNOWLEDGMENTS

My gratitude goes to the many students who have read portions of this book in its evolution and responded to its writing assignments, while showing me ways to enliven and clarify the work's conceptual approach. We explored philosophers' autobiographies in classrooms that include the Smithsonian Associates Program in Washington, D.C., the University of North Carolina at Asheville, University of California, Santa Cruz, The Little Schoolhouse in Nors, Denmark, the Thurston County Senior Center and the Evergreen State College in Olympia, Washington.

Many colleagues and friends have shared this journey with me, foremost my roommate in graduate school, Harry R. (Rick) Moody. A late-night debate over whether philosophers actually lived according to their ideas led us to teach a first college course in Philosophical Autobiography. My wife Gail has provided enthusiastic support and encouragement to sustain my energies to bring this book to fulfillment. And my editor and publisher, Peter Stansill, has shown uncommon guidance, care and attention to detail, rare qualities in today's publishing world.

Thanks also to Denise Snodgrass and Eric Weinberger who reviewed proofs of the book and made valuable editorial suggestions.

To all these individuals and institutions I extend my deepest appreciation, recognizing that whatever shortcomings the book may have are a product of my own limitations.

Ronald J. Manheimer, Ph.D.
Asheville NC 28804

To my teachers,
George and Finvola Drury,
who guided me to the threshold
of philosophy and poetry

CONTENTS

1

THE MALKOVICH TRANSFORMATIONS

The protagonist in the 1999 fantasy film *Being John Malkovich* is Craig Schwartz, an out of work puppeteer. One day Craig discovers a hidden doorway behind some cabinets in an office building where he has landed a temporary job as a filing clerk. Intrigued, he crawls into what seems to be a damp tunnel. Suddenly the entry door slams shut behind him and Craig is hurtled through a space-time vortex that thrusts him into the mind of the film's namesake, actor John Malkovich.

Later, back in the office, Craig tells the story of his amazing experience to his coworker, the opportunistic Maxine. She speculates that other people might be willing to pony up for a brief sojourn in a famous person's head. They place a newspaper ad and soon people are lining up at the portal after work hours with cash in hand. Delivered through the tunnel, the mind travelers delight in experiencing the world through the eyes of a celebrity, even if he is engaged in such mundane activities as ordering towels over the phone, rehearsing lines for a play or flagging down a taxi.

These mind trips are short-lived. The eavesdroppers are again sent flying through the vortex only to come tumbling down into a ditch beside the New Jersey turnpike just outside the Holland Tunnel. Craig retrieves the dazed travelers and guides them back home. These mind ventures seem to have an effect like travel to a foreign country. The sojourners not only have a vicarious experience of another person's life, they also gain new insights into the existence from which they were temporarily extracted.

Summing up the experience, Craig exclaims to Maxine: "I don't think I can go on living my life as I have lived it." For him, the journey "raises all sorts of philosophical questions about the nature of self, about the existence of the soul."

What we might call the Malkovichian transformation is an exaggeration, or perhaps even a parody, of what can occur when we read a work of fiction, watch a play, study a painted or photographed portrait, or participate in other acts of the imagination. We are released from our current preoccupations and drawn into the life and times of other human beings. We may feel the guilt of Dostoevsky's Raskolnikov, the sorrow of Shakespeare's Ophelia, the joy of the figures in Matisse's painting, The Dance. Characters and scenes stay with us as if etched in memory and come back to us, unexpectedly, in times of struggle or triumph or boredom.

Though it is not quite like reading a novel or looking at a painting, delving into the autobiographical works of individuals who have made the life of the mind their central preoccupation – certain highly influential philosophers – can produce something along the lines of the Malkovichian transformation, triggering for us, as it did for Craig Schwartz, important questions about "the nature of the self, existence of the soul." How this might happen can be found in Danish philosopher and religious thinker Søren Kierkegaard's account of his literary strategy in his 1848 auto-biography, *The Point of View for My Work as an Author*.

KIERKEGAARD PLAYS MALKOVICH

In this autobiographical essay, Kierkegaard explains that in many of the books he wrote under pseudonyms he intentionally set out to lure readers into philosophical perplexities by creating conflicts of beliefs, attitudes, values, even theological positions, leaving it to the reader, as he has one of his pseudonyms exclaim, "to put two and two together." In this way, Kierkegaard provides a mirror to the reader's own confusions and uncertainties.

Aligning himself with a great educative tradition stretching back to Socrates, Kierkegaard argues that only through a process of "personal appropriation" would compelling truths about how we lead our lives have meaning and value. Teaching us to think abstractly about ideas is inade-quate unless we can make use of these ideas, consider them part of our own experiences, subject them to critical analysis, measure them against both familiar and unexpected circumstances, in short, become what Kierke-gaard dubbed an "existential thinker." In his novelistic work, *Either/Or*, he has one of his characters, Judge Wilhelm, insist in a letter to his young poet friend "only the truth that edifies is truth for you." Advancing a Socratic position, Wilhelm asserts you have to not only "know yourself" but also tackle the equally difficult task: to "become yourself."

Aiming to promote individual authenticity in an era of emerging Euro-pean mass societies, Kierkegaard uses the term "enabling dialectic" to sum up his literary-philosophical strategy. By engaging us in a conflict of diverg-ing viewpoints, he invites us to go through the inventions of his literary and philosophical mind to discover our own inner truths. These truths are not arbitrary. Kierkegaard, like every philosophical autobiographer, has an agenda, a direction in which he seeks to guide his readers. Still, were he alive today and had he seen the Malkovich movie, Kierkegaard would assent to a similar journey of transformation – not for you to become another Kierkegaard but, though standing dazed and disoriented outside the Holland Tunnel, to become yourself.

Each of the philosophical autobiographies to be encountered in this book possesses an "enabling dialectic" because each seeks to communicate transformative moments brought about through choices, challenges and crises. Consistent with the authors' philosophical ideas, each self-reflective narrative would take a different form that might "enable" the receptive reader to actively participate in a journey that not only retraces but also reenacts discoveries in the life of the mind of that thinker. As a genre, these philosophical autobiographies themselves have a history.

Philosophers who chose to write autobiographically belong to a unique tradition that can be traced to an ancient and seminal figure. Writing in the fourth century of the Common Era, Augustine, Bishop of Hippo, put forth an early and remarkably candid first-person narrative, the *Confessions*. He reflected not only on his life experiences but also on the capacity that makes writing an autobiography possible – the function of memory, the powers of the mind and the nature of the soul. He is in awe of the very process he's undertaken. Augustine discovers he possesses an ability to investigate what he calls "the palace of memory," one that is "large and boundless." He wants to understand how the mind can interrogate itself and yet never fully encompass itself. Are we not, he wonders, a mystery to ourselves? And in a literary crescendo that comes at the end of his contemplations, he proclaims: "A great admiration rises upon me; astonishment seizes me."

How should we understand the nature of memory and personhood? How should we understand the identity of the one who remembers relative to the one who is remembered as having had a certain experience? Augustine is so enthralled with these questions that he adds several chapters to his autobiography. In them he speculates on the nature of memory, time and language. From the very origins of the autobiographical form initiated by a philosophical mind arise critical reflections on the very possibility of writing about oneself.

We find similar concerns in the 18th century Swiss-born visionary, Jean-Jacques Rousseau who, with an ironic nod to Augustine, also entitled his autobiography *Confessions*. When Rousseau remembers childhood punishments, youthful love affairs, and political crises of his adult life, he asks: When we remember love, hate, fear, anger or joy, do we re-experience those emotions or only the idea of having had them? Can we know that the remembered emotional past is really the way it was or only the way it now seems?

It's clear that when philosophers set out to write first-person narratives, they cannot help but to ponder epistemological problems that other autobiographers may take for granted. Insofar as their lives are the fabric of their work, their narratives form the weave of the philosophical autobiography.

In the philosophical autobiographies we will be considering, we are going to encounter reflections on the very foundation of ideas that would support and lend shape to an autobiography: theories of selfhood, memory, language, identity, ways of knowing, time, causality, nature, the spiritual and the scientific. We won't find every one of these concerns expressed in every autobiography of the philosophical sort but, as good detectives, we will find several in all of them. Not always explicitly stated, these concerns will sometimes be inferred between the lines as the philosopher points us to other places in his or her writings. Pursuing clues in this Malkovichian manner, we will have our moments of discovery, seeing the philosopher's world from the inside out.

PLACES IN THE MIND

Each philosophical autobiography that we are about to encounter will be found to contain one or more depictions of a place or space that functions as a metaphor or allegory of self-change. Each serves the autobiographer as a conceptual construction in which the interplay of what changes and what endures is played out. These places in the mind take many forms.

For example, gardens figure prominently for the scripturally oriented Augustine. In Book 9 of the *Confessions*, Augustine describes a conversation with his mother, Monica, while the two are standing together on the second-floor inner balcony of a friend's house in the port city of Ostia. There, awaiting the ship that will take them home to North Africa, they are gazing down into a central garden. His account is of a conversation that moves from perceptions of the immediate physical environment to conceptual ideas, then to awareness of the functioning of the mind itself, and beyond that to an experience of what lay above the human mind – the realm of a timeless, divine intelligence. Moving from what is below to what is above, Augustine invites his reader to make a similar ascent, one that aims to reconcile Greek philosophy with Christian metaphysics.

The French philosopher Jean-Paul Sartre, in *The Words*, describes the setting of childhood within the rooms of the bourgeois family household of his maternal grandparents, where he lives with his mother. Listening to a conversation around the dining room table, he comes to the shocking realization that a child is little more than the mirrored projections of the adults around him. Dismayed, he vows to renounce these projections by reinventing himself through an imaginative use of language. Making up heroic tales, the little Sartre opens a path to his future – he becomes a story-teller. His first experiments with writing as an act of self-formation will lead to his famous claim: "Existence precedes essence."

Gandhi, the Indian activist and philosopher recounts in *My Experiment with Truth* that he wrote its chapters episodically during his two years in the Yeravda prison following his conviction for civil disobedience against the British Crown then ruling India. While outwardly crusading against injustice, he has been trying to live inwardly in such a way as to attain *moksha* – liberation from the cycle of reincarnation through a process of self-purification and through renouncing, by means of self-control, distracting passions and pleasures.

Readers quickly realize that Gandhi's cell is a metaphor for other kinds of imprisonment – the imposed restrictions of a foreign power, the urges and impulses of the physical body, impure thoughts. This is the metaphor-ical space in which he seeks personal liberation while aiming to liberate his country and countrymen.

The choice and details of a setting may seem accidental or simply matters of fact. But by its placement into an autobiography the setting takes on special significance. Twentieth-century German philosopher Martin Heidegger understood the importance of place when he described the relationship between "building, dwelling and thinking." He pointed to the rustic farmhouses built by Black Forest peasants who, in their receptive relationship to their surroundings, located their homes below the wind-protected south-facing summit of a woodland vale, close to a natural spring; making sure that its overhanging shingle roof had just the right slope to "bear up under the burden of snow." The interior, says Heidegger, would include "the altar corner behind the community table, the childbed and the place for coffins."

For Heidegger, the way the peasants situated themselves was practical and profound. Attunement to weather, faith, family, work, life and death, they "let earth and heaven, divinities and mortals enter in simple oneness into things." For Heidegger, these peasants reveal how it is to be at home on the earth. He intimates that when it comes to thinking, philosophers should seek a similar simplicity and oneness of being.

By placing their transformative life experiences into the settings of rooms, gardens, country and mountain paths, cafes and prisons, philo-sophical autobiographers show how they dwelled in thought. Few were as harmoniously situated as Heidegger's peasants. Theirs was often a search-ing, sometimes wandering way of dwelling.

Through its stage setting the philosophical autobiography gives us a picture of how an important thinker lived. But should anyone with an interest in philosophy really care? Consider that Heidegger, in a work on Aristotle, said of the ancient philosopher that he lived and died in a certain place during a certain time, which is all we need to know about his life. Only the credibility of Aristotle's thoughts should concern us.

IMPERSONAL TRUTHS

Philosophical autobiographies raise many red flags for the academic philosopher. For one, scholarly critics will object that the specifics of a philosopher's life have traditionally not been considered especially relevant to the veracity of their ideas and concepts. These have to stand or fall on their own merits. When philosophers do occasionally fall back on examples from their personal lives, it is usually to support or exemplify some broader truth. Consider the famous scene in Plato's dialogue, *Phaedo*, where Socrates, when released from his prison shackles, begins a discourse on how frequently opposites such as pleasure and pain occur together. Generally, philosophers adhere to an unstated yet implicit rule: "Do not obscure the impersonal truth with the incidental details of your personal existence."

Second, references to how philosophers lived, what sort of family life they had, how and where they were educated, and so on, are generally viewed as valuable for understanding the history of philosophy and the cultural and social contexts that formed the background to a thinker's conceptual work. However, a biographical approach to the realm of philosophy could lead one to speculate that the most profound insights can be traced to the nursery, to a mother's breast or its absence, a father's harsh or soothing words, the childhood or adulthood conditions of poverty or wealth.

Once we walk this pathway, philosophy turns into psychoanalytic theory, ideas become the sublimation of unconscious wishes, and the life of the mind turns into a hall of smoke and mirrors.

To argue that there are no pertinent connections between philosophers' lives and their ideas seems an artificial and arbitrary dogma. What we need is a more useful way to frame our understanding of the relationship between impersonal and personal truths. We can find this by exploring how, in any particular life, ways of thinking, feeling, imagining and of conducting one's life are interrelated. We are not inquiring which one is the cause of the other – transitive life experiences or enduring ideas – but how the processes of becoming oneself and discovering and embracing ideas mirror each other.

Still, very few renowned thinkers have written autobiographies and those that have are almost exclusively males who grew up and lived in Western cultures. Though not whole books, a bounty of letters, diaries and journals of important philosophers, male and female, East and West, does exist in abundance, and several valuable anthologies of extracts have been assembled.

An example is Amélia Oksenburg-Rorty's anthology, *The Many Faces of Philosophy* (2003). In the introduction she cautions us that in their scholarly writings philosophers prefer "a method of demonstration to a narrative of discovery." In other words, philosophy is based on carefully reasoned arguments and logical proofs, not an appeal to personal insights and experiences. I hope to show that a small handful of influential thinkers have also employed a discovery narrative as a method of demonstration. However, the fact that a philosopher has written an autobiography does not automatically qualify it as a philosophical work.

We'll take some modern examples. Bertrand Russell's autobiography (1967) is a rich source of information about his family of origin, his education, marriages, friends and enemies, political causes and, to a certain extent, the development of his ideas. But Russell's autobiography does not challenge the reader's mind with knotty issues such as we would find in his famous little book, *Our Knowledge of the External World* (1926).

Russell does not present his autobiography as a philosophical work, does not subject it or us to the rigors of philosophical argument, or lay the work out in such a way as to take the reader through a series of logical or developmental stages. When Russell presents the scene of a life-changing, "quasi-mystical" revelation, he does not engage us in the discovery process, but rather gives us a list of his insights and life-guiding principles as if they had fallen from the sky.

The mid-20th century Harvard mathematical logician, the notable Willard Van Orman Quine, wrote an autobiography, *The Time of My Life* (1985), also detailing his family background, education, career, working habits, the stressful conflicts of his first marriage to a woman he regarded as mentally ill, his second much happier marriage, and so on. But there is scant evidence of Quine's logical brilliance in the book and no more insight shown about his relationships than we might expect from the average reflective person.

In addition to this important distinction, the genre of the philosophical autobiography is limited in several ways. Historically, we find relatively few works from women, among which we could point to the 16th century Spanish mystic and Carmelite nun St. Theresa's *The Life of St. Teresa of*

Avila by Herself (1957), Simone de Beauvoir's four memoirs, and American feminist philosopher Mary Daly's *Outercourse* (1992). Secondly, few auto-biographies of this nature are found in the Eastern tradition; notable exceptions include Medieval Sufi philosopher Al Ghazali's *The Deliverance from Error* (1999), 20th century Indian mystic Yogananda's *Autobiography of A Yogi* (1972) and Indian political crusader and national liberator Mohandas K. Gandhi's *The Story of My Experiment with Truth* (1927-29).

And thirdly, there is an insufficient range of exemplars to represent the diverse schools of thought in the philosophical tradition, raising the question whether the appeal of the autobiographical is only compatible with certain types of philosophical positions.

A fourth issue is that the vast majority of philosophers have shown little inclination to write an autobiography. Not because they were so terribly humble but because, as far as they were concerned, their personal life was no one else's business and did not affect the infallibility of their axioms and proofs. The philosophers would tend to point us down the hall to the history or literature department. Well, suppose we take that walk and open the door to the literature department's lounge. Eavesdropping, we just might find we're back not only in the domain of philosophy but in political science, too.

THE LITERARY POLITICS OF AUTOBIOGRAPHY

It is difficult to isolate the philosophical autobiography from the broader context of the genre of autobiography in general. There is much to learn about how that genre has fared in recent times, because that will influence not only how others – that is, scholarly types – have judged and reinter-preted both well-known and lesser-known autobiographies but also how contemporary readers are likely to react to these personal narratives now.

The point is that the genre of autobiography has taken quite a beating from critics of all kinds – postmodernist, psychoanalytic interpreters, Marxists, feminists, to name a few. Their criticisms and interpretations reflect major changes in our culture and consciousness. Knowing some-thing, then, about the literary legacy of autobiography will help us put things into greater perspective.

Philosophers' life stories fall within the larger genre of the literary auto-biography, a form of writing that traditionally occupied a low rung on the status ladder of literature until the middle of the 20th century. It was not that autobiographies weren't read and admired for their historical and artistic qualities; it's just that literary critics saw them mainly as a sub-category of historical writing or of biography.

Meanwhile, historians saw them as a subcategory of literature, albeit a potentially important resource for learning about a particular period or set of events. Historians would then compare the autobiographer's account of the facts with other sources. The idea that the autobiography might hold some special place, a unique niche in the realm of literature and history, came in part from the work of Georg Misch, an early 20th century German philologist, whose 1907 *History of Autobiography in Antiquity* profoundly influenced European and later – when the work was translated (1950) – English-speaking scholars.

Misch, embracing the philosophy of Hegel, was convinced that auto-biographies of significant public figures provided insight into the "spirit of the times" in which the authors lived, or what Hegel called the *Geistes-geschichte*. Publicly important or world historical figures were those through whom impersonal or universal currents of transformation in consciousness moved. For Misch, "autobiographies are bound always to be representative of their period." So what better way to capture the spirit of historical movements than to study them? An eloquent statement of Misch's view is found in his treatment of Augustine's role in a time of spiritual unrest, the disintegration of Roman domination and the rise of Christianity.

> In such epochs the making of an autobiography depends
> on how the autobiographer understands his life as a
> whole, inquiring into its direction, its ends and aims, its
> meaning. This tendency gives his autobiography a philo-
> sophical status: in dealing with his own experiences, on
> which his understanding of life is based, he brings into
> view the nature of human existence as he has learnt to
> fathom it in the course of his life's work. (1950, p.633)

Misch traces the autobiographical impulse as far back as Egyptian tomb inscriptions, from there to the stone-inscribed deeds of Babylonian and Assyrian rulers, and to other ancient examples that used the first-person mode of narration. He then works his way through Roman emperors to bishop and philosopher Augustine and finally to the late sixth century Roman Empire philosopher, Boethius. It was not until after Misch's work reached the English-speaking world that scholarly criticism began to challenge what would be regarded as his "great man" approach to auto-biography.

Those critics recognized that Misch helped to elevate certain auto-biographies into the Pantheon of high culture where they came to rest among the great novels, dramas and works of poetry considered worthy of serious study. But his approach established a narrow, elitist view of the first-person narrative that marginalized the autobiographical writings of individuals who were, based on the Mischian criteria, not significant public figures from the point of view of the mainstream historian. These would include the life narratives of women, minorities, people living under European colonial rule and the many others whose story and stature would not fit what later scholars deride as the "master narrative," the normative type of autobiography that reflects a single historical trajectory, that of the dominant classes and nations.

Breaking out of this constricted field of study and the assumptions that promoted a "canon" of the representative life narrative, contemporary scholars have revolutionized the approach to autobiography. In fact, what at first looks like literary criticism soon turns into a philosophical battleground, as big guns come to bear upon key assumptions of the humanistic tradition, including the status of the autobiographical narrative.

The early 1970s saw an outpouring of critical studies that began to challenge the great, representative public figure approach and its assumptions about the true status of the life depicted. The impact of Marxist analysis of subtle class identification, of Freud's challenge to the idea that the individual is primarily a rational actor, and linguistic insights into the power of language as a culturally coded system of meanings, all combined to cast doubt on what had formerly passed as unquestionably given, such as the idea that each person possesses a singular, continuous, core self.

Three generations, or "waves," of literary and philosophical criticism have swept over the genre, according to scholars Sidonie Smith and Julia Watson in their *Reading Autobiography, A Guide for Interpreting Life Narratives* (2001). The great representative-man approach, typified by Misch, they now regard in retrospect as the first generation.

The second "surge" is variously traced to Belgian critic Georges Gusdorf's essay "Conditions and Limits of Autobiography" (1956) and to publication of Francis R. Hart's essay, "Notes for an Anatomy of Modern Autobiography" (1970).

Gusdorf argues that the life narrative is really an art form rather than a history. The autobiographer is not just telling the story of his or her life as if it had been frozen in time and thawed out for the purposes of the autobiography. Rather, the writing constitutes a creative revisiting and reconstructing of the past in the present. The work delivers up a cultural artifact that, if successful, reveals the consciousness of the writer and his or her ability to shape "the unity of a life across time."

An implication here is that the autobiographer does not have privileged or direct access to the past, as someone like Misch would assume, but that even these life experiences are imaginatively refashioned through the powers of memory to reconfigure earlier experience in light of subsequent ones. All recollection is then interpretation, a reevaluating looking-back from some present that is in continuous dynamic interaction with the past. The autobiographer's art is to capture that process in all its richness and complexity.

Following out the implications of Gusdorf's work, James Olney demonstrates that the multiple forms autobiographies take reflect multiple modes of self-understanding and interpretation. In his *Metaphors of Self: The Meaning of Autobiography* (1972) he asserts that, at its core, meaning is a human projection, a function of the "metaphorizing imagination." For Olney, those who search for laws and forms independent of human construction ultimately discover a "man-in-the-moon" mirror image of their own minds rather than an independent reality. Olney's mirror to the mind of the maker is his metaphor for the autobiographer in action.

Hart's critical analysis of autobiography focuses on the variety of forms or categories that reflect the autobiographer's intentions: the confession, the apology, and the memoir. Self-reflective narrators set out to address certain projected readers and, depending on what the authors aim to achieve, choose different ways to enact that communication, preferring one manner of discourse, or voice, rather than another. In an essay appearing in 1989, French critic Philippe Lejeune calls this rhetoric of engagement an "autobiographical pact" that the writer aims to establish with the reader.

While individuality and greatness remain enshrined in the theoretical approaches to autobiography of these two scholars (e.g. Gusdorf is a big fan of the famous Enlightenment thinker Rousseau's), their work shifts attention to autobiography as a source of not factual but fictional truth. They help to open the doors of doubt, leading to further suspicion about the stability of the narrating self and narrated subject, the role of imagination and not simply memory, and the political and ideological investments that autobiographies make in trying to persuade readers to accept the perspectives and values of the writers.

Further exploring the philosophical foundations of autobiography, Karl Weintraub, in *The Value of the Individual: Self and Circumstance in Autobiography* (1978), traces the expanded prominence of the genre toward the end of the 18th century to the rise of a new mode of self-conception – that of "unique and unrepeatable individuality." For Weintraub the increasing popularity of the secular autobiography, for both writers and readers, is a reflection of ideologies that emphasize the importance of the individual citizen and the variety, not uniformity, of individual lives. Like Gusdorf, he regards autobiography as a product of the distinctly Western mind, a Christian-influenced, apocalyptic oriented mentality in which is ingrained the notion that history is the progressive movement toward some *telos* or culmination point and that we individuals (but not just Westerners) are carried in that movement as microcosms of the larger historical development.

If the second generation of criticism makes autobiography a psychologically richer and philosophically more complex literary form, the third generation makes it seem as analytically difficult to achieve as the oddly shaped bumble bee to fly. Critics belonging to this "third wave," writing in the 1970s and 80s see the autobiography as a "practice of subjectivity" so severed from the old anchors – historical fact, singular, immutable selfhood, universality, male superiority, linguistically neutral representation, and unity of meaning – that one might assume the genre of the autobiography has collapsed in upon itself.

In their eyes, autobiography is an act of theatrical-like "performance" that is creative of an idealized projected character with whose likeness the narrator would like to be identified (Bruss, 1976). In this way the autobiographical writer is an "impersonator" (Renza, 1977) who, in carefully selecting what to tell, both hides and reveals simultaneously.

Taking this a step further, for French critic Paul de Man (1979) the autobiographer is actually invented by the medium of language itself, since it is only within the established pathways of culturally encoded, linguistic norms of self-representation that one knows how to present oneself. This realization will, in turn, produce the anti-autobiography, such as the case of Roland Barthes whose intentionally fragmented narrative, *Roland Barthes* (1977), dissolves the certainty of self-knowing.

Still another take on the status of the autobiography is found in French philosopher and critic Jacques Derrida's (1974) analysis of Rousseau's *Confessions* (among others) that the narrator may declare overtly "what he wishes to say," while also revealing "what he does not wish to say." In other words, the autobiographer directly asserts certain claims about his or her role in events, certain theoretical discoveries, certain principles of life, but in giving readers descriptive accounts of scenes and relationships and related ideas and emotions, readers sense a contradictory truth coming to the surface.

Adding to this challenge, the reader may also find contradictions between the autobiographical work's claims and assertions and those stated in philosophical works by the same author. Is one version to be preferred over the other; if so, on what grounds? For Derrida the act of interpretation falls within the texts themselves. There is no "real" independent historical figure to which we can appeal to learn a final truth about the life of the autobiographer. However, if our goal is to understand the meanings that the autobiographer ascribes to his or her life, then we must, so to speak, enter into the narrative by investing our own seeking after meaning.

Prominent within this third wave of critical theory, scholarly works in women's studies seek to reveal the male preponderance of the first-person narrative as characterized by a preoccupation with reporting the author's progressive achievements – in other words, the genre is dominated by male narcissistic narrators whose stories, stripped of their niceties, amount to a lot of chest-pounding. They point to the distinctly different genre of the female autobiography in which concern for others and the richness of relationships find a more prominent place in the narrative. The relationship-oriented female narrator is echoed in the developmental theory of Carol Gilligan whose *In a Different Voice* (1982) challenged as gender-biased the then-predominant theories of developmental stages.

An arena in which a parallel debate occupies feminist, postmodernist, structuralist and minority studies scholars is the debate over the *bildungs-roman*, the novelistic form emerging in the 18th century in which a heroic narrative tells the story (*roman*) of a usually male character's passage through a series of developmental (*bildung*) stages through to the completion (or failure) of a heroic life task.

In a study of the female version of the *bildungsroman*, Pin-chia Feng (1998) traces the autobiographical elements in the autobiographical works of novelists Toni Morrison and Maxine Hong Kingston, arguing that, though in need of reformation, the genre still has life in a post-bourgeois, postmodern, multicultural world. Autobiography does not have to be the egoist's favorite genre, its uses can be turned toward the communal and in service of cultural and political critiques, she argues.

Stripped of its pretenses, privileges and presumptions, autobiography becomes "performance," an imaginative act of self-representation in which one knows or at least suspects he or she is pretending to be the same person telling the story as the subject told about. The telling or narrative is dependent on culturally approved or established norms ("master narratives") that are so ingrained that author and reader are both unaware of them.

Only those who have felt the pain of exclusion – enslaved peoples, marginalized classes and ethnic groups, social outcasts, those labeled as deviants, and so on – may be aware of these preconscious assumptions and constructions because they have lived outside of them. Given the chance to tell their stories, they must invent new forms; find new voices to gain audibility in the culture. In the past thirty years, the genre of the auto- biography has burst open with renewed attention to the vast collection of African-American slave narratives, narratives of survivors of genocide, abused children, political exiles, former hospital and prison inmates, prostitutes, gay and lesbian writers and myriad others who would not have qualified for serious consideration under the Mischian criteria of repre- sentative world historical figure.

CONTEMPORARY PHILOSOPHERS' ATTITUDES

But what do philosophers themselves have to say about autobiography? While literary scholars, first Continental and then Anglo-American, have turned into philosophical critics of autobiography, given their traditional indifference to the autobiographical, few contemporary philosophers have explicitly addressed the relationship between philosophy and auto- biography.

A seminal contribution that aims to rescue philosophers' auto- biographies from reductionist psychoanalytic theory and to elevate philos- ophers' rational reflection and efforts of self-determination comes from Schlomit C. Schuster's dissertation and subsequent book, *The Philoso- pher's Autobiography: A Qualitative Study* (2003). Taking a position counter to the third-wave approach to autobiography, trained in philosophy and psychology, Schuster focuses her attention on the capabilities of the mature mind and its rich psychological makeup.

Her brilliant, systematic genre study credits thinkers as diverse as Augustine, Sartre and Bertrand Russell with genuine self-insight and authentic engagement in the history of their times. Still, as Schuster acknowledges, some philosophers exhibit a sharp dichotomy between their professional and personal lives.

What will probably seem strange to readers unfamiliar with currents in contemporary academic philosophy is that there are several recent auto- biographies written by philosophers who proudly declare that while they want to share the "excitement and passion of the subject" – pursuing philosophy – theirs will be strictly an "intellectual autobiography," one that sharply limits commentary on their personal life except for events, influences, and relationships that have been central to an academic career (McGinn, 2002).

These kinds of intellectual, career-development narratives give the reader a view of the philosopher's "mental furniture" – the then-current hot issues with which certain schools of philosophy were preoccupied, such as theories concerning determinism, the relationship between mind and brain, the concept of necessity, whether human minds can comprehend reality directly, and so on. In these academic philosophers' auto-biographies, one gets the sense that the lived personal life ran parallel to, but never seriously intersected with, the life of the mind – aside from intellectual rivalries and departmental politics (Honderich, 2001).

An important exception is found in Harvard philosopher Stanley Cavell. In his *A Pitch of Philosophy* (1994), Cavell writes about the events in his youth that turned him from pursuing a career as a classical music composer (hence the allusion to musical "pitch") to finding his voice as a professional philosopher (the allusion to "pitching" ideas).

Cavell speculates that for philosophy and autobiography, "each is a dimension of the other," because "each life is exemplary of all, a parable of each." Does this sound like Misch's "representative" or great man theory of autobiography, now with a democratic twist that makes it more inclusive? Cavell does believe that "the autobiographical dimension of philosophy is internal to the claim that philosophy speaks for the human, for all; that is its necessary arrogance." Going counter to the postmodern trend, he finds that each life story represents something universal to all other lives and that storytelling is our legitimate claim on a way of seeing the world. In fact, we cannot help making this claim since, consciously or not, each of us is carrying the banner of some personal quest and there are only so many quests to be championed.

Cavell uses the term "arrogation" to describe the mix of prerogative, ascription, and the right to claim a position and give it voice. He draws on the Transcendentalist philosopher and poet Emerson who famously pro-claimed that if a thinker pursues his or her most personal "presentiments" (inklings, intuitions, ideas) far enough, he or she would arrive at something that transcends the purely subjective. Whether he or she will thereby speak "for the human, for all," or only for those who happen to identify with the ideas and experiences of the writer or speaker, though that is perhaps a great many, remains to be seen.

"A great many" doesn't quite get us to what Kant would call the "neces-sarily and universally true" but it does give us the idea of each life as a parable, a symbolic story with far reaching implications that link us to the lives of others. We will find a similar sentiment in the opening pages of the second volume of Simone de Beauvoir's memoir, *The Prime of Life* (1962).

Anyone who writes honestly about his or her life, she assures us while reassuring herself, cannot help but to "illuminate the lives of others." De Beauvoir's task, she tells us, is to "find out now or never" a "pattern" in her life that she believes will come to light if she lays out the fabric of her experiences, thoughts, choices, relationships and actions. Implied, though in very different ways, by Cavell and de Beauvoir is the expectation that the autobiographical narrative will reveal a pattern, a parable, a framework of ideas that helps to shape the meaning and quality of life. Is there practical value in what may at first seem like a mainly self-memorializing activity? Would anyone so inclined find value in giving form to a philosophical autobiography?

TAKING UP THE CHALLENGE

An answer comes from Charles Taylor, the McGill University philosopher whose influential study, *Sources of the Self: The Making of the Modern Identity* (1989), provides an analysis of the philosophical roots of modern ideas of identity. Taylor argues that without a framework within which to think, feel and judge what actions and choices are to be preferred, we fall into a life that is spiritually senseless. Taylor regards such senselessness as a malaise of our time.

By contrast, those who have such a framework possess what he calls a "moral ontology," a commitment to some end, such as human dignity, love of God, the attainment of freedom, striving for social justice, or a search for personal salvation. The quest for such a framework, Taylor implies, is a goal shared by more than an elite few. And this may account, in part, for the wide acclaim of his study of the modern self and perhaps for the enormous popularity of first-person narratives such as autobiography, memoir and letters, for it is in these that we often find the pattern of convictions.

Turning from reading philosophical autobiographies to writing one may be like the shift in studying a foreign language. You cannot acquire a language passively by simply learning the rules for how to decline a verb or construct a sentence. At some point, you have to start using the language. That is why students frequently find they learn more in a few months about how to use a language by living among its speakers than from years of classroom study. Moreover, they may also find they project a somewhat different personality in their new language.

To help the adventurous try their own hands at writing a philosophical autobiography I have included writing exercises in each chapter, designed so that readers might get a feel for what each philosophical autobiographer sought to accomplish. These exercises are derived in part from the methods we will find in the philosophical autobiographies explored in this book. Just trying a few of these exercises may deepen readers' appreciation of what qualifies a first-person narrative as a philosophical one.

Would the contemporary fledgling philosophical autobiographer be challenged by the second- and third-wave debates over issues of truth and authenticity, gender bias and cultural differences in the construction of a life story? Yes, implies Taylor, because these issues reflect major dilemmas of our time. There are no fixed moral ontologies, frameworks of meaning, that we can easily embrace, free of uncertainty, hesitation or downright disbelief. In other words, taking on the challenge of writing a philosophical autobiography is an act of critical self-reflection.

Finding the meaning in life is a task on everyone's agenda, according to Taylor. Had we lived in earlier, less democratic times, we might feel the heavy hand of moral authority, an inescapable weight that could quash the spirit of an independent mind. But the modern seeker's existential challenge is quite the opposite – weightlessness. In comparison to former times, little moral authority is imposed upon us. We take on our own spiritual ballast or, foregoing the quest for moral autonomy, submit ourselves to prepackaged rules and guidelines of some dominant political or religious ideology.

Reading and writing the philosophical autobiography may serve as an ideal proving ground for examining issues of meaning and identity, being and belonging, language and selfhood, ideas and actions, skepticism and belief, adaptability versus ideological inflexibility. The challenge is daunting, but the effort will be worthwhile.

In addition to reflective writing I also suggest some activities, what I am calling "philosophical fieldwork," that might help readers put themselves in the shoes of these influential thinkers, though in a present-day context. Contemplative walks, a day of fasting or an interview with a stranger become pathways into the mindset of great seekers.

BECOMING HISTORICAL TO ONESELF

If the central task of autobiography is to articulate meanings that give sense and purpose to our lives, then it falls to each of us to evaluate what makes an articulated life convincing. The point at which we become historical to ourselves, gaining awareness of the irreversible and contextual character of time and memory, is the moment our personal historical consciousness is born and with it the autobiographical self – fictive, fragmentary and multiple though it may be.

The difficulty is to capture the process of historical self-becoming rather than simply reporting the results as if the narrator always knew what was going to happen next. The most valuable philosophical self-narrators are those who can communicate the process of self-change in such a way as to inspire others. Their communicative power rests in their ability to tell a story that is at once emotional and conceptual, though not everyone need agree with their interpretations. The authors make known both the impasses they reached and the ways they found to surmount them. In reinterpreting the past perhaps they have distorted the facts so that brief moments become whole chapters or, conversely, by compressing time a few terse sentences or telling metaphors say it all. Such distortions may help to magnify the meanings of experience.

The philosophical autobiography is an excellent embodiment of a lived-in framework and a moral ontology of flesh and blood. Discovering and articulating a moral ontology, a framework for interpreting experience, is what some people seek in crafting an autobiography and in reading the life stories of others. These works are not only mirrors of the minds of great thinkers; they become mirrors to the mind of the reader.

Still, we have to be on the alert. It is exciting to read de Beauvoir telling us that writing her autobiography is going to be an adventure for her, a discovery process, and that we readers may come along and share in that experience. Of course the discovery or discoveries have already taken place, so that leaving this statement in the opening pages is again something of an "impersonation" because she is asking us to pretend that she still doesn't know what "pattern" she's going to find. But if she can convincingly make us feel that she captured the discovery process then, like a good novel, we are going to value, and feel honored by, her willingness to invite us into the café where she writes and smokes cigarettes with Sartre, or the bedroom she shares with him and, at times, with others, or the hiking paths she tramps along while thinking up ideas for her next novel or essay. We can also make our own separate discovery that de Beauvoir has indeed left out a good deal if we read one of several critical biographies that suggest the pattern she presents to the reader is rather like a jigsaw puzzle with more than a few pieces missing.

UNDER THESE COVERS

Which autobiographies will be gathered under the covers of this book and why? We have to start with Augustine's *Confessions*, without which it is impossible to understand the form and substance of subsequent auto-biographies. Whether they consciously or unconsciously emulate or seek to break with the Augustinian ur-genre, they still spring from the soil that Augustine tilled.

Next, to take advantage of our understanding of the new genre and to contrast its secular use over a thousand years later, we turn to Rousseau's rollicking and self-justifying *Confessions*. In making this historical leap, we leave out a multitude of Augustine-inspired spiritual autobiographies of the Middle Ages. There are numerous works by philosophers whose writing has an intimate quality, such as the 16th century French writer Montaigne's highly personalized *Essays*. We get a good sense of Montaigne's view of the world but we don't necessarily gain in-depth understanding of the life experiences that led him to his views.

Descartes' fascinating self-narrative of the ideally rational man, his *Discourse on Method*, is another work that marginally qualifies as a philo-sophical autobiography. Descartes tells us a little bit about his schooling and studies, his travels, and about the night of an epiphany in an "over-heated room." He even draws analogies between city planning, building houses and following the correct rules for rationally constructive thinking. But Descartes uses the first-person narrative mainly to persuade us that if we reflect along with him we will surely reach the same conclusions, regardless of our personal idiosyncrasies or life experiences.

So we will skip ahead historically to take on the great soul psychologists of the 19th century, Nietzsche and Kierkegaard. Next, we turn to John Stuart Mill and, through her letters, his Platonic partner and later wife, Harriet Taylor, the two great champions of women's suffrage and social liberty. Another duo, Simone de Beauvoir and Jean-Paul Sartre provide much modernist material that already presages the postmodernist era.

We will draw out the philosophers in Carl Jung and Mohandas Gandhi, who were certainly deeply reflective, speculative individuals inclined to metaphysical inquiry. Though Jung would claim that he was chiefly a scientist, the world disagreed. An honorary Harvard doctorate in 1936 praised him as "a philosopher who has examined the unconscious mind" (Bair, 2003).

There is another reason to include Jung. His intensely personal, theoret-ical work emphasizes the power of the unconscious as a source, a gateway to the myths and symbols of primordial experience. If Jung is correct that our conscious, external life is merely a veneer, what then becomes of the status of the philosopher's consciously reflective process and apparently rational ideas? Hopefully, Jung's autobiography will provide some answers.

Gandhi's autobiography, written mainly while he was in prison for acts of civil disobedience, captures life lessons that exemplify teaching by example. Beneath the apparent surface simplicity of Gandhi's narrative there is a profound reformulation of Hindu spiritual philosophy combined with theories of government, economics and social reform. Twentieth century Jewish philosopher Martin Buber's brief autobiography will keep relationships between people and with their deity in the forefront of our minds.

DIALOGUE AMONG THE PHILOSOPHERS

The sequence of chapters follows a rough chronology of the lifetimes of the philosophical autobiographers. However, several overlap in historical time. I have tried to arrange the order so that the background and influences of one philosopher that is important to understanding another become apparent.

For example, when Rousseau chose to title his autobiography his *Confessions*, he was clearly playing off of Augustine's work. Gandhi was familiar with John Stuart Mill and the philosophy of utilitarianism but even more so with Mill as part of the British Raj since Mill and his father both worked for the East India Company that held considerable power over the Indian people. Buber wrote an important letter to Gandhi trying to convince the Mahatma that the emerging state of Israel had a legitimate right to exist and that non-violent civil disobedience would not work in Nazi Germany. Buber was also deeply moved when in his youth he read Nietzsche's *Thus Spoke Zarathustra*. And Buber knew Jung and his wife, Emma, and attended one of the annual Jungian conferences in Switzerland in 1934. Jung taught a long running seminar on Nietzsche. Jung and Buber exchanged letters that reflect ships passing in the night. Sartre and de Beauvoir inherited the legacy of Nietzschean "transvaluation of values." Their form of radical subjectivity and existential freedom depended on Nietzsche's exaltation of the power of the will and his anti-metaphysical critiques.

In short, there are all manner of both direct and indirect connections between our philosophical autobiographers and in many cases the autobiography of one had significant influence on how another was written. I will try to bring this out as we transition from one figure to another.

Stepping into the shoes and minds of certain philosophers through their life stories is one way to go beyond a packaged whirlwind tour of philosophy that is sometimes the character of courses and books that purport to introduce us to philosophy. The approach is different from reading those simplified treatments of particular philosophers that sometimes reek of sarcasm when the author has taken the assignment for pay and has only disdain for the philosophy at hand.

What an inquiring reader wants is an acculturation process that leads to an appreciation of what a philosophical world view looks like from the inside. Then he or she can render judgment on the inhabitants and bring back whatever souvenirs are deemed memorable. Hopefully, in most cases something of value will be brought home

The book's last chapter, Uniting Contraries, aims to extract the accounts of self-change in each philosophical autobiography, compare them, and trace a common theme that runs from the first to the last.

PATHFINDING

My goal is to encourage readers to get hold of some or all of these auto-biographies and to enjoy them and take from them what they find useful. To that end, I provide links to those autobiographies that are freely accessible through the Internet and to other works that can be downloaded for a modest fee. I hope to guide readers to portals that provide access to the philosophical autobiography in question and help them find ways into places in the mind, whether that is an interior garden, a country lane or a subterranean tomb. There, I want to be the reader's pathfinder, doing so without blocking the view.

The subsequent chapters of this book will, with some necessary flexibility, adhere to the following structure. Each will:

1) Depict a central setting, a conceptual "space" or "scene" in the auto-biography that embodies and enacts self-change.

2) Enlarge upon this scene of self-change by exploring the background and the historical context in which each autobiographer lived and worked in order to better grasp the challenges each philosopher faced.

3) Show how each philosopher's theories concerning language, memory and time make the telling of his or her story a creative possibility though often with self-identified limits.

4) Educe the concept of identity that is embodied by the shape of the narrative.

5) Highlight the overall lessons we learn as readers about what it means to dwell within a uniquely structured moral universe or as Being Philosopher X.

6) Suggest ways to engage in reflective writing to explore aspects of constructing one's own philosophical autobiography and occasionally to offer

some activities that may deepen our appreciation of a philosopher's journey.

7) Provide a reader's guide to other works by the philosophical autobiographer, and in some cases to secondary sources, that allow opportunities to get further acquainted. Where journal articles cited are available online, a link will be provided.

REFERENCES

Arendt, Hannah (1999), *Deliverance from Error and Five Key Texts*. Trans. R. J. McCarthy. S.J. Louisville, KY: Fons Vitae

Bair, Deirdre (2003). *Jung. A Biography*. New York: Back Bay Books/Little Brown and Co.

Barthes, Roland (1977). *Roland Barthes*. Trans. Richard Howard. New York: Hill and Wang.

Bruss, Elizabeth (1976). *Autobiographical Acts: The Changing Situation of a Literary Genre*. Baltimore: Johns Hopkins University Press.

Cavell, Stanley (1994). *The Pitch of Philosophy: Autobiographical Exercises*. Cambridge, MA: Harvard University Press.

de Beauvoir, Simone (1962). *The Prime of Life*. Trans. Peter Green. Cleveland: World Publishing Co.

Derrida, Jacques (1974). *Of Grammatology*. Trans. Gayatri Chakravorty Spivak. Baltimore: Johns Hopkins University Press.

Descartes, René (1905). *The Meditations*. Trans. John Veitsch. Chicago: Open Court.

Feng, Pin-chia (1998). *The Female Bildungsroman by Toni Morrison and Maxine Hong Kingston, a Postmodern Reading*. Peter Lang.

Folkenflik, Robert (1993) ed. *The Culture of Autobiography: Constructions of Self-Representation*. Stanford: Stanford U. Press.

Heidegger, Martin (1971). "Building Dwelling Thinking," in Martin Heidegger, *Poetry, Language, Thought*. Trans. Albert Hofstadter. New York: Harper and Row.

Honderich, Ted (2001). *Philosopher: A Kind of Life*. London and New York: Routledge.

Lejeune, Philippe (1989) "The Autobiographical Pact," in Paul John Eakins, ed. *On Autobiography*. Trans. Katherine Leary. Minneapolis: Minnesota University Press.

McGinn, Colin (2001). *The Making of a Philosopher: My Journey through Twentieth-Century Philosophy*. New York: Harper.

Misch, Georg (1950 [original German publication, 1907]). *A History of Autobiography in Antiquity* (two volumes). London: Routledge and Kegan Paul Limited.

Olney, James (1972). *Metaphors of Self: The Meaning of Autobiography*. Princeton: Princeton University Press

_____ (1988) ed. *Studies in Autobiography*. Oxford U. Press (see especially essays by Eakin, Harpham and Bree).

Renza, Louis A. (1980). "The Veto of the Imagination: A Theory of Autobiography." In Olney, ed. *Autobiography: Essays, Theoretical and Critical*, pp. 268-295. Princeton: Princeton University Press.

Rorty, Amélia Oksenberg (2003). *The Many Faces of Philosophy*. Oxford: Oxford University Press.

Rousseau, Jean-Jacques (1782/1992). *The Reveries of the Solitary Walker*. Trans. Charles E. Butterworth. Hackett Publishing Co.

Russell, Bertrand. (1966). *The Autobiography of Bertrand Russell, 1872-1914*. London: George Allen and Unwin.

_____ (1926). *Our Knowledge of the External World as a Field for Scientific Method in Philosophy*. London: G. Allen & Unwin.

Saint Theresa of Avila (1957). *The Life of Saint Theresa of Avila by Herself*. Tr. J. M Cohen. London: Penguin Books.

Schuster, Shlomit C. (2003). *The Philosopher's Autobiography: A Qualitative Study*. New York: Praeger.

Smith, Sidonie & Watson, Julia (2001). *Reading Autobiography: A Guide for Interpreting Life Narratives*. University of Minnesota Press.

Smith, Sidonie (1993). *Subjectivity, Identity, and the Body: Women's Autobiographical Practices in the Twentieth Century*. Indiana U. Press.

Weintraub, Karl Joachim, (1978). *The Value of the Individual: Self and Circumstance in Autobiography*. Chicago: University of Chicago Press.

ADDITIONAL REFERENCES

Benstock, Shari (1988). *The Private Self: Theory and Practice of Women's Autobiographical Writing*. U. North Carolina Press.

Eakin, John Paul (1988). *Fictions in Autobiography: Studies in the Art of Self-Invention*. Princeton: Princeton U. Press.

Goodwin, James (1993) ed. *Autobiography: The Self Made Text*. Twayne Publishers.

Griffiths, A. Phillip (1992), ed. *The Impulse to Philosophise*. Cambridge U. Press.

Murdoch, Iris (1997). "Literature and Philosophy: A Conversation with Bryan Magee," in *Existentialists and Mystics*. New York: The Penguin Press.

Norton, David (1976). *Personal Destinies*. Princeton, NJ: Princeton University Press.

Scharfstein, Ben-Ami (1980). *The Philosophers: Their Lives and the Nature of Their Thought*. Oxford U. Press.

Spengemann, William C. (1980). *The Forms of Autobiography: Episodes in the History of a Literary Genre*. Yale U. Press

FREE ONLINE OR DOWNLOADABLE AUTOBIOGRAPHIES COVERED IN THE BOOK

Augustine's *Confessions* in the Edward Pusey translation at
http://www.sacred-texts.com/chr/augconf/aug01.htm

Rousseau's *Confessions* translated by Conyngham Mallory at
http://ebooks.adelaide.edu.au/r/rousseau/jean_jacques/r864c/)

Autobiography of John Stuart Mill at
http://www.gutenberg.org/cache/epub/10378/pg10378.html

Ecce Homo, autobiography of Friederich Nietzsche translated by Anthony M Ludovici, at
https://archive.org/details/TheCompleteWorksOfFriedrichNietzschevol.17-EcceHomo

The Words, autobiography of J-P Sartre, at
http://www.ebook3000.com/The-Words--The-Autobiography-of-Jean-Paul-Sartre_56106.html

Memories, Dreams, Reflections, autobiography of C.G. Jung, at
https://archive.org/stream/MemoriesDreamsReflectionsCarlJung/Memories%2C%20Dreams%2C%20Reflections%20-%20Carl%20Jung#page/n3/mode/1up

The Story of My Experiment with Truth, autobiography of M. K. Gandhi, at
http://www.mkgandhi.org/autobio/autobio.htm

AVAILABLE AS AN EBOOK FOR FEE

Meetings, autobiography of Martin Buber, at
http://books.google.com/books?id=3UjaAAAAQBAJ

2

THE GARDENS OF AUGUSTINE

In a famous scene in Episode V of the film epic, *Star Wars*, we listen in as the impish Jedi Master, Yoda, attempts to teach the saga's protagonist, Luke Skywalker, about the cosmic contest between the forces of light and dark. In place of his swampy planet Dagobah, Yoda could have been standing on a street corner in Rome, planet Earth, in the fourth century of the Common Era. For when he admonishes Luke to "Beware of the dark side of the Force," he echoes the ancient teachings of a Christian sect known as the Manicheans. They, too, regard the universe as a battleground between counter forces of good and evil, revealed metaphorically as the powers of light and darkness.

Neophyte Luke asks Yoda how one tells the difference between the forces of light and dark, and how the warrior can attune himself to the one and not be lured in by the other. Again sounding Manichaean, Yoda answers: "When you are calm, at peace. Passive." The emotions of fear and anger lead to hate and aggression, which, in turn, make one susceptible to the dark side. Every Jedi Knight, instructs the 900-year-old Yoda, must learn patience, discipline and humility. He or she must subdue emotion so that the rational mind can hold sway.

Manichaeism is thought to have died out centuries ago, yet vestiges of the sect's beliefs about the battle between the powers of good and evil and the dualistic nature of the cosmos remain with us in popular culture. In *Star Wars* the Jedi Knights possess knowledge of the "force," which is represented by the "light saber." The Jedi-trained followers' mind can harness what amounts to the "force" of good in doing battle with the "dark side," the equally powerful force of evil. Yoda, the cave-dwelling hermetic teacher of the mysteries of the force is a prophet-like creature who speaks in riddles and paradoxes. He advises Luke that the follower who practices self-mastery and who realizes that the force of evil thrives on anger, fear and violence, will be able to lead a purified life and "go with the force" – no doubt the force of good.

This Star Wars account of the dualistic nature of good and evil forces and, caught between them, of the human condition, is intuitively more understandable than monotheism's paradoxical explanation of how a singular, omnipotent and benevolent deity is also the source of evil. As in the Book of Job, monotheism's God will sometimes allow evil to run its course without intervening because it is part of a larger plan that mere mortals can never fathom. We read in the book of Isaiah, "I form the light, and create darkness; I make peace, and create evil; I am the Lord, that doeth all these things." The Manichaean system of independent and antagonistic cosmic powers seems easier to grasp, though from a Judeo-Christian perspective it opens itself to polytheism and the pagan idea of multiple spiritually infused dominions.

The doctrine had a similar appeal to a young, North African-born spiritual seeker by the name of Aurelius Augustinus. He became not only a follower of the secret order but "converted" others away from both competing pagan beliefs and Christian ones, so ardently did he believe the Manichees held a superior intellectual and spiritual position. The man we now call St. Augustine would later turn against and do battle with the Manicheans, declaring their beliefs heretical to those of the Catholic Church. To do battle this spiritual warrior would not take hold of a sword of light but a cross of wood. More scholar than swordsman, Augustine was a prolific writer who set down the story of his own religious struggles in a book most scholars credit as the first fully realized spiritual and philosophical autobiography, *The Confessions*.

A DISTANT TIME AND PLACE

By the fourth century of the Common Era, the high plains and valleys of the region of North Africa known as Numidia lay refulgent in fields of grain, the terrain crisscrossed by good roads connecting a wide network of prosperous towns. Under the influence of the Roman Empire the lands south of the ancient port city of Carthage had experienced an economic boom. Known as Rome's granary, Numidia's prosperity extended far into the hinterlands reaching almost to the Sahara. One of the small towns of this region (now the country of Algeria) was Thagaste (modern-day Souk Ahras), located on a plateau 2,000 feet above sea level, about 60 miles inland from the Mediterranean Sea. It was there that Aurelius Augustinus was born in 354 CE.

By the time of his birth, Rome had been officially Christian for four decades and Thagaste securely Catholic, though various Christian sects (such as the Manicheans), splinter groups and adherents to pagan rites continued to attract followers. Given the dominant influence of Roman culture and his family's middle-class social position, Augustine would grow up speaking Latin, not the native Berber language commonly used by the slaves who tended his father Patricius's vineyards.

By virtue of his family status and his native intelligence, Augustine was destined for a place in the Roman bureaucracy in which Patricius held a minor local office. While Augustine's father, still then a pagan, had lofty expectations about his son's worldly success, his mother, Monnica (the original Berber spelling though now generally rendered as Monica), had other hopes for him. An illiterate, devout Christian, she wished that Augustine would follow in the righteous path of Christ the Savior. And since Augustine was very much his mother's son, he did just that, but only after considerable emotional turmoil, intellectual exploration, and soul searching.

Eight decades later, in the third month of the siege of the Mediterranean city of Hippo by Christian Visigoth invaders, Augustine, then Bishop of Hippo, fell ill of a fever and died on August 28 in the year 430. The 76-year-old Catholic authority had become the most important leader of the North African church, having produced a large body of written works (232 according to his own catalogue, the *Retractations*) ranging from treatises defending the Catholic faith against numerous competing theologies to sermons, letters and commentaries on Scripture. His framework of doctrines and theological investigations became known as Augustinianism.

Augustine harnessed his intellectual brilliance, literary skills and spiritual passion to formulate a profound integration of several sources: the centuries-earlier Greek philosophical and contemplative tradition arising from Plato and the neo-Platonic mystics, the narrative-based messages of the Hebrew Bible and its evocation of a singular, all-powerful God, and the teachings of the New Testament concerning the daring idea of a God-man, savior and redeemer. Augustine affirmed the faith in a divine being who mediated between the infinite God and finite human beings, carrying a message about the nature of the human soul that in turning to itself through inquiry and reflection, turned to God, and knew itself through the love of God as the heart of creation.

The chief problem for the Christian believer was that while this act of turning required the free exercise of the human will, the act could not be accomplished by volition alone. This omniscient and omnipotent God had to empower the act. This would seem to make the soul's journey to itself both paradoxical and enigmatic. Augustine accepted that perplexity announcing, more than once, that in his soul searching, he had become a mystery to himself.

Among Augustine's most famous works is the first-person narrative charting the course of his spiritual odyssey, *Confessiones*, a term that can be variously translated as "testimony" or "confessions." Let us remember that Augustine was not a saint when he wrote this volume and, while he held considerable authority in the church, the *Confessions* was still an unprecedented experiment in religious writing, a veritable spiritual self-exposé. Drawing on his considerable skills as a teacher of rhetoric (the art of persuasion crucial to judicial and political processes), Augustine created a unique literary work of remarkable candor. He built it from his personal life with all its ups and downs, sordid particulars, materialistic ambitions, and complex relationships to parents, teachers, lovers and rulers, and his ideological struggles.

He was so successful that today we may come upon that work and find it unremarkable. Perhaps because of the heavy freight of prayer and theological argumentation the work carries, it may strike the reader as too doctrinaire to be believable and too conventionally pious to possess originality. If the *Confessions* seems derivative, that is because Augustine made the mold from which thousands of spiritual and secular autobiographies have since been cast or, rejecting it, the mold they sought to shatter. Our challenge is to come at it with fresh sensibilities.

THE TWO GARDENS

The *Confessions*, organized as a series of "Books" containing multiple "chapters," can be conceived as having three parts. The first, Books 1-9, tells the story of Augustine's life from birth up to the time of his conversion to Christianity and, a year later, the death of his mother. This remembered past section is followed in Book 10 by Augustine's intense reflection on the current state of his soul and on the gift and mystery of memory – the faculty that enabled him to write the previous nine chapters. Finally, the third section, made up of Books 11-13, inaugurated through meditation on the opening verses of the Book of Genesis, finds Augustine pondering issues of Christian metaphysics.

The work departs from an already existing genre of conversion stories in which the authors tend to dismiss the significance of their lives before conversion as just so much confusion, ignorance, sin and suffering that is no longer relevant to their newly found way. Augustine does not follow this literary pattern. Instead, he simultaneously evaluates, interprets and retells his life story as if it was happening both with and without benefit of the revelations he believes he's gained through God's grace. He interprets the most elementary aspects of life, such as nursing at his mother's breast, learning to speak, playing childhood pranks and choosing a career, as profoundly revealing of both earthly desires and needs, uncontrollable impulses and temptations, and as evidence of the omnipresence of God at every moment. To Augustine, every event of a person's life contains sub-conscious messages calling the individual to union with the divine.

The *Confessions* is a continuous, though selective, life history narrative, frequently interrupted or embellished by prayers of gratitude and expressions of remorse that reflect Augustine's movement toward this ultimate goal, as he understands it in hindsight. This anticipation of an ultimate culmination (Augustine's spiritual conversion and his mystical experiences) lends drama to the story, what literary scholars call narrative drive. He seems to be reliving his experiences in the retelling of them. This dramatic quality invites his readers to follow along, which is certainly his intention. The didactic purpose of the *Confessions* is to provide a model for those who would follow the pathway to a new conception of an invisible and intangible God, a journey that leads through a process of doubt, confusion, and travail to redemption.

Augustine implores his creator in Book 1 of the *Confessions*: "My soul's house is narrow for you to enter; will you not make it broader?" Not through doorways or windows will his God come find him, but through open spaces under the heavens. The two revelatory and life-changing scenes of the *Confessions* take place in gardens. The most famous scene, in Book 8, is Augustine's account of his conversion. Along with his mother, Monica, his mistress, who remains unnamed, his son, Adeodatus, and several close friends, Augustine is taking a break from his duties as a well-respected teacher of rhetoric in Milan, which was then the seat of government for the Roman Empire. They have retreated to a nearby country villa where the group is engaged in philosophic study and contemplation.

We have to imagine a period of great instability, as the most powerful empire on earth is in decline and threatened on all sides by revolts of its various conquered peoples and from marauding hordes of so-called barbarians (non-Romans). Christianity has eclipsed but not eliminated the practice of earlier Greek and Roman religions while several Christian sects compete to gain the upper hand in controlling the interpretation of Christ's teachings and the establishment of the earthly church.

In Book 8, Augustine is 32 years old. His baptism a year later coincides with the Christological year, the age at which Christ died and was resurrected. We find Augustine, who has struggled for years to find a resolution to his spiritual hunger, caught in the turmoil of his era and his life. "I was displeased with the worldly life which I was leading," says Augustine (Book 8, 1). He has achieved the ideal of a conventional Roman upper-class life. He is a member of the intellectual elite, a noted teacher of the art of persuasion, which was an essential skill for politicians and speechmakers of all kinds, and has a circle of loving friends and family. Nevertheless, Augustine finds his life deficient on almost every level, yet he cannot make the leap to a new life committed to chastity, austerity and indifference to worldly pursuits.

Over the years he has embraced several systems of belief, foremost Manichaeism, not exactly the Star Wars version but a compelling forerunner. It is important here that we have a fuller understanding of why Manichaeism held such a powerful attraction for Augustine.

Preeminent among the issues that plagued the philosophically minded Augustine during the decade before his conversion was the perplexing question: what is the source of evil? For Augustine, this is not only a speculative question of theodicy (arguments to justify to mortals the ways of an omnipotent and benevolent deity in a world marred by such evils as war, pestilence and injustice), it is a personal inquiry into the causes that distracted him from leading what he imagined as the less anxious, more tranquil life of the contemplative seeker.

Why, for example, could he not master the lust he felt toward his mistress, the anger toward his nagging mother, the temptations of earthly power, and the pleasure of dominating others in philosophical arguments? Where did these and other such urges come from, urges that in their extreme could lead to disastrous consequences for individuals and their societies? And if the God of the Christian faith were in fact benevolent, then how could this omnipotent deity allow the evils of the world to be perpetuated? Or was this God, the creator of all life and substance, also the controller of evil itself?

The young Augustine found a temporary solution to these tormenting questions in the teachings of the third century Persian prophet, Mani, whose followers, the Manichees, formed secret societies to protect and perpetuate their teachings. The Manichees explained the presence of evil by positing a dualistic system in which forces of good and evil collided. The Christian God did not create evil, argued the Manichees; rather, evil is a separate force against which the Christian God has sent his son to do battle. The battleground of good and evil is human experience, since human beings are imprisoned by the physical sensuousness of the body against which the spiritual parts, the mind and soul, struggle for independence. Those who choose an ascetic life (the Manichees favored celibacy, vegetarianism and contemplation) in rejection of everything of the lower realm may thereby gain entrance into the higher. The Manichees claimed their tenets were strongly based on the teachings of St. Paul and they regarded themselves as an elite, enlightened group of true Christians. Through rational understanding of the need to subjugate evil in themselves and through the practice of an ascetic lifestyle, they believed they could escape the snares of all human depravity.

Augustine had hoped that Manichaeism would satisfy his intellectual and spiritual longing. He identified with and participated in this sect for many years. Gradually, given the force of his analytical mind and his continued restlessness, he began to find flaws in the tenets of the cult. Augustine faulted the system because it attributed the active principle to the force of evil as it sought to invade and overwhelm the seemingly more passive force of good. Moreover, the dualism of separate forces harkened back to the pagan idea of realms of multiple gods, not the Platonic and Christian belief in a single deity reigning over a unified and coherent universe. Augustine believed the framework did not pose an adequate solution to the impulse to do evil since rational self-control did not, in his experience and through his observations of others, prove sufficiently effective. Besides this, the system made human beings unaccountable for evil ways (in the vernacular of *Star Wars*, 'it was the dark side that made me do it') and left them in an unredeemable position since there seemed to be no place in the system for the intervention of a superior, redemptive power – a savior or redeemer of souls.

By this moment in the *Confessions'* narrative he has finally figured out that the concept of God espoused in both the Hebrew Bible (to him the "Old Testament") and New Testament is meant to be understood allegorically, not as an external power that dwells in either a literal heaven above or underworld below but is invisibly, immaterially and intimately part of oneself. He sees before him the path of self-denial: the true Christian will give up the things of this world such as earthly desires and attachments and fame and fortune. He believes a first step onto the path will lead him to the great goal implicit in his deepest question: "How shall I find rest until I find rest in Thee?" But until now he has put off that step for some future time – captured in the often quoted, "Lord give me chastity and continence: but not now" (*Confessions*, Bk. 5).

Wandering around the country house garden wracked with "gnawing anxieties," Augustine throws himself down under a fig tree and weeps, berating himself that he lacks the strength of conviction to surrender to God. His good friend Alypius tries to console him but to no avail. Suddenly, Augustine harkens to the singsong voice of a child coming from a nearby house. "Tolle, lege; tolle, lege," goes the Latin chant, "take up and read; take up and read." Perceiving this unfamiliar exhortation might be a divine command, Augustine arises, steps over to a table where he has placed a copy of the Epistles of St. Paul, opens the book and reads at random Paul's inviting words: "No reveling or drunkenness, no debauchery or vice, no quarrels or jealousies. Let Christ Jesus himself be the armor that you wear; give no more thought to satisfying the bodily appetites." And miraculously these words suddenly enable Augustine to step onto the path of the dedicated Christian believer.

The story of the conversion is told with great dramatic slowness in order to evoke the intensity of the seeker's longing as he strains to break the discord between two wills, carnal and spiritual, only to find he cannot force the transformation of self-change that he seeks. Only God's intervention through earthly, highly symbolic means, such as the voice of a child coming through the trees, and through the words inspired by the son of God's apostle, could make this possible. Had Augustine been able to will his conversion, he would have undermined the central point of Christianity by making unnecessary the role of divine mediator and redeemer. Of special importance also is the fact that Augustine is not alone when he experiences this transformation. His friend and student, Alypius, witnesses his conversion and is so moved that he, too, immediately experiences this spiritual self-change.

Augustine deems the setting, which is probably historically accurate, essential to the retelling. Augustine's readers and commentators would quickly associate this enclosed garden and its fig tree with the Biblical Garden of Eden and its tree of life and the tree of the knowledge of good and evil. Mythologically, Romulus and Remus, the legendary founders of Rome, were suckled by a she-wolf under a fig tree. From ancient times revelations frequently take place under trees, and paradise, a place of perfect oneness, has been associated with gardens from time immemorial. Augustine's turn to God is his return to Edenic oneness and perfection, made possible by the bridge maker, mediator, Christ, through the words of his apostle, Paul. Keeping these elements – garden, book, voices, tree, friend – in mind, let us turn to the second garden scene recounted in Book 9.

Augustine and his mother, Monica, are standing together, he tells us, "leaning in at a window," through which they gaze upon the interior garden of a friend's house in Ostia, the port of Rome on the Tiber River. He doesn't offer us any details about trees, flowers or shrubs, or whether there would be birds nesting or singing in that roofless inner courtyard. Only that they stand alone, "conversing together most tenderly," sharing a moment of contemplation in which each, in turn, seeks to compare the visible light and life around them with the invisible quality of eternity that the Christian faith promises is the world beyond time. Monica, age fifty-six, is tired and Augustine remarks that she does not look well. He is troubled because his mother drops hints that her mission in life, witnessing her son's conversion to Catholicism, is now complete. Though they are resting in preparation for a sea journey across the Mediterranean from Italy back to Thagaste, it dawns upon Augustine that this may be the moment of his mother's final journey on earth.

Augustine is both exhausted and exhilarated. A year earlier he had resigned from his position as professor of rhetoric, a vocation that once meant everything to him but which he now claims was little more than "a seller of words." He has given up power, fortune, the pleasures bestowed upon the well-educated citizen of this highly evolved Greco-Roman civilization. And, for what? To contemplate eternal life?

The usual sorts of exchanges that might be overheard among the porticos of a single-family home in the fourth century harbor town were the shouts of dockworkers and tradesmen, the haggling of shopkeepers and customers, and the hawking of artisans selling their wares in open market places. Ostia (the Latin means "mouth," as in the mouth of the River Tiber) would be noisy, though nowhere as tumultuous as densely populated Rome, a fifteen-mile journey inland. The inhabitants would be living in three and four-story tenements, or *insulae*, built of brick, mortar, and stone. A few, the more affluent, would live in a *domus*, a house with luxurious accommodations like interior gardens (*peristylia*) with spouting fountains. So though he personally disdained wealth and possessions, Augustine was apparently well connected to those who did not.

Augustine and his mother, he tells us, are "removed from the crowd." We know this is both physically and mentally true, since they're standing within the quiet space of a room shuttered against the busy streets, and have spiritually sequestered themselves among the members of a small sect of intensely devout Catholics, the servi Dei, servants of God, who yearn for a life separate from the turmoil of political upheaval, the constant threat of invading armies, the decay and impending collapse of the Empire.

Such conflict is another reason for their delay in Ostia. The harbor is currently under a blockade by the fleet of General Maximus who is seeking to wrestle power from Emperor Theodosius in yet another civil war. The Roman Gods – though they might bring fortune or failure – cannot comfort them. What they seek is release from the bondage of earthly suffering. More than that, they seek union with the one divine being, the sole creator of the universe and all its inhabitants. They yearn for a glimpse of the beatified life, like that of the saints, Paul and John, who, in their minds, inhabit a timeless realm of perfection and absolute security far removed from the balconies, arched doorways and the atria of stone-built houses and enclosed gardens in a harbor town in Italy.

Adding a few details of our own, let us take the liberty of picturing Augustine and his mother gazing down on a lush garden of date palms, lemon, orange and pomegranate trees, bird of paradise flowers and fragrant shrubs that might have filled the interior courtyard of their friend's house. Then one of them, let it be Monica, asks: 'How should we understand the meaning of eternity?' And considering the matter this way and that, as was his habit, Augustine responds, 'Maybe it is not enough for us to trust to understanding. But let us nevertheless use our rational minds and proceed to search, one level at a time, through all manners of things.' And raising his arms and pointing, he would add, 'including the heavens themselves, where sun and moon and stars shine above the earth.'

Then Monica responds, 'Yes, my son, perhaps there is a glint of eternity in that drop of water on a palm leaf, or in the sparkle of a star, like a diamond set into the velvety black canopy above. Yet these things we perceive through the physical senses do not seem worthy of comparison to eternity, which has neither beginning nor end, neither growth nor decay.' And in unison they would sigh and look into each other's eyes, seeing themselves looking and feeling suddenly that something or someone was looking upon them. Not from above, but looking through their eyes as if there were a seer positioned at the back of each one's head.

Augustine, who has a fondness for doing everything in threes, breaks the silence: 'Mother, let us take three steps in turn. First we shall consider, then we shall speak of that which we consider, and then we shall wonder of the matter of which we speak.' And she acquiesces to this method of contemplation, since she knew her son was steeped in the ways of the Greek philosophers while she could not read Greek and, in truth, little of any other language. His path has been that of the mind while hers has been that of the heart. Intuitively, she senses that these paths will intersect.

Like the shape of a triadic chord, the fingers of their minds progress up the frets of this instrument, this lyre of consciousness. "Meditating, speaking and looking with wonder" – how one mode leads into the other, round and round, upward and upward. "Step by step," says Augustine, they "passed over all material things... even the heaven itself." They know this sensation of soaring above the things of the world will bring them only as far as themselves. "And we came at last to our own minds," says Augustine, who loves this endless turning upon oneself because it always leads to the infinite regress of asking what power gives the ability to inquire into the basis of our knowledge. And at this juncture he pauses, pleased with himself for recognizing their dependency on a power, which is a gift they could never have bestowed upon themselves.

And they "pass above themselves," he says. Did they grow light headed from their lofty speculations? No, insists Augustine, they attained the place in which dwells the Greek Goddess of wisdom, Sophia, which he now experiences not as a state of intellectual contemplation through which one would recognize the timeless, abstract forms of all things, like a pure geometry of space and time, but instead as the female presence of a divine being who creates everything and to which everything belongs.

And in this moment, which has neither beginning nor end, since, says Augustine, Wisdom "is not made, but is as she has been and forever shall be," they have an uncanny experience. Their mouths continue to form the shapes of words but no sounds issue forth. While this frightens Augustine, it does not surprise Monica because she knows the greatest gifts come in silences that harbor what cannot be said. And Augustine comes to truly know what he has espoused but never fully realized, that human words are finite, having beginnings and endings, yet the realm of Wisdom is without beginning or end. Words fall short. Like rungs of a ladder, words provide a foothold for thoughts, which helps them to climb until they arrive at the moment beyond words. In that moment, the place of enormous silence, mouths agape, the ladder falling away, the radiant light from the back of the eye streaming through them, their silent stammering turns to soft moans, and joyfully they "touch the spiritual harvest."

Augustine possesses the artistic ability to endow a physical place with transformative meanings and to use the senses to evoke spiritual ideas. He says that attaining wisdom is like tasting some incredibly delicious food. Throughout the *Confessions* he reiterates how the soul "hungers and thirsts for the changeless truth" (Book 3), for "incorruptible food." He chooses the metaphoric language of tasting to characterize his spiritual quest rather than less sensuous, visual metaphors that speak of clarity of vision that one finds among the ancient philosophers. Augustine says of mother and son's mystical ascent: "We attained to the region of abundance that never fails, in which you feed Israel forever upon the food of truth."

His account is filled with allusions to tasting fruit, language that harkens to the rich sensuousness of the Biblical Book, Song of Songs, and its ecstatic lovers who, in their amorous encounters, do a great deal of tasting. In fact, one may wonder why this subsection of the *Confessions* has been entitled "The Vision at Ostia," since it is the metaphor of taste, not sight, that animates it. Almost everything about the "vision" is oral and metaphorically gustatory. Perhaps Augustine is reminding us of the idea of incarnation and communion, the symbolic (some would argue literal) eating of the body of Christ reenacted in the Eucharist.

Augustine's brilliance lay in revising the traditional Greek philosophical idea of the rational ascent. In this model the knower progressively moves upward from the stage of untested opinions, arrived at through the senses, to eventual contemplation of the cosmic order, as understood by means of abstract concepts. Like Plato in his dialogue on love and desire, the *Symposium*, he dramatizes the steps that bring the philosopher to the abstract idea of Beauty as the ultimate quest of desire, but he gives the process a mystical reformulation, imbuing it with all the yearning and sighing of a Christian seeker. Augustine turns the traditional Greek ideal of wisdom – contemplation of the laws of human and physical nature – into a station along the way in the mind's search for God, the lawmaker and creator of the universe. By turning the Greek figure of the Goddess Sophia into a nurturing, food-giving mother Goddess, he deftly displaces the classical humanists' belief in the soul's *a priori* possession of wisdom as something to be drawn out through education and reflection. Now access to wisdom requires divine assistance, the intervention of the Christian God.

Augustine and Monica's ascent is also a descent, a turning back to what is most human – frailty, dependency, hunger. As classics scholar Martha Nussbaum points out, in Augustine's formulation "Christian love both ascends and descends, both purifying the will and recovering a receptivity and vulnerability that the Platonist ascent had surmounted." (Nussbaum, 2001)

Augustine's garden scene is multilayered with allusions to Adam and Eve in the Garden of Eden, only now reversed as the banishment edict is apparently, at least momentarily, abolished, and they reenter the place of original innocence and oneness; and to the "enclosed garden" of the Song of Songs, the wonderfully erotic poem of the Hebrew Bible which by Augustine's time was interpreted from a strictly allegorical point of view in both the Jewish and Christian tradition as variously depicting the Hebrew God's love for his people, Israel, or the individual soul's love of God. In the Song of Songs, tasting is the central metaphor of delight, as in the following. "And my beloved among the young men/is a branching apricot tree in the wood. /In that shade I have often lingered/tasting the fruit" (Bloch and Bloch, 1995). And certainly readers were still touched by Augustine's account in the previous Book 8 of his Milanese garden experience.

For those immersed in the Christian tradition, the characters of Augustine and Monica easily become allegories of the relationship between

Church and the Holy Mother. Augustine's allusion to "first fruit" is at once evocative of the fruit of the trees of both life and of good and evil, and of his mother's breasts. I say this not through some half-baked Freudian interpretation but in relation to Augustine's own words earlier in the *Confessions*.

> *From my tenderest infancy I had, in a manner, sucked*
> *with my mother's milk that name of my Savior, Thy Son; I*
> *kept it in the recesses of my heart; and all that presented*
> *itself to me without that divine name, though it might be*
> *elegant, well written, and even replete with truth, did not*
> *altogether carry me away.* (Book 3)

For Augustine everything that happens in life, from the most elementary to the most sublime, bespeaks the presence of God. In his universe of discourse, all things are connected and relatable. What better way, then, to evoke the blissful oneness with God than to compare the mystical union to the relationship of mother and infant before the infant experiences separation and differentiation? The Madonna and child is certainly one of the great themes of Medieval and Renaissance iconography and its evocative power is both psychological and spiritual. And why not allude to infantile hunger and thirst as having become the adult version of the spiritual quest for absolute security and self-unification as the tension of inner conflict is finally resolved?

The five elements of the Milanese garden are re-evoked in the garden of Ostia. The perspective is slightly different, as Augustine is looking down into the garden from a second floor window rather than locating himself at ground level. His friend this time is his mother and their epiphany is simultaneous rather than sequential. While there is no literal tree (e.g. the fig tree of Book 8), there is frequent allusion to fruitfulness and to the fruit of the Biblical trees of Eden.

The Epistle of St. Paul as a text left sitting on a table is absent in this second garden; instead, Augustine's description of the ascent is sprinkled with quotations from Proverbs, Psalms, and the New Testament, and his vision of Sophia, the Goddess of wisdom, evokes the entire Greco-Roman philosophical literature, most especially his favorite pre-Christian thinker, Plotinus. As to a voice conveying heavenly messages (the child's distant, "take up and read" of Chapter 8), there is again a reversal in the garden of Book 9. For here it is the silence that comes before and after voices make sounds that Augustine emphasizes.

As part of Augustine and Monica's ascent, they address all the elements of earth and heaven, asking, "Are you God?" And all the things of creation respond in the negative, insisting in one voice, "He made us." Even more insistent is Augustine when he describes a kind of silent *glossolalia*, ecstatic speaking in an unknown language, that overcame them. Their mouths moved as if they were speaking but no audible sounds came out. This is Augustine's way of pointing to the ineffable character of their experience. It was beyond the reach of descriptive language, was in fact pre-linguistic because the experience was finally completely unmediated by human ideas and concepts, as is the essential nature of ecstatic experience – literally, a step out of place and, we would add, time.

Bishop Augustine realizes that as an important authority on such matters as sacrament, wisdom and grace, he must explain that the soundless voice they heard was not conveyed by a metaphorical peal of thunder, nor by an imaginary angel, nor through pure contemplation of the glorious works of God's creation. He takes pains to assure his reader that the mother and son's path to knowledge was related to, and may in fact have utilized, the Greek speculative mysticism of the famous student of Platonic philosophy, Plotinus and other pre-Christian mystics for whom the God of creation, the One, would always be unfathomable. But unlike these seekers, it was the true God's voice, heard directly, that Augustine reports experiencing with Monica. Together, he claims, they achieved an authentic, singular connection to the wisdom of the creator. In doing this, he claims their "election" by God as two of the chosen.

Following their edifying experience, mother and son agree that the delights of the corporeal world have lost what little luster had remained, have even become "contemptible." Monica then tells him she finds no delight in "anything in this life." All her hopes in the world have been fulfilled. Earthly happiness holds no further value. A few days later she falls ill and after a short period of decline, dies. Following her wishes, Augustine buries his mother at Ostia rather than transporting her body back to Thagaste. This ends the life history narrative portion of the *Confessions*.

Perhaps, like any skeptical reader, we ask of Augustine: "Did it really happen this way, your life like one long allegory?" We will find that he winks back, offering a sort of disclaimer. At the very end of Book 9, after recounting the vision, Augustine adds, almost as a footnote: "Such things I said, although not in this manner and in these words." Augustine is like Socrates, who after presenting an elaborate allegory or mythic tale as a parallel to the quest for timeless knowledge adds, "Anyway, it was something like this." Words help but may also hinder and mislead. Augustine's wink tells us his account is still only a semblance. For the real thing, he intimates, we have to look into our own souls; we have to make our own journey.

If the ultimate experience that human beings seek cannot be captured in words but can only be described by analogy, metaphor and allegory, how then should these functions of language be understood? And if Augustine is using these means for retelling the experiences that were so decisive as to change his life (and, consequently, the lives of millions of others whom he would influence through his doctrinal teachings), how is he able to remember what happened ten years earlier without worrying that his memory is distorted by subsequent experiences and by that erosion of time we call forgetfulness? As a founder of the genre of philosophical autobiography, Augustine sets himself the task of looking into these very questions for they are part and parcel of the mystery that is the divinely blessed human life.

PALACE OF MEMORY

Every autobiography depends on memory, though few autobiographies mention or question the act of remembering to investigate the presuppositions that underlie it. And every autobiography depends on language and on the autobiographer's ability to capture the remembered past in sentences that have the power to make the past present. A compelling autobiography will tell a story in such a way that when making the past present it also creates anticipation in our minds of what is to come. In this sense, at any point in an autobiography the author is remembering the past, attempting to understand it in the present moment of writing, and pointing toward or anticipating what part of the story will unfold next.

Even though we hold such a book in our hands and know that the work, like the life, is already completed, if the work is effective we should nevertheless find ourselves moved by the writing as if the events were still taking place. And we should feel the suspense of not knowing, while caring about how the narrator's future will turn out.

Augustine is well trained as a rhetorician and he knows from reading other first-person narratives that without the tension created through conflict, a literary work quickly turns into a treatise that, because it loses forward momentum, may lose our interest. Simply put, Augustine's narrative conflict is the apparent irreconcilability of his inner and outer life. But by the time we reach Book 10 of the *Confessions*, that tension is dissipated. Augustine has arrived at his goal, knowing God, a terminus whose accomplishment was foreshadowed from the very beginning of the story. Instead of continuing the account of his life to bring us up to date to the time of writing the *Confessions* ten years later when he has become Bishop of Hippo, Augustine chooses to change modes and turns his and our attention to these presuppositions about memory, language and time that make the autobiographical act possible. As readers, we will need to have been sufficiently fascinated by his life history, and the search for adequate concepts by which to frame his life and interpret his experiences, in order to feel motivated to follow him into some convoluted meditations. We may easily wonder why he appends Chapters 10-13 to the narrative.

First, Augustine wants to justify why it was necessary for him to write the *Confessions*, not just to have had the experiences that led him to undergo his conversion and become an important ecclesiastical authority. Second, he wishes to make his life an example of a lost soul that finds its way to God so that others might follow. In this sense, he is a spiritual pathfinder, a Christian seeker who will do for other would-be Christians what, years earlier, the Roman writer Cicero did for him. Augustine's reading of the pagan Cicero's *Hortensius*, a work urging the reader to pursue wisdom by renouncing worldly ambition and physical pleasure, opened the door to the philosophical and inward life. Third, Augustine is blessed with a philosophical mind that wants to understand the nature of its own functioning. Call it a compulsion. Augustine cannot stop with the fact that he is capable of writing a first-person narrative (the term "autobiography" does not emerge until the 18th century). He wants to dig beneath the soil of those gardens of ecstasy and study what underlies his ability to remember, write and know in time.

Focusing on the third purpose of his philosophical reflections, we note that Augustine employs several metaphors for memory. He calls it the "stomach of the mind" (Book 10, 14) because the faculty of memory enables us to digest a great quantity of experience and, like a ruminating cow, to bring it back up again for further digestion. He speaks about memory as a "palace" of many rooms (Book 10, 8) that we can wander through as we remember and investigate scenes from earlier life events.

There must be some special purpose for this remarkable gift that not only allows us to retrieve names, faces, places, and feelings that otherwise would have disappeared but which seems to have a power of its own as when memories flood our minds without our seeming to have requested them. Unbidden memories carry a kind of insistence – that we make connections we had not formerly understood, that we are reminded or alerted to a task or quest from which we had been distracted. Memory offers the possibility of seeing larger patterns and pictures of our lives, ones made up of thousands of smaller images, fragments whose composition we could not have understood earlier. Accepting the challenge of writing a philo-sophical autobiography, employing not only the pen of the confessional but also the scalpel of critical analysis is an act of moving toward greater wholeness. And Augustine, to speak colloquially, is all about discovering the unity of experiences. But he is also well aware of the impediments to the unitive vision. Language itself is one such impediment.

Without the use of language there could be no autobiography. Writing is a method of recollection. A sentence that invokes a fragment of memory often leads to another, and another. But this kind of discursive language is, says Augustine, "motion subject to the laws of time" (Book 11, 6). And time, as Augustine understands it, is the incapacity of the present instant to hold still (Book 11, 11). Augustine encounters a problem that would seem to make an autobiography, if not an impossible, then at most a very restricted activity. The sequentiality of writing, in which one sentence must follow another, mirrors the experience of (to use a fancy term) "human temporal-ity," in which the divisions of time – past, present and future – form what seems analogous to an arrow whose leap from the bow consists of three parts: departure, flight and destination. The arrow's trajectory travels through a series of infinite imaginary points like a line divisible into segments.

Discursive language has this same limitation. Syllables, words, sentences and paragraphs are serial, with one following the other. Yet memory and the remembered past are not serial but are somehow parallel, a palace whose many rooms hold both what we remember and even what we've forgotten. Given this initial spatial understanding of time as distance travelled and of language as sequential, it would seem we humans would never be able to grasp, let alone represent, the whole or simultaneity of our experiences and realizations. We would only be able to lay out the story bit by bit, discretely moment by moment, in an endless sequence, like the arrow in Zeno's famous paradox that could never reach its destination since it must pass through an infinite number of points. Were this true, every autobiography would be doomed to failure or would, at best, serve as a factual chronology of disconnected life events.

If Augustine is going to successfully capture the completeness suggested by his and Monica's temporal transcending vision (or taste) at Ostia and by his dramatic conversion experience, a completeness that provides him with the ability to examine and recount his life story not only in retrospect but as a preformed predestined whole, then he needs to come up with an alter-native way of understanding the functions of time, language and memory. Otherwise, remembering and writing will never bring him, or us, closer to the transformative experience than to a distorted and inadequate account that would seem uneventful in its retelling. His solution is to shift from thinking of time as an independent quality of the external physical universe (the equivalent of distance traveled by a body in motion), and to reconsider time as the regulative function of the human mind. Just as Augustine in Book 9 shifts from his account using the analogy of vertical ascent from earth to heaven, from body to mind, and from sight to taste, so he veers away from spatial projections of time to reflect on the way we experience sound and music.

Augustine considers the following possibility. Suppose someone wishes to utter a prolonged sound and decides beforehand how long he wants it to last. He can rehearse that sound in silence, commit it to memory, and then begin to make the sound until the rehearsed duration elapses. Augustine says: "It sounds until it reaches the limit set for it or rather, I should not use the present tense and say it sounds, but the past and the future, saying that it both sounded and will sound" (Book 11, 27).

Augustine takes other, related examples. When someone is reciting a familiar text, say a poem or passage from Scripture, he and his listeners both retain what has been uttered, hear what is currently being said, and anticipate what is coming. Similarly with music, we retain portions of the melody that have sounded, hear the notes currently affecting our ears, and anticipate the notes that will come. Without this capability, we would never experience the continuity of a song, poem or psalm. Songs, poems and psalms have a way of telling us something while preparing us for what is yet to come until we reach the end. Repetition fixes the whole in our minds yet, if the work is compelling, we remain attentive to its repetition despite knowing how it will end. Without being capable of understanding this relationship of parts to whole, we would never understand the relationship between the stories and chapters, or the paragraphs, sentences and words of Augustine's autobiography. Nor would he be able to shape his experiences into an interrelated whole.

Once Augustine is able to make the shift from understanding time and language in strictly spatial terms – quantifiable projections or points on an imaginary line, he is able to articulate the qualitative dimensions of human time consciousness. He now understands that when we recite a poem, tell a story or listen to a piece of music, intuitively we have the whole before us even before the sounds of voices or instruments begin. The moments of a story or melody do not vanish into oblivion. By continuing to pay attention we add to what we have heard. And because we anticipate what is to come next, we establish the continuity of the unfolding experience. In this way the human inner experience of time is shaped by the three qualities:

retention, attention and anticipation. The unity of the three makes experience continuous and whole.

By shifting to sound Augustine avoids slipping into an "objective fallacy" based on analogies from sight perception. Sound is invisible and while it has an objective physical reality as vibration in space, we know it most intimately and directly as an activity of the ear and mind. We are both the receptive sounding board and, through voice or instrument, the potential maker of sound. Sound, story, music, these seem to happen inside our minds. To be perceived, appreciated and understood, they depend on our subjective responses.

Memory itself has a triadic character similar to the experience of hearing or making sound. We can make the past and future present by remembering, retelling and writing as we activate what we have retained, pay attention to its content, and anticipate what comes next. Memory saves experiences from disappearing. The act of writing from memory preserves the past and helps to make it whole, enabling us to explore multiple possible meanings. And if, as Augustine does, you believe that these meanings, like the story, are already ordained, already whole in the mind of God, then you have the opportunity to perform a parallel aesthetic and epistemological function by taking the fragments of your life and assembling them into larger wholes – to, as it were, hear the melody of your life.

What is true of the human capacity to discover the unitary quality of a life, says Augustine, is also true "of the whole history of mankind, of which each man's life is a part" (Book 11, 27-28). The parts of a life contribute to the whole and the whole of a life to a larger whole, the story of humankind. Our identity, who and what we truly are, will turn out to be amplified by the larger context to which we belong.

IDENTITY: TEMPORAL AND ETERNAL

The concept of identity has diverse meanings that have emerged through human history. While kinship and group loyalty are key attributes of tribal societies, autonomy and uniqueness are critical features of modern economies and political ideologies that place great value on individuality. Western, mainly secular societies are now said to reflect post-modern forms of identity characterized by multiple and more fluid senses of self.

As a contributor to this history of the idea of identity, Augustine has frequently been described as the first "modern" autobiographer precisely because he ascribes to the individual a larger degree of autonomy and culpability than had previously been granted to a person and because he views each individual's life as not just a cyclical mythic journey but also as a uniquely historical one (perhaps spiral or helical). In fact, Augustine bestows the qualities of parable upon the mundane details of an individual's life. Regarded in this way, our lives are both more and less than they may seem, as we are actors using a script written by God the director from on high, a God who delights in giving to every action and event a double meaning depending on the lens through which you view it: temporal or eternal, literal or symbolic, or both.

Augustine presents the biographical aspects of his identity within this dualistic temporal-eternal framework. In the last personal narrative section of the *Confessions*, the last few chapters of Book 9, he provides us with details about his parents. For example, his father was a temperamental fellow who was sometimes verbally (though, claims Augustine, not physically) abusive toward his wife, while she was overly involved in her son's life – though for that he is now grateful. Augustine does not deny that an important aspect of his identity is his family position as the son of these particular influential parents. He describes other relationships in which he is a friend, a father and a lover. Augustine is also a rhetorician, a professor, a Bishop, writer, and North African Roman (of Berber descent). He plays many roles and acquires many attributes through playing them – he is at times ambitious, competitive, eloquent, intelligent, reflective, dogmatic, dutiful, humble and proud.

By virtue of his own theology, Augustine regards himself as possessing free will and therefore he feels responsible for, and often remorseful over, his past actions. He claims for his self-portrait a strong degree of autonomy as a self-regulating, willful person, an agent from whom decisions, vows, actions, and words come forth. He makes the even stronger case that, as a being brought into existence by the creator, he is a dependent creature whose innermost identity contains a spark of the divine. At one moment, in the height of his ecstasy, going beyond mind and rationality, he appears unfettered by his mortal ego and at one with God, a soul almost completely shorn of finite human qualities. This taste of eternity is still temporary and, though the experience defines who Augustine has become, he cannot remain in that moment of rapture. His "sad weight," he says, makes him fall back from the "sweet delight" of spiritual ecstasy, leaving him "swallowed up by normality" (Book 10, 40).

Augustine establishes the paradigm of the spiritual pilgrim as simultaneously a creature of the finite and infinite, of the temporal order and the eternal realm. Somehow, if we believe him, he can see things both ways – through human eyes and from the viewpoint of the deity, from mundane time and from eternity. As finite human beings, we are subjected to the whims of mood, the urges of passion, and the willfulness of disobedience to authority, especially the supreme authority of God as revealed through the words and actions of Jesus Christ and his disciples.

As creatures, we participate in the infinite by virtue of possessing, through memory, ideas and ideals that could not (Augustine argues in following Plato) have been derived from experience, since what we experience through sense perception is always the concrete particulars, the mutable, the imperfect. Through free will we can lead our lives in a disciplined way that more closely corresponds to the ideals of virtue, obedience and love. In this way we are more in awe of the divine authority than that of human Caesars, generals and landed gentry, while not transgressing God's messengers – the hierarchy of the institution of the Catholic Church and its spokespersons, the priests, bishops, cardinals and the Pope. The latter are the leaders of the "city of God," the former are those of the cities of mankind.

Though Augustine does his utmost to Christianize the pagan contemplative ideal of the soul's return to its eternal home as espoused in the teachings of Plotinus (205-270 CE), the embers of that compelling mythology remain aglow under the cooling ashes of Augustine's mature theology. What Plotinus articulated, communicating through his disciple Porphyry who wrote all this down in *The Enneads,* was a vision of life that saw the material world of political upheavals, bodily sufferings and bewildering changes as the degraded forms of a truer and purer reality that was immutable, eternal and unitary. Because human beings are alienated and separated from The One, the principle of a perfect and complete order embodied in a unitive being from which individual souls emanate and are embodied in matter, they must seek to transcend this earthly home, break free of time and change and follow the yearning of the soul for its lost true home. This then, from the Plotinian point of view, is the human condition: to belong simultaneously to a perfect all-encompassing order and to an egoistic and fragmented particular life, the result of freely chosen actions.

The solution, the pathway homeward, is available only to an elite few who are able to pursue a life of leisured withdrawal from the trials and travails of daily life. These individuals must devote themselves to intellectual mastery that enables them to differentiate between the particulars of the world and the universal being of the eternal order from which they come. In addition, the gifted seeker will come to understand the interrelatedness of what has been called "the great chain of being," which is the arrangement of the complete order of beings, from the most perfect to the most imperfect, as the multiplicity that makes up the unity of The One. This continuum then becomes the stairway of ascent for the mind that recognizes the steps that lead upward to an ultimate reunion with The One.

Could such a union be achieved during this lifetime? No, according to Plotinus, but we are capable of momentary glimpses of the final union that would come after death.

Augustine sees himself as belonging to just such an elite, who longed for a home quite different from the one they found in Rome or Milan or Thagaste. If they had to put up with this earthly life, they would at least do so in the most detached manner possible. Where Augustine departed from the Plotinian journey and lifestyle was in his belief that it would take more than philosophic contemplation to find his way home; it would take the intervention of God to bring redemption from his fallen nature, from sin. And that, he believed, could only come from a personal God who so willed his return to the place where the wandering soul may finally rest.

Augustine's picture of human identity seems to make our life an unfortunate but somehow necessary departure from an ideal state of timeless perfection. We are fated to live in a fallen state of finite temporal unfolding that makes our individual history of self-becoming a parable of the soul's yearning to find its way back home. Augustine did not invent this archetypal story; he simply crystallized it by synthesizing the thousand-year long dream of a pagan intellectual elite with the four-hundred-year, comparatively "new" version that erupted through Christianity.

Though many would subsequently condemn Augustine for his misanthropic attitudes towards women, his prudishness about sex and the pleasures of the body, his intolerant views of other faith traditions or versions of Christian belief, and his insistence on the dominant authority of the church as the sacred equivalent of the Roman Empire, his mythology, if we can call it that, appealed to a receptive audience. When we turn to other philosophical autobiographies, even secular ones, we will encounter vestiges of the Augustinian myth and the identity of the homeward-bound journeyer. This paradigmatic structure of origin, departure or exile and return has become so commonplace in life story accounts as to go almost unnoticed. For that reason we need to do a little archeology. Augustine's palace of memory is built on a conceptual foundation, much of which remains hidden from view.

FOLLOWING SAINT AUGUSTINE

Augustine derived his interpretation of the tenets of Christianity that form the foundation of Catholicism (and his life story) from three sources: 1) Scripture (including both the so-called Old Testament, or more accurately, Hebrew Bible, and the New Testament); 2) widely accepted Jewish, pagan and Christian beliefs of the period; and 3) from his observations and analysis of human actions.

We may summarize these views as follows. 1) The world is created and directed by an omnipotent, omniscient and benevolent God; 2) everything that happens, including human actions, is influenced in varying degrees by God's will; 3) nevertheless, human beings are free agents insofar as they can choose what lies within their power to affect – a position that is sometimes referred to as "voluntarism"; from which it follows, 4) that humans are responsible for their actions and are capable of choosing wisely or unwisely, failing from weakness of the will to choose in accordance with God's will and, hence; 5) prone to sinfulness, as is their fatally flawed history from birth; and therefore 6) because of their errant ways, the unrighteous will be punished (if not in this life then in life after death); while 7) only the "elect" will receive God's grace. This last tenet, the predestination of the elect, comes to prominence in Augustine's late writings but is not asserted at the time of the *Confessions*.

Explicit in this complex set of tenets are the familiar theological doctrines of predestination, original sin, individual free will, personal salvation, as well as several of the major attributes of the God of Western faiths (e.g., all-knowing, all-good, present everywhere). Augustine's strong view about predestination incorporates emphasis on human free will while advancing the argument that simultaneously everything humans do is foreknown by God, caused by God. The concepts of predestination and foreknowledge are subtly different. A God who is atemporal knows past, present and future simultaneously, but this God may not possess the power to cause the future or may cede this power to his human creatures (hence, preserving their free will). The God of Augustine's *Confessions* seems to possess more the attribute of divine foreknowledge than of predestination, understood as causing whatever happens to happen.

Still, we must ask, could one argue that all existence is divinely foreknown while insisting that humans have the capacity of free will? Both propositions cannot be simultaneously true. Something has to give. Or does it? What Augustine relinquishes is a linear conception of time that would imply that each moment is the cause of the next. What he acquires is a qualitative, dual temporal understanding of time that allows him to, as it were, stand in two places or imagine two perspectives – one of a human being with a biographical mind and one of a deity with a transhistorical consciousness. The narrative oscillation between the two perspectives can be disorienting to the reader of the *Confessions*.

Augustine's theology is something like life in Kafka's fictive Castle, a realm where the rules seem contradictory, where you're never certain where you stand, who is truly in charge, or how or why you got into your life situation, and yet you have this terrible longing to discover the hidden truth of the place, which is somehow the hidden truth of your own self. The paradoxical character of human experience only became more pronounced as Augustine grew older. So perplexing and pessimistic were Augustine's later theological views that they caused great distress among the monks of monasteries in both North Africa and on the Continent. Some monks even rebelled against the authority of their abbots, arguing that since nothing a person can do will alter whether he or she receives God's grace, their sole preoccupation must be to pray and to passively surrender themselves to God's will. Hence, they will not bother with the mundane day-to-day chores of the monastery.

The great influence of Augustine's theology derives in part from its systematic nature and from its spiritual (or at least psychological) persuasiveness. From the time of ancient Judaism and even in Greek philosophy by the time of Plato (fifth century before the Common Era), a conviction came to the fore that a single all-powerful God ruled over a universe obedient to his laws. This God concept eclipsed (while often incorporating) earlier views of a more capricious universe controlled by multiple Gods that reigned over specific domains such as the sea, mountains, earth, poetry, fortune, war, love, reason and justice. These Gods often made humans playthings in their unpredictable competition. The post-polytheistic Gods, Yahweh in Judaism, the demiurge in Plato, the Prime Mover in Aristotle, are mainly masculine in attributed powers, though the Jewish God has feminine aspects or manifestations – the Judaic *shechinah* or Sabbath Bride. In Augustine's time the Greek Goddess Sophia had become the wisdom figuration of the deity.

Judaism gave us the all-knowing and all-good deity and the edict that the people of Israel were obliged to bend their collective will to the commandments (numbering 613) of that supreme God. Judaism did not promulgate the concept of original sin or the fall, though the book of Genesis conveys a story about disobedience and sexual self-awareness. The Garden of Eden tale is a reformulation of many earlier myths concerning the separation of the human and the divine, the curse or gift of mortality, sexual differences, temptations and the power of procreation. Judaism preserved the idea that the nation and the individual could always turn and return directly to God in atonement for sinful thoughts and actions. Nor was the concept of Predestination as logically educed in Judaism as in Augustine's formulation.

Regarded from a strictly abstract point of view, the set of tenets or foundational building blocks (some would call dogmas) articulated for the faithful placed them in a wholly and holy unified universe ruled over by an "imperial" (Scott, 1995) deity who held them accountable for following his laws as fully revealed through the life, actions and words of his son, the Savior God. Christ then becomes the single mediator between the human and the divine, a now (theologically speaking) otherwise unbridgeable chasm separating human beings and their creator, between the mortal and immortal. Moreover, while a person's salvation depended enormously on leading a life of moral purity and obedience to the rules and regulations of this religious system, only an awe-inspired and fearful love of God would qualify in approaching the status of the true believer and follower. Yet, even at the most extreme version of piety, the individual should have no expectations of persuading the imperial deity to grant the favor of grace, that is, the experience of a direct knowledge and encounter with the divine authority.

From a psycho-spiritual point of view, as the great scholar Rudolf Otto pointed out in his *The Idea of the Holy*, there was and still is something powerfully compelling (he uses the term *a priori*, which means prior to experience, not derived from but preceding it) that is triggered by the idea of holiness and of a supreme deity who created heaven and earth. That idea, historically speaking, inspired millions of people to assent to a system of interlocking doctrines that account for the human condition in a theistic universe. Besides the political imposition of this religious system by converted rulers, how else can we explain the rapid spread of Christianity as it swept away or engulfed centuries of long-dominant myths and cults, even among the most isolated tribal cultures?

The juxtaposition of these religious tenets brought about conflict right from the beginning, as they were promulgated. Which is why Augustine's younger contemporary, Bishop Julian of Eclanum, attacked his concept of original sin, arguing that it "makes it seem as if the Devil were the maker of men" (Brown, 1967). Nevertheless, Augustine prevailed against numerous objections from within Catholicism and without, though all the elements of his system have since been reinterpreted according to the nuanced beliefs of the various Protestant denominations and, within these as within Catholicism, through gradations of interpretation ranging from ultraconservative to ultra-liberal and yet, be it noted, without being abandoned completely.

There is more darkness and pessimism in the Augustine of his later years, when these doctrines were fully formed, than is apparent in the *Confessions*, a work begun when he was 42. Perhaps this is due to the

Visigoth invasion of Rome that had set back the clock on the coming of the Kingdom of God. Perhaps this is because Augustine, as a church father, had to build ever higher and more solid walls against the many heretical movements that challenged Catholic Christianity. Consequently, the moderate austerity he championed with regard to sexual desire, to take one notable example, around the time of the *Confessions* – that the quality of sexual intercourse might be transformed through the permanent friendship of two people in marriage – became in his later writings the complete condemnation of sexuality as a "torture of the will."

The hardened or inflexibly defensive set of doctrines that have come down to us as Augustinianism may seem unappealing, except to those who hold the strongly orthodox positions of a monotheistic faith. Though well-schooled in the humanistic traditions of Greek and Roman culture that placed the human being at the center of the universe, Augustine came to reject this philosophical orientation and instead placed the supreme God at the center not only of the universe but at the innermost core of the human soul. For what more intimate relationship could a mortal being have with an immortal than to discover the God as operating from within one's innermost self at every moment? So when Augustine says, "truth lies in the inner man," he directs the Socratic exhortation to "know thyself" toward a mystical act of self-surrender.

The Augustine of the *Confessions* appears like another, kinder and gentler person whose psychological insights, philosophical depth, and emotional accessibility form almost an antidote to the ascetic sternness of the later teachings. And it is in the *Confessions*, in the very structure of that work, that we may find an explanation of the seeming paradox of Augustine's theology. For foremost, the *Confessions* contains, indeed embodies, a dualistic view of time that allows sudden shifts in perception and attention and points toward a unitary conception of human experience that is at once secular and sacred, one in which what God already knows (the viewpoint of eternity) and what humans seek to know and do (a viewpoint from within human history) are perhaps not irreconcilable, though, for all that, remain all the more mysterious. We will find that Augustine seems capable of a three-dimensional space-time perspective when he writes from the eye-view of the deity and from that of the mortal self – from the viewpoints of eternity and temporality.

BEING ST. AUGUSTINE

Homer's *Odyssey* tells of Odysseus' heroic sea journey to do battle at Troy and there, once victorious, to complete an arduous return voyage to the home island of Ithaca. The saga illustrates the virtues appropriate to the noble warrior and to loyal members of the royal household, and portrays the human struggle with the capricious nature of the gods. Augustine reinterprets this and other Greco-Roman heroic journey legends by over-laying the Christianized biblical narrative of the expulsion from the Garden of Eden and the quest to find a way back. Augustine, too, sails away from home, tackles fame and fortune in Rome and then Milan, achieves success, finds disappointment, battles with temptations, wins a victory, sails back to North Africa and sets up to rule over his wayward flock.

In Augustine's version, the single God is like the pagan multiple Gods in manipulating events and even one's inner motives to determine the outcome of the journey. Paradoxically, we rather pitiful human beings are still supposed to do our utmost to live and act virtuously, love and fear the God, suppress our baser instincts and try to live obediently to follow what this God wants of us. Augustine seems perfectly happy with this arrange-ment. Though his version of earthly life comes across as one long lament, he is capable of delighting in contemplating his humble existence, because in it he discovers all the wonderful gifts that God has bestowed upon him, such as a memory capacity in which he can differentiate the permanent and timeless from the impermanent and changeable. So here is the new hero: the ascetic, celibate administrator-monk with the capacity of double vision (temporal-eternal) and dual existence (mortal body-immortal soul), a living image of a certain ideal of the divine. He also has an exquisite sense of taste and a great love of liturgical music.

None of us could, and few of us would want to, be St. Augustine. Never-theless, a democratized version of the Augustine myth of the soul's journey to its true home permeates Western culture, from the writings of Medieval mystics to 20th century, symbolist poet T.S. Eliot's *Four Quartets* and James Joyce's *Ulysses*. If you were like St. Augustine, you would see every detail of life, every event, every thought and emotion as both literally what it is and figuratively as a sign directing you to the path that you (the true self, not the ego) should follow. The stories of the bible would be your stories, the life of Christ, your life. And though you would and could not be other than who you are – this concrete individual, living in uncertainty, equipped with the capacity and ability to make choices, especially moral choices, prey to temptation by which you would often choose the lesser over the greater good because it was easier and more pleasurable – this unique and unrepeatable You would nevertheless belong completely to God and to the will of God. Regarded in this way, you would be a mere temporary atom of

existence but unfortunately an atom that would have to suffer the consequences of your errant ways or enjoy the bliss of your virtuous ways (if you
were one of the elect) for eternity after death.

Augustine's meaning making is at once radiant and pervasive, elitist
and, in contemporary terms, sexist. He perpetuates the myth of the female
temptress. Yet the rich sensuousness of his pursuit of Sophia and the triune
(mother, son, God) consummation of his search suggest that beneath the
armor of dogma there beats the amorous heart of the passionate seeker. So
for those who do not accept the narrow Augustinian pathway there are still
vivid traces of the universal journey homeward emblazoned by Augustine's
brilliantly soulful questing.

FIELDWORK AND REFLECTIVE WRITING

Augustine's marvelous skill is that he can conjure up the eternal in the
unity of time. He knows that most of us dwell in time's disunity as if we
were living out a parable of exile, wandering and return. For Augustine, it
is our sinfulness that causes our separation from the divine. So here is the
writing exercise. Consider, in the manner of Augustine's *Confessions*, your
own possible experiences of theft, drunkenness, debauchery, lust, gluttony,
arrogance, moral vacillation, desire and divisiveness. Feel free to add to this
list.

Now start another list alongside this first one, placing on it other words
familiar from the Augustinian discourse, doing so in the form of gerunds –
e.g., saving, praising, gazing, tasting, sucking, touching, searching, won-
dering, surrendering and renouncing.

Next, pair up or connect a word that "lights up" in your mind from one
list with a similarly glowing word from the other list. Take this pair as your
theme – e.g., "surrendering lust," "sucking arrogance." Use this pair of
words to write by free association whatever comes into your head for about
five minutes. Then try another pair and write for another five minutes.

Do as many of these pairing exercises as time and energy permit. Reread
and give each of these five-minute exercise pieces a descriptive title (try to
be specific). Now imagine that your editor is a good-natured God with a
great sense of humor. How would your God arrange these pieces to show a
path toward self-forgiveness?

Here are three fieldwork explorations to consider, the first about
gardens, the second about dogmas and the third about evil in movies.

Gardens, ancient and modern, are ideal places for quiet contemplation
and intimate conversations. Augustine's gardens are part of the built
environment even if they suggest something Biblically Edenic – a naturally

endowed paradise of perfection and innocence fashioned by the Deity. Today's gardens range from the humble strawberry patch in the backyard near the commuter railroad tracks to the sprawling, glass-enclosed botanical gardens found in most cities and towns across the world. In emulation of Augustine, take yourself to a garden that is easily accessible, a garden where you can spend an hour of quiet time without being disturbed. Ideally, there will be seating or, if unavailable, your own collapsible fabric chair or a blanket. Alternately, you might choose to take a stroll through an outdoor garden, one with scenic pathways.

Gardens help to remind us of our place as conscious beings in a realm without consciousness yet alive with growth, reproduction, seasonal cycles, beauty, decay, majesty, interdependence, competition, diversity and adaptive ingenuity. We can almost not restrain ourselves from projecting human concerns, motives and affairs into the "conversations" among trees and grasses, orchids and philodendrons, succulents and fungi.

The purpose of this contemplative visit is not spiritual conversion or mystical communion (though these are not prohibited either), rather our purpose is to explore the relationship between the existence of a self-aware being – that is, our own personhood – and the non-conscious realm of organic nature. Aiming to set aside, at least for this one hour or so, our assumptions and opinions about the meaning of human presence in the natural world, we aim to reenact Augustine's inquiry in which he asks of flora and fauna, wind and cloud, sun and stars: "Are you God?" Our goal is to allow the garden's inhabitants to speak unhindered by our educated, indoctrinated and opinionated minds. Our goal is to refine our capacity for receptivity. Afterwards we can allow all of our filtering judgments and categorizing perceptions to return to their dominant positions.

If you are a member of a faith tradition and belong to a religious body, consider for fieldwork interviewing some of its older members to ascertain how the practices of that faith have changed or remained the same during the past three or four decades. The interviews should be conducted on an individual basis to avoid interruptions and heated arguments among multiple interviewees. In all likelihood, you will be encountering issues about egalitarianism (e.g. the ordination of women or their access to participation in religious ceremonies), the uses of traditional source languages (e.g., Latin, Hebrew, Arabic and Sanskrit), the place and role of clerical authority, the group's stance on abortion and homosexuality, changing interpretations and uses of traditional symbols, and so on. Do the older congregants view the changes as improvements or signs of spiritual decline? How do they understand the reasons for the changes?

If you have limited knowledge of the theological ideas, historical controversies and tensions that underlie your devotional practices, you might find it helpful to get hold of a popular yet scholarly book, Karen Armstrong's *The History of God* (1993). Armstrong's book can be a valuable resource for gaining insight into the intellectual battles that have been waged over the conflicting concepts of a Supreme Being and the derived religious practices ascribed to the commandments of the God or Gods.

Another activity, to refresh your memory of the Manichean heresy, is to get hold of one of the *Star Wars* episodes and watch it while paying attention to how the story accounts for the battle between good and evil. Note how resolution of the conflict is handled, the role of superhuman powers, the place of human courage and initiative, and the film's subtext about history and destiny. Consider also how the plot of *Star Wars* accounts for the origin of evil in the universe.

READER'S GUIDE

There is no better place to start exploring the heart and mind of Augustine than the *Confessions*, of which there are numerous English translations, several of which are freely accessible through the Internet. For those who prefer a translation rendered in the contemporary idiom that makes the text sound more natural to the modern reader's ear, the 1963 Rex Warner version (reprinted multiple times), *The Confessions of St. Augustine*, is ideal. For those who enjoy a translation that aims to capture something of the Latin idiom of Augustine's writing and is a more scholarly rendering, consider James J. O'Donnell's 1992 three-volume *Augustine, Confessions*. For readers who would like to know more about the times in which Augustine lived, T. Kermit Scott's *Augustine: His Thought in Context* (1995) is a valuable resource.

The reader's challenge is to read the *Confessions* slowly and carefully, paying attention to the way Augustine weaves the mundane facts of his life with quotations from scripture, as passages from the psalms, the book of Proverbs, from the gospels and from the Song of Songs illumine his life and speak through him. The post-autobiographical books 10-13 will challenge readers unfamiliar with philosophical thought. Still, even for those lacking familiarity with the works of Plato or the Hebrew bible, Augustine's meditations on time and memory, rich with observations from everyday life, remain thought-provoking.

Two outstanding biographies, one brief and the other lengthy, will prove helpful in giving the reader an overview of Augustine's life and times. Gary Wills' *Saint Augustine* (1999), one in the series of "Penguin Lives" inaugurated by Penguin Books, is an outstanding encapsulation of Augustine's development and a defense against what Wills calls "academic conjectures" that assert what he considers ill-informed psychological interpretations of Augustine's writings.

Peter Brown's 1967 more fully elaborated *Augustine of Hippo* is still considered one of the most trustworthy scholarly and readable biographies of Augustine. Brown helps the reader understand the historical context in which Augustine lived and wrote, the literary and philosophical sources that influenced him, and the political and economic changes that helped shape the battle between paganism and Christianity and led to the downfall of the Roman Empire.

For readers who would delve further into Augustine's work, *On the Trinity* provides a fascinating exploration of Augustine's triadic consciousness – how three (e.g., memory, will, intellect) become one in Augustine's meditations on temporality and the workings of the human mind.

Additional resources cited in this chapter: Ariel and Chana Bloch's beautiful translation, *The Song of Songs: The World's First Great Love Poem* (1995), Rudolph Otto's frequently cited *The Idea of the Holy*, first published in German in 1917, thereafter in numerous English editions including one in 2010, and Martha Nussbaum's *Upheavals of Thought: The Intelligence of Emotions* (2001) that includes a wonderfully insightful section on Augustine's *Confessions*.

3

Rousseau on the Road to Vincennes

Augustine's *Confessions* found many imitators in the spiritual communities of the monastic Middle Ages. Most embraced a two-part, before-and-after narrative approach. For example, in her spiritual autobiography, *Life*, the 16th century Spanish mystic, spiritual reformer, and founder of Carmelite convents, St. Teresa of Avila, devoted three times as many chapters to her "new life" following her conversion experience as to the first part of her life, despite the fact that the first part encompassed thirty-nine years (birth to conversion experience), while the second part covered only eight.

Writing primarily for the monastic community of her confessors and spiritual directors who requested this work, it is not surprising that, having reported on her parentage and upbringing, St. Teresa would concentrate on "the favors and kind of prayer" she says she felt the Lord had granted her. Augustine's *Confessions*, a Spanish translation of which she read in 1554, profoundly influenced Teresa's writing of the *Life*, published in 1565. One of the many who would fulfill Augustine's hope that his evocative story might impact others' lives, Teresa exclaimed that she saw her own difficulties in Augustine's testimony of his spiritual struggles. And when she read the description of his conversion and the voice in the garden experience, she "totally dissolved in tears." According to her autobiography, Teresa's "new life" represented a complete break from the past, so much so that the story following her conversion qualified in her mind as a "new book."

This was not so in Augustine's case. Despite the fact that the *Confessions* gives the appearance of being composed of two quite different parts – the childhood to conversion experience and his mother's death recounted in Books 1-9 and the meditation on time, memory and creation of Books 10-13 – the latter comprise more a celebration of the vantage point Augustine achieved in synthesizing his knowledge of ancient Greek philosophy with his fresh interpretation of meaning in the Old and New Testaments and writings of the Christian saints. Augustine struggled throughout his life with what he called his "two wills" – one drawing him to the sensuous, earthly life and the other to the immaterial and eternal. Had it not included accounts of the urges, passions, desires and aspirations of the period of his childhood through to his attainment of worldly success, Augustine's *Confessions* would have long been relegated to the genre of spiritual literature known as the lives of the saints. In his narrative the sustained tension of the two wills continues to give Augustine's *Confessions* contemporary relevance.

Thirteen hundred years later another confessional narrative containing scenes of self-transformation – both similar and radically different from Augustine's accounts – appeared before the literate public. This time its language was French. Like St. Augustine and St. Theresa's narratives, the story also featured a dramatic before and after turning-point scene. Only this self-transformation was not of a traditional religious kind, nor did it serve to make the early years of childhood, youth and adulthood secondary to what came after. On the contrary, the account of the narrator's childhood and youth turned out to be crucial to his own, and subsequently his readers', understanding of the influential person that he became. As for the matter of having two wills, this next autobiographer will describe the struggle he experienced as the possessor of both a natural and an unnatural or distorted inner self.

This dramatic, one might even say paradigm-transforming literary and philosophical innovation came from the pen of an individual who would put nature (*la nature*) where Augustine had placed God (*Deus*), and would point to the emotion of shame where the Saint had uttered sin. The Geneva-born 18th century confessional writer, a Protestant who flirted with Catholicism for a period in his youth, did not open the book of an Apostle to experience redirection to a new life. Rather, browsing in a literary magazine, he came upon an advertisement announcing an essay contest whose topic questioned the moral values of the times. Though he would later rue the day of this transformative experience, it put our next philosophical autobiographer on the path to becoming one of the most famous figures of the European Age of Enlightenment.

One could say that Jean-Jacques Rousseau (1712-1778) was a child born of literature. When he entered the world a frail and sickly infant, his mother departed, dying of complications of childbirth. She bequeathed to the household of his father, Isaac Rousseau, a large collection of Greek and Roman classics as well as a fair number of the romantic novels of which she was so fond.

Rousseau's father would read these literary works to the young Jean-Jacques, inadvertently providing him with a precocious education not only in the intellectual realm of ideas and history but also in the life of feeling. Jean-Jacques recounts that as he quickly became literate, he and his father would sit up at night taking turns reading from the novel of the moment and would become so enthralled with the story that they might carry on until daybreak. The effects of this literary communion between father and son were a sharing in the joy and tears of each heroic tale, conjoined in the sadness of the lost wife and mother, Suzanne. For the child Jean-Jacques, these literary evenings provided an education in a range of sentiments far in advance of his actual life experiences.

Rousseau says that he had "a knowledge of the passions" that was unique in a child his age. While he had no conceptually formed ideas of "things in themselves," of the youthful Rousseau he asserts "all the feelings of actual life were already known to me. I had conceived nothing, but felt everything." Since he had not yet acquired the powers of reason, these emotions, initiated through literature, placed a stamp on his personality, giving him a romantic view of life that later experience and reflection could never erase.

Referring to this precocious education in the life of feeling, Rousseau says it was both a blessing and a curse. It created the colorful palate of his emotional life, later helping him to cultivate his talents as a composer of music and of words, while it burdened him with an unusual susceptibility to feelings to which other less highly-strung mortals would be insensitive or indifferent. Rousseau would claim that he counted this early encounter with books as the source of "the unbroken consciousness of my own existence."

When his clockmaker father got into trouble because of a quarrel with a French captain and had to flee from their walled city, the ten year-old Jean-Jacques was put into the care of his Uncle Gabriel Bernard, who soon sent him along with his own son, Abraham, to live in the household of the scholarly Calvinist Pastor Jean-Jacques Lambercier, where the boys would study subjects such as mathematics and Latin. There, in the village of Bossey, Jean-Jacques acquired a passion for the study of nature and a different passion for the Pastor's daughter, Gabrielle. He found he enjoyed the occasional spanking he received from the older girl's hand for some minor infraction. In this way emerged Rousseau's self-revealed sado-masochism – not exactly the usual topic for a life story of the period. But then, Rousseau's story was not typical.

Two years later the boys would return to Rousseau's uncle's home and shortly thereafter Jean-Jacques was placed in the household of an engraver where he earned his room and board as an apprentice. After three years of unhappy toiling, he ran away, eventually ending up in the manor of an attractive widow who took in young men willing to receive indoctrination as Catholic converts. The widow, Madam de Waren, had a fondness for handsome youths. So in addition to his theological training, she provided Rousseau with an initiation into the life of adult sexuality. Along the way of his meandering apprenticeships and religious and erotic education, the mostly self-taught Rousseau acquired knowledge in musical performance and composition, secretarial skills and, through continued extensive reading, familiarity with the expansive literature of the arts, humanities and sciences that were to suffuse the Age of Enlightenment. He also experienced hardships, betrayals, unrequited love, poverty and a debilitating addiction to masturbation – the latter, compounded by his fertile imagination, becoming a substitute for his many unrequited infatuations.

In the contemporary idiom we might say that Rousseau gives us TMI, too much information. And we might wonder why anyone would choose to reveal such intimate, and for most people, humiliating details about himself? Do they help us understand the world-famous ideas for which such an individual became renowned?

From Rousseau's point of view, the answer to the latter question is yes. He regarded his life history as a reflection of the social values and attitudes that could distort an innocent child's development. Rousseau makes his life a case history that becomes the context for understanding the clash between emerging ideas of freedom, justice and knowledge and religious dogma, social stratification and enculturated beliefs and attitudes of his day. In all its intimate details Rousseau made his personal life a laboratory for the study of social change. Though he would claim that his was a unique existence, and that it was Nature herself that "broke the mold" in which he was cast, Rousseau would still cry out his justification for making public his self-revelations. He would appeal to both his own and to the nature of humankind that his story serves to illumine the lives of countless others. In his life story one would learn about how the formation of passions such as greed, anger, envy and sexual obsession distort the person endowed with the simple gifts of natural being. By depicting the negative Rousseau believed the positive could be revealed.

Though it is perhaps unfair to impose a modern psychological framework on Rousseau, it is difficult not to regard him as a "marginal" personality. In his three major self-narratives written in his mid and later life (and published posthumously) Rousseau depicts himself as the repeatedly misunderstood and alienated, indeed frequently banished, citizen of one kingdom or duchy of northern Europe after another, the odd man out of one group of would-be friends, colleagues, protectors or benefactors after another. He believed that not only his enemies but even his friends were in conspiracy against him. He could trust no one, was always on the outside of society – whether the households of wealthy aristocrats (many of whom would lose their heads to the guillotine of the French Revolution) or middle-class intellectuals and artists, some of whom would help to see those heads roll.

This alienated outsider complex was his unfortunate burden but also his gift, because as one who always put himself at a distance – though he would claim his outsider perspective was imposed upon him by others – Rousseau acquired the skills of observation, detachment, independent and critical thinking, combined with a fertile imagination. These qualities would be crucial to the originality of his work and thought. He possessed the power of envisioning the possible where others only saw the necessary and unchangeable.

Rousseau even dressed differently from his contemporaries, donning loosely fitting Turkish pantaloons instead of the then-socially fashionable culottes or knee breeches. He also sported a turban. While this baggy costume concealed an embarrassing problem of incontinence due to a life-long urinary tract disease, it also befitted Rousseau's contrarian disposition and eccentric personality.

Rousseau challenges his readers to understand how a peripatetic, emotionally orphaned, wandering music teacher could transform himself into an epoch-making philosopher whose words, "Man is born free and is everywhere in chains," has echoed through the centuries as a clarion call to revolution. Rousseau was presumptuous enough to believe that when he dubbed his life story *The Confessions*, it would eclipse the work of the famous Augustine. Where there had been original sin, the world would now discover original innocence.

A COUNTRY ROAD

Jean-Jacques Rousseau, age thirty-nine, is walking the six miles from his solitary room in central Paris to the chateau prison of Vincennes where he is going to visit his friend, Denis Diderot, man of letters, philosopher and soon-to-be editor of the first compendium of the enormous expansion of the world's knowledge, the *Encyclopédie*. Diderot has been imprisoned for the boldness of his philosophical writings. The ruling segments of French society, besieged on every side by revolutionary movements, are highly sensitive to anything that suggests a challenge to the mutually supporting authority of church, king, and nobility. Diderot, a free thinker, has argued against divine revelation in favor of a rationalistic religiosity and championed the Enlightenment view that empirical observation – knowledge gained through the senses – is more trustworthy than appeal to innate ideas that only the highly educated secular elite and the priesthood possess. Among his wild scientific speculations, Diderot has suggested the blind may learn to read through the sense of touch.

It is a warm autumn day, recounts Jean-Jacques in Book Eight of his *Confessions*, and though he is an ardent rambler, he would rather have hired a carriage for this journey, could he have afforded the fare. Poor Rousseau has worn himself out by striding along at a rapid pace. He should rest a moment. Unfortunately, and here we get a tiny foreshadowing of Rousseau's campaign against the distortion of nature and the natural, the trees that line the road are "lopped after the fashion of the country" and afford little shade.

Usually he brings a book to read while walking but today, in haste, he has tucked a copy of the monthly magazine, *Le Mercure de France*, under his arm. Struggling along, perspiring in the late afternoon heat, Rousseau begins to glance through the pages of the magazine. Suddenly, his eyes fall on an announcement. The Academy of the University of Dijon is offering a prize to be awarded the following year, 1750, for the best essay answering the question: "Has the restoration of the sciences and arts tended to purify morals?" In a flash his mind is filled with ideas and phrases.

Who better than he, thinks Rousseau, to address such a question? He has taught music to young ladies in the finest of French households and written several operas, though because of others' jealousies and conniving none have been successfully produced. Self-educated, he has immersed himself in classical as well as popular literature, studied the history of civilizations, traveled widely, received instructions in both his native Calvinism and Catholicism, observed the working of governments, kings, tyrants, and even recently served as assistant to the French ambassador to Italy, though that assignment ended disastrously. If the arts and sciences, revived under the banner of the Enlightenment, have improved the condition of mankind, then surely he, Jean-Jacques, is in a position to know and to address the Academy's question. He must immediately stop to make notes.

Rousseau spots a large oak tree whose shelter can provide the respite for him to quickly sketch out the line of argumentation he will use in writing the essay. If only he could capture a fraction of the ideas and insights that flood his mind. Half an hour later, putting away his pencil and paper, he hurries on to Vincennes and his friend.

Diderot, released from the towering dungeon after a month of solitary confinement, may now meet with his wife and friends on the grounds of the chateau. "In a state of agitation bordering upon madness," Rousseau tells about the contest and reads his preliminary sketch to Diderot, who encourages him to seek the prize. How fortunate he is to have an intelligent, supportive friend like Diderot. Yet Rousseau cannot help but reflect on the occasion of his earlier visit just after Diderot was released from the dungeon. Distraught about his friend's health and sanity, Rousseau had flung himself upon Diderot, embracing him with cries and sighs, "choked with tenderness and joy." And Diderot's response? He turned to another visitor, a priest, and said: "You see, sir, how my friends love me!" Strange, thinks Rousseau, "this would not have been the first idea that would have occurred to me had I been in Diderot's place."

Is Diderot a false friend, merely using Rousseau's affections for his own ulterior ends? What has happened to people that the more cultured and sophisticated, the less sincere they become? Have noble speeches replaced noble actions; do manners and customs alienate people from their own honest and genuine natural selves? These reflections will become part of the theme of Rousseau's essay – the decline of moral virtue under the influence of cultural and intellectual refinement. People were better off when they lived in huts and formed close-knit bands to guarantee their survival, he would argue.

In the ensuing essay from his scribbled notes, Rousseau alludes to ancient Sparta and the austere nobility of its proud citizens, comparing them to the Athenians who, he says, grew soft and careless through luxuriating in their cultural and scientific achievement. His thesis is not original. Commentaries on the superiority of nature over artifice, the primitive over the civilized, had already flowed from the pens of thinkers such as Montesquieu, Fenelon, Seneca, Plutarch and even the ancient Plato.

Still Rousseau's line of argumentation flies in the face of many of his friends, the *philosophes*, who believe in the benefits to mankind of scientific advancement such as the worldview-altering discoveries of Isaac Newton and the flourishing of music, drama, literature and the visual arts. Had not the great Voltaire written eloquently on the progressive improvement of human conduct in light of modern Europe's slow awakening from dark centuries of superstition and ignorance, guided by the advancement of learning and science? True, thought Rousseau, but why listen to that skeptical windbag, Voltaire? Jean-Jacques would show the world that too great a price had been paid for so-called enlightenment.

From the moment he read the words about the prize of Dijon, says Rousseau, he "beheld another world and became another man." From then on Jean-Jacques, destined to win the prize, would become the visionary spokesman for life liberated from false manners, stultifying customs, repressive governments, and forms of education insensitive to the natural development of the child. He would be caught in the middle of political and social controversies, and become suspicious of his friends to the point of paranoia, a victim of intrigues and deceptions, himself capable of maligning others and abusing their hospitality. Though his name will be known the world over, he will pay a great price for "this moment of madness" on the road to Vincennes.

Following his essay on the arts and sciences, known as the First Discourse, Rousseau later extended his visionary critique of society, writing a series of passionate essays on freedom and autonomy that led to the Second Discourse, three years later, on the origins of inequality among men. His impassioned words concerning the natural dignity of mankind became a banner for the French Revolution, and he its posthumous prophet. Yet during the remainder of his life, Rousseau was harried from country to country, denounced in one, embraced in another, only to be denounced again there. Eventually he decides to tell his story as a confessional tale of daring candor and originality.

Readers already familiar with Augustine's *Confessions* will note the teasing parallels to Book 8 of his testament. We remember from the previous chapter how Augustine, pacing around in the garden with his friend Alypius, agonizes over his desire and resistance to accepting the life commitment of a Christian believer. We recall the childlike voice that chants playfully: "Take up and read; Take up and read." And how Augustine, as if receiving a divine command, picks up his copy of the Epistles of Paul in which his eyes fall on a certain passage concerning relief from a life of longing and vice. This vehicle serves to open his passageway to the conversion experience.

That Rousseau's Book 8 also offers readers a dramatic account of his life-changing experience is no mere coincidence. He too has read a passage containing a challenging question about the possibilities of living a virtuous life. He too flings himself under a tree. And he too hears a voice, though an inward one, that tells him how to respond to the question. And though his friend is not immediately present, as was Augustine's, Rousseau has his Diderot as intellectual and spiritual companion near enough to soon share in his revelation. And though it is not located in a courtyard garden, the scene of Rousseau's transformation is also outdoors, under the sky and a sturdy oak, not fig, tree.

Rousseau's revelation has to take place out of doors and metaphorically echo an arduous journey on foot. How else would the man who extolled nature find his way? And how could he not, like Augustine, realize what this act of self-change would mean in terms of the difficulties he would have to face as the apostle of the natural man? Augustine gained fame and power. Rousseau gained fame and sorrow. Augustine pointed to the misdeeds of Adam and Eve in the Garden of Eden as the source of human misfortune from which only the new Redeemer could bring the power of redemption, the soul-cleansing blood of sacrifice. Rousseau rejected this account as anthropologically impossible since humans in a hypothetical state of nature would have no idea of deception or disobedience. Sin was not the original state but only emerged when humans aggregated and formed social groups and hierarchies. Human beings created sins through the exaggerated affects of the passions. Given the right upbringing and education, a new and more genuine human could come about who would be free of these passions and resultant vices. Humans, Rousseau proclaimed, have to save themselves. What's more, they have the power to do so.

Curiously – though not unlike Augustine in Book 9 of his *Confessions* – in the middle of presenting this vividly recollected and depicted story of the circumstances that changed his life, Rousseau pauses for a moment to reflect on the possible fallibility of one's memory. He has, says Jean-Jacques, "a lively recollection of the impressions" which this life-changing occasion produced upon him, yet he admits "the details have escaped me." This is understandable, since almost twenty years have passed since the moment of his "illumination." No, it is not simply the passage of time that has induced forgetfulness, says Rousseau. Rather he finds that once he has committed an experience to paper, in this case sharing the story a few years afterward in a letter to his friend Monsieur de Malesherbes, he ceases to remember it. For Rousseau, writing something down causes the particularities of the event to disappear from memory. If that is so, then just what is the status of the epiphany under the oak and other scenes depicted in Rousseau's lengthy autobiography? Once again, the philosopher interrogates the workings of his own mind and reveals his autobiographical method.

WRITING AND MEMORY

Rousseau discusses two interrelated issues about writing and memory. Both have to do with a goal to which most writers aspire: capturing emotions, thoughts and remembrances and bringing them alive on paper. Writers call it creating a sense of "immediacy."

Because writing induces forgetfulness for Rousseau, he has devised a method of composition that he first used in preparing the second Dijon essay. Prone to insomnia, he would stay awake at night contemplating his feelings and ideas for the essay and gradually fashion them into sentences that he would mentally rewrite and then commit to memory. A hired secretary, Madame Le Vasseur, the mother of Therese, the woman with whom he would later live and produce offspring, would arrive at his apartment in the morning and, while he was still in bed, Rousseau would dictate the memorized text to her and she would write it down. This way he would not forget the sentences of his nocturnal composition, which, if he were to get up and take the time to wash and dress, would lose their freshness and vibrancy. Besides, by not writing down his own thoughts and impressions, presumably Rousseau would better be able to retain them. Rousseau says he encountered the same problem with music. He could easily learn songs by heart. But once he acquired the skill of notational sight-reading, he was no longer able to recall melodies he had learned spontaneously.

So much for sidestepping the mechanics of writing in order to retain the freshness of thought and feeling. Today this would be like using a dictation machine or voice-activated word processing program. What happens after Rousseau has, in fact, written an account he has shared with other readers? Here is where Rousseau helps to usher in the Romantic era of literature. The second issue for Rousseau is how to recover, recapture and communicate the felt immediacy of the remembered past.

Rousseau makes it clear that he is less concerned with reproducing exact accounts of past experience then he is in revisiting past scenes to try to revive feelings he had at the time. These feelings, more than facts, hold the meanings that Rousseau regards as crucial for both self-understanding and for justifying himself to his readers. There is little question but that Rousseau as much re-imagines past experiences as remembers them. This doesn't trouble him, because his goal is to make vividly present the felt meaning of the past. In this sense, he seeks to achieve two perspectives simultaneously. One perspective is to bring to life what an experience felt like in his childhood, youth or young adulthood (e.g. the epiphany under the oak). Another perspective is to retell this experience drawing on insights that could only come later and yet not let this retrospective interpretation blunt the immediacy of the original experience.

And here we have the essential elements of the Romantic movement of the 19th century – emphasis on the inward truth, the life of feeling, spontaneity, the transcendence of reason, the expressive self – a movement whose authors, painters and composers would often refer back to Rousseau.

Rousseau's reflections on thought, feeling, memory and writing lead him, as they did with Augustine, to further exploration of time, language, history and the self – crucial aspects of the autobiographical act.

THE USES OF REVERIE

Rousseau's theories of time, history, memory and language are completely intertwined and are enacted and embodied in the *Confessions*. To understand this, we have to look again at his second Dijon essay, the work known as the *Discourse on Inequality*. Here we find a quasi-historical, quasi-mythical theory of how human beings have developed over thousands of years, emerging from primitive, mute and isolated creatures to socially organized and linguistically equipped beings. This may sound to us like a precursor to Darwin's theory of evolution. In the post-Darwinian era the "ascent of man" was increasingly associated with ideas of human progress and social betterment and with the uses of intelligence as a mechanism of successful biological and social adaptation.

But Rousseau does not embrace the idea of a progressive improvement of mankind as the dominant earthly species. And though he postulates "perfectibility" as a motive of human freedom, he pictures an ideal condition that belongs not to the future but to a primordial past, when human beings were consciously transparent to themselves and to one another, as they had not yet taken on the falsifying social pretenses and inequality-making class systems of subsequent European civilization.

We might recall a similar-sounding rhetoric that surfaced in the counterculture of the 1960s and was exemplified in works such as Norman O. Brown's *Life Against Death* (1959) and *Love's Body* (1966), the latter describing the conflict between the liberating "polymorphous perversity" of erotic love and the repressive forces of civilization. One might also call to mind Herbert Marcuse's *Eros and Civilization* (1955), a Marxist-Freudian exhortation for a classless and non-repressive society. These authors extolled the idea of a pure childhood self that is uninhibited by social convention and repressive cultural taboos. They seem to echo Rousseau's yearning to recapture a golden age or primal innocence that could be found in both early human development and in an ideal childhood.

Rousseau's method for recovering this authentic self has some of the elements of Freudian psychoanalysis but instead of a couch and a mostly silent therapist who would listen to the patient's free associations, dreams, fantasies and tales of childhood and parents, Rousseau drew upon solitude, reminiscence, countryside ambling, and an approach to writing that would enable him to delve deeply into not only his personal remote past but, by implication, the remote past of mankind.

When popular 60s rock band singers Crosby, Stills, Nash and Young crooned Joni Mitchell's Woodstock Festival anthem, "We've got to get ourselves back to the Garden," they, like Rousseau, were equating an idealized Edenic period of childhood with the authentic self. Going against the socially ingrained belief in progress made possible by industrial technology and modernity, the singers question the idea of perfectibility as something toward which mankind is moving in the future. Instead, the decline or demise of the authentic self is represented not by a biblical Fall but a lost innocence and stifling artificiality that has emerged over centuries of social conformity and emotional repression. A historically lost authentic nature is at the same time one's own hidden true nature and this can be recovered and redeemed through abandoning oneself to exploration through memory and experimentation, which in the 60s would likely have included the use of psychedelic drugs. For his part, Rousseau seemed able to produce his own reverie states while in either a trance-like daze or on a solitary stroll.

Rousseau's approach in the *Confessions* is to showcase his exemplary and daring attempt to use the power of memory – albeit with a good admixture of imagination and literary technique. He calls upon uncensored language to simultaneously discover and express an inner person and, in turn, to invite readers to see themselves in the mirror of his descriptions.

In a later autobiographical work, *Dialogues*, Rousseau praises the "solitary and retiring life" that allows a person to dwell in a state of reverie as a means of shedding the self-falsifying disguises of pretense and self-deception that obfuscate a vision of one's native or intrinsic self. A person willing and able to set about engaging in soul-searching reverie would be like a painter using palette and brushes to bring forth a self-portrait that penetrates outward appearance, truly revealing the artist's inner self. Likewise, this is Rousseau's task in the *Confessions* and in two subsequent autobiographical works, *Reveries of a Solitary Walker* and the *Dialogues*.

His fondness for country walks becomes a metaphor of inward discovery, as Rousseau turns a pathway though the landscape of physical nature into the temporality of a journey through the nature of the self, a trip through one's life from the present moment to the distant past, especially the past of childhood when the individual was closest to his or her unaffected and undistorted self.

Rousseau aims to create a narrative that simultaneously revives past experiences as though they were occurring in the present moment of writing, while he seeks to renew these experiences once again. This dual time perspective has parallels with the pictorial representation of space and foreshadows, by analogy, the landscape and portrait paintings that Cezanne would compose over a hundred years later. Aiming to capture a childlike immediacy of perception, Cezanne compressed the close and distant elements of a landscape, redefining linear three-dimensional perspective by creating visual planes that the viewer's eye sees as receding and advancing colors. He depicted different sides of trees, houses, even the planes of a face, simultaneously through a flattening of perspective. And through emotionally associative color, not realism, he captured the feelings evoked by the very scenes and faces he was painting. In this way, the process of seeing and painting remains vitally alive in the finished work. Not surprisingly, Cezanne was a great fan of Rousseau's.

Just so, the literary predecessor of this post-Impressionist artist who embraced his views about childhood, Rousseau recreates the immediacy of a long past or distant moment as immediately felt memory, while simultaneously evoking his present experience of revisiting that scene as it strikes him under the conditions of a current mood or situation. And as Cezanne would paint his beloved Mount Sainte Victoire over and over in an effort to capture the sacred geometry of this landscape, so would Rousseau repeatedly return to his self-portraiture to discover yet another nuance of his personality and a new facet of meaning.

Rarely is an artist satisfied with making art for his or her own pleasure, stashing away the paintings or manuscript for no other eyes to behold. The impulse to exhibit what one has made invites participation in the creative act and gives the work an ongoing life that affirms the value and stature of its creator. But this exhibitionist tendency also opens the author to the interpretation and judgment of others – appraisals that are difficult, if not impossible, to control. Moreover, the viewer's gaze leads to questions about the maker of this art – his or her originality, choice of influences, apparent moral or political message, and intimated life story. Rousseau wants to take the position of both judge and judged, exercising a sort of authorial intrusion into the reader's role as critic. The issue? Who and what is the truly "natural," that is, undistorted human being?

SHAPING IDENTITY

French literary critic and philosopher Jacques Derrida (1974) offers a highly nuanced reading of Rousseau's *Confessions* in which he contends that there is a radical discrepancy between what Rousseau "declares" to be the truth about the major events of his life and what he "describes" in evoking the emotions of these events. So that while Rousseau will claim that even when he did something not completely honorable, such as telling a lie or casting blame on someone he knew was innocent, he nevertheless remained a virtuous person deep down inside. Circumstances, weakness of character, excessive passion caused by the distorting influences of his childhood and youth serve to explain these dishonorable actions, argues Rousseau.

One could easily imagine him appearing on the Oprah TV show to make his case before the studio audience. Like some contemporary tell-all auto-biographers who appear on talk shows, he will seek to expunge his sense of shame and perhaps guilt through public confession, hoping to win the audience's applause for his candid disclosures. Through his act of soul-baring he aims to persuade readers just what a kind and noble human being he truly is.

But Derrida doesn't buy it. If Rousseau only wanted to convince contemporary and future readers that deep down inside he still possesses the goodness of the "natural man" who has been misaligned and poorly judged, then why would Rousseau provide the reader with such evocative accounts of his romantic encounters? Why revive scenes such as his enjoyment of being physically punished, his subtly referenced acts of self-pleasuring and other tantalizing descriptions? These suggest to Derrida that the *Confessions* is less modeled on the paradigm of St. Augustine's fall and redemption narrative than on another sort of genre – the highly popular libertine novel published anonymously by certain of Rousseau's contemporaries. Today, we would classify these works as soft pornography. Rousseau is no fool. He anticipates his readers' possible moral judgments and he aims to head them off, doing so right from the very beginning of his story.

Rousseau opens the *Confessions* with this claim: that he is putting before his reader an unprecedentedly candid account of an absolutely unique life, an account that is nothing less than an epoch-making literary act that not only has no predecessors but that will have no successors or "imitators." Therefore, unless they are equally willing to rise to the challenge of producing even a remotely similarly soul-baring literary work, no reader is in a position to judge him adversely. To do so would only reveal the confessional competitor's self-deceit and inability to acknowledge the real, that is, authentic, Rousseau. From the very beginning of his *Confessions*, Rousseau claims the right to be the sole authority for creating himself as a character and for judging his life. Moreover, he puts the reader on guard. If they don't watch out, they'll find themselves in a fencing match.

Should the reader attempt a lunge of negative criticism, he will soon find himself parried by the nimble Jean-Jacques.

Rousseau's life and his *Confessions* are replete with contradictions about the nature of authentic identity. And while he describes his own search for self-transparent honesty, Rousseau admits to having been an impostor. He pretended at times to be an accomplished music teacher passing himself off under an alias as the composer Vaussore de Villeneuve, when in actuality he had scant knowledge of music. Later he would disguise himself as an Englishman by the name of Dudding. He also admits that because of his own timidity and fear of acting incorrectly in social situations, he rejected the norms of social manners and adopted his own socially eccentric behavior. Rousseau even plays at being Rousseau, "Citizen of Geneva," when in actuality he had abandoned and rejected that Calvinist city of his early years.

And as for turning his five illegitimate children over to an orphanage where, he claimed, they would be more suitably protected and raised than in his own chaotic household, his readers can only roll their eyes in disbelief that this is the same person who wrote *Emile*, the highly influential treatise on the education of youth. The odor of guilt co-mingled with self-justification wafts off the pages of Rousseau's several autobiographical works. How can readers believe Rousseau's claim that sincerity saves and transfigures the soul because it enables the individual to overcome an inner division, to "become what he ought to be"?

ROUSSEAU'S THOUGHT EXPERIMENT: THE STATE OF NATURE

The question that Rousseau inherited was both personal and historical: what is the world of physical nature trying to communicate to those whose nature is human? Rousseau believes he is uniquely qualified to answer. His own unusual upbringing, personal inclinations and conflicts, sexual desires and career ambitions caused him to wonder, worry about and justify just what sort of a man he should become. Historically speaking, he was born into an age that was burgeoning with new knowledge about the laws of physics, biology and astronomy that called for fresh ways to understand not only the physical world of nature but also the idea of nature as a cosmological process. Nature, his enlightenment contemporaries believed, possessed an inherent goal or *telos* that to them echoed the quest for human freedom. So for Rousseau understanding the nature of nature, his own and the larger world's, was an intertwined enterprise. What then was Rousseau's contribution to these students of nature?

For at least a century after his death, scholars grouped Rousseau with three famous French political, philosophical and scientific figures – Montesquieu, Voltaire and Buffon, dubbing them the "four bright lamps" of the 18th century. Montesquieu was a social commentator and political thinker famous for his articulation of the theory of legislative and judicial "separation of powers," taken for granted in modern discussions of government and implemented in many constitutions throughout the world. Poet, playwright, novelist and historical and scientific essayist, Voltaire, was an outspoken advocate of social reform whose writings played a major role in feeding the fires of both the American and French Revolutions.

Yes, one might say, we've heard of these famous individuals. But who on earth was Buffon? Once considered one of the foremost naturalists of the 18th century, an author of what, in its day, was among the century's "best-selling" multivolume works, the *Histoire Naturelle, Générale et Particulière*, Buffon served for decades as the superintendent of the Jardin du Roi, France's most important scientific laboratory for the study of botany and natural history. Buffon was a gifted writer who extolled the natural world and used the results of both contemporary scientific experiments and the questionably scientific literature of earlier centuries to expound theories on everything from the importance of the biological mother's breastfeeding her child (as opposed to the popular middle- and upper-class preference for the use of wet nurses) as a way to ensure the immunity against diseases of childhood, to the possibilities of life on other planets. Mainly based on his work as a scientific experimenter and theoretician, Buffon's reputation would not survive subsequent scientific discoveries that cast his name and published works into oblivion.

Buffon's importance to Rousseau is that he was among the leading intellectuals of his day who sought to apply reason, animated by a healthy dose of Cartesian doubt (inquiry based not upon received opinion but on reasoned analysis), not only to natural phenomena but also to the domains of human behavior and social arrangements – in other words, to ethics and politics. Proof or justification of theories in all areas of human interest and concern would no longer be justified by referral to biblical sources, ecclesiastical authority or to ingrained cultural attitudes but to demonstrable evidence and convincing logical argument. This meant that almost any inquiry into the knowable world could eventually lead the bold reasoner – who was willing and able to publish his or her results – to condemnation by the clergy, crown or powerful members of the aristocracy. Nevertheless, the projects of Enlightenment thinkers such as the "four bright lamps" illumined every aspect of human life, though their authors would sometimes have to pay a heavy price for their efforts.

Rousseau is said to have once made a pilgrimage to Buffon's study and knelt at the door in adoration of the famous man. Though Rousseau would learn a great deal from him, his and Buffon's idea of what the term nature implied were vastly different. To understand the importance of this divergence, we need a little background that will lead us back in a moment to Buffon.

Rousseau was part of a small group of rebellious thinkers known as the *philosophes*. Their task was to give a foundation to philosophy that was independent of any particular tradition, culture or religion and to advance and justify their thinking by the use of reasoned argument. A key element in their methodology was to conduct thought experiments in which they would attempt to pare away every attribute of the human being that could be identified as the result of social conditioning and acculturation. They would attempt to imagine instead a creature existing in a hypothetical "state of nature." What, they asked, were those remaining intrinsic (we might also say, primal) human characteristics that revealed universal and unchanging qualities? This may seem like a naive question but it constituted a radical starting point for inquiry since the Enlightenment project would seek to determine the optimal and legitimate forms of government and social organization that befitted this pristine human being rather than accepting the ones that happened to then exist.

Prior to Rousseau's contribution, the two most famous accounts of this state of nature were those of Thomas Hobbes and John Locke. Hobbes argued that self-interest was the driving force of the natural being. Consequently, without a form of sovereign government designed to suppress an inevitable war of every person against every other, chaos and anarchy would prevail. Life, in this state, would be, as Hobbes famously described, "solitary, poor, nasty, brutish, and short." Locke's intellectual experiment with the state of nature exercise led him to a far different view. Locke identified an inherent sense of obligations arising between human beings, obligations that manifested themselves in terms of natural rights to life, liberty and property.

Rousseau likewise engaged in this state-of-nature thought experiment but he drew on actual accounts of so-called savage tribes whose (from an 18th century European point of view) uncivilized condition might reveal the natural, pre-civilized or primary characteristics of humans. He argued that Hobbes' portrayal was flawed because it simply took already civilized human beings and removed laws, government and technology from their surroundings. For humans to be at war with one another, Rousseau asserted, they would already need to possess complex thought processes that included concepts of property, calculations about the future, perception of other human beings as threats, and minimal language skills. These attributes, Rousseau insisted, were undeveloped in mankind so Hobbes' speculations were in error. By contrast, Rousseau's infamous "noble savage," a being as yet unshaped and uncorrupted by civilizing forces, was amoral, neither virtuous nor vicious. Rousseau believed these early humans were isolated, since they did not yet form groups for mutual benefit and protection. Yet they exhibited qualities of timidity, tranquility and muteness – lacking in the powers of articulation, since spoken language had not yet emerged. In addition, their perceptions of time were markedly different from those of civilized humans, as they were indifferent, because oblivious, to the anticipation of a future situation.

Rousseau's natural human beings, like Hobbes', do exhibit the motivation of self-preservation, but this is balanced by the capacity for "pity," which Rousseau describes as "an innate repugnance to see his fellow suffer" (Second Discourse). What makes humans different from other animals is their inherent capacity to function as free agents and, though still undeveloped, their inherent power to reason. Freedom and reason, pity and self-interest, these are the essential and inherent characteristics that make up the natural human. Thousands of years would be required for mankind to evolve into the modern social creature that wears *culottes*, kneels before crosses and kings, writes romantic poetry and wages endless wars over territory and belief. As we shall see, Rousseau wishes to point back to this original condition of human beings as an ideal template upon which development might build. This precursor to civilized human beings would be corrupted by the artificiality of life in cities, towns and villages and by the modern state. But there might yet remain a way to reclaim and redeem the primordial being – not by a return to the life of the solitary forest dweller but by rediscovery of the inner person and of the pure self of childhood.

It was against this background that Rousseau studied Buffon's *Natural History* to learn about the forms of primitive man. Buffon's chapter on "Varieties within the Human Species" informed Rousseau that the human race was not, as many of his contemporaries believed, composed of different species but was one species that, through influences of climate, diet, disease and ways of life, manifested itself in divergent ways. By implication, different social systems that evolved did not follow ironclad rules but possessed relative merits depending on the circumstances through which they arose. Therefore there was no one right or divinely mandated form of social organization. Moreover, argued Buffon, this original savage being from whom human diversity sprang and in whom contemporary civilized people might still be able to see themselves, exhibited a gentler, more tranquil and calmer soul than so-called civilized man, a creature misshapen by vices that only emerge in society.

Besides the single origins of humans, Buffon undertook to determine the age of the earth and the original emergence of mankind. Drawing on both geological and astronomical data provided by his contemporaries, Buffon calculated that instead of the Genesis account of six days of creation and one of rest, dating back to 4004 BC, there were actually "seven epochs," the last of which saw the appearance of animals and humans among them. He calculated that the age of the earth was close to 75,000 years.

Especially important for Rousseau (and countless other Enlightenment thinkers, including Thomas Jefferson), was Buffon's conviction that Nature was fully malleable under the dominance of Man. From the domestication of animals such as the dog and horse, to agricultural cultivation to progressive improvements in human social organization, Buffon's Seventh-Epoch human beings exhibited godlike powers. Buffon foresaw a glorious future for the human species now in possession of the skills of the arts, industry, metallurgy, and other branches of scientific knowledge. While Buffon was not a political agitator and sought to avoid all possible controversy with ecclesiastical and governmental authorities, nevertheless his contribution to theoretical knowledge of his day inadvertently aided the camp of social reformers who would appeal to these newly discovered scientific facts to justify a revolution.

Where Buffon looked optimistically on the emerging powers of human reason and the products of artistic and scientific discovery, Rousseau remained skeptical. To him, the world had gotten worse, not better. He was not an advocate for progress moving toward some future paradise. Paradise had already occurred and been lost. The question was: could it be recovered?

Using this state-of-nature methodology, Rousseau, like Buffon, created humankind's elementary form, a sort of culturally unclothed figure, as yet unembarrassed because unself-conscious, whose most fundamental and authentic character and inherent dignity required those forms of social organization that would enhance and endow its essential nature rather than distort and diminish it. Rousseau then attempts a critique of the stages of development such a "natural" being has passed through and might yet evolve toward. The aim of achieving perfectibility of the human experiment through the capacity and exercise of freedom and reason is Rousseau's rallying cry. Yet paradoxically Rousseau's concept of time and history does not point forward or even backward, but inward. Human betterment depends not on more achievements in the arts and sciences but on a truer and more genuine relationship to self and to others – a state of being that once existed but has been lost. How this primordial condition was lost (and might, therefore, be restored) becomes one of Rousseau's main preoccupations.

How long-standing assumptions were subject to critical debate is reflected in the essay contest question put forth by the Academy of Dijon in 1753: "What is the origin of inequality among men; and is it authorized by the natural law?" Even to raise such a question meant taking something that was viewed as part of the fixed nature of society and holding it out for speculation and, if justified, for change. Rousseau had already won the Dijon Academy prize in 1750, writing on whether contributions to the arts and sciences had improved the moral condition of mankind. Not surprisingly given his own precocious experiences with literature as one of the sources of his life-distorting passions, Rousseau argued the rather anti-Enlightenment position that they had not. In response to the new contest question Rousseau took a more positive stance.

Like Buffon, Rousseau argued that humans had evolved over millennia and had passed through numerous stages in their development. His quasi-historical account depicted early forms of social organization arising from small groups of humans banding together temporarily to face certain tasks such as the slaying of large beasts or the construction of shelters. Later when the arts of agriculture and metallurgy were discovered and specialization through division of labor occurred, individuals grouped together with some doing physical labor, others making tools and still others organizing work. From this, distinct social classes and newly adopted ideas of private property emerged which, in turn, created conflict and warfare.

Agreements to form pacts for mutual protection were, argued Rousseau, really no more than ways for those in power to keep their powers by convincing those with less power that it was in their best interest to do so. Inequality is, therefore, not determined by fixed principles of nature but is a byproduct of evolving social arrangements. By their deceptive ways, a cunning few were able to convince the many to pursue an illusion of freedom through which, instead, they "ran to meet their chains."

Once an account of how natural development became distorted gains credence, it tends to point to the possibility of a better, more just and fair state of mankind. The barriers that have been erected to hold back change now begin to weaken. For it is not because of suffering and repression that people eventually rise up in protest, rather it is when a vision is held up that a better condition of life is possible. Rousseau would go on to apply his criteria for authentic, dignified and virtuous human development to areas such as love, marriage and sexuality (*Julie, or the New Heloise*, 1761), political philosophy (*The Social Contract*, 1762), and education (*Emile*, 1762). Each of these works brought him greater fame and greater trouble. Against the background of this hypothetical experiment with the natural conditions of mankind, Rousseau eventually turned his method upon himself.

By now a figure of considerable controversy, Rousseau decided in 1764 to begin writing the first of several autobiographical works, his *Confessions*. While he never says so, Rousseau likely chose this title in order to play opposite to Augustine's narrative of redemption from sin. Rousseau would not need a divine intermediary to accomplish his task. He, the inwardly natural man, already possessed godlike qualities. It was just that they were hidden under layers of fashion finery and concealed by masks of social posturing. His purpose was to show the true persona of Jean-Jacques Rousseau as contrasted to the many false images that had been fabricated by others, either because of jealousy, political opposition or presumed moral superiority. To do this convincingly Rousseau would have to be more self-revealing, self-critical and transparent than any of his contemporaries and, perhaps, more than any author of the past and even, so he claimed, the future.

ROUSSEAU'S INFLUENCE ON ANTHROPOLOGY

We owe a personal debt of gratitude to Rousseau because, directly or indirectly, we have absorbed into the fibers of our being aspects of his contribution to politics, literature, philosophy and education. Our very cultural milieu still echoes Rousseau's exhortations and invitations to heed the inner voice of nature that speaks through the individual self if we are willing and able to quiet the multitude of distracting noises of modern life such as the voices of envy, greed, avarice, pride, egotism and arrogance. Somewhere in each of us is a pure and virtuous soul, an authentic identity that connects us to our prehistoric ancestors and to every living creature, man or beast, mineral or plant. And if sometimes we exhibit some of the excesses of Rousseau's ultra-sincere human, blaming others for our shortcomings, feeling suspicious about other people's intention concerning our welfare, excusing the injuries we have done to others as simply misguided moments due to stress or poor judgment, then maybe we have also to thank Rousseau for these foibles.

Rousseau's philosophical and literary works continue to be read by students of history, political science, anthropology, literature, psychology, education and philosophy. They are essential to an understanding of the

fermenting movements that led up to the French Revolution, to comparative assessment of forms of democratic government particularly regarding
issues of human rights and moral obligations both individual and collective, and to tracing progressive changes in theories of childhood development and, by implication, the education of children and youths. Rousseau's
theory of the naturally good person, who through free will and the capacity
to reason can self-legislate his or her own rules and obligations autono-
mously yet within a consensual civic association, had a powerful impact on
subsequent philosophers such as Immanuel Kant (1724-1804), although the
latter would substitute rational and universal principles for Rousseau's
notion of the "general will" of a particular community.

While Rousseau is certainly not the only philosopher to emphasize the
importance of feelings as well as reason, he is among the relatively few
major thinkers who could serve as predecessors to popular contemporary
notions such as "emotional intelligence," understood as the self-controlled
use of emotional responses as both a guide to creative and constructive
behavior regarding others and as a source of self-awareness and personal
conviction.

Similarly, the important development of ethnography and cultural
anthropology to self-critically identify Eurocentric prejudices in judgment
and categorization regarding so-called "primitive" or "savage" people has
led to more highly refined skills of observation and greater appreciation of
just how "sophisticated" were and are many tribal peoples across the world
in terms of their understanding of natural medicine, weather forecasting,
animal behavior, artistic representation, tool making, and complex forms
of familial and tribal relationships and rituals. Some anthropologist have
strongly identified with Rousseau, both the philosopher and the man of
solitude, and his framework for appreciating both past and present primordial human being. A case in point is the French cultural anthropologist, Claude Levi-Strauss (1908-2009).

Levi-Strauss is noted as a "structural anthropologist" because he put
great emphasis on how human socialization into the use of language leads
to perceiving what we call reality through categories of difference and
distinctness. Levi-Strauss saw these language-informed structures as based
on a system of binary oppositions. He claims that it was Rousseau's description of the gradual rise of linguistic usage from early humans' mute state of
nature – a development caused by the division of labor, sense of possessions and hierarchy within groups that taught human beings to see one
another as different and themselves as special and separate – that led him
to study how language structures reality. Levi-Strauss identifies with
Rousseau's aim in the Second Discourse to search for a condition of primal

human beings which "no longer exists, which perhaps has never existed, but of which it is nevertheless essential to have a sound conception" in order to judge our own society.

Unlike Rousseau, Levi-Strauss did make direct empirical studies of various tribal peoples in the Amazon and elsewhere in whom he sought to find the simplest or underlying forms of emerging social organization. He studied tribal languages in order to discover how tribal people defined and classified the world around them and established laws and rules regarding family relationships. But he did not presume that his anthropological vantage point enabled him or any other non-tribal observer to gain direct insight into the culture of the Other. Rather, the anthropologist, at best, perceives another people's categories through his or her classifying and categorizing system as bequeathed by cultural upbringing.

The anthropologist positions him or herself somewhere between categories of personal subjectivity and the categorizing mind of the subject under study. While this observer may attempt to suspend judgment, this can only be done to the extent that one is reflexively aware of how he or she perceives the world of others as different. Levi-Strauss did seek to find universal abstract structures that define kinship and thus to find common ground with the peoples of the world, whether literate and modernized or non-literate and tribal. Levi-Strauss praised Rousseau for awakening this awareness of what all people share with one another as a single species united by universal principles of mind. So in titling one of his most important books, *La Pensée Sauvage* (*The Savage Mind*, actually a bit of a play on words that could also be translated as "The Wild Pansy"), we see Levi-Strauss tipping his hat to Rousseau's noble savage.

Traces of the Rousseauean fascination with the "noble savage" can also be found in Theodora Kroeber's account of the Yana Indian whom her husband, anthropologist Alfred Kroeber, studied and looked after at the University of California anthropological museum in Berkeley. He was discovered wandering, disoriented, starving and practically naked in the corral of a slaughterhouse near Oroville, California one morning in August of 1911. The man they would later name Ishi ("man" in his native Yana language) turned out to be the last living member of an Indian tribe thought to have completely disappeared. Ishi belonged to a Stone-Age clan that lived in small roving bands occupying an area of rugged country in the foothills of Mount Lassen. For decades Ishi and a small surviving group of five people managed to elude white men who had over the years intruded into their territory, displacing and sometimes murdering Ishi's fellow clansmen. But at the last there was only Ishi, who decided that rather than finding an isolated place to die he would venture into the white man's world and give himself up to whatever happened.

Theodora Kroeber, working with her more elderly husband and a mass of field notes and papers some forty years later after Ishi's death, published her account in the poignant *Ishi in Two Worlds: a Biography of the Last Wild Indian in North America* (1967). While there is no mention of Rousseau, there is ample appreciation of the dignity, modesty, cheerfulness and industriousness of this primordial man. Quoting her husband, she writes that Ishi was "the most patient man I ever knew... [who had] mastered the philosophy of patience, without trace either of self-pity, or of bitterness to dull the purity of his cheerful enduringness." Remarkably Alfred Kroeber and several of his colleagues developed intimate friendships with Ishi, learning to speak some of his language and teaching him theirs, bringing him into their family lives as well as into their professional research. Ishi showed them how he made arrowheads, quills and other tools, as well as clothing and fires. They sympathized with Ishi's unique loneliness as the only one left of his people and they saw in him what is most human and most essential, a compassionate concern for others.

Where others, ignorant of tribal people or prejudiced against Indians as dangerous and inhuman, failed to find any commonality with those they deemed uncivilized, the Kroebers and their colleagues delighted in their association with Ishi and helped to alter popular attitudes by showing the humanity of this last Stone-Age man. Indeed, reports Theodora Kroeber, people from all walks of life were drawn to Ishi as to a lost part of themselves. They made pilgrimages to the Berkeley museum for a chance to glimpse the Stone-Age man. Rousseau would have loved to be one of them.

BEING ROUSSEAU

While Levi-Strauss shares a common language with Jean-Jacques and can easily find links of history, culture and even personality that enable him to identify with Rousseau and his times, the Stone-Age man Ishi seems worlds and eons apart from the often bombastic, self-preoccupied Citizen of Geneva. Of course, this is the Rousseau of the essay, the narrative of self, the dialogues and discourses. It is hard not to assume that as he wrote he also spoke, that his literary tone and rhetorical style are identical to his demeanor in person. Yet Rousseau tells us that he was shy and timid, almost to a fault, and that because of his urinary tract affliction, he constantly feared embarrassment in public situation, many of which he avoided. He was a country walker, a person who loved solitude though he lived for many years with an uneducated linen-maid, Therese Le Vasseur, whom he finally married after twenty-three years of cohabitation and with whom he had the five children.

What seems most amazing about the life of Rousseau is the surprising transformation of the impersonating, largely self-educated, troubled and impoverished young vagabond into the famous thinker so closely associated with the French Enlightenment and the Revolution. The occasion of reading about the Dijon Academy essay contest seems to have functioned as a catalyst that suddenly enabled Rousseau to gather into a focused whole what had hitherto been divergent ideas, interest and impressions. Like many visionaries, he reports this experience as though he were a kind of medium or messenger of the gods, an intermediary between heaven and earth like the mythical Greek god Hermes.

Winning the prize not only changed his stature in the eyes of others, it also changed his image of himself as an actor on the world stage. And he learned to play that role to the hilt by continuing to tap into both what he knew and what he felt. It is Rousseau who is the man of reason and feeling, of sympathy or pity towards others, and of intense self-interest. He is the guilty and the innocent, the memory sojourner, the skillful master of spontaneous self-expression; the man who sought to push Augustine aside from under his fig tree and plant himself there instead. Though Rousseau never mentions Augustine by name in the *Confessions*, he contrasts his views on resignation and a loving deity in his last autobiographical work, *The Reveries of the Solitary Walker*, exclaiming at the end of the Second Walk: "I do not go as far as St. Augustine who would have consoled himself to be damned if such was the will of God."

FIELDWORK AND REFLECTIVE WRITING

In the spirit of Rousseau, go for a walk without a companion who might distract you by conversation. It doesn't matter whether your walk is along forested paths or city sidewalks. Bring along a small paper or plastic bag. Your task is to collect five objects that you happen to come across during your walk. The objects will have to be relatively small to fit inside your bag. They could be organic or inorganic, ranging from a tree leaf to a scrap of newspaper, a dandelion to a rusty nail, a smooth round stone to an empty matchbox. Once you return to your abode, spread out the five objects on a surface and study them carefully. Each will serve you as a metaphorical aspect of human nature. For example, the leaf represents the cycle of seasons that may parallel the "seasons" of one's life. The discarded matchbox speaks to you of the element of fire and energy and also of habits such as smoking a cigarette. Limiting yourself to these five metaphorical items, construct an account of human nature in the form of a short essay such as a modern day Rousseau might conjure up.

On this or a separate walk, equipped with a small note pad and pencil or pen, write down five questions that five things you see raise in your mind. For example, a noble tree might suggest the question: What happened here seventy-five to a hundred years ago when it was just a sprout? Or a curbstone might ask: How does the imposition of a human built edge alter a natural landscape? When you return home, allow the things you have noted to speak through you and onto paper.

Rousseau was a crusader against injustice, using himself as the primary sounding board. These unjust acts could be anything from a raised eyebrow or upturned nose (a snub) to the denial of one's freedom to practice a religion of choice or to proclaim a new scientific theory. Consider injustices in your life or ones experienced by family members and friends. Recreate through writing the situation of one such injustice using your imagination to supplement known or remembered facts. Use Rousseau's bifocal technique of recreating a scene as if it were occurring in the present. Try using present tense, bits of dialogue and sensory descriptors. Then switch perspectives by reconsidering the recreated memory and giving it a different interpretation from the vantage point of hindsight. Draw out the moral lessons that could be extracted from this second perspective. Could these moral lessons be put in the form of maxims that might be useful to others?

READER'S GUIDE

Besides the Internet-accessible translations, the English language Penguin Classics paperback edition of Rousseau's *Confessions* (1953) is widely available. At almost six hundred pages, the work may tax the patience of contemporary readers, especially since in the later parts of the book Rousseau becomes increasingly obsessed with his belief that conspiracies to harm him are being plotted left and right. Reading the *Confessions* as bedtime literature in small draughts, like imbibing a nightcap, will bring the reader much pleasure over Rousseau's eloquence and storytelling ability and less impatience over the frequent sighs and moans of the melancholic, though sometimes comedic, author.

We find a particularly good edition that includes Rousseau's correspondence and letters to Malesherbes in the 1995 University Press of New England translation by Christopher Kelly. *Reveries of a Solitary Walker* is a later, shorter and more compact piece of writing, offering the reader a somewhat more lyrical retelling of many of the same tales as in the *Confessions* though from a more reconciled perspective.

To experience Rousseau's philosophical anthropological mind in action, the Second Discourse on inequality is a must read. Numerous English-language editions containing the First and Second Discourses are readily available in paperback. Excellent studies of the mind of Rousseau are found in Jean Starobinski's *Jean-Jacques Rousseau: Transparency and Obstruction* (1988, translation by Arthur Goldhammer) and Ronald Grimsley's *Jean-Jacques Rousseau: A Study in Self-Awareness* (1969). Kelly is also the author of Rousseau's *Exemplary Life: The Confessions as Political Philosophy* (1987).

On Levi-Strauss's indebtedness to Rousseau, see T. M. Luhrmann, "Our Master, Our Brother: Levi-Strauss's Debt to Rousseau," *Cultural Anthropology*, Vol. 5, No. 4 (Nov., 1990), pp. 396-413. The University of California Press published Theodora Kroeber's *Ishi in Two Worlds* in 1967. David Edmonds and John Eidinow have written *Rousseau's Dog: Two Great Thinkers at War in the Age of Enlightenment* (2006) about the clash between Jean-Jacques and David Hume, the Scottish philosopher famous for his major work, *An Inquiry Concerning Human Understanding*, practically the Bible of British empiricism. Hume gave Rousseau shelter and protection in the English countryside when (1766) Rousseau had to flee Geneva late in his life. The book is cleverly constructed to build toward the ill-fated meeting of the two philosophical greats, however it falls short of the coauthors' highly accessible and philosophically engaging *Wittgenstein's Poker* (2001). To understand Jacques Derrida's critique of Rousseau's theory of how the written word evolved from the spoken, that is, his theory of language, see Part II of Derrida's *Of Grammatology* (1967).

Readers intrigued with St. Teresa of Avila will enjoy her *Autobiography* (sometimes titled *Life*) in a new translation by E. Allison Peers (2010).

4

The Incubus of John Stuart Mill

"Now what I want is facts," insists Mr. Gradgrind, the imperious school teacher in Charles Dickens' novel, *Hard Times*. Facts, he berates his young pupils, not "fancy," not the frivolousness of imagination, will prepare these children to take their places alongside the humming textile machinery of Coketown, the novel's fictive, Victorian-era northern English manufacturing metropolis. Apparently, Mr. Gradgrind has not read Rousseau's *Emile* or, if he has, he's dismissed it as just so much sentimental nonsense from the Continent about the preciousness of childhood. Right from the start, insists Gradgrind, young people must know that the good of society derives from each person harmonizing his and her happiness with the happiness of all. And as a man of "facts and calculations," Mr. Gradgrind knows how to tally up the units of pleasure that each act will render in yielding "the greatest happiness for the greatest number of people."

The schoolmaster has heard this powerful slogan as attributed to the eminent social philosopher, Mr. Bentham, and he is certain that it provides the correct guidance for the future of this booming industrial society. However, as if to rebuke her father's happiness theory, the young Louisa Gradgrind has fallen into a state of depression. Can she not see how much future happiness she will derive from accepting her father's "business proposal" that she wed the wealthy mill owner, Mr. Bounderby, a mere thirty years her senior? Perhaps if she had been less smitten with fancy, she would be better off.

First published in serial form in 1853, Dickens' *Hard Times* is one in a series of satirical novels that attack the evils of industrialization, the use of child labor, and the abuse of childhood itself in denying young people the cultivation and nourishment of their imaginations. Dickens is also ridiculing the newly popular social philosophy with the faintly industrial sounding name, Utilitarianism, whose founder, Jeremy Bentham, actually did devise what he called a "felicific calculus" for determining the amount of pleasure or pain that any given act might produce.

Moreover, though Dickens could not have known this at the time of writing his novel, another young person, similarly educated to dwell on facts and disregard fancy, would likewise recount a serious depressive episode, though for him it came at age twenty. He would attribute his "mental crisis" to a dearth of attention to the life of feeling and imagination in his education and upbringing. He would find the path to recovery in exactly the neglected realm of the imagination – the world of literature and poetry.

If there was ever an education antithetical to Rousseau's edict that "children should be children before being men," and that they should be reading directly from the book of nature through the uses of their five senses before being forced to sit starring at a printed page, it was the one that John Stuart Mill received. And if there was a philosophy that contradicted Rousseau's assertion that children are born with an innate sense of moral goodness that only needs careful nurturing, it is the epistemology of Utilitarianism, a theory that holds we come into the world with nothing in our heads. We are a blank slate, a *tabula rasa*, upon which sense experience inscribes its coded messages.

John Stuart Mill (1806-1873), born of a Scottish father, James Mill, and a Yorkshire mother, Harriet (Burrow) Mill, was an inheritor of the British allegiance to the philosophy of experience known as empiricism, which stretched historically from John Locke to his father's friend and fellow social reformer, Jeremy Bentham (1748-1832). Not only was John Stuart educated according to principles suggested by Mr. Bentham, for several years the Mill family actually lived for about six months each year with the Bentham family at a country estate, Ford Abbey, where Bentham tutored John in various subjects. Projecting the tradition forward, John Mill and the woman who would eventually become his wife, Harriet Taylor Mill, were chosen as godparents to a child by the name of Bertrand Russell (1872-1970) who, when he grew up and became a mathematical logician and political firebrand, turned out to be one of the most important British empiricists of the 20th century.

Given this lineage, we can only wonder whether adopting a philosophy such as empiricism and Utilitarianism, is a matter of temperament, upbringing, education, culture, social class, or even heredity. Though the seeds of a philosophy may be planted early, the soil will vary from one generation to another so that as a species matures, it may look very different from its parent stock. This would certainly be the case for John Stuart Mill.

John Mill grew up during the reign of a king famous for his war with the New World colonies and for his madness, George III (1760-1820), and he matured during that of a queen whose imperial dignity and strong sense of moral propriety lent her name to an era, Queen Victoria (1837-1901). The early decades of the 19th century saw England turn from an agrarian society to an industrial one, with all the wealth and misfortune that followed, depending on where you stood in the hierarchy of the social classes. "Rule Britannia" was still the theme song of the era as the great island kingdom held sway as a colonizer of vast portions of the world, most notably India, managed initially through the East India Trading Company in whose stately London headquarters father James Mill, and later son John, spent the major portion of their working careers.

The rise of a growing merchant class and with it the emergence of new small industrial towns led to a growing middle class that clamored for a voice in the running of government. The influence of the French Revolution and other social upheavals that sought to dismantle the aristocracies of Europe further intensified the call for democracy. The sharp reaction to the terrible suffering exacted by unhealthy and inhumane factory systems, child labor, dangerous mines and the rampant spread of diseases, such as cholera, through the narrow lanes of urban sprawl, found expression in the new Dickensian type of literature.

The Philosophical Radicals, a minority party, championed reforms to make the British Parliament more responsive to the needs of the populace and more independent of the monarchy. The Radicals goaded the liberal but complacent Whig Party to pass the Parliamentary Reform Act of 1832, which led to the enfranchisement of thousands of small property owners and expansion of Parliamentary representation. This was the first of three reform acts that would diminish the power of the House of Lords and its non-elected noblemen and lead to a more representative democracy.

James Mill was one of the founders of the Radical Party. He wanted to do away with the privileges of inheritance that sustained the aristocracy, the landed gentry, and the House of Lords that dominated English law. He championed a society that rewarded merit based on democratic choice, the fuller expression of human rights through male suffrage (he took a weaker position on women's right to the vote), and an entire way of making laws and shaping institutions based on principles that linked self-interest and the individual's pursuit of happiness to the overall happiness of the majority – one's fellow citizens.

To advocate for liberty and democratic participation through representation of the masses, you would have to believe in the good will and responsible character of the ordinary person. You would also have to believe that ordinary people, born with a blank slate for a mind, could be educated to become reasonably intelligent citizens who sought, as you did, continuous self-improvement. James Mill's first guinea pig for his educational theory was his son John.

Adhering to a theory that today we would describe as behaviorism, James believed that if you could control a child's education and environmental influences, you could produce a thoroughly rational individual equipped with the powers of critical analysis that would help to free that person from prejudices of every sort. So he schooled John at home, keeping him under strict supervision and restricting him from contact with other children (apart from his siblings who would eventually number nine) who might lead him astray. He taught John Greek starting at age three, then Latin at seven, logic at twelve, and so on, and held John accountable to produce summaries in both written and oral form of the various books he had been studying. John and his father would take walks during which the son would recount such matters as the history of the Peloponnesian Wars or summarize a treatise on political economy.

A key element of the educational theory was this process of conditioning by which John would associate pleasure with intellectual accomplishment and pain with indolence and indifference. The theory of association, derived from the psychology of David Hartley (1705-1757) with which James Mill was quite familiar, was a critical ingredient of his pedagogical method. If, as Mill and Hartley believed, all knowledge was derived from the senses, then careful observation of the sequences in nature would yield general impressions of the chain of causality linking the first to the last in the order in which they occur. The ability to recall the order of the sequences would lead to an understanding of the regularities in nature. The more carefully trained in detecting these regularities was the child's mind, the more enduring the power of induction. Such training would free the child from superstitions and unexamined opinions.

The combination of the theories of empiricism, associationism, induction, and conditioning that led to experiencing pleasure and pain in accordance with learned behavior (and the requisite critique of received opinions, blind faith and intuited assumptions), would lead to the ideal form of education, which prepared one for a leadership role in bringing about an ideal society. Associationism is a key psychological theory because it accounts for the power to combine into a whole both sensory experiences that eventually become generalities – ideas, and to associate these ideas with either positive or negative emotions. John Stuart Mill was supposed to be the crowning example of the success of this educational theory and its philosophical underpinnings. However, as in the case of Louisa Gradgrind, something went amiss.

A BOOK IN MIND

In the narrative simply entitled *Autobiography*, John Stuart Mill describes the scenes of his childhood. We see him sitting beside his father at a table in a crowded living room with infant siblings howling in various corners attended by his mother, as John does his homework assignment and his father continues to pen the multi-volume *History of British India*, a task that would eventually land him his East India Company employment. In this home schooling environment, John is developing his father's habits of mind and catching his reformer zeal. As one scene leads to another, we find the teenaged John handing out pamphlets on methods of birth control in public places, an act for which he would be arrested on a charge of distributing obscene literature.

Moving ahead a few years, we find that the now twenty-year-old John, thanks to his father's influence, has been working at the East India Company for three years and is now handling correspondence concerning the administration of certain Indian states. He has gone straight from home schooling to work, not attending one of the famous English universities because his father regarded places such as Oxford and Cambridge as havens for idle rich young men. Besides, as John Stuart himself exclaimed, as far as education was concerned, he was already a quarter of a century ahead of his peers.

John had passionately embraced the philosophy and goals of the reform movement as well as the central tenets of empiricism. He became an advocate for the moral philosophy that emphasized usefulness or benefit, an ethical framework he gleaned both from the writings of and family visits with Jeremy Bentham and his circle of admirers. A champion of both interrelated causes, John had begun to publish essays on political, social and cultural topics of the day in a new Radical party journal, the *Westminster Review*.

We might regard him, as did some of his acquaintances, as a youthful version and so perfect a product of his father's teaching as to be, as John said of himself, "a thinking machine." That he had a highly skilled analytic mind is evident as is the fact that he was committed to improvements in the conditions of his fellow citizens. How these are interrelated is revealed under the banner with which both son and father were known in philosophical circles – the school of thought known as Utilitarianism.

Utilitarianism is an awkward and frequently misapplied name for a moral philosophy maintaining that human happiness is the end and the test of right and wrong decisions and actions, that it is the abundance of pleasure over pain that guides happiness, and that based on our experience of that which maximizes pleasure (and minimizes pain) in our choices and conduct, we could formulate certain guidelines that should hold not only for ourselves but for all others. In this way our individual pursuits of happiness, taking care not to infringe on others' similar pursuits, would combine to produce "the greatest happiness for the greatest number."

What is remarkable about Utilitarianism, a species of what philosophers call a normative ethics (because it supplies us with norms for how we should act to favor good over evil), is its foundation on a principle that goes back at least to Aristotle – that happiness is the ultimate objective of life. Aristotle said that happiness was activity in accordance with virtue. But in Jeremy Bentham's formulation, embraced early by John Stuart, happiness is dependent not on some abstract moral qualities but on what we might think of as almost biological or instinctive properties – physical and emotional pleasure and pain.

Unlike other normative ethical systems based on our sense of doing the right thing (duty), or following religious commandments derived from the edict of a supreme being, or based on direct intuition of some inherent human attributes such as an instinct for sympathy or cooperation, Utilitarian ethics was rooted in a lowest common denominator, what lies simply in the nature of being human. This is why Utilitarianism, or this early version of it, is considered a naturalistic ethics. And why, since it emphasizes the consequences of choices and actions, and less a person's motives or intentions, it is classified as teleological (the Greek, *telos* = end or goal).

Tallying various types and degrees of pleasure and the avoidance of pain to derive the good of all mankind, may seem to require leaping over a vast intellectual chasm. And, in fact, given the impact of Utilitarianism on a great many democracies, making this leap would ever after challenge their governing bodies to balance the rights of individuals to pursue happiness and the needs of society to guarantee the rights of all to pursue the happiness that sustained and nourished the aggregate whole. John Stuart Mill had to face this challenge in his early adulthood.

At this time Mill's objective in life was, he says, to be "a reformer of the world." His view of his own happiness is inextricably linked to this purpose. It gives him a "durable and distant" goal toward which he believes he will always be making progress and provides him with a community of fellow believers with whom to associate in a common enterprise. Everything about his life seemed to be going splendidly, when, he says, he suddenly "awakened from a dream."

The twenty year-old John asks himself a simple question: "Supposing all of your political and reformer goals were achieved so that the improvements you project into the future for society and its institutions were accomplished. Would you then experience joy and happiness?" And an irrepressible voice answers back: "No." At this, Mill says, his "heart sank." The seemingly sturdy intellectual structure on which he had based his life "fell down" like a house of cards. He is mortified and compares the ensuing bleak epiphany to that of a Methodist's "first conviction of sin." Such a conviction bursts forth when a person realizes there is something terribly wrong with his or her life, some fatal error that condemns the person to darkness from which they will need to seek redemption.

Over several pages of the *Autobiography*, Mill creates a picture of his growing desperation. He carefully enumerates why he had nowhere to turn for help, applying his usual logical precision to his self-diagnosis of depression. Lacking a long-term, stable purpose in life, he was, he says, "a ship without a rudder." He no longer finds enjoyment from the usual sources such as books or music. He has no one to share his experience with because of a lack of friends and of closeness to his mother or his siblings. For despite living together in close quarters, the family atmosphere was emotionally restrained.

He finds he cannot discuss his situation with his father because his condition has no place within the system of James Mill's theoretical constructs. And, with his love of music, he arrives at the disheartening conclusion that all musical combinations of harmonious notes must have been exhausted so that no new musical composing is possible. Concerning other factors such as loss of sleep or appetite, classical symptoms of modern-day clinical depression, he remains silent.

Relating how he had "nothing left to live for," Mill introduces something new into the pages of his autobiography, a poem. He says the lines of the melancholy piece, "Dejection," by one of the English Lake Poets (so called because they lived in the beautiful Lake District of rural northern England), Samuel Taylor Coleridge, perfectly echo his situation though, chronologically, he did not encounter this poem until several years after the event he is recounting.

> A grief without a pang, void, dark and drear,
> A drowsy, stifled, unimpassioned grief,
> Which finds no natural outlet or relief
> In word, or sigh, or tear.

Mill reconstructs the sequence of events that led to his "mental crisis" so as to highlight their significance. He is not attempting to render an unfiltered recollection of how the events unfolded at the time; rather he seems to be following the aesthetic method of another of the Lake Poets, William Wordsworth, who aimed to depict "emotion recollected in tranquility." This tranquility was an achieved perspective that Mill only later could utilize to reconstruct the events of 1826-27. We may be surprised that it is Coleridge, a religious conservative who defended the traditional family and whose philosophical views were deeply influenced by German Idealism (a species of Continental Rationalism) that Mill draws on for insight. We will see that his choice was highly strategic.

Though he was raised to associate pleasure with noble deeds and good thoughts ("all things beneficial") and to associate pain with the opposite ("all things hurtful"), this educational method did not enable him to establish sufficiently strong associations to withstand "the power of analysis" in which he had also been trained. The connections were "artificial and casual" and lacked a "natural tie," he concludes, because the "analysing spirit remains without its natural complements and correctives." Just what might this be? Mill, the persistent empiricist, believes that while analysis can strengthen your grasp of "the permanent sequences in nature; the real connections between Things," without cultivation of feelings sufficiently strong to bind pleasure and joy with such natural knowledge, we are left unfeeling about that for which we should otherwise espouse great sympathy. In Mill's case, this meant indifference towards the well-being of others.

Contemporary readers might simply conclude that Mill's idealism was dashed and that he realized the inadequacy of the theory of association, because it gave too mechanical a picture of the way the mind worked and consequently led to methods of conditioning that were ultimately doomed to failure. In short, he was all head and no heart. His instinctive life was stifled. It's not surprising then that Mill should awake as if from a dream. It was someone else's dream, his father's. From our contemporary psychological perspective, we might conclude that Mill needed to regain his self-esteem and to get out from under his father's domination. But this was not the way Mill reconstructs and retells his story of what happened during the "melancholy winter of 1826-27."

Mill paints a remarkable picture of isolation, hopelessness and, because he could not imagine continuing his life indefinitely in this way, suicidal thoughts. Despite this inward struggle, we know from his account and that of biographers that he continues to maintain his professional responsibilities. People around him remained unaware of his psychological condition.

Concerning how he will deal with his depression, much hangs in the balance. Not only his life and sanity, but also an entire philosophical tradition of which he was once the proud recipient and is now more a victim. John Stuart is now a deviant whose mental collapse would stand as an indictment of the whole edifice of Utilitarian thought – a suitable topic for a Dickens novel.

Mill tells us this story for a purpose, as he tells us earlier in the *Autobiography* about how a child of ordinary intelligence is capable of far more than any school might require, since "a pupil from whom nothing is ever demanded which he cannot do, never does all he can." Now we know that there is something that Mill cannot do, namely, produce his own happiness. Nevertheless, he will seek to cure himself of depression, though how he does this, he says with deliberate qualification, is in part "accidental." His choice of this word is, however, not accidental. If we remember how Augustine just happened to a hear a child's voice singing something like "take and read," and how by a stroke of good fortune he happened to have the epistles of Paul lying close at hand and happened to open the book to just the right passage, we will be alert to the way seemingly insignificant or circumstantial factors can become a catalyst for momentous change. In Augustine's case, he cannot cause nor will his conversion. It requires divine intervention. And Rousseau just happens to have a copy of a magazine announcing an essay competition when he has his road to Vincennes inspiration. Rousseau, the Natural Man, already has all the resources he needs. In the case of John Stuart Mill, something akin to, and yet distinctly different from, these accidents is happening

Mill cannot exactly will his recovery because that would mean using reason to take control of emotion, and that is in Mill's eyes the very basis of his problem. Nor could Mill pray for divine intervention, since he was then an agnostic and remained so throughout his life. Whatever happens, it must come from emotion, not reason and analysis. Mill's liberation should not arise from yet another theory but display a pre-conceptual or spontaneous character. In this sense "accidental" implies undetermined or gratuitous, definitely not preordained by an omnipotent power.

The scene of Mill's transformative recovery, or at least his ascent from the descending spiral of despair, occurs not as it does in other philosophers' autobiographies – in some physical setting such as a garden or country lane. Rather, for the highly cerebral Mr. Mill, it occurs in a scene in a book. Mill explains the situation like this. During this period of depression he happens to get hold of a memoir of the minor Romantic, 18th century French novelist, Jean-Françoise Marmontel (1723-1799). While reading, he comes upon a passage in which Marmontel "relates his father's death" and how, though still a young boy, Marmontel proclaims to his family that he will become their savior, aiming to take "the place of all that they had lost."

Mill says, "A vivid conception of the scene and its feeling came over me, and I was moved to tears. From this moment my burthen grew lighter." His capacity to respond emotionally to the story shows the despondent Mill that he still has some spark of feeling and compassion left in him. And from this moment he begins to awake from the nightmare of depression. He offers no further explanation of this event.

Was it the release of an unconscious wish that his own father was dead or the memoir's inspiring tale of courage and capability that stemmed the tide of sadness, or both? Mill doesn't say, nor does the master of analytical explanation provide further commentary on the exact cause of his recovery. Mill's reticence in matters such as the source and cure of his depression leave uninterpreted several key moments described in his *Autobiography*. Consequently, these have proven fair game for any number of scholarly investigators who employ critical frameworks that might aid them to tease out meanings seemingly hidden from the author, Mill, himself.

For example, in a 1945 journal article, the researcher A.W. Levi theorizes that an oedipal death wish can be found lurking in John Stuart's comments about his father's stern and dominating demeanor toward him. And scholar Peter Glassman in his 1985 monograph, *J.S. Mill: The Evolution of A Genius*, follows up with a psychoanalytic study of Mill's first-person narrative, insisting that subliminal and unconscious forces shaped Mill's life and that an important function of his literary career constituted an unconscious effort to recover from the emotionally abusive treatment Mill had received at the hands of a father who regarded his son as a great experiment in the formation of genius.

In contrast to these views, Professor John Skorupski, in his 1989 comprehensive reevaluation of Mill the philosopher, argues that it was Mill's "crystalline vision," a courageous, honestly intense, and rigorous pursuit of truth, that accounts for the periods of anguish and depression in his life and that interpreters who create edifices of psychological speculation on Mill's rather colorless and meager passages are wasting time and ink when they would be better off seeking to improve their understanding of Mill's highly nuanced epistemology. This is the tack that we will take.

Librarians call the psychologically restorative uses of literature "bibliotherapy." Mill's session of bibliotherapy centers on the story of a father's death and the son's sudden maturation. And this is exactly what happens in Mill's narrative of his recovery. Mill will go on to criticize what he sees as the weakness in his father's theory of education and he will propose modifications that enable him to preserve his father's philosophical legacy while overcoming the limits of that theory. He also underscores the weakness of the Utilitarian presupposition of how pleasure and pain serve as the non-cognitive, quantifiable measures of the highly cerebral system of the ethics of the "greatest happiness principle." Yet, instead of rejecting it, he will rescue Utilitarianism by adding a qualitative dimension to the theory's mainly quantitative one. Finally, he also builds a bridge between what is known as the Enlightenment Project (described in our previous chapter), the 18th century intellectual movement stemming from the French *philosophes* that gave the physical sciences preeminence in explaining and gaining mastery over the human predicament, and the 19th century Romantic turn to philosophical idealism that invades Britain from Germany with the poet, Coleridge, who champions feelings and imagination as superior to the empirically oriented physical sciences. Erecting this conceptual bridge is a neat trick if you can pull it off.

Mill says he derived two crucial principles from his experience with depression and recovery: first, do not make happiness your direct goal, rather let happiness come as the indirect result of dedicating yourself to the improvement of mankind and the happiness of others; and second, do not neglect the cultivation of your "internal culture" or "passive susceptibilities" by concentrating solely on "the ordering of outward circumstances."

So balancing affective and cognitive capacities becomes Mill's new credo. Mill's ordeal is not only a personal lesson for he sees in his own plight the circumstances of other young Englishmen and women similarly raised in an atmosphere of suppressed affection and emotion. "I felt the flaw in my life must be a flaw in life itself," he exclaims, turning the microscope of self-analysis into a telescope for looking outward at the wider culture. It is the English in particular who lack the capacity for expressing tenderness and other emotions, says Mill, that is at the root of not only an educational flaw but a flaw in the national character.

Perhaps that is another reason why it is not merely "accidental" that he read the poignant story from the pen of a Frenchman that had the power to release him from the fetters of the English national character. Mill loved the French and fondly remembered his year with Jeremy Bentham's brother's family in France where he found the warm and playful family life was so unlike the emotionally austere existence beside the Mill hearth. John and the woman who would, after a twenty-year Platonic relationship, become his wife, Harriet Taylor, eventually moved to Avignon in Provence after they were married. That is where Harriet died and was buried and where Mill lived for many years after her death.

Besides arriving at these two major lessons, John Stuart gained related insights. Returning to his efforts for social and political reform, if attainment of the various freedoms (to vote, speak out, have control over one's body) were achieved and if physical comfort were secured for all the members of a society, yet they were still not truly happy, then that simply showed the limited goals of social reform. People need to develop the capacity to enjoy life through poetry, music, philosophy and the natural environment. Small wonder then that Mill embraced the sentiments of Lake Poet Wordsworth and felt drawn to the champion of imagination and feeling, Coleridge. Though Mill little valued Wordsworth as a thinker, he was moved by the poet's ability to evoke "the love of rural objects and natural scenery." And he greatly admired Coleridge's celebration of the powers of the imagination as not a distortion of reality (as perceived by the senses) but an intensifying of those senses.

For Mill imagination, as a productive power of the mind to see things whole and to grasp their meaning, compensated for the shortcomings of learned associations between sense impressions and feelings of pleasure or pain – the theory of memory training firmly endorsed by James Mill. Yet he still did not completely abandon this so-called associationist theory, rather, following Wordsworth, with whom he became friends and who also held the theory of association, he aimed to balance associationism with a theory of the creative imagination.

In the Preface to the *Lyrical Ballads*, Wordsworth says the poet's role illustrates "the manner in which our feelings and ideas are associated." While the poet and the scientist pursue similar avenues toward knowledge, the poet is in touch with "our natural and inalienable inheritance" of feeling and sympathy, while the scientist represents the gradual acquisition of knowledge, an achievement that does not lead to a "habitual and direct sympathy connecting us with our fellow beings." Mill would accept this formulation and conclude that science must be supplemented by art, intellect by imagination.

While the fabric of his "old and taught" opinions was giving way, says Mill, he never allowed them to fall to pieces. Rather, he was busy weaving them anew. So how did he manage to let the results of his earlier education unravel while he knitted up the tattered fabric?

First, Mill replaced praise and disapproval and a mainly quantitative calculus of pleasure and pain with a more qualified, nuanced, and more authentically "natural" notion of how associations should work. He did not seek to replace learning through experience with a theory of intuition or innate knowledge. He simply argued that education should put equal emphasis on training the child or young person to appreciate the intrinsic beauty of the natural world and of works of art that communicate joy and the human capacity for happiness. For only by cultivating one's inner culture could an individual learn to discern lesser pleasures from loftier ones.

Second, philosophically a person could not be reduced to being simply a reactive bundle of pleasures and pains because there exists an irreducible identity and a quality of self-worth that belongs to each person, even if it is just his or her pure and unfettered capacity to be a center of desires and to seek happiness. Pleasure and pain, now understood qualitatively, point us to happiness but they are not mere physical sensations nor strictly exterior causes, since at some point in the formation of character they become internal, taking the form of what Mill frequently calls our "opinions," which correspond more closely to what, today, we would call convictions or beliefs.

THE PROBLEM OF SELF-CHANGE

There is one key issue that remains unexplained or unaccounted for in Mill's story of his recovery – how could it have been possible? He does not completely reject any of his earlier theories (Mill published a major essay on Utilitarianism in 1854 and a book on the subject in 1860, both many years after his revelations about the weakness of his father's and Bentham's versions), nor does he repudiate his education (in fact, even with its flaws, he recommends his education as proving what is possible for a child to accomplish).

So how can he account for the effect of a few tears and a poignant moment while reading a book for not only snapping out of depression but also setting out to reeducate himself by reading poetry and developing his "passive susceptibilities"? From his own philosophical point of view, what in his mental makeup could fuel the engine of self-change? Or to rephrase the question and apply it more broadly, what capacity enables us (if we are Utilitarians and Empiricists like Mill) to pursue self-improvement and self-reformation?

If, as Mill does, we hold a developmental theory about a life having stages, what accounts for the movement between stages? This is a particularly difficult question for Mill (and for most other human development theorists) because his system of thought seems to preclude any notion of an autonomous free will, or of an innate soul with inherent qualities waiting to come forth or, in a more religious vein, intervention of the hand of some deity who could lift us to a higher plane. It will turn out that we have to approach this question by examining Mill's theory of history, for the concepts embedded in this theory show how he might have understood his own individual life history.

If the pattern we have hypothesized about philosophical auto-biographies holds, we should find an account of time, memory and language in Mill's narrative. Mill held the view, elaborated in his *A System of Logic*, that memory can be understood as "intuitive knowledge." He held this position because his theory of association seemed to adequately cover how experiences became bound up with similar experiences and how pleasure and pain further entwine to produce empirical generalities that the mind stores up. Reviewing these bundled associations retrospectively would, for Mill, be an act of intuition that produced knowledge (predictable patterns). A concept of memory as such is not a major concern of Mill the autobiographer and we will not find a discussion of it in Mill's chapter on his "mental crisis" or anywhere else in the *Autobiography*. This absence may seem to dash our expectations. However, further examination of the chapter will show Mill shifting to a related topic; instead of memory, he offers a theory of historical change.

History could be described as the evidentiary science or art of collective memory. Historical accounts give us glimpses into what Mill would call "human nature," that is, general patterns of thought and action influenced by circumstances such as geography, technology, belief, education, custom and so on. That historical narratives might describe predictable stages through which societies pass, was a powerfully speculative idea emerging during the 19th century, one that would culminate in the grand theories of people like Hegel and Marx.

Mill examines this trend of thought because it was part of his intellectual life during the period of his crisis, but it turns out that an account of historical transformation – which raises important questions about historical determinacy, intersects with Mill's reflection on his personal plight and the possibility of self-change. So it is history, not memory that becomes the key issue. Perhaps this should not surprise us if we remember what Mill says on the very first page of his *Autobiography*, namely that in an "age of transition in opinions" such as the era in which he lived, there was benefit in "noting the successive phases of any mind which was always pressing forward." Mill's conviction is that his own "progress" mirrors the intellectual developments of his time.

Mill makes no effort to conceal the fact that he has reordered and reconstructed the story of his past by weaving in references to poems and poets he only encountered several years after he had recovered from depression. These help him understand and explain his condition, the deficiency in his upbringing, the larger flaws in society, and the cure – the cultivation of feeling and imagination. We understand our past in hindsight by seeing more completely what had been occurring bit by bit. What remains open to uncertainty is whether our retrospective glance falsely identifies causes of insight and self-change, and in this way mythologizes some past episode, or whether hindsight, taking advantage of new perspectives, ultimately enables us to realize the true meaning of what we at the time could not have understood.

Does the explanatory framework really matter as long as the narrative reconstruction leads us to a state of greater happiness, freeing us from the pain we may have experienced at that earlier time? For most people not particularly concerned with theoretical certainties, probably not. But for a John Stuart Mill who, after all, is espousing the validity of a philosophy that encompasses what we know, how we know, and how we therefore should live, and whose life story is meant to serve as both a guide and cautionary tale for others, the explanation or account does matter. In fact, it matters a great deal.

Within the framework of the *Autobiography* it is equally crucial, Mill's reevaluation of the importance of feelings leads directly to the next chapter. There he depicts how he falls in love with Harriet Taylor, the woman who becomes his soul mate, partner in social reform and the intellectual muse for his most famous books. Mill has to convincingly describe how he manages to progress from Chapter Five concerning his "mental crisis" in order to be ready to arrive at Mrs. Taylor's door to attend a dinner party in Chapter Six.

We should not be surprised then that near the end of Chapter Five, Mill addresses the crucial problem of self-change. First, he reemphasizes that the "new impressions" and "turning points" that contributed to "a definite progress in my mode of thought," though they produced "new light," also enabled him to "reconcile" some errors in his earlier views. The upheaval in his life led to critical reevaluations. Still, he insists, "while they modified the truths less generally known which lay in my early opinions, and in no essential part of which I at any time wavered." In other words, Mill could be both faithful to and critical of his earlier training. But there was one crucial opinion from his earlier education that, he says, "Weighed on my existence like an incubus," the doctrine of "Philosophical Necessity." Here is how Mill describes the incubus, or evil spirit:

> *I felt as if I was scientifically proved to be the helpless*
> *slave of antecedent circumstances; as if my character and*

> *that of all others had been formed for us by agencies*
> *beyond our control, and was wholly out of our own power.*

Readers should keep in mind Mill's choice of the word "incubus" as the weight on his chest. For an erudite individual such as Mill, the choice of this word must have been quite intentional. It is likely that Mill was acquainted with the work of Henry Fuseli (1741-1825), the Swiss-born artist who resided in London and whose most famous painting, "The Nightmare," (which Mill might easily have seen) depicts an incubus, an ogre-like demon, sitting on the chest of a somnolent woman, while the head of a fierce horse (the "mare" of "nightmare") pokes into the scene from behind a curtain. A great deal could be made of Mill's choice of words to express oppression. Once again, the dutiful son, the devoted lover, and the rational philosopher are one and the same person. Mill's task is to exorcize the incubus.

Mill admitted being a determinist. He believed there were empirically derived laws of causality that could account for the entire universe of human experience and that these could be reduced to general laws of cause and effect. Causation is the constant relationship between a phenomenon and the observable conditions that produce it. That nature is uniform such that the laws of causality found in one place would be expected in others is an underlying assumption of the form of empiricism Mill embraced. The question was: could human actions be attributed to the type of seemingly infallible laws that made the planets revolve in their orbits or apples fall at a certain rate from trees?

The basic premise of Mill's education was that conditioning (upbringing and education) and environment shaped the character and opinion of both a person and, by implication, that of a nation. So how could either the individual or a collection of individuals change unless human nature and national character were amenable to development? Mill clearly does believe that personal change is possible but what if that change also follows laws of causality? Wouldn't this be an external force, not an internal one, and hence inconsistent with the idea of developing one's "inner culture"?

Though perhaps only in retrospect, Mill sees the problem of his own development and the need for a principle that can account for self-change and self-improvement. Mill's solution is to uncover "a misleading association" in the concept of "necessity," an association that was "the operative force in the depressing and paralyzing influence which I had experienced," in other words, the conditions and theories that led up to his depression.

The solution that Mill puts forth is free will, "the conviction that we have real power over the formation of our own character." Our own desires, says Mill, enable us to influence our circumstances. We are not only passive agents but also active ones. This assertion would eventually lead Mill to write his most famous or at least most enduringly read essay, "On Liberty," a testimony to the human powers of self-formation and, correspondingly, of responsibility for one's actions.

But how on earth does Mill import a theory of free will into what until now has seemed like a completely deterministic system of the shaping of human character? He does not provide this explanation in the *Auto-biography*. He just reports it. Either we are convinced by the testimony of his account of self-change or we are not. To find the more detailed solution, we have to go elsewhere.

In Part Six of Mill's *System of Logic,* entitled "On the Logic of the Moral Sciences," the work which made him famous in his own time, Mill tries to show that liberty is compatible with determinism. The solution hinges on critiquing a theory of causality that would insist that all behavior is necessitated by motives that are out of our control and are, in that sense, involuntary. Certainly, some conditions such as absence of food or air will cause death. That is involuntary.

But attempting to take our own life through use of poison, one of Mill's key, and perhaps self-revealing, examples, is not involuntary ("except in some cases of mania") nor necessary, since we can choose otherwise or we can take an antidote or have our stomachs pumped, says Mill. But suppose that, too, is caused by prior conditioning; that the belief in free will is itself an illusion created by indoctrination? Not so, answers Mill, because it is by our powers of reasoning that we can adjudicate between motives and choose the one that is best. That would make us morally accountable, rational agents. But where does this power of reason come from since it is beginning to sound like it belongs inherently in the given nature of the individual, which would imply a transcendental self such as that espoused by the Kantians, and not a naturalistic-based account that would derive the capacity to reason, i.e., to engage in induction, solely from experience?

Mill's solution is to argue that there are many and sometimes competing motives to our actions, and in that sense we are not like planetary orbits or falling apples. We are able to reflect on the consequences of our motives based on prior experiences (e.g., too much alcohol will give me a hangover so I am not going to have another beer) or can reflect on possible dangers through observations based on prior observations (e.g., the edge of that cliff looks unstable and might break off under my weight, therefore I'm going to hang back), and so choose to act from the motive or motives that are likeliest to continue our course toward happiness. In this way Mill makes room for a range of freely chosen acts of self-determination while retaining aspects of a determinist system of causality. He relates this approach to his theory of historical change.

No matter how influential the circumstances of birth, environment and education, a person still possesses the capacity for further development. An individual, like a society, goes through phases of growth. And even if these phases are determined from the outset, as Mill came to believe through accepting a particular theory of historical change, still the element of free will is never completely subsumed by the force of circumstance alone. Mill's father, James, took a rather more ahistorical and non-developmental approach to societies. He thought that national character was fixed, determined largely by race and environmental circumstances. Bentham was far more appreciative of these differences and their relative merits (he admired the culture of India and recognized the richness of its classic period).

James Mill classified societies as either barbarian ("rude") or civilized. Though he was well aware of and claimed to accept theories of societal development, he employed the more static rude-versus-civilized, classification. Eventually, rude societies (which, for James, included all Asian ones) might progress, but for now he thought it best to simply clear the deck of what he deemed inferior beliefs and practices. These customs and laws would be replaced by drawing on the rational principles of Utility (Greatest Happiness). James Mill assumed that self-interest was the primary motivation for each person but through the imposition of laws and educational methods each individual would be set on the right course by channeling self-interest toward advancing the common wellbeing or happiness of all.

Unlike his father, John Stuart Mill, following the French social philosopher, August Comte, embraced the theory of historical development that postulated stages of society that constituted "the natural order of human progress." In one view, that of the Saint-Simonians who advanced a kind of mystical socialism, there are alternating "organic" and "critical periods" of society. The organic period operates from a general cultural consensus that allows the society to move forward without serious internal dissention. The critical period is caused by the failure or collapse of the organic period due to loss of conviction in the beliefs and assumptions formerly considered invulnerable or not even recognized as presuppositions. Clearly, Mill has himself passed from the organic to the critical and is working his way forward to another organic period.

It is difficult not to regard Mill's seemingly contradictory theory of free will as an act of self-deception or sophistry. We may, perhaps commonly, tend to see the actions of others as completely consistent with their personalities (or what Mill would call character), as if they could not do otherwise than they do, yet see ourselves as less determined by our own pattern of preferences and responses. But then free will, attributed only to ourselves, is either self-deception or a lack of generosity in how we view others.

A second way of looking at the matter is to argue that Mill is altering his idea of necessity, shifting from causality to correlation. Certain actions may correlate with certain results (e.g., proper diet and exercise correlates with longevity), yet not be the cause or not the sole cause of the result (some trim, athletic people die at a young age from congenital diseases, accidents, suicide and so on). And a third possibility is what we would call indeterminacy – that there are simply too many causal factors to reduce them to just one or a generalizable few. But indeterminacy, understood here as limited empirical law, is still not an adequate foundation for free will, understood as autonomy, or the capacity for self-governance.

There is another way to defend Mill's view. Many of us have taken personality tests or inventories and found the resultant profile uncannily accurate. We may conclude that we are simply "wired" a certain way and in this sense whatever we do is "caused" by our inherent disposition. Given this point of view, the theory of determinism would hold. Yet, our psychological typology cannot account for the particular decisions we make among a variety of choices, though it could account for the range of choices among which we narrow our options. So in this sense though free will is limited, it does operate.

His subtle concept of free will saves Mill from the logical consequences of his deterministic empiricism. When his version of free will is combined with his assessment of poetry's ability to emancipate feeling from pure causation, conditioning and the habits of analysis, he produces a wonderfully humanistic conception of the individual. Whether this account of his psychological and epistemological recovery from depression can truly explain how Mill was now prepared to fall in love with a married woman with three children after he had had little or no prior experience with the opposite sex and how he would persist in this quest for her undying affection, remains hard to comprehend.

From the outside, Mill's romantic actions seem like a giant leap, a true act of free will, and a break with the autobiographical figure of the narrative's first five chapters. Other less generous interpreters may disagree, proposing that John did not undergo such a dramatic change. He merely replaced the incubus of his father with the succubus (female form of the incubus) of his wife. Perhaps so, but for us the clue to Mill's psychological emancipation and readiness for love lies in his new appreciation of language, the other piece of the puzzle of self-change we have discovered in other philosophers' autobiographies.

Early in the *Autobiography*, Mill explains that his father warned him about the misleading influences of emotive language in poetry and literature. Not unlike Plato's recommendation of the censorship of poetry and drama because they appealed to the emotions and were in this way unreliable (emotions fluctuate), James Mill limited John's exposure to such works. Now we find that emotive language is part of John Stuart's cure. Among his many talents and skills, John Stuart Mill was also an improvisational pianist. He found this form of self-expression an outlet for feelings that otherwise seemed to have little place in the domain of the family philosophy. But feelings he had, and when they came into conflict with the efficient operation of the analytical mind some major modification would be called for.

We have already had ample testimony to the saving power of poetic language and its ability to awaken "not mere outward beauty, but states of feeling, and of thought coloured by feeling, under the excitement of beauty," and through this means to "draw from a source of inward joy, of sympathetic and imaginative pleasure, which could be shared in by all human beings."

This newfound ability to share feelings would certainly qualify Mill to begin a relationship with Harriet Taylor. Still, Mill is also skeptical about the uses of language, as exemplified by his critique of the misleading force of association with the word "necessity" that imposed such a barrier to his and others' thoughts. Mill's analysis of language, "the main instrument of thought," and the meanings of propositions, is extensive and comprises the first Three Books of his *System of Logic*. At the heart of his view of language use is that all "real" propositions are based on experience, none are *a priori*. This is entirely consistent with the way he understands his life as recounted in the *Autobiography*.

IDENTITY OF THE THINKING MACHINE

Interpreters of Mill's autobiography have been struck by its self-effacing tone and Mill's tendency to attribute his accomplishment to others, mainly to his father and to Harriet Taylor Mill and secondarily to people such as

Jeremy Bentham, and the poets, Wordsworth and Coleridge. The grandiloquent way that Mill describes these two primary figures, his father and his wife, suggests that he has idealized them beyond the level of "real" propositions and turned them into godlike creatures. Is Mill guilty of false humility or is this placing others in the limelight consistent with a Victorian-style propriety in which, even in an autobiography, one strives to avoid appearing prideful or self-centered? Perhaps a better explanation is that Mill is simply being consistent with his philosophical views about education and circumstance as etching themselves deeply in one's mind and in the formation of one's character. James Mill and Harriet Taylor are vital aspects of John Stuart Mill's life. So when he attributes certain qualities and influences to them, he is also describing himself.

Certainly Mill's story describes how he gained possession of his life and exercised the freedom to use his great knowledge, intellect and, later, enlarged capacity for feelings to modify his outlook and prepare himself for the exchange of affection and intimacy he found with Harriet Taylor. Mill's ability to become a "circumstance" to himself and accept the challenge to synthesize aspects of empiricism and radical reform with Romantic idealism and its more politically and theologically conservative views, also suggests Mill's self-emancipation from the doctrines on which he was raised. Still, scholars disagree sharply over whether Mill really did liberate himself from being his father's "thinking machine," because he continued to defend Utilitarianism, even though some of the refinements he brought to the moral theory would not have gone over well with James Mill, and he put himself under the domination of yet another forceful person, Mrs. Taylor. Readers of the autobiography and the published letters between John and Harriet can decide for themselves.

The related and more philosophical question is even more knotty: Did Mill's development lead him to believe in the idea of an autonomous self and would he have attributed to such a self the capacity to exceed the limits of materiality, finitude and causality? The disputed philosophical concept is known as the "transcendental ego" or "transcendental self."

A transcendental self sounds almost mystical (and is sometimes used in the context of Eastern mysticism) but in the work of Kant and others it does not quite have that connotation. Rather, the transcendental ego is the principal of a unified empirical self-consciousness, a hypothetical and yet necessary feature of mind that is the very condition of the possibility of knowledge. As one might guess, the transcendental ego is not a natural byproduct of experience, rather it must be a presupposition for the possibility of generating knowledge from experience through, for Kant, the categories of understanding such as space, time, number, causality and so on, which are simply the ways the developed mind processes experience.

Mill could have sought to integrate this concept of a generative and unifying self-consciousness as he engaged with the so-called "Germano-Coleridgeans," who were deeply influenced by the German Romantic philosopher, Fichte. Had he accepted this position, he would have all but repudiated his lifelong commitment to philosophical naturalism, the school of thought that insists that knowledge is the product of human participation in the laws of nature which, by means of experiences, they come to understand these laws as also their own. The trouble with naturalism is that it is hard to understand how having countless experiences and making countless choices among motives adds up to a coherent sense of personal identity and the capacity for self-regulation (imposing moral guidance on one's own actions). Such a naturalistic identity seems like little more than a bundle of habits that makes up one's character, where character seems like little more than predictable behavior.

Do we have any evidence in the *Autobiography* as to Mill's position on the autonomy of the self? Early and late in the *Autobiography*, Mill makes it clear that he never ceased to argue and campaign for women's voting rights, even when his father stood less insistent and even accepted the idea that women might be well enough represented by their husbands, brothers and fathers. His vehement disagreement with those who opposed women's suffrage surfaces numerous times in the *Autobiography*.

Mill makes reference to the fact that both his wife and his stepdaughter, Helen Taylor, were actively involved in producing the famous essay that became a chief weapon in the suffrage battle in later years, "The Subjection of Women." In that essay, Mill says that his contemporaries can have little idea of who women are because the conditions under which they live and the restrictions imposed on their liberty are such that their development is stifled and their individual character is as yet unrealized. Without the full exercise of freedom, understood as human rights, a person remains only the shadow of their possibility. Exercising one's rights and expressing one's opinion are the keys to what today we would call "self-actualization" and "civic engagement."

If Mill's *Autobiography* has one main message, it is that if John Stuart could emancipate himself from the tyranny of his upbringing and use the gifts that he received, then so can others. However, critical to one's identity as a fully realized person, besides the exercising of one's rights and preferences, is making the happiness of others our highest priority. Seeking to ensure that laws, social customs, rights and opportunities are for-mulated in such a way as to promote the greatest good for the greatest number is not just a moral axiom based on abstract thinking.

For Mill, the individual's progress is completely tied up with society's progress. That is why he tried to convince the members of Parliament to support universal education. Only an informed and literate populace would be able to bring about a just society in which everyone benefits. The drift of this kind of reasoning should sound familiar since it is the basis of much of American beliefs about opportunity in a democratic society. Those who support this view are only too well aware of the internal tension caused by what seems a tenuous conjunction between the pursuit of self-interest and private goods, and concern and respect for the good of a society that would make that pursuit possible.

BEING JOHN STUART MILL

Mill's life story with its simple, straightforward title, *Autobiography*, is a work of careful construction. He wrote and revised it, in close collaboration with his wife, over a period of years, the earliest draft dating to 1853-54, when he was in his forties, and the final to 1869-70, twelve years after the death of Mrs. Mill and two years after he had been defeated for reelection to Parliament. The *Autobiography* was finally published in 1873, immediately following Mill's death, as indicated in his will.

The tone of the *Autobiography* might be characterized as understate-ment or disinterested reportage. In part, this was the style in which Mill wrote most of his essays and books, and he treated his own life story no differently. Even if it is told in a matter of fact way, the narrative is not without powerful emotional content. The events and relationships about which he speaks are deeply human matters that may evoke strong responses in readers. Perhaps this is why, of all of Mill's works, the *Auto-biography* is still among the most read while the majority of his other works (aside from the high school or college requisite, *On Liberty*) receive little or no attention. Mill's story of his remarkably precocious education, socially daring love affair, his friendships, the books and authors who influenced him, and his political activities is the stuff of great drama. Yet the unaffected prose style forms a calming surface over the rough seas that bore the ship of his life. This toned-down, analytical style may put off some readers, who may find Mill a stuffy, obtuse, self-repressed character. But to the reader who comes to the *Autobiography* with tolerant and patient sensibility, that reader will find the story both passionate and rewarding.

Should Mill's life story be recast in the manner of an English period-based film like Ang Lee's *Sense and Sensibility* (based on the novel by Jane Austen), we would watch a scene that takes place after supper as John improvises at the piano for Harriet's enjoyment. When she asks what is inspiring his composition, he might answer, "Clouds driven before a storm," or a dirge, a procession, a battle. And she would smile and nod as she returned to editing one of their political essays. However, it would be difficult for a film director to convincingly depict the subtle way Mill came to recover from depression. Showing the downcast Mill reading a book and then bursting into tears would not be sufficiently compelling, though followers of self-help books might drive up demand for a paperback reprinting of Marmontel's *Memoires d'un Père*. There would certainly be a revival of interest in Wordsworth and even Coleridge as mental health muses.

Psychologists would appear on TV talk shows to confirm the need for the expression of affection between parent and child, especially when the parent is a highly exacting home educator. Educators would speak to the value of the cultivation of feelings through the arts as an important balance to emphasis on analytical training in the sciences and logical training in philosophy. The fundamentalist-oriented believers would probably condemn the film for its apparent approval of a love affair outside marriage unless they argued that there was nothing in the film to suggest that Mill and Taylor had sexual relationships out of wedlock and that theirs was a perfectly chaste relationship (scoring a point for abstinence). Left-leaning political critics would disparage both father and son's denigrating views of Indian civilization and point to the great evils committed under the rule of first the East India Company and then the British government who drained the Indian subcontinent of wealth and self-respect.

Members of the women's movement and feminist scholars would criticize Mill for taking too much credit for what were Harriet's ideas and for not placing her name beside (or even above) his on the title page of various books and essays. They would applaud Harriet's pronouncement that if women gained equality with men, then their experience of sexual pleasure would also increase; that if women were educated on an equal par with men, few would bother entering marriage, scorning the conventions of marriage as prescribed in Victorian England. They would cheer Harriet's assertion that if women lacked equal access to education, then they should at least have recourse to quick and easy divorce.

Harriet Taylor Mill wanted to rename the law of divorce, "Proof of Affection." Harriet pictured an ideal society with perfect equality between men and women. There would be women in every conceivable type of job, in government, in the pulpit. Women wouldn't have babies unless they wanted to, and they would realize they were accountable for this decision. Under ideal circumstances women would find sexual experience the best and most beautiful sensation, a transformation of the five senses of the material world into a feeling of infinity, the fulfillment of the end of creation. "Who enjoys most is most virtuous," wrote Harriet, a year after meeting John Stuart Mill, a year after the birth of the third and last child of her first marriage, Helen.

Would it be difficult to imagine being John Stuart Mill? True, few of us have been so precocious in our educational advancement and few would have the presumptuousness to decide that a flaw in their lives must be a flaw in society. But in many ways we are all cultural offspring of J. S. Mill and Harriet Taylor Mill. We are inheritors of a highly empirically-based, technocratic, post-industrial social order, a secular society struggling with the demands for equal rights of a wide assortment of social minorities, non-conformists, in short, people who lead what Mill called "experimental lives." We acknowledge that each person has the right to pursue his or her happiness but we are not sure how elastic a society can be before it shatters into fragments. Even now, we chafe at the idea of national character because that term sounds too coercive in its suggestion of uniformity. But with our highly individualistic pursuits of happiness have we become what cultural analyst Christopher Lasch called the "Narcissistic Society"?

As for the sexual liberation hinted at by Harriet Mill, could she have foreseen the accepted levels of sexual experimentation or imagine the pornography industry's growth, which had just gotten underway during the Victorian period?

The backlashes against liberalism that Mill identified in an important social leader like Coleridge who lauded the Anglican Church, social traditions, the traditional family and the life of feeling and intuition, are also part of our culturally conflicted society. The rise of evangelicalism, embracing of ancient spiritual practices, even the popular revived architectural derivative of the English Tudor and Georgian home styles, suggest harkening back to a more certain, more stable, more genteel period. Mill saw himself as an adjudicator between the claims and goals of the 18th century Enlightenment Project and the 19th century Romantic Movement. His life and his *Autobiography* embody both the richness and the perplexing contradictions that arise in the meeting of the two philosophical currents.

FIELDWORK AND REFLECTIVE WRITING

John Stuart Mill was a great believer in the social value of individuals' eccentricities. Protecting peoples' rights to non-injurious and non-infringing ventures and alternative lifestyles in arenas such as work (creative, scientific, political), family and community (co-ops, communes, ashrams), and public expression (think of the famous Hyde Park soapbox speakers) were to him positive attributes of a liberal society. The diverse ways in which people lead their lives constitute an ongoing social experiment that enables a society to test out new directions. Not every lifestyle experiment will flourish or be found beneficial but society reaps the benefits of unusual minds and personalities.

We might think of people like John Ruskin, Mary Wollstonecraft, Bertrand Russell, Einstein, Wittgenstein, Eleanor Roosevelt, and Buckminster Fuller as examples. They are not simply geniuses but ingenious people who, as the saying goes, marched to a different drummer. As a consequence, they were at times castigated by critics as radicals, impractical dreamers, immoralists or social deviants. But each served to broaden the picture of the world held by contemporaries and subsequent generations.

We all know at least one person whom we regard as "different," "unique," or "special." Perhaps this person is a non-conformist. At least, that is how we perceive them. But how do they perceive themselves and estimate the value they bestow upon others in their world? Consider conducting an interview with such a person. The interview should be informal. You might just want to invite this person to have lunch with you. You may have to drum up an explanation if this is a first-time social encounter. Be inventive. Keep in mind the assumptions you hold about this person in advance of the interview and whether you have to alter them as a consequence of what you learn.

The person you interview could be anyone – from a distant uncle or cousin to a coworker or to the teenage daughter of a friend or family member with whom you have rarely exchanged more than pleasantries and polite conversation. To insure that the conversation does not turn into a self-fulfilling prophecy because of how you (perhaps unconsciously) impose your assumptions on this person, take a look at some of the websites advising on "how to start a conversation" or "how to conduct an oral history interview." The key lies in how you ask questions and show openness and interest rather than judgment or irritation. The conversation should not be one-sided. You will want to share something of your life in exchange, and what you share should be more or less equally risky to what your interview partner is willing to share in the sense of making you feel similarly vulnerable.

Here is a writing exercise. Following the fieldwork above, let's assume that each of us is, in some ways, an eccentric. A little edge of nonconformity sticks out here and there. But do we aim to nurture the growth of this edge if it's healthy and helpful? Each one has to come to terms with the tension between leading a life according to necessity (what must be) and that of freedom (what could be). Social conventions, the seeming dictates of temperament, talent and intelligence, our social class, gender, sexual orientation, and race, these and other factors influence how we fashion a life story and frame our possibilities.

When our life story feels restrictive rather than enabling, we find ourselves pushing against the barriers of necessity. Our sense of the possible grows more distant and feels unreachable. Perhaps it is naïve to think that we can break free of the impasse of necessity simply by rewriting our personal narrative. Probably this cannot be accomplished as a single act. But rewriting some aspect of one's personal narrative can be a liberating step in combination with others. Mill did it to get the weight of the incubus off his chest and to awaken from a paralyzing determinist nightmare. He embraced indeterminacy as an opportunity for personal initiative.

Mill was an improvisational pianist. We recall his other nightmare that all musical inventiveness (combination of notes) had been tried and no new music would be forthcoming. The reader's assignment is then to write a series of variations on a theme – the theme of "one way in which I extend outside the mold of the average, normal, conformist person." Choose just one way, not many. The idea is to write a paragraph (or maybe two) to describe this in a very specific way. Then write another description in which there are slight variations. Do this at least five times. Next, ask yourself, when rereading the last variation, how pursuing this eccentricity benefits a wider sphere of people such as family, friends, your community, and so on. For example, I have a rather introverted friend who decided to take a workshop on how to become a clown. She became so enamored of this "alter ego" that she began to hire out to entertain at children's parties and, eventually, for hospitalized children.

READER'S GUIDE

There is no better place to start exploring Mill than his *Autobiography*, and there are several editions of it in print, the most authoritative being Jack Stillinger's 1969 version, a revision of John Jacob Coss's earlier (1924) edition based on the original manuscript owned by Columbia University.

Dedicated readers may want to examine the drafts of the *Autobiography* contained in Volume I of the *Collected Writings of John Stuart Mill*. Next the reader might go to *The Complete Works of Harriet Taylor Mill*, published in 1998 and edited by Jo Ellen Jacob. This single volume contains Mrs. Mill's essays on a wide variety of subjects, especially the lives of women (for example, see the essay, "Enfranchisement of Women") and it contains an important selection of her letters to John Stuart Mill, to her first husband John Taylor, to friends and family, and to her daughter, Helen. This collection will give the reader an additional outside perspective point from which to put John Stuart in perspective.

For modern readers, J. S. Mill's rather convoluted syntax and, to us, mannered style may be off-putting. If you think of it as a foreign language that you, somehow, seem to be able to decipher, that will help. Getting used to it takes time, but the passage into this great mind and his time is worth the effort. Mill's "The Subjection of Women" is not only a brilliant defense of women's suffrage but also a wonderful essay through which the reader sees how Mill applies the main tenets of Utilitarianism to human rights and human development. Similarly, his essay on "The Utility of Religion" shows Mill practicing his philosophical naturalism by appreciating the human need for religiosity (he is clearly the precursor of William James' *On the Variety of Religious Experiences*) and, after a critique of what he considered the harmful influences of religion, he puts forth his notion of a "religion of humanity."

For those who might wish to read a biography of Mill, two outstanding contributions are Michael St. John Packe's *The Life of John Stuart Mill* (first published in 1954), and the more recent (2004) *John Stuart Mill: A Biography*, by Nicholas Capaldi. A readable and updated treatment of Mill's importance can be found in John Skorupski's *Why Read Mill Today?* (Routledge, 2006). These sources will lead still eager readers to many other works by Mill.

5

Kierkegaard's House of Melancholy

John Stuart Mill is not the only philosopher to suffer from depression and a dominating father, or the only one to transform that state of despair into reenergizing philosophical insight. Our next philosophical autobiographer, whose life time overlaps with Mill (though no mutual influences are reflected in the work of either person), not only suffered from but made despair (*angst* in Danish) a central concept in his philosophical writing, a body of work both deeply personal and yet revealing of larger human dilemmas.

When Søren Kierkegaard (1813-1855) uses the phrase, "my activity as an author," he means to include the whole corpus of his written work: not only the novelistic philosophical essays, the sermon-like discourses on Christian scripture, his philosophical/theological/psychological critiques of mid-19th century philosophers such as Hegel and Fichte, but as well the vast collection of journals and diaries that he bequeathed to posterity. By the time of his death at the age of forty-two, Kierkegaard had produced a remarkable and extensive literature, employing his native Danish in inventive ways unlike anyone before or since.

Kierkegaard identifies himself with his "authorship" (*forfatterskab*), a term highlighting that though he possessed an advanced university degree in theology, he spoke with the authority neither of the minister nor the professor. In modern-day terms, he was an independent scholar who paid for his books to be published and who thought of himself as one individual addressing another.

Little of what Kierkegaard published was well understood by his contemporaries or for many decades, though at least one of his books, the novelistic *Either/Or* (1843) with its risqué section, "The Diary of A Seducer," was the Danish equivalent of a bestseller. This lack of understanding was the result of several factors: the elusive, often ironic and even paradoxical, character of his diverse writing styles, that he published under several pseudonyms as well as under his own name, because what he had to say was so radically unprecedented, that it was written in a language accessible to only the most literate inhabitants of this little northern European kingdom whose population at the time numbered about 1.3 million, and finally because the author was such an odd character.

Though well known among Copenhagen's intellectuals and literati as an eccentric yet engaging conversationalist, Kierkegaard led an extremely private life. When in his mid-thirties he was parodied in a popular Copenhagen tabloid, *The Corsair,* he was thereafter regarded by a wider public as a comical, if not rather pathetic, figure. In the last years of his life Kierkegaard was an outspoken critic of the Lutheran state church and there was even a fistfight at his burial. By his own reckoning, Kierkegaard was both exceptional and an exception.

Kierkegaard's great intellectual and spiritual gifts were first discovered by scholars who read his works in German translation, for it was in Germany that he gained posthumous recognition as an original mind with an important message. By the early decades of the 20th century his authorship had made a profound impact on European philosophers – secular, Christian and Jewish alike. He eventually became regarded as one of the seminal figures of a philosophical movement that did not receive a label until a French journalist in the 1950s dubbed as "Existentialist" certain thinkers preoccupied with issues of freedom, human finitude, and the challenge to live an authentic, self-liberated life. Because such "existential" thinkers as Sartre, Simone de Beauvoir, Gabriel Marcel and Heidegger frequently referred to Kierkegaard in their books and essays, his authorship became entangled in theirs. Kierkegaard's works were not translated into English until the 1950s, which then led to a second round of discovery and appreciation in the UK and North America.

Kierkegaard penned the narrative describing the strategy of his authorship, *The Point of View for My Work as an Author* (hereafter the POV) in 1848. The book's subtitle, "A Direct Communication, Report to History," reflects Kierkegaard's effort to clear up certain misunderstandings about the intentions of his role as an author.

> *The contents of this little book affirm, then, what I truly*
> *am as an author. That I am and was an author is related*
> *to Christianity, to the problem of 'becoming a Christian,'*
> *with a direct or indirect polemic against the monstrous*
> *illusion we call Christendom, or against the illusion that*
> *in such a land of ours all are Christians of a sort.*

He was reluctant to publish the POV during his lifetime for fear that it might seem self-congratulatory. Instead, he left instructions to his brother, Peter Christian Kierkegaard, then a bishop in the Danish Lutheran church, to bring the short work out after his death. P.C. Kierkegaard did so, though apparently reluctantly, since the work did not appear until 1859, four years after his controversial brother's death. While the POV is more a defense and explanation of the purposes that lay behind his literary productivity and includes a very compressed account of the decisive biographical influences that motivated him, Kierkegaard left a large collection of handwritten journals, papers and diaries that he somehow knew would eventually find a wide readership. These writings were crated up and shifted from one place to another, gathering dust along the way. They were finally, and fortuitously, organized and published by a scholarly, devoted acquaintance, H. P. Barfod. The first volume appeared in 1869, 14 years after Kierkegaard's death.

Kierkegaard is one of those remarkable people who believe absolutely in the immortality of their words. There was no question in his mind but that, since his mission was of a higher calling, not only his books but his personal papers would eventually see the light of day in published form. He was also certain that the footprints of his personal life inscribed in the POV would eventually lead future readers to this vast treasure trove packed with intimate details of his life. In this sense his posthumous writings form one interconnected body of work, a legacy that turns Kierkegaard's life into a case history, one that both invites interpretation and challenges the reader's capacity for self-understanding. Kierkegaard is one of those thinkers who, when you think you're finally gazing upon his true visage, you discover he is holding up a mirror.

There is no salient architectonic space representative of Kierkegaard's way of inhabiting his thought in the POV. But his commentary in the POV concerning the profound influence his father, Michael Pedersen Kierkegaard, had on the young Søren is expressed in no uncertain terms. And while Kierkegaard claims he is reluctant to give anything but a very brief account of his personal life, and especially of the influences on his childhood, he asserts in the POV that through the formative relationship with "the melancholy old man" he was, he says, decisively "predisposed from my earliest childhood, and step by step through the whole development, to become exactly the sort of author I became." By following the footsteps that lead from the POV to his journals we discover the formative architecture of the Kierkegaardian soul.

IMAGINARY WALKS

When he was a child, Søren Kierkegaard tells us in his Journals, he went for walks with his father. Lots of Danish children went for walks with their fathers in Copenhagen's extensive system of parks, especially those surrounding the royal castles with their formal gardens and their tree-shaded gravel paths. But unlike these children, Søren Kierkegaard's walks with his father were conducted indoors, and not after the workday but in the morning or early afternoons. We can image them walking hand in hand through the parlor with its massive horsehide-covered oak couch, and over the Persian carpet-lined hallways that led to the big sitting room and the library with its walls of bound leather volumes that might have smelled to Søren like butterscotch.

Søren's father, Michael, known to his associates as Hosier Kierkegaard, an occupational title bestowed on 19th century Danish shopkeepers who dealt in woolens, such as socks, scarves, suits, and gloves, retired early from the business in which he had made a small fortune so he could spend his time as he wished. And what he wished was to take charge of his eight children's upbringing. He did not trust the judgment of his wife, Ane, formerly a domestic servant in the three-floored house until Michael's first wife, Kirstine, died childless after only two years of marriage. And then, before the year of mourning was out, this uneducated servant girl, a distant relation, delivered the newly (and hastily) married couple's first child. Numerous pregnancies followed their marriage until the last, the caboose, produced little Søren.

Michael Pedersen Kierkegaard was a haunted soul. He was both melancholic and agoraphobic. Outside were people, neighbors, shopkeepers, ministers and bankers who, he imagined, would whisper about his shameful indiscretion. Little did they know of an even graver sin. Long before, as a poor and hopeless shepherd boy living out on the western moors in a region remote from the hustle and bustle of Copenhagen, he had cursed God for the injustice that he felt was his impoverished life. Because he grew to become a deeply religious man, well versed in theology and Christian scriptures, this act of blasphemy continued to weigh heavily upon his heart. Few knew about his burden, not even family members, no one except little Søren with whom he walked, traversing the floors of the grand house at number 2 Nytorv, there beside Copenhagen's city hall.

Inside, father and son might take an imaginary walk out through the city gates to a nearby country palace. Or they would go to the busy harbor, or stroll the tree-lined boulevards and narrow cobblestone streets of the town. Father would point out the pastry woman's tempting fare, the fine lines of the dappled grey that drew a handsome carriage, how light glinted off the golden globes atop the highest turret of the Frederiksberg Palace. So vividly familiar to Søren were these sights and sounds that he would often grow weary. Half an hour's stroll around the house was like the passing of an entire day.

They were not alone on these excursions. Michael Pedersen Kierkegaard invented conversations with passersby, interviewing them by posing difficult questions of Christian theology, conversations into which he drew young Søren as though the boy were but a miniature adult. Søren felt a swelling in his head. His mind was growing so fast and so large that his small skull could not contain its contents. But of this frightening growth whom could he tell? His brothers and sisters, too, suffered under the dark cloud of his father's joyless piety and benevolent tyranny. But they had not received the attention that had little Søren, nor were any of them their father's confidante.

In the POV, Kierkegaard laments his "crazy upbringing." To be treated like an adult when still an impressionable child, and to have the terrible burden of a depressed father's despair as his legacy, was nothing less than "frightful." He, too, then, a victim of melancholy, learns to accept also his greatest gifts – imagination, a precocious intellect, the power of solitude, and the art of concealing oneself through donning the mask of the ordinary. So with his secret unhappiness and his art of dissimulation, Kierkegaard embarks on a life of divided identity.

We know from reading Kierkegaard's Journals that as an adult and unlike his father who only entertained a small circle of houseguests, he managed to spend a good deal of time in the streets of Copenhagen. There he made it a habit of meeting and talking with both acquaintances and complete strangers. He also attended several of the various Lutheran churches of Copenhagen, though he was rarely happy with what he perceived as a too comfortable, culturally embedded and domesticated version of Christianity, which he referred to as "Christendom." He was also, to a highly unusual extent, a public person and a private one. He deliberately sought to present an image to the outer world that was in direct opposition to the private Kierkegaard, sequestered in his home, where, moving from one writing stand to another, he was busy composing several books at one time, some under his actual name and others under invented ones that would hide him but serve his purposes.

Kierkegaard was a self-described "spy in a higher service, the service of an idea." Like the great mystics, he was in the world but not of it. His chief social occupation, whether at the theater or in the marketplace, was observing the behavior and habits of his countrymen and -women, following the newspapers and magazines of the day, and engaging in conversation about issues great and small. But this social persona was a disguise, since all along he was mining information that, like the coal in the ornate iron stove that heated his home, he stoked into the roaring furnace of his mind to power his authorship.

In the POV he attributes to his father both his interest in the Christian experience and his melancholic (today we would say depressive) predisposition. For it was with his father that he first explored the public and private worlds and developed his method for moving between them, a method that became the hallmark of his authorship and the framework within which he led his life. Kierkegaard is most truly at home when his inward reflective and suffering nature is channeled into the service of an authorship that pretends to be what it is not – at times aesthetically frivolous, at other times metaphysically speculative and detached, or humorous as in the great seriously comic tradition of a Shakespeare or, in more recent times, a Kafka or Beckett. Setting out into the world from the home of his melancholic upbringing, Kierkegaard describes his journey.

> *So I fared forth into life – initiated into all possible*
> *enjoyments, yet never really enjoying, but rather (to*
> *indulge the one pleasure I had in connection with the pain*
> *of melancholy) laboring to produce the impression that I*
> *enjoyed.*

Eventually young Søren becomes the grown up Herr Søren, and not only that but Magister Kierkegaard, since he had achieved the academic rank of Master, equivalent to a doctorate in theology. This occurs once he had successfully defended and published his dissertation, *Concept of Irony*, on the history of literary irony and in particular on Socrates' uses of irony as depicted in *The Dialogues of* Plato. Writing the dissertation was, says the ironic Kierkegaard, "as difficult as describing an elf whose hat makes him invisible." A few years later his father dies, leaving him a sufficient inheritance so that, if carefully managed, he will never need to work for a living. It is around this time, in his mid-twenties, that Kierkegaard falls in love with the fourteen-year-old, Regina Olsen. He woos her and they become engaged when she is all of seventeen. But then Kierkegaard panics. He alludes to this in POV as the "factum," and knows that the dedicated reader will eventually have to go to his published Journals to learn the "facts" of the matter.

In its simplest form, the story goes that Kierkegaard realizes he will make an unsuitable husband because of his deep and, he believes, permanent condition of depression and because of his devotion to a version of the Christian life that leaves little room for ordinary domestic bliss. Contemporary readers may have trouble accepting this account and even more trouble with the way Kierkegaard chooses to break off the engagement by running around like a playboy to convince her that he is a mere scoundrel.

He then rushes off to Berlin for a couple of months where he writes the second volume of *Either/Or* by inventing the fictive Judge Wilhelm's letters to a young friend, the "poet" of the first volume, and then adding the sermon of a country parson. All the while he attempts to give the impression that he's just out having a good time. Kierkegaard then returns to Copenhagen, sends back his engagement ring and writes the planned first volume of *Either/Or*, the poet's pieces. A few months later in 1843 the whole book is published under the pseudonym of the purported editor, Victor Eremita.

So with melancholy as the "thorn in my flesh," devastated that he can never marry the love of his life, and possessed of the knowledge that he could never be like others but would always be a man apart, an exception, Kierkegaard proclaims, "Thus I became an author." Yet is it so inevitable that a person should choose the life of the pen because he has a melancholic personality, suffers from an inability to lead a normal life, to love in a normal way, has an almost uncontrollably active imagination, and possesses considerable literary gifts? To Kierkegaard, the answer is affirmative. His calling is inevitable because he believes a higher authority, what he calls "Divine Governance," directs his life.

Some people believe they have a religiously sanctified vocation, others believe in fate or predestination as determining their course of life, and still others, perhaps the majority, believe they create their own destiny by the way they respond to or interpret circumstances and opportunities. Kierkegaard believes that the troubles and sorrows that have befallen him, accidental as they may seem, were really intended all along to press him into the service of calling others to a Christian life. Not only that, but he finds that it isn't so much that he writes these quirky, exotic, often polemical, often lyrically poetic books, but that they write themselves through him, the Danish language messenger. This attitude, explicitly claimed in the POV, can be regarded as a supreme form of pride or of humility. Here's Kierkegaard's account.

> *Since I became an author, I have never for a single day had the experience I hear others complain of, namely a lack of thoughts or their failure to present themselves. If that were to happen to me, it would rather be an occasion for joy, that finally I had obtained a day that was really free.*

No lack of inspiration for Kierkegaard. Instead, following an imperative of restraint so that he does not diverge from his divinely ordained mission, he writes as if taking dictation, "quietly and placidly as one performs a prescribed task." And here he is again on the work that he calls his "productivity."

> The whole productivity has had in a certain sense an
> uninterruptedly even course, as if I had nothing else to do
> but to copy daily a definite portion of a printed book.

Kierkegaard does not assume that his productivity comes directly from God, as if he were taking dictation, but that his activity as an author is in obedience to God's will. In this he follows in the great tradition of Christian spiritual writers going back to Augustine who see themselves as servants to and messengers of God. They believe that in bearing witness to the power that has transformed their lives, through their writing they may enable others to experience a similar, though always unique, transformation. Yet there is a paradox in Kierkegaard's case, because all along he has employed a strategy of indirect communication as the best way to bring about this transformation and now, with the POV, he is stepping out from behind his masks of deception to communicate directly with his readers. If he has been correct, all along, that direct communication is inappropriate when attempting to help people change their lives, then why should he contradict this approach with a direct communication, especially when he knows the effort will be futile?

To truly arrive at an understanding of Kierkegaard's dilemma, we need to appreciate his remarkable insight that the art of rhetoric is to interrelate the stages of life with appropriate modes of communication.

KIERKEGAARD'S DUAL THEORY

The strategy of Kierkegaard's authorship rests on a dual theory of life stages and communication. Kierkegaard observed that as people develop they occupy one of several life attitudes or outlooks. He proposed three main stages of development: youth, in which we place great value on feelings and moments of fulfillment through infatuation or delight in beauty, though these are still external to us; adulthood, in which we "give birth to ourselves" by discovering the power of the will to create value through ethical reasoning and gain an advantage over time by making durable commitments to career, a life mate and to friends; and finally, in mature adulthood, embracing a life based on the belief that one is completely dependent on God who, for Christians anyway, enters the individual's biographical existence through the pathway of the mediator, the Christ.

For Kierkegaard, the essence of Christianity is the birth of a God-man, a being who is at once both mortal and immortal, finite and infinite, a person who suffers and yet is able to transcend suffering. The figure of Jesus is a mirror to the human soul. That is the genius of Christian belief, according to Kierkegaard. For him Christianity is not so much a body of theological ideas as it is a way of life centered on the task of reconciling the human duality that we have a foot in each of two worlds, the here and now and the forever. This formulated spiritual tension of unresolved duality has sometimes been called "crisis theology."

It is this duality that spurs us forward through various stages of development in which we try to achieve reconciliation through appropriately integrating or balancing what is possible and what is necessary, living our finite historical lives while striving for something that will outlive the historical. So Kierkegaard puts a great deal of emphasis on human freedom as the problematical gift that allows us to march bravely into the unknowable future, making ourselves up as we go along. Since no one can lead our lives for us, we become increasingly aware that we are solitary figures, certainly capable of love and fellow feelings, nevertheless unaided by other mortals in resolving our dual nature.

Paradoxically, though we strive mightily to come to terms with our existence as singular subjects, we can never achieve our goal through independent actions of the will because, in the end, we are ultimately dependent on the love and care of an infinite being whom, in one of his philosophical books, Kierkegaard calls "the God." Kierkegaard's impact on other religious thinkers comes through this message that the spiritual life entails the constant risk of uncertainty and paradox, for him the authentic way of engaging with ourselves and with others. Kierkegaard returns Christianity to the realm of experience as an ongoing developmental process ("becoming a Christian") and so, by implication, followers of other faith traditions may come to see their own religions in similar process-like terms.

Besides these stages, which Kierkegaard called the aesthetic, the ethical and the religious life outlooks, he identified two intermediary ones – irony and humor. The ironic standpoint grows from dissatisfaction with the fleeting prospects of romantic love or poetic rapture. You become worldly and disdainful of the illusoriness of momentary pleasures. Instead, you adopt a distancing superiority that immures you against the temptations of elusive pleasures as well as from the perceived dullness and boredom of a respectable life. Hence the feigned superiority of the ironist who seems to hover over ordinary life, glancing down with a wry smile. Such was the character of the young poet of Kierkegaard's *Either/Or*, Vol. I.

The transitional ironic stage falls between the aesthetic and the ethical. As for the boundary condition of humor, this has a different origin. Should you discover the core of happiness that comes from the lasting benefits of the ethical life and membership in the community of good and caring human beings, still you might feel something missing. This is sometimes referred to as the "more" in the phrase, "Yes, but isn't there anything more to life?" Then you might become aware of the incompleteness of human affairs, of the irresolvable nature of life's contradictions and paradoxes. Once a source of irritation and despair, now softened by the calm that comes with age, life's contradictions are now changed into a deeper appreciation of life's irreconcilables.

Picture a grandfather listening earnestly to the teenage woes of a granddaughter, knowing that empathy, more than advice, is the most useful response. The elder knows that the sorrows of today will only blossom into the sorrows of tomorrow but that there will be times of great joy, though the dialectic of life will never end as long as one is alive. The grandfather thinks how long it has taken him to reach this point of acceptance while his son and daughter-in-law will argue with the child or try to persuade her through rational means.

Kierkegaard's genius was to carry this life stage theory into another dimension. He reasoned that if each person at any given time in life dwelt primarily within one dominant outlook, then this attitude would be the filter through which all moral and intellectual communications would be received and interpreted. Therefore, for an author to penetrate this filter, that author had to understand the basic outlook of the reader and write in such a way as to engage that reader through depictions of thought, feeling and action that anticipated and addressed that reader's mind set. Then and only then could such an author present dilemmas and challenges that might cause such a reader to have second thoughts and insights or trigger a process of further development. Such a form of communication could not be direct but must employ a strategy of benevolent deceit, tricking the person, as it were, into following a story, a character or line of thought into a perplexing thicket of disorientation from which he would have to struggle to find his way. A perfect example of his method is embodied in *Either/Or*.

The book opens with an account by its purported editor, Victor Eremita (the "Victorious Hermit"), who tells us how he was sitting in his attic room trying to finish a letter when he heard the blast of the postman's horn.

Frantically searching for an envelope in his newly acquired antique secretary, he finds the envelope drawer jammed. Infuriated, he grabs an axe (which just happens to be lying nearby) and delivers a blow to the desk. Behold, a secret compartment springs open, revealing a parcel of papers and letters. He finds an envelope, seals it and rushes downstairs to meet the postman's carriage. Then he rushes back up several flights of stairs in excited anticipation of perusing this apparently hidden treasure.

Tied in bundles, one packet of papers turns out to be a set of short, witty essays and aphorisms written, apparently, by a young man whom he dubs the poetical Herr A. The other set is made up of two lengthy letters written by a lower court judge, a well-settled, well-adjusted middle-aged man whom he identifies as Judge Wilhelm or Herr B. The letters, apparently, were sent to Herr A. as the wise guidance of an older man to one younger. A single, additional item, a sermon, written out by a country parson, a friend of Judge B's, is also among the papers.

How they would end up in this secret compartment remains a mystery. Nevertheless, Victor deems it important to publish these works in two separate volumes that, as it were, speak to each other in a three-way debate between life attitudes – that of the passionate and impetuous, young poet, that of the stable and sober, middle-aged, rationalistic judge, and that of the pious parson, seemingly the same age as the judge but of yet another mindset, that of the humble reflective individual grappling with what it means to become a true Christian. Each of the three authors writes in a way that reflects his life stage. The poet expresses himself in short, clever, often ironic and erotic, essays and aphorisms. The judge expostulates in two very long, sometimes pompous but psychologically insightful epistles. The minister employs the sermonic style of the day, a homily based on a passage from Scripture.

Kierkegaard invites his reader to identify first with the young and eloquent poet, then with the mature judge who exhorts the poet to abandon a life of futile and elusive pleasures and instead to "give birth to yourself." And finally, when the reader might have concluded that the Judge, who stands at what would seem the pinnacle stage of moral autonomy, living as a contented and exemplary citizen, has finished giving his advice, the reader is offered one last item. The book ends with this text of a country parson's sermon in which he argues that "we of ourselves can do nothing," and "only the truth that edifies is truth for you." By implication, this sermonic theme has already shaken the foundations of the Judge's calm existence by challenging the idea that a person can complete him- or herself or rest secure in the arms of a rationally based ethical orientation.

"Reader," asks Kierkegaard from behind the mask of Victor Eremita, "which version of the ideal life do you choose?" Many are those who over the years have read and reread *Either/Or* and identified most strongly with now one, then another, and maybe, finally having achieved one's own individuality, with no single one of its characters, yet find the life stage theory useful for personal reflection concerning self-change. *Either/Or* is itself among the literary works that Kierkegaard would label "aesthetic" writings, while the more traditionally philosophical monographs such as *The Concept of Dread* or the *Concluding Unscientific Postscript* challenge the reader's conceptual abilities and require some familiarity with Christian theology and with the philosophy of Hegel, who was during Kierkegaard's lifetime one of the most influential European thinkers. And while Kierkegaard was remarkably prolific in producing these various books under various pseudonyms, he was also writing religious works under his own name. Eventually, the Kierkegaard of many names found himself ensnared by his own devices.

A CRISIS OF IDENTITY

In the middle of his thirties Kierkegaard found himself in an awkward position. It came about in this way. For years he'd been going around in public pretending to be a carefree fellow whose inheritance meant that he didn't need to work. But secretly he had been laboring mightily, using these Latinate names with such literal meanings as the Victorious Hermit, the Hilarious Bookbinder and John the Climber, to produce deep, difficult books aimed at demolishing the biggest, most fashionable ideas of the day and at making the Christian path not easier to tread but more difficult, more perplexing and more personal. In his mind he was the Socrates of 19th century Copenhagen. Like the Athenian gadfly, he wanted to trick people into scrutinizing their opinions, to learn to reason for themselves and pursue the golden imperative – know thyself.

But Kierkegaard also wanted individuals to embrace their unique calling or destiny, to become themselves. He assumed that in each person there dwelt an authentic, unique self, striving to be born out of the conflicting passions of youth and the unfulfilled dreams of midlife. To assist them he wove thoughts in such a way as to perplex and provoke through what he called the "dialectic of communication."

Kierkegaard, seeking to emulate the master of transformative education, Socrates, the midwife (*maieutiker*) to others' ideas, also called his method the "enabling dialectic." But he got caught in his own literary devices. A popular magazine called *The Corsair*, something like a highbrow version of our *National Inquirer*, that took delight in satirizing the politicians and intellectuals of Copenhagen, published a series of caricature that cruelly, though perhaps all too accurately, depicted Magister Kierkegaard gadding about with his umbrella, stovepipe hat, long-tailed coat, and pants with the comical quality that one leg length was invariable shorter than the other. Perhaps he should have been honored to be included among the celebrities teased by the magazine's editor, Meïr Aron Goldschmidt, and in fact he had encouraged the editor, who had been an admirer of his writing, to parody him like he had other public figures of the day.

A tailor could have solved his problem. But his pant legs remained unchanged and he did not feel honored. Instead, his preexisting state of melancholy deepened. At the age of thirty-five, by then a frail sickly sort of person, Kierkegaard lived in a state of perpetual despair. As a consequence of *The Corsair* cartoons, children chased him in the streets of Copenhagen, yelling his first name, Søren, which became for more than a century thereafter a term of ridicule (*"Nej, for Søren!"*), something like the American expression, "Oh, for Pete's sake!" Danish parents ceased for several decades giving their children that name.

In his diary for 1848, the year he wrote the POV, Kierkegaard commented despairingly that people must see him as a superfluous soul, having neither wife nor children, no visible means of support, and completely idle except for producing some boring religious commentaries whose message was hard to understand. Kierkegaard was truly the odd man out. But to him, so was Socrates, and even more so Jesus. At least he could take solace in the fact that he belonged to a tradition of great outsiders.

The magazine had not only parodied him but also revealed Kierkegaard as the pseudonymous author of a great many annoying and perplexing books. The man everyone thought was a bon vivant turned out to be a ponderously difficult, serious-minded philosopher and theologian. Kierkegaard felt devastated. Those reputable individuals who had encouraged Kierkegaard's attacks on the satirical tabloid (having the highest circulation at the time in Denmark) did little to defend him. Instead they took secret and cowardly delight in seeing the brilliant author outfoxed. His whole complex literary strategy was toppling down like a house of cards. His efforts were misunderstood as the inconsistent rambling of an eccentric genius. Now the master of irony had been played the fool. Was he a benign genius or an intellectual bully? No one could be sure. Which meant people would have even less idea of what to make of his books. And there was an even more disturbing problem for Kierkegaard.

Some critics who gradually realized the full scope of Kierkegaard's authorship and life-stage theory concluded that, like many other writers, he must have started out as an aesthetically-oriented, hedonistic author who, as he left his youth and found his professional calling, became an ethical one. They surmised that finally in midlife he discovered his faith and the centrality of Christianity in his life. They were applying Kierkegaard's own developmental theory to his life's work. But no, said Kierkegaard, that was quite wrong.

Kierkegaard wanted posterity to understand that throughout his adult life he was a deeply inward-seeking Christian. Not necessarily the conventional type of Christian they would recognize – a pious churchgoer who found little difficulty accepting the dogmas of the faith. Rather, he was a passionate believer in the mystery of the birth, death and resurrection of Jesus as reflecting the mystery of his own inner life. But if this were so, wouldn't he be an exception to his own theory of moral and spiritual development? And if indirect communication was the only way to reach and move the reader from one stage to another, then what good would be a direct communication that explained the strategy of the authorship? It would be a futile gesture.

Nevertheless, to set the record straight and to defend the integrity of his authorship for posterity, Magister Kierkegaard decided to compromise his authorial position by explaining and justifying his complex charade. So he wrote the lengthy first-person essay to help contemporary and future readers understand not only his intentions but also the correct "point of view" (*synspunkt*) for surveying the works of his authorship.

The formerly secretive Kierkegaard decided that for readers to understand his literary strategy they would also need to know what led him to undertake it in the first place. Though he presented only the barest outline, perhaps knowing or believing that someday dedicated readers would find their way to his Journals to fill in these abstract shapes, he sketched out the plight of a child whose loving parent's guiding hand drew him down into a melancholic state he could never overcome.

Readers might have remembered the words of his own *Either/Or* in which Herr A. asks: "What is a poet?" And then, answering his own question, says: "An unhappy man who in his heart harbors a deep anguish, but whose lips are so fashioned that the moans and cries that pass over them are transformed into ravishing music." That was his plight, which became his calling, his cross, and his legacy to mankind. It is quite clear that Kierkegaard interpreted his life as a parable of what it meant to become a Christian, that he experienced his life as Christ-like, though in making this identification he knew he stood on the edge of heresy and the sin of hubris.

The year in which Kierkegaard wrote the POV, 1848, was an auspicious one in European history, marked by widespread political upheavals driven by constitutional reformers seeking to topple their monarchs. It was the year Marx and Engels published the *Communist Manifesto*. It was also a time of rampant nationalism as small kingdoms and city-states were forged into nation states. Denmark was itself undergoing huge changes in 1848, as King Christian VIII was about to concede to a bloodless revolution that would make Denmark a constitutional monarchy. That same year, Denmark raced headlong into yet another futile war. The country, which had once dominated much of Scandinavia, had already lost large territories, including Norway. Now the Danes were about to fight a losing battle with Prussia over Denmark's southern provinces, Schleswig and Holstein, whose mixed population of Danes and Germans had divided national loyalties.

Kierkegaard seemed indifferent to these political transformations. He showed no patriotic enthusiasm for the war and was of two minds about democratic rule by the rising middle classes. As an aside, 1848 was also the year that, with his father deceased and only one brother still living, Kierkegaard sold the family home at number 2 Nytorv and moved into a newly furnished apartment nearby.

KIERKEGAARD'S DUAL IDENTITY

Kierkegaard was at war with the crowd mentality and with Danish Christendom at mid-19th century. He had girded for battle but was caught in the awkward elaborateness of his own armor. All he could do was to take it off and show how its gleaming beauty hid his own spindly-figured nakedness. After he had put the works of his authorship in proper perspective and declared that, even though there appeared to be some kind of linear development reflecting the author's own maturing, nevertheless he stood outside or above the individual works, as if simply placing pieces into a jigsaw puzzle that would eventually be complete and reveal a whole picture. Yet there is a puzzling twist in how Kierkegaard saw the completed whole.

> *I must truly say that I cannot understand the whole, just because to the merest insignificant detail I understand the whole, but what I cannot understand is that now I can understand it and yet cannot by any means say at the instant of commencing it I understand it so precisely --*

> *though it is I that have carried it out and made every step*
> *with reflection.*

A way to understand this statement is to see that Kierkegaard had two different "I"s in mind and two different "understandings." The one "viewpoint" came as a momentous experience of feeling that he had received grace, which he reports in his Journals shortly before writing the POV, and the other came when his mission was fully revealed to him as a necessary and meaningful consequence of his striving and suffering. Only then did he understand where his life was leading because he now saw that it was God who directed him. This point of view echoes that of Augustine in the *Confessions,* who uses a dual time perspective to tell his story from the temporal positions of before conversion and after. Apparently, the transformative experience of receiving God's blessing does not obliterate one's memory of what life was like previously, though it changes forever how one would interpret one's life.

The two "I"s in Kierkegaard's statement of the paradox of self-comprehension are directly linked to another book, which he called, "one of the best I've written," conceived and published in the same year as the POV. In the prolog to Sickness Unto Death, a psycho-spiritual study of despair, Kierkegaard defines what it is to be a human being.

> *The human is spirit. But what is spirit? Spirit is the self.*
> *But what is the self? The self is a relationship that relates*
> *itself to itself, or is that in the relationship by which the*
> *relationship relates itself to itself; the self is not the*
> *relationship but that the relationship relates itself to itself.*
> *The human is a synthesis of the infinite and the finite, the*
> *temporal and the eternal, freedom and necessity, in short,*
> *a synthesis. A synthesis is a relationship between two.*
> *Conceived this way, the human is yet not a self.*

Utilizing (some say, parodying) the then-popular Hegelian terminology of self-consciousness as a dialectical process animated by the interplay of opposites (e.g. self/other, being/nothing), Kierkegaard guides the Hegelian-initiated reader along a familiar path – toward convergence in a mediated third moment that preserves while uniting differences. Kierkegaard accepts and builds upon Hegel's notion of the self as not a fixed thing but as a dynamic activity, a series of self-opposing relationships that culminate in an increasingly encompassing unity that, for Hegel, ultimately leads to "thought thinking itself." But this self-possessing, all-encompassing form of contemplation is not the destination Kierkegaard believes possible for human beings in all their concrete individuality. His description is certainly convoluted and we would do well to slow it down for a moment.

The first sentence harkens all the way back to the early Greek philosophers' notion that what animates life is *thumos*, breath. When one dies, breath departs, disappearing into the great unknown. Kierkegaard uses the Danish word "*aand*"(modern spelling *ånd*, pronounced similar to English "on"), which means "spirit" as in spiritual, spirit of the times, the Holy Spirit and similar uses. At first, spirit is still undifferentiated since every life possesses a principle of animation. When a creature with spirit announces itself through the capacity of self-consciousness, the self becomes critically differentiated as a singular and unique being. The process could end there.

If you were to stroll through any Danish cemetery, you would find the graves marked thus: Blacksmith, Jens Pedersen; Teacher, Aage Nielsen; Housewife, Birthe Hansen; Farmer, Kristian Skammelsen – and then something about family members. Your identity would be a combination of your parentage, your occupation, your Danish citizenship and inheritance of Danish history, culture and religious upbringing. The matter would be settled. But Kierkegaard does not equate self-identity with role, nationality, gender, marital status, religious affiliation or physical description.

The self is a word that stands for a relationship that is inward, not outward. We do not simply have an identity as a fixed possession because who then is the possessor and what is the possessed? The relationship is dynamic, a set of reflections seemingly without end. Well, but there's the rub. There is an end, death. So we know the process will come to an end even if a hereafter follows. How does that knowledge affect our experience of reflectivity? It makes us a bit dizzy, off balance, incomplete. If we could take a snapshot of the process, we could hold up the psychographic image and say, "There I am, this self-relating being." Or we could argue that because language itself is linear and finite it can never capture the dynamic process, and that the experience of becoming a self is ultimately pre-linguistic or ineffable.

Kierkegaard doesn't stop there. He insists the self is not identical to the relationship process but points to what makes the process possible. We may have the capability of being self-constituting, because we are self-relating selves. Understood in this sense, the self is radically free. But how does human self-consciousness account for that freedom? That is the mystery toward which Kierkegaard wants to direct us by insisting on the tension – that to be human is fundamentally to experience oneself as a synthesis, or better, conjunction, of oppositional qualities. Granted, the opposing qualities remain preserved in the hypothetical synthesis that could be understood as the apex in the triangle of opposite terms. Yet the triangle is not completed as long as we are still defined by duality.

Let us also note at this point that Kierkegaard's concept of self is situated but undetermined. Preserved is the condition of freedom to choose oneself, to accept or even more, to embrace the condition of what it is to be the creature whose task it is to become a self. That is the situation. And placed in the context of a concrete life, the situation is multilayered with the facts and factors of what Hannah Arendt called our "natology," that is, what comes to us with our birthright (e.g. parentage, culture, historical moment).

But Kierkegaard does not propose, as philosophers before him would likely have done, an essential self, a highly specific something that already exists in its potential. This leaves open the challenge: how is one to become a self? And this question, more than what it is one becomes, is the central issue for Kierkegaard and, indeed, as we will see in the chapter on Sartre and de Beauvoir, the focus of the inheritors of Kierkegaard's philosophy of existence. Please also note that the self is sexless, that is, as an activity, a how of being, it has no gender, nor is it influenced by gender or any other contingent factor on which the process might depend. There are no male and female roles for the process of becoming a self or, in Kierkegaard's mind, becoming a Christian. Simone de Beauvoir and the various schools of feminist philosophy will challenge this view mightily.

For Kierkegaard, we are not some self-completing beings as are acorns that turn into the oaks. Here are the two "I"s, the duality of self and the urge toward integration of opposing tendencies. But the process is inconclusive, the resolution incomplete. Searching for one's identity, one knows one is searching, so there is a doubly reflective process – I see myself searching for myself. But then isn't that who I am, the searcher, the seeker? Such an image of identity as an ongoing developmental process provides an authentic, partial resolution to the tension of inner duality. "At least," one might say, "I am in motion, on my quest, my journey. Isn't that what this life is all about – searching?"

The psychologist of the spiritual, Kierkegaard knows this ploy. In its most advanced form, wistful acceptance of the paradoxical in life, it is the transitional stage of humor. But the dynamic self of humor, while a resting place of sorts, is also from Kierkegaard's point of view, a self-deception because, in his version of reality, there is only unrest. If a human being were only one half of the dialectic – wholly free, wholly mortal, purely a creature of necessity, then there would be no struggle, no quest to resolve the mirror play of self-relating.

Alas, comes the Kierkegaardian sigh, would that this was the case. We are the creature that knows itself as this duality – finite and infinite, impermanent and yet enduring. The question for such a self-relating being, argues Kierkegaard, is whether the self "must have constituted itself or have been constituted by another." Kierkegaard argues for the latter position, that the freedom that is identical with self-consciousness is nevertheless dependent on another who has bestowed this gift. The key to the resolution is the "Power" that underlies and makes possible the process of reflection itself. Kierkegaard attributes the power to a higher or transcendent source. Kierkegaard offers us an analogy for understanding this process.

In *The Concept of Dread* Kierkegaard uses the analogy of a multistory house constructed with a cellar, first-floor living area, and second floor presumably of bedrooms. By analogy, the cellar is the space of physicality, the bodily and the senses. The first floor is more spiritual, at least consisting of the thoughtful, the reflective, the caring. The upper floor would then be the more fully spiritual.

It's a typical vertical notion of ascent through the hierarchy of being that we know from Plato and Augustine and that, though attacked on all sides, persists as a habit of mind to this day. Kierkegaard says that the majority of people choose to live in the cellar because that is where they are most "at home," in preferring physical comforts to all else and trusting the material world as the most real. If someone were to point out that they possess a great deal more, the space of a whole house in which to roam, indeed that it is their own property, still, says Kierkegaard, they will insist on remaining below ground. The quest for Kierkegaard is not to solely occupy the upper floor but to be a householder, living fully on all floors. But to do that, one has to explore the upper levels and know what is possible. However, while there is a stairway connecting the cellar and the first floor, Kierkegaard implies that the stairway to the second floor must, metaphorically speaking, be lowered from above.

If what it means to become a self rests ultimately upon a mystery, and depends on a Power that makes self-becoming possible, then one's identity is similarly a mystery, a dizzying paradox. To be sure, this vertiginous language of the self-relating self has driven scholarly interpreters to despair. Their reactions range from Louis Mackey's declaration (in *Kierkegaard: A Kind of Poet*) that the attempted definition of self is just so much "Gobbledegook," meant to show the impossibility of arriving at a satisfactory definition, to Mark Taylor's claim (in *Journey to Selfhood*) that it is "the most complete and explicit definition of the structure of selfhood" that Kierkegaard has to offer in the context of contrasting his view with that of Hegel. If they take seriously Kierkegaard's use of pseudonyms and his claim of indirect communication, interpreters have to decide whether the "real" Kierkegaard is speaking through a pseudonymous author who is therefore a fictional narrator, or whether Kierkegaard is characterizing how a thinker in a given stage of life would tend to see matters and articulate them according to his, but not Kierkegaard's, life stage.

Indeed, some will argue, in the vein of Louis Mackey, that even if Kierkegaard wanted to, he could not explain how this mystery gets resolved. The powers of reason are not adequate to the task. It cannot be communicated directly. That is why, according to Kierkegaard and many of the great religious teachers, spiritual language is a language of parables, proverbs, koans, mythologies and other forms of discourse that are indirect because they do not just come right out and tell us how to understand our lives but require interpretation and personal appropriation. They hold the power to assist in self-transforming the reflective listener or reader. Even Kierkegaard's religious writings, published under his own name, are not direct communications, except that we know the name of the actual author. They are more like guided meditations on a Scriptural theme. They remain indirect forms of discourse.

If all of Kierkegaard's work is indirect, then either the POV is an aberration, a misguided step in the authorship, a failure of nerve, or it is yet another tactic of indirect communication. Is this intentional, is Kierkegaard aware of this, or is Divine Governance once again moving the hand of the melancholy father's melancholy son? I would submit that Kierkegaard's first-person narrative intentionally corresponds to and is consistent with his notion of the self as a dynamic interplay of self-relatedness.

To see the irony in this situation, we turn to the "Conclusion" section of the POV.

> I have nothing further to say, but in conclusion I will let
> another speak, my poet, who when he comes will assign
> me a place among those who have suffered for the sake of
> an idea, and he will say: "The martyrdom this author
> suffered may be briefly described thus: He suffered from
> being a genius in a provincial town. The standard he
> applied in relation to talents, industry, disinterestedness,
> devotedness, definition of thought, &c., was on the

average far too great for his contemporaries; it raised the
price on them too terribly, and reduced their price too
terribly; it almost made it seem as if the provincial town
and the majority in it did not possess dominium
absolutum, but that there was a God in existence.

The Latin phrase means "absolute dominion," as in having control over one's destiny. Kierkegaard anticipates the coming of the secular society. He lets his poet go on in this way, proffering a eulogy about how unjustly Søren was treated because his countrymen believed Kierkegaard was too prideful and deserved to be punished, whereas it was their pettiness, jealousy, envy and resentment against anyone who would argue that becoming a Christian, or just as truly, becoming a person, was the most strenuous and difficult task set before an individual. His poet declares, that by his work the author "transmuted his suffering into a treasure for eternity," yet he cannot take credit for his authorship because it was Governance that moved him and guided him. His poet can honestly say that though the author died historically of a mortal disease, "poetically" he died "of longing for eternity." And for that, he had "nothing else to do but to thank God."

Of all the voices to invoke at the end of his story, where we might have expected an imaginary eulogy coming from his deceased father, his brother the bishop, or perhaps a country parson, it is instead the very archetype he had long left behind – the poet, the figure he associated with the aesthetic stage of life. How could someone from the bottom of the ladder, the cellar of the house of moral development, speak knowingly of one who had reached the upper floor, even climbed the lowered stairway? It is because of one of Kierkegaard's favorite ideas, "repetition," the strange and the familiar co-mingling when we experience, a second time around, something that had previously seemed unique and unrepeatable.

The occasion for the POV, he tells us in the introduction, coincides with his decision to allow *Either/Or* to be published in a second edition. This time, everyone will know that he is the author who has given voice to each of the characters, that the four – the editor, Victor, the poetic, Herr A and Judge, Herr B, and the parson, are really voices from one head. The whole of the authorship is beginning to come back for a second time, and who knows how many more repetitions? It is therefore fitting that he allows his poet to have the final word. It is only a poet, someone who lives in the moment, who allows his enthusiasm to get the better of him, who would dare to confer literary immortality on the melancholy Kierkegaard, as the dramatist Plato made the mortal Socrates an immortal hero of the life of the mind. The poet's "second coming." How Christ-like.

Yet this poet's prophetic words are not poetry as such but highly lyrical prose. More than that, the poet's eulogy reads like the libretto for late Romantic opera, a tragic-comic melodrama full of *sturm und drang*. Given this, can we accept Kierkegaard's claim that the POV represents his effort at direct communication or, as he states on the title page, "A Report to History"? I think the answer is no. For this book is a knock on the door of the Pantheon, a report in the sense that one reports for duty, that he has arrived at the threshold of becoming an historical figure and asks to be let in. Kierkegaard, the author, disappears. He has passed into eternity. And those who have maligned and misunderstood him and his message will now realize the errors of their ways and suffer remorse.

BEING SØREN KIERKEGAARD

Kierkegaard says the purpose of his authorship is to serve the reader.

> *This is the secret of the art of helping others. Anyone who has not mastered this is himself deluded when he proposes to help others. In order to help another effectively I must understand more than he–yet first of all surely I must understand what he understands. If I do not know that, my greater understanding will be of no help to him.*

This "servant" role requires great humility, patience and self-control. The servant must be able to put himself in the place of the other in order to know how to address him or her in such a way as to enable, not dominate. If a would-be helper lapses into the pride of superior knowledge, he will alienate the one he seeks to help. If he becomes angry at being misunderstood or misjudged, he will have failed in his mission. And if he becomes enamored of his own brilliant image reflected in the public's appreciation of his artistic accomplishments, then he will end up believing in his outward persona, deceiving himself. Kierkegaard's servant is a Socratic educator.

Are we committing the intentional fallacy if we accept Kierkegaard's claim in the POV that he passed through no developmental stages as an author or as a person but that somehow his adult life from early on embodied a Christian moral perspective, one that allowed him to masterfully shape his authorship in such a way that he could pretend through his many characters to speak from now the aesthetic life view, now the ethical, now that of the ironist, the humorist, and simultaneously that of the Christian religious thinker?

The school of literary interpretation that held sway in the 1940s through 1970s, the so-called "New Criticism," argued that only the work itself, the world that work created for the reader, should be considered, not the author's biography and certainly not overlaid theories that claimed to have privileged insight into the author's private meanings and purposes. Authors lie, they make up tales and create mythologies around their work and their life stories at the time of publication. Then they change their minds and reinterpret what they meant from the vantage point of later years. In short, they cannot be trusted to know more about their own work than a reader who comes freshly upon the scene.

But here we have an author who owns up, lets the cat out of the bag, reveals his purpose, indeed, continues to harangue the reader about what a sham and a hypocrisy it is to claim to be a Christian as if it were the easiest thing in the world and you didn't even have to go to church, read the Bible or, if you had, to take its words all that seriously. Perhaps, like many friends and enemies of Kierkegaard who wrote about him after his death, one would allow that while he said all these and many more harsh words about his countrymen and the clergy, we can account for his behavior because he was a physically and mentally afflicted person who dispensed half-truths and sought to stir up unrest out of his own desperate condition. This was an easy way to dismiss a challenging thinker and many articles on the subject were published in the Danish press in the decades after Søren passed away.

We cannot worry about what Kierkegaard's contemporaries thought when they read the POV after the author's death. What is *our* point of view for Kierkegaard's work as an author? Are we among the betraying townsmen, including the clergy, who resented his sharp criticism of conventionalized Christendom, the children running after him in the street mocking him, an adoring reader who has become a devoted Kierke-gaardian, the critically detached scholar who takes no position, the crafty literary critic who classifies his work as yet another type of rhetoric, the analytically trained philosopher who dismisses Kierkegaard's theorizing as hopelessly mired in metaphysically nonsensical statements? Actively or passively, ever reader takes a stance.

Using the Malkovichian transformation, I suggest we occupy a middle ground. Let us allow ourselves to enjoy the mental journey in the mind of Kierkegaard before we plop down on a grassy slope beside the entrance to the Hudson Tunnel. Kierkegaard has invited us into the parental home from which his authorship was born. We have followed him out into the street and into the pages of books, journals, and a Copenhagen tabloid. The last thing he wants is for us to become followers, cloned Kierkegaardians.

Our task, he asserts, is to become ourselves, to take the risk of embracing our uniqueness rather than modeling ourselves on others. And if the price we must pay is a certain amount of suffering, anguish, despair and loneliness, we can take solace in knowing that the seeker's path is blazed by these signs of difficulty. And that what lies at the end of the path is unspeakable joy.

FIELDWORK AND REFLECTIVE WRITING

The term "point of view" (Danish: *synspunkt*) in Kierkegaard's endeavor to sum up the strategy of his authorship is another way of saying that the narrators of varied works is one person with one overarching purpose. And now that this narrator is speaking to us directly in order to put his authenticating seal on the correct understanding of the corpus of his work, we as readers are in a better position to possess a similar overview. By virtue of Kierkegaard's own theory of communication and life stages, he knows that we cannot relinquish our point of view to step into his. We are going to respond from our point of view. But what is our point of view, each as a reader and as a maker and inhabitant of a life?

Becoming self-conscious of how we interpret experience is as problematic as the indeterminacy paradox in physics. The instrument of analysis distorts the object under scrutiny. Perhaps that is why some of us enjoy taking personality tests and attitude quizzes or having our horoscope done. Now, with something externally produced, we're offered an outsider's portrait of ourselves. Of course, we respond to this portrait from our point of view – whether to deny its accuracy ("Oh, I'm not like that at all. The test must be flawed."), or to claim that it reveals the way we truly are ("Yes, I am an introverted, intuitive, feeling, perceiving type. Eureka!"). Self-awareness is always an approximation.

Given these limitations, consider Kierkegaard's theory of life stages and the attributes he assigns to each – the aesthetic, ethical and religious, as well as the two transitional stages of irony and humor. With which stage do you currently most identify? Describe the events or experiences that mark the transition to this stage from a previous one. Stay focused on the transition, and try to describe it slowly and carefully as if you were putting a movie scene into slow motion. What in your narrative would account for the possibility of self-change and what would account for the resistances?

READER'S GUIDE

Kierkegaard would be horrified to learn that his authorship had been placed among the writings of the so-called Existentialists. True, he has in common with them a concentrated focus on the self-becoming of the individual as a finite subject whose task is to construct a life through a series of willed choices, blessed or cursed with the freedom to leap into the unknown. But for Kierkegaard the landing point is preordained and the universe structured with moral meaning, even if ultimately we must make a leap beyond those meanings when we come up to the chasm that separates our finite lives from nearness to the eternal. It is to become contemporary with Christ, to live in a way that illumines and is illuminated by the life and words of the Savior. The parable of the God-Man awaits us. We can choose it.

A few among the Existentialists might hold similar positions, most would not, instead favoring the notion of the absurd, that there are no independent and impersonal meanings or paradigms that await us other than the ones that we invent. Placing Kierkegaard within a school of thought only serves to blunt his indirect communication to his reader as "that individual." We would be reading him as an entomologist – here is another type of idea, let's label it and add it to our collection.

Should we accept it, our task is to find something of value in Kierkegaard's many-sided authorship. Granted, this is not an easy task. But Kierkegaard has given us guidance: to start with our own most compelling questions is the way to find the right entry point, a way that may make Kierkegaard relevant. Still, we will face several obstacles. Many of Kierkegaard's philosophical and theological commentaries assume the reader is already familiar with some aspects of the western philosophical tradition, especially with the German philosophers Kant and Hegel, and possibly Schelling, Schiller, and Hamann, to name the most important. His intellectual Danish readers would certainly have known about the important theologians of the day to whom Kierkegaard frequently alludes, such as the religious leaders H. L. Martensen and Jakob Peter Mynster.

Critically important also would be awareness of the growing movement among the followers of N.F.S. Grundtvig, Denmark's most important religious figure, who profoundly changed the role of the church as a key element in the modernization of Denmark through a Christian appreciation of Nordic mythology and an emphasis on community-building, adult education and agricultural cooperatives. Finally, Kierkegaard would assume his reader is fully versed in both Jewish and Christian scripture and shared his belief that only the essence of a Protestant understanding of Christianity could lead to salvation and grace.

Those who have not yet acquainted themselves with any of the above or just a little, and who would be offended by Kierkegaard's prejudices, may throw up their hands in despair. Better, they might say, to simply read some secondary source that will give us a summary of what Kierkegaard is all about, expressed in laymen's terms, than to bother with what seems an arduous and time-consuming activity. And with that reader, I couldn't agree more. If one had to study Kierkegaard to achieve the resolution of faith, there would be few Christians. And if one had to peruse the authorship in order to become a self, then... Well, I think the point is clear. But for that persistent reader who is sufficiently intrigued to go further into the Kierkegaardian household, I offer this guidance.

Either/Or is a great starting point for those who enjoy literature, find fascination with theories of life development, feel caught between the pulls of spontaneity and commitment, and welcome the challenge of being called upon to adjudicate between the conflicting moral worlds of the book's characters. Those who have found the story of Abraham and Isaac, known in Hebrew as the *ahkidah* or sacrificial obedience story, intriguing for its provocative portrayal of faith, will find *Fear and Trembling* a valuable place to experience Kierkegaard at his most meditative. In *Fear and Trembling,* he circles around and around this Biblical account to intensify the incomprehensible and irreducible meaning of faith, a meaning he saw eclipsed by reliance on rationality in all matters of life. Individuals who may have been attracted to the literature on the quest for the historical Jesus that was extremely popular from the mid-nineteenth century forward may find easy access to Kierkegaard's *Philosophical Fragments,* a small book in which he compares Socrates and Jesus as teachers and examines whether "an historical point of departure" can serve as a pathway for delving into the Christian experience. He contrasts this with another approach that aims to achieve a contemporaneity with the Christ story by short-circuiting a good deal of church history and rationalistic theology. For those individuals who are well on their way in spiritual appreciation and practice, the little book, *Purity of Heart* ("is to will one thing") is a moving testimony to a well-oriented spiritual path.

There are hundreds, if not thousands, of books written in countless languages about Kierkegaard's authorship. Some appreciate him most as a literary figure of inventive genius (e.g. Louis Mackey's 1971 book, *Kierkegaard: A Kind of Poet*), others for his critical analysis of German idealism and rationalistic theology (e.g. Mark C. Taylor's 1980 work, *Journey to Selfhood: Hegel and Kierkegaard,* and his *Kierkegaard's Pseudonymous Authorship: a Study of Time and the Self,* 1975). Kierkegaard continues to be reinterpreted in the context of new intellectual trends. And so we have, for example, a post-modernist account, *Kierkegaard & The Problem of*

Writing by Pat Bigelow (1981). There are several good biographies, including the earliest in English by the major Kierkegaard translator Walter Lowrie (1962), and then Alastair Hannay's *Kierkegaard, A Biography* (1982) and, one by the former co-director of the Kierkegaard Society, Joakim Garff's *SAK, Søren Aabye Kierkegaard, A Biography* (2000).

An excellent and highly readable scholarly study that places Kierkegaard into the context of Danish cultural and political history is Bruce Kirmmse's 1990 work, *Kierkegaard in Golden Age Denmark*. Readers with access to major public or university libraries should find the multi-volume collection of Kierkegaard's *Journals and Papers*. Several thematically organized selections from the journals and papers are available in paperback editions. There are also numerous Kierkegaard web sites on the Internet such as Dr. Anthony Storm's Commentary on Kierkegaard (http://www.Sørenkierkegaard.org) and various encyclopedias of philosophy (e.g. the *Stanford Encyclopedia of Philosophy*) that can provide the reader with quick thumbnail sketches of the various thinkers to whom Kierkegaard refers. For the reader who hears the call to "that individual," there is plenty of material to keep you involved for years to come.

6

NIETZSCHE'S PYRAMID

If you could only retain one memory to carry with you into an imagined timelessness of life after death, what would you choose? That is the question put to the migrating souls of the deceased in *After Life*, the 1998 Japanese language film by writer, editor and director Hirokazu Edo. *After Life* tells the story of twenty-two people who arrive at a fog-enshrouded way station between death and what lies beyond. Having stepped across the threshold of what looks like an abandoned school building, the wayfarers are informed by a group of guides that they have three days to select one memory that is particularly meaningful to them and another three days to work with resident filmmakers to recreate the memory. This single remembered event, reenacted on film, will be the only piece of earthly life they may take with them into the next world where they will dwell with it forever. Here is a true test of autobiographical selectivity.

Faced with this daunting challenge, the life reviewers, who represent a wide spectrum of ages at death, grapple with memories. These range from a sexual encounter, childbirth, a dance lesson, riding on a train on a summer's day, to a final cigarette during a WWII battle and, for a teenager, a visit to Disneyland. The characters gradually let go of what had seemed the high points of life, regarding many of these initial choices as moments of shallow or illusory happiness. Each wayfarer recovers a less obvious, more inward and completing moment, such as a quiet conversation on a park bench with a loved one, or a unique adventure piloting a small plane through a dangerous storm.

Though the film makes no reference to the German philosopher, Friedrich Nietzsche's idea of "eternal recurrence," it echoes a theme that Nietzsche (1844-1900) puts to his readers in several of his most famous works such as *Thus Spoke Zarathustra* (1885) and *Twilight of the Idols* (1888). Nietzsche's version goes something like this. If a demon came to you and told you that everything you had done in your life would be repeated over and over again for all eternity, would you react with a cry of anguish or a shout of exaltation? And he asks: Should we not live our lives as though eternal recurrence of all that has been were true and, thus, affirm each moment of existence as a decisive celebration of human creativity? Not in some hypothetical afterlife, the promise of many religious traditions, but in the immediacy of our present lives would we incorporate this view of the perpetual revolution of the world. We would do so "as if" this cosmic revelation were our highest truth.

Sagas of great cosmic cycles of destruction and creation, as well as individual reincarnation, can be found in the mythologies and beliefs of many peoples, especially in Asian religions such as Hinduism and Buddhism but also in ancient Greek cosmology. To live, indeed, to thrive, despite this vision of the endless repetition of every moment of one's being, to abandon any notion of reward or punishment in a hereafter, to relinquish any hope of preexisting meaning, may seem to defy the powers of human reason and require a rock solid endurance of will. And that is exactly what Nietzsche attempted to cultivate.

As if he had set out to pry up the already deteriorating veneer of late 19th century European civilization, Nietzsche relentlessly attacked the fundamental ideas, beliefs and presuppositions on which Western culture was built: the superiority of human reason as man's highest faculty, the presumed difference between good and evil, the importance of collective social values and virtues, the omniscient God of Christianity and Judaism, the formation of nation states such as the then-new Confederation of German States, the wisdom of supposedly great philosophers, especially Socrates and Plato, the laudability of ancient Athenian culture that had long been regarded as the apogee of civilization, the emerging ideals of a democratic society, the common man, goodness, world peace, a disembodied self, and on and on. No wonder the would-be demigod Hitler had himself photographed admiring a bust of Nietzsche. Ironically, Nietzsche also attacked anti-Semitism and the ethos of the ethnically unified *Volk*.

Nietzsche wrote with extraordinarily captivating power and energy. He is often considered, with Kierkegaard, the parallel founder of the philosophy of existentialism. Yet unlike Kierkegaard, he was not a theist, nor a practicing or believing Christian; rather he labeled Christianity a "slave morality" that in admonishing followers to "turn the other cheek," inadvertently fostered a repressive culture of deep-seated "resentment." Like Kierkegaard, he had a profound distrust of the coming egalitarian society, the metaphysics of 19th century German idealism, especially the system-building philosophies of Kant and Hegel, and in general the privileging of the faculty of reason over that of the will. Nietzsche ridiculed the idea that humans had the capacity to grasp timeless truths, he scorned the value of so-called objective knowledge and denied the usefulness of conventional scholarship, logic and philosophical discourse. None of these, asserted Nietzsche, would prove useful for living a robust and creative life.

One might wonder, with all this negativism, what appeal would such a thinker have? Somehow, it is as if Nietzsche had read the subconscious doubts and anxieties of the leading thinkers, literary figures and theologians of his day. He could seemingly peer into the dark or suppressed side of their meditations and eavesdrop on their long simmering suspicions about such matters as the existence of God, the intelligibility and benignity of the universe, the underpinnings of conventional values and morality, the orderliness of creativity and the grandeur of Western civilization. Nietzsche heard and saw the coming sounds and sights of an industrial, technological, bureaucratic, utilitarian-oriented capitalist society whose fixation on wealth, productivity and progress would quash the little that remained of human life intoxicated by its own creative energies. So Nietzsche's critique anticipated the science of the unconscious – Freudian psychoanalytic theory – which was later applied not just to diseases of the mind but also more broadly to what Freud aptly titled one of his books, "civilization and its discontents."

After an initially successful career as an academic philologist (his first appointment to the faculty of philology at the University of Basel came at the young age of twenty-four) specializing in the scholarship of Greek and Roman antiquity, Nietzsche began to write controversial and polemical books that fell outside the usual bounds of academic respectability. He also developed numerous chronic ailments (nausea, vision problems and headaches) that interfered with his demanding teaching schedule, which required that he temporarily take leave of his position. Eventually he was relieved of his duties but went on to write and publish one book after another, each more daring than the previous.

Nietzsche was passionately drawn to the philosophy of Arthur Schopenhauer and to the music of his contemporary, Richard Wagner, with whom he became a close friend, and was a member of Wagner's circle of ardent admirers. But eventually he turned against both the philosopher and the composer.

Like Rousseau, Nietzsche was a wanderer and a walker. Because of his illnesses, he sought out warm, sunny climates, which necessitated frequent relocations to various places in Italy, France, Germany and Switzerland, depending on the season and his state of mind. An inveterate trekker, Nietzsche loved to roam the valleys and mountain regions of Italy and Switzerland. It was on one of these outings that a life-changing vision came to him.

A PYRAMIDAL BOULDER

The circumstances under which Nietzsche wrote *Thus Spoke Zarathustra*, he tells us in his autobiography, *Ecce Homo*, occurred in August of 1881, when he was staying in Sils-Maria, a small village in the Upper Engadine Mountains of southeastern Switzerland. It was during one of his many strenuous walks around Lake Silvaplana, Nietzsche reports that he "stopped near Surlie by a huge, pyramidal boulder" and there, exhilarated by the high mountain air and the majestic panorama of mountains and lake, had a powerful revelation.

Already fascinated by the creative impulse that had distanced him from the academic world, Nietzsche reports in *Ecce Homo* that he now saw that the truly creative individual must rise above ordinary existence. Experiencing an exalted state, Nietzsche embraced becoming a "mere medium of overpowering forces" that produced "a storm of feeling of freedom, absoluteness, power, divinity." As if the sheer force of existence empowered him with an exquisite receptivity, Nietzsche found that "things themselves were approaching and offering themselves as metaphors." Among the metaphorical "things" that Nietzsche encountered was the voice in his inner mind of what would become his avatar, the reincarnation of Zoroaster, the Persian prophet, whom Nietzsche would call Zarathustra.

A seemingly incidental detail Nietzsche includes in an otherwise pre-sumed but undescribed setting of his ecstatic receptivity to the Zarathustra figure, who will speak volumes of prophecy to him, is the pyramid-shaped boulder beside which his vision occurs. What Nietzsche does not tell us is that the pyramid or ziggurat shape is closely associated with several ancient belief systems, especially Zoroastrianism. Consciously or not, Nietzsche gives us a physical and metaphorical landmark for his life-transforming experience. Both an instance of myth making and an orienting reference point in his narrative, reference to the pyramidal boulder is no mere happenstance. Nietzsche is an exacting author who chooses each word carefully. The pyramidal boulder symbolizes the arrival of Zarathustra at this juncture in Nietzsche's life.

The Zoroaster-like prophetic voice was not completely original to Nietzsche, as interest in what was then called Orientalism had become quite fervent in Europe in the latter part of the 19th century, leading to numerous translations of the sacred texts attributed to Zoroaster (the Greek name of the Persian prophet Zartosht), who purportedly lived sometime between 1750 and 1500 BCE.

Nietzsche explains in *Ecce Homo* that he had actually begun the book while staying in Rapallo, a fishing village on the Ligurian coast just east of

Genoa. There, walking up a steep hillside path, while "looking over pine trees and far out to sea," he first heard Zarathustra speaking to him and had to quickly make notes to capture the wisdom of this prophet. But it was while standing in proximity to the pyramid-shaped boulder at Sils-Maria that Nietzsche marks the dramatic turning point of his thinking and literary work. He did not just conjure up Zarathustra as, say, the poet Tennyson conjured up the ancient Greek seafarer Ulysses (for the poem of the same name); rather Nietzsche says he was "overpowered" by the emergence of Zarathustra. Of this gift of inspiration, he admonishes the dubious: "You listen, you do not look for anything, you take, you do not ask who is there; a thought lights up in a flash with necessity, without hesitation as to its form." To this revelation Nietzsche proclaims: "I never had any choice."

Nietzsche insists that the inspiration that transformed his life was "involuntary." The subsequent images and metaphors that Zarathustra would utter just "offered themselves up" as the "closest, simplest, most fitting expression." And as for precedence to such experiences, Nietzsche says, "You would have to go back thousands of years to find anyone who would say: 'It is mine as well.'"

Nietzsche points to other sojourns that took place during this pivotal year of the writing of Zarathustra. For example, during his stay in Nice he had "unforgettable moments," once again during a "tiring climb," in this instance from the railway station to a mountain plateau. He could, says Nietzsche, "hike in the mountains for seven or eight hours at a time without any thought of tiredness." He slept well, "laughed a lot," and enjoyed "the most perfect vigour and patience." In each place, echoing Zarathustra, Nietzsche does not just write, he learns to "ride on every metaphor to every truth. Here words and word-shrines of all being jump up for you; all being wants to become a word here, all becoming wants to learn to speak from you."

What better picture of euphoria, inspiration, and visioning than that of the high altitude explorer who dwells in "azure solitude" and listens to the voice, not just of nature but of sheer being? But to the skeptic, Nietzsche's account must seem like just so much self-mythologizing, confirming the critics' view that the autobiographical mode at best lends itself to egoistic performances and, in the case of Ecce Homo, to the antics of the self-appointed court jester, if not the madman. Many have made this claim but how, then, to account for Nietzsche's infectious spirit?

Though Nietzsche's prolific outpouring did not immediately find favorable reception, shortly after his complete mental collapse in 1889 at the age of forty-five his writing began to capture the attention of artists, intellectuals, and political figures across Europe. His *Lebensphilosophie* (life philosophy) called forth the creative energies of a new generation ready to cast aside the conventionally esteemed values of rationality, piety and the comforts of middle-class life. Nietzsche's enthusiasm for the rejuvenating spirit of war and the warrior ethos was a harbinger of the madness of the Great War. It should come as no surprise then that, besides the Bible and Goethe's *Faust*, Nietzsche's *Thus Spoke Zarathustra* was read in the trenches, a gift from the German government intended to inspire its soldiers.

But Nietzsche has also been an inspiration to peace-loving poets, novelists, dancers, painters, psychologists, philosophers, sociologists and social revolutionaries. His writing style is highly enigmatic and open to multiple interpretations because, like Kierkegaard, he chose to communicate his vision through forms of indirect discourse such as the aphorism, myth, parable and metaphor.

The problem of understanding Nietzsche is similar to that of understanding Kierkegaard. Just as Kierkegaard dedicated his authorship to "*hin enkelte*," "that individual," so Nietzsche subtitled *Thus Spoke Zarathustra*, "A Book for Everyone and Nobody." Unless the student of their words is willing to be lifted off the ground and shaken by the collar, reading their works as though each individual was the one and only reader to whom these writers addressed themselves, then mere detached comprehension is irrelevant, as are any scholarly commentaries on the two. The admittedly arrogant Nietzsche warns us: "Those who can breathe the air of my writings know that it is an air of the heights, a strong air. One must be made for it. Otherwise there is no small danger that one may catch cold in it."

For Nietzsche, *Zarathustra* marks the change from writing books that still retain a semblance of the tone and style of the academic scholar or the self-doubting poetic thinker. Now he has achieved what he describes as "a perfect state of being outside yourself, with the most distinct consciousness of a host of subtle shudders and shiverings down to the tips of your toes." He has experienced a profound joy that, rather than excluding "the bleakest and most painful things," allows them to become the conditions, the "necessary shades within this sort of excess of light." Personal suffering is vindicated by the miraculous results of self-transcendence. Not by means of self-absorption and contemplation, nothing so heady, but through persistent cheerfulness, through the intensity of living each moment, through an almost precognitive encountering via the physical world, the mountain path, of a nature that is so completely indifferent to the human that it crushes the truly surrendering listener only to make possible his rebirth. Nietzsche asserted that "what does not kill you will make you stronger."

CONJURING RILKE

For those who are familiar with his work, it is hard to read these passages of Nietzsche's *Ecce Homo* and not think of another artist, the visionary German poet, Rainer Maria Rilke. Some three decades after Nietzsche's ecstatic vision, Rilke is pacing around on the stormy cliffs overlooking the Adriatic Sea on the grounds of the privately owned Duino Castle, where he is a guest.

He has not written any major poems for eleven years. Having abandoned all hope of further inspiration, Rilke is suddenly seized by a voice coming out of the wind that utters this astounding question:

> *Who, if I cried, would hear me among the angelic*
> *Orders? And even if one of them suddenly*
> *pressed me against his heart, I should fade in the strength*
> *of his stronger existence.*

And rushing back to the castle, Rilke continues to hear additional phrases and in this, the first of the ten Duino Elegies, rhapsodizes:

> *... For beauty's nothing*
> *but the beginnings of Terror we're still just able to bear,*
> *and why we adore it so is because it serenely*
> *disdains to destroy us.*

Here, in this J. B. Leishman translation, is expressed the extraordinary self-overcoming that turns the one seeking into the one found, the hearer for whom a voice was waiting for the opportune moment or, as Rilke says of the poet's creative receptivity: "a star was waiting for you to notice it," or "a violin yielded itself to your hearing." The poetic genius is the vehicle through which the being of things can become heard. And here, too, is the Nietzschean idea that the beautiful, along with the painful and even life threatening, can become transformed into a source of awe and source of strength.

THE MUSTACHE OF HYPERBOLE

Nietzsche's *Ecce Homo* is primarily an account of his authorship, and in that way bears a striking resemblance to Kierkegaard's *The Point of View for My Work as an Author*. Both books could be regarded as intellectual autobiographies since they concern themselves mainly with the authors' written works and only secondarily with other particulars of their lives such as parents, upbringing, formal education, health and so on. Both books include brief references to family members – mainly fathers, and to other influential people such as teachers and friends. And, as in the other philosophical autobiographies we have been considering, they also include references to scenes of life changing moments.

Nietzsche tells us next to nothing of his upbringing, except that his father, a Lutheran clergyman who died at the age of thirty-six when Nietzsche was five, was a kind though rather sad man who seemed to have just passed through life without really living it. Yet he draws a parallel to his father, stating that he, too, at the age of thirty-six has experienced a crisis of health. Due to his symptoms – headaches, impaired vision, partial paralysis, Nietzsche, whose career was already in trouble, was granted leave from his professorship at the University of Basel where, as mentioned, he taught classical philology.

He did not die then but underwent a dramatic change, turning from his career as a brilliant academic to a life of increasing eccentricity, sporting an enormous mustache that hung down to his chin, suffering from restlessness and periodic illness, while maintaining a prolific literary output. His scholarly works became ever more polemical, costing him his academic reputation but gaining him notoriety among a small circle of admirers. He began the life of a wanderer, moving from one city or village to another in search of the right climate and environment that might help relieve his symptoms. Climate, Nietzsche believed, affected metabolism, which influenced energy and therefore one's capacity for greatness.

Ecce Homo was among Nietzsche's last books, written shortly before he famously embraced two horses whose master was beating them in the town square in Turin, after which he collapsed and succumbed to a complete mental breakdown. Most scholars believe the cause of Nietzsche illness was syphilis, which he contracted in his youth; others believe he suffered from a brain tumor. He died in the year of the new century.

Nietzsche's literary autobiography is provocative because the usual autobiographical conventions of modesty and self-effacement are completely missing. Nietzsche's style is to proclaim his greatness. He does so in a manner that would embarrass most other writers of the narrative self though most of them probably would feel pride in their accomplishments and station in life. They just wouldn't dare to express their self-esteem so blatantly. But here we have what appears to be the most arrogant first-person narrative one could imagine, with chapters headed with phrases like: "Why I Am So Clever," "Why I Am So Wise," "Why I Write Such Good Books."

Like Kierkegaard's small book, Nietzsche's *Ecce Homo* summarizes his authorship as a series of strategic literary moves with their own internal logic of succession, an account to posterity of a literary output he knew had confounded his contemporaries as it would both perplex and dazzle future generations of readers. Nietzsche's literary voice has been described as hyperbolic, that is, he intentionally expresses himself in exaggerated overstatements. This would seem opposite to the literary style and voice so endearing to academic writers, including philosophers, of monotonic reasoning, and occasionally irony or tongue-in-cheek understatement. Nietzsche touted the greatness of his literary feat in comparison with the smallness of his contemporaries' lives. The very Latin title, "Behold the man," borrowed from the Gospel of St. John where Pontius Pilate utters these words while pointing to Jesus wearing the crown of thorns before his crucifixion, reveals Nietzsche's grandiose self-image. Yet who is the reader supposed to behold – Nietzsche as the crucified or the crucifier? Perhaps both.

Another way to understand and appreciate Nietzsche's voice in *Ecce Homo* is to picture him (as he was purportedly once glimpsed, in the nude, by his landlady through a keyhole) dancing as he performs the art song of his life and work. Nietzsche, himself an improvisational composer and pianist, frequently evokes the image of the dancer and has his Zarathustra proclaim, "Only in dance do I know how to speak in parables of the loftiest things." And though he only watches the dancers ("and now my highest parable stayed unspoken in my limbs!"), it is in the song and the dance that the prophet points toward the will to power, the self-transcendence that connects the dancer to the creative spirit.

Anyone who has performed a tango or watched a modern dance production knows that dance is exaggerated movement that expresses and releases the life of feeling, ideas, the very physicality of being alive. Another word for this exaggerated exuberance is euphoria, a condition associated with hallucinogenic drugs (including those used in rituals, such as peyote and mescaline) and with highly emotional religious rituals that may involve chanting, dance, mandalas, and meditation. Did Nietzsche hope his euphoric writing style would be contagious and draw the reader into the trance-like state of the narrator? Certainly that seems to be the case in the form of language he gives to his Zarathustra

There are certain remarkably prolific individuals, geniuses perhaps, who regard themselves as the vehicle through whose writing the wisdom of a higher being or power is revealed. They do not construct sentences and paragraphs like most mortals but seem to pluck them out of the air and write them down as if the gods had chosen them. It is their personal destiny to serve as a lightning rod, conducting highly charged language with remarkable originality and daring from the top of their heads down through the arm and fingers and out onto the page before the ink of the previous sentence has time to dry. Moreover, such prophetic thinkers know that merely informing or educating the reader is not enough to trigger a fundamental change in outlook.

Kierkegaard attributed his unique style and enormous literary output to the role of divine "governance," noting that his melancholic upbringing and his painfully isolated life were the necessary precursors to his religious and philosophical calling. Not exactly that these circumstances shaped his beliefs – that would be, in effect, a denial of their validity – but that the conditions made him an "exception" to the common lot of mankind and to the conventional thinking of the day. Of course, he believed that everyone could be an "exception" if they truly sought to become "that individual."

Nietzsche made no such claim, though during certain single years of his life he wrote and published more books that became world famous than most great thinkers might produce in a lifetime. He took full responsibility, insisted on his sole authority for his calling and his works. If, as he declared, he was a witness to his age and a prophet of its demise, he was also a profoundly influential figure of that era.

"The harm the good do is the most harmful harm," says Nietzsche. Why? Because the good "cannot create, they are always the beginning of the end." Nietzsche had no use for people of conventional morality, the conventionally good Christian, good Jew, the good citizen. They resent those who are truly great and seek to pull them down to their level of mediocrity or else they put the creative geniuses on a pedestal and give them prizes, like trophies for thoroughbreds or show dogs. And these honors tame the wildness of the great, classify them, and label them. Elevated as ideals, the great ones are made exceptions, beautiful monsters afflicted with exceptionality.

Nietzsche believed it was his duty to unmask civilization, to set the record straight because, for him, self-deception was "uncleanliness," a sin against true greatness that would make the perpetrator sick with moral depravity. Nietzsche described himself as "dynamite," a "lightning bolt of truth." Despite this menacing self-portrait, I think Nietzsche actually regarded himself as benevolent, as a crusader against a civilization bent on its own destruction, or at least as a prophet of that self-destruction.

But hadn't his words lent themselves to the Nazis who proclaimed themselves the *Übermenschen,* the Supermen who were destined to rule the world and who, with the help of Nietzsche's sister, an adamant Nazi believer, usurped Nietzsche's language of purity and uncleanness to purge the Aryan race of those they deemed inferior? Even though Nietzsche's writings demonstrate he was not a racist or anti-Semite, he bequeathed a language of ruthlessness and violence that fit the Nazis' purposes only too well.

Ironically, with his abhorrence of nationalism, his mental and physical frailty, his marginal existence, Nietzsche too would have been drummed out of their society, sent into exile somewhere in Switzerland, somewhere in the Alps from which he would see his ideas twisted to purposes he could not have imagined. Or, refusing exile, he would have been anonymously exterminated along with the "horde" he despised, gassed ignobly along with the pious Jew, the nomadic gypsy, the zealous Communist, the feeble and, like himself, the mentally impaired. To have seen that famous photograph – Hitler contemplating a bust of Nietzsche – that would have done him in.

Nietzsche admired those who stood above conventional morality, above the traditional distinction between good and evil. This classical moral distinction was, he thought, a strictly human invention, not ordained by a higher being, not dictated by laws of nature, not even the logical outcome of rational principles. The dichotomy, good and evil, was only a distraction from a more profound truth – that we make our values and bear responsibility for creating our lives through a primitive, even biological, inner urge to shape our own destiny. This Nietzsche called the "will to power." And it was in acts of greatness, the superhuman achievements of the sublime poets, composers, philosopher – those who shaped the world to their way of seeing, hearing and thinking – that the will to power was most clearly demonstrated.

AN OVERTURE FOR REDEEMING THE PAST

We might assume that for an author to survey and comment on his literary output over a number of decades, that author would presuppose the continuity of the biographical narrator as agent and by implication that of an enduring or unitary self. Moreover, for a continuous self to carry out such a review, that self or agent would have to possess the capacity to remember. And clearly Nietzsche does remember, since he recounts the circumstances of geography and the influences of people under which his various books were written and even evokes the mood and intensity of certain inspirational moments. Yet Nietzsche's *Ecce Homo* reflects not an unchanging point of reference, a character's sameness, but a self-overcoming one.

For example, his radically shifting assessments of Schopenhauer and Wagner, among others, and even of his own written works, suggest major discontinuities and upheavals in Nietzsche's attitudes towards the past and a revision in remembering. His Zarathustra announces Nietzsche's attitude toward the past: "To redeem what is past and transform all 'it was' into 'that is what I willed!' – that is the only thing I would consider redemption." Memory is inseparable from will, unless a person presents himself as an automaton, a victim or the passive product of his times. He presents and represents renewal and regeneration. Not for the past or even the present age does he write, but for the future.

Nietzsche regarded himself as the prototype of the *Übermensch* and consciously penned his works with all of humanity in mind; not only his contemporaries but also, more importantly, readers as yet unborn. That is why he declares in the "Why I Am a Destiny" section of *Ecce Homo*:

> *Someday my name will be associated with the memory of something tremendous, a crisis like no other on earth, the profoundest collision of conscience, a decision conjured up against everything that had been believed, required, and held sacred up to that time.*

So how does Nietzsche, as the autobiographical narrator of *Ecce Homo*, capture the dynamic of self-change without giving the impression that his one and only life reflects a totalizing of all that has come before? If the singular Nietzsche is a fiction or illusion fostered by the accident of the same name being printed on the title page of each book, then what it means to remember must also be viewed with a certain amount of skepticism.

Ecce Homo, though it comes as one of the last scenes of his literary and philosophical life, may, by analogy, be appreciated as like an overture to a symphony or opera. An overture usually serves to create interest and anticipation in the audience, as it introduces segments of the musical themes that will be further elaborated and through which tension will be built toward the climax or final resolution of the piece. Nietzsche's retrospective as a "monument to a crisis" is directed toward the future, as are the prophetic words of sages, seers and saints. As an analysis of the decline of both the society and the individual, they are initially addressed to their contemporaries as both warnings and predictions.

The "crisis" to which Nietzsche refers is both his own personal struggle to liberate himself from self-deception and the falsity of received values and knowledge (e.g. the teachings of Christianity, idealism in European philosophy, the Romanticism of Wagner, the nihilism of Schopenhauer, and what he judged as scholarly misreadings of antiquity) and the crisis of European civilization that continues in a downward spiral through absorption of the deeply ingrained falsehoods upon which society is built. However, for Nietzsche to state optimistically that "someday" his name will be associated with a realization that his life and work reflects this disaster suggests that his words will not have been in vain.

Nietzsche's enterprise is to remember for the sake of the future just as his life and work have moved toward self-liberation. Nothing less than a conception of freedom from the past is at work here. What is called for is a critical attitude toward personal and public history, because the function of memory is itself a major part of the problem, the "crisis." If we remember that Rousseau traced the origin of human language to the rise of class differences and the tyranny of one group over the other (the origins of inequality), so Nietzsche traces memory as an emerging capacity that is associated with the making of "promises."

Before this evolutionary change (Nietzsche was a reader of Darwin though he had his own take on evolution) human beings were like other animals – mainly instinctual, with no capacity for remembering. Rather, they had the "faculty of oblivion" that Nietzsche observes in creatures such as cows. But memory evolves as the consequence of social organization that enforces and ingrains the "herding values" that make a person beholden to others and to the group. We learn to remember (i.e. internalize) the rules of our own suppression of drives and instincts. Religion, philosophy and the resultant moralities are devices of human evolution that function to establish conscience as the inner voice of self-suppression, what Nietzsche terms "bad conscience." This could not happen without memory.

This depiction may sound strange until we consider the rise of psycho-analytic theory not long after Nietzsche penned his vast opus. Isn't this what Freud claims, that a whole internalized realm of Greek gods (e.g. Oedipus, Electra, Eros) dwell within us in the unconscious mind and reenact the dramas of the instinct of sexual desire, rage, revenge versus the instinct for self-preservation. That, according to Freud, is how tribal rites and rules came into being as taboos against incest, adultery, defilement of what has been deemed sacred such as tribal totems, and so on – in other words, the foundations of civilization are built on self-repression as the necessary component of social organization. If we understand what Nietzsche is saying in light of Freud, his ideas seem much less far-fetched.

Nietzsche's enterprise is to practice spiritual self-surgery, to free himself and his authentic reader from self-suppression, to liberate the individual, as he believes he has managed to liberate himself. And to do that he has to delve into the very depths of the human mind, which is also patterned into human physiology (and, for Nietzsche, these are inseparable because we are our bodies), to root out and destroy the most deeply presupposed elements of what has passed for centuries as knowledge.

This requires a critique of the function of memory itself. So there is a way that memory can, as it were, redeem itself. For one thing, memory gives the individual a sense of continuity and insofar we can recognize the herding instinct in ourselves, we can create a degree of personal sovereignty. When memory is guided by the will, its work is no longer merely retrospective and passive, reinforcing bad conscience, but futural and critical.

In his well-known essay on "The Uses and Abuses of History for Life" Nietzsche identifies three potentially positive attitudes towards the past: the monumental, antiquarian and critical types of history. The first enables a society to pay homage to the great achievements of the past and the struggles of a people to expand the idea of human being, providing ideals for what contemporary people might also accomplish. The antiquarian, by contrast, sees the preservation of the past as an end in itself, and in doing so helps people to appreciate their lives and culture. Finally, the critical historian's stance toward the past is to identify the flaws and failures in a culture's past in order to take what is deemed useful for the sake of the future, rather than to be slavishly attached to the past. Through this third method, the interpreter of history uses his or her power to break open the narrative of the past and dissolve it through condemning it. This irreverent judgment is rendered neither by righteousness nor mercy, says Nietzsche, but by "life alone, that dark, driving, insatiable self-desiring force."

These three approaches to the past each have their validity according to the needs, goals and aspirations of a people at a particular time and in their particular cultural setting. As for the time in which he is writing and to which he addresses himself, the end of the European 19th century with its rising prominence of the natural sciences (e.g. Darwinism, the emerging laboratory-based life science of psychology and physiology) and new technologies (e.g., the railway, telegraph, typewriter and photography, and the industrialization of work) and with the explosion of historical scholarship that scrutinized the past in new ways, Nietzsche warns of the pitfalls of too much knowledge of history. For one, the burden of historical information tends to overshadow the present, making it seem just another episode. In this way historical knowledge may stifle creativity, give the individual the sense that he or she is relatively insignificant in the vast sweep of historical forces, that somehow everything of importance has already been done and that the best one can do is to be an imitator of past greatness.

If what Nietzsche has to say about types of history also applies to the function of memory, then we get a better idea of what he saw as his task – the critical history method applied to both the past of civilization and one's own culture as well as one's own past. Paradoxically, we would need to know a great deal about the past in order to judge its flaws and failures, and in doing so could easily sink into the vast amount of information, succumbing in humility to the legacy that the past contributions to our culture has given to us. We might even be tempted to fabricate a pattern or system we perceive in historical events. And while we would gain an advantage of understanding history as a generative pattern of development, we might lose a sense of our role and responsibility within that vast matrix.

This is exactly what Nietzsche saw happening as numerous all-encompassing explanations of history emerged from the German idealist philosophers such as Hegel and Fichte but also the economic theorist, Karl Marx. Fortunately, says Nietzsche, we human beings are equipped with the power of forgetfulness and can ignore or set aside the past. We can reframe the historical to extract "that which bestows upon existence the character of the eternal and stable, towards art and religion."

NIETZSCHE'S STYLE AS PHILOSOPHY

Corresponding to his redeeming the past through the judgments of the will and the multiple selves that he and we behold in his intellectual biography, Nietzsche (again like Kierkegaard) refers to the crucial issue of communication. In *Ecce Homo* he tells us that the meaning of every literary style is to communicate, "an inner tension of pathos, with signs, including the tempo of these signs." Moreover, that since he has "an extraordinary number of inner states," he has "the most multifarious art of style than anyone has ever had at his disposal." Nietzsche did not resort to pseudonyms, as did Kierkegaard. But like Kierkegaard, he employed or deployed a wide range of communicative styles including aphorisms, parables, songs, poems, Biblical-style prophetic utterances, myths, traditional scholarly analysis, and especially what Nietzsche calls the "dithyramb."

Originally a hymn to the god Dionysus, the dithyramb was a choral lyric that involved exchanges between a single figure, the leader, and the chorus. Scholars believe it arose in the extemporaneous songs of the Dionysian festivals. These wine-inspired ecstatic chant-songs of praise and adoration that brought followers of the cult of Dionysus to a frenzied oneness with the god and with each other, eventually developed into the literary form to be found, for example, in the dithyrambs of the 5th century BCE Greek lyric poet Bacchylides. Over time, it became freer in its meter and more musical. Additional leaders or speakers eventually became the characters that acted out the drama, while the chorus grew to represent and express the larger cosmic forces of destiny.

For Nietzsche the greatness of the Greek tragedy – especially the plays of Aeschylus and Sophocles – was the quality of their evocative performance that enacted the collision of the boundary-breaking spirit of irrational ecstasy of the Dionysian spirit with that of the boundary seeking, anti-chaotic, form-giving rationality of the Apollonian spirit. In classic Greek tragedy the hero yearns for superiority over the mysterious, the fateful, and the destined but is ultimately defeated by universal forces represented by gods whose dominion cannot be overthrown. This depiction of the human condition provides access to the most profound truths of life and death, suffering and redemption, creativity and destruction. Even though the hero must die as part of the tragic plot, this death represents the reincorporation of the individual into the primordial oneness of the cosmic mystery.

Rather than serving to "arouse fear and pity," as Aristotle famously theorized in his treatises on tragedy, Nietzsche rejects this Apollonian-leaning interpretation offered by the marvelously rational Aristotle, pointing instead toward the sacred non-rational ritual experience that would have brought Greek audiences to emotional surrender.

In Zarathustra, we have the leader who encounters numerous individuals and groups during his wandering and preaching. These figures might be construed as chorus-like. And Nietzsche's own life, as he tells readers of *Ecce Homo* how his contemporaries reacted to his various books, provides a similar set of choral responses – mainly negative, though he insists that he has highly receptive and brilliant readers in cities around the world. Yet these are not the voices of cosmic destiny – far from it. So it is likelier that his books enact both leader and chorus as their inner drama draws the reader into the collision of the Dionysian and Apollonian.

Nietzsche presents his life as a reflection of the sickness of his cultural milieu and his literary production as a cauterizing treatment that uses pain to counteract pain. His surprising posthumous success can be attributed in part to the fact that he was in the vanguard of diagnosing certain flaws and failures of European civilization, making observations on the impact of modernization, dominance of the scientific outlook, and the rise of the bureaucratic nation-state – issues that resonated in the hearts and minds of countless others throughout the world.

Rilke and, as we shall later see, Picasso represent hundreds if not thousands of creative people who responded to Nietzsche's Zarathustra's exhortations and his Dionysian calling. And like Nietzsche, they recognized the need to find fresh ways to use or to "hear" or "see" the language of their art form in ways that broke with the conventions of their day. The risk they ran was the judgment of unintelligibility, which was the case, at least initially, for most of them and, to an extent, is still the case today as viewers ponder a Picasso cubist painting and proclaim, "I just don't get it."

The problem of Nietzsche's style and his theory of language as initially a form of auditory enslavement through memory-training obedience and later as the medium of an energetic world waiting to be heard through its metaphoric function, created a totally divergent response among Nietzsche's readers. To many of the artists, writers, poets and dancers of the 20th century, Nietzsche seemed to understand the non-rational, physiological or kinetic, spiritual and lyrical way of experiencing existence. For European philosophers such as Karl Jaspers, Martin Heidegger, and others critical of the Idealist metaphysical thinking that Nietzsche either was unintelligible or symptomatic of political despotism.

Even as recent a study of Nietzsche written by the analytically trained academic philosopher, Christopher Janaway, reflects this dichotomy, as Janaway admits in the Preface to his monograph, *Beyond Selflessness: Reading Nietzsche's Genealogy of Morals*, that reading Nietzsche made him "nervous and insecure" (Janaway, 2007). Janaway notes that it is possible to read Nietzsche selectively so as to choose only those propositions and arguments "that sound plausible and sensible to today's academic philosophers." He goes on to admit that approaching his writing in this way "does not mesh with my experience of reading Nietzsche." And he recognizes that part of Nietzsche's task is "disrupting our confidence in philosophy." In other words, it is difficult to approach Nietzsche's work without feeling confronted by the question: Who am I, the reader of this man's work? Not narrowly the "I" who practices academic philosophy but the "I" who asks: What does it mean for me to be a person? What is the basis of my identity?

IDENTITY

Nietzsche's approach to the identity of the individual is most easily apprehended through tracing his influence of negation. Like Kierkegaard,

Nietzsche sought to rescue the individual from succumbing to meta-physical systems that would meld the free and autonomous person with all-encompassing concepts such as Spirit (Hegel), a universal moral self (Kant), the cosmic will (Schopenhauer), or the thinking subject of the *Cogito ergo sum* (Descartes). The individual, argued Nietzsche, is not to be understood as a copy of an ideal form, a mode or moment of an historical process, or an immaterial mind encased in a material body. Nor will the individual find solace in the ascetic life of renunciation of pleasures, desires, or by relinquishing the quest for happiness. Not if there is to be any joy in life. Rather, an individual is one who practices self-creation and self-legislation through a reevaluation of values. Truly, Nietzsche's power of the negative is a force to contend with.

But how great is the victory if the Nietzschean individual is a creature left in a state of detachment from everyone and everything and bereft of any received formulations of meaning? A conventional solution is to postulate that each person has a destiny or inner purpose and that his or her quest is to discover and actualize this special uniqueness. Theoretically this could be accomplished by undergoing a battery of personality assess-ment tests that reveal how a person is oriented as a character type with particular motives, capabilities, dispositions, strengths and weakness. But the fact that standardized tests could perform this analysis means that individuals are only apparently unique, whereas in truth they are simply instances of an aggregate of characteristics and ultimately sortable into some categorical type – in other words, one exemplar among many, many instances. If this were so, we would have to redefine uniqueness to mean "different relative to most but not to all other people." From an outside observer's point of view, this is probably so.

Nietzsche does hold that each person has a fixed psychophysical con-stitution, which makes him or her a particular type of person. Each "type" can then develop his or her sovereignty only within these limits. So our options are not infinite after all and we do, in a sense, have an inherent disposition to contend with. For contemporary equivalents, one might look at the popular theory of the Enneagram for such a character typology or to the Myers-Briggs "types" that were derived from the work of Carl Jung. However, neither of these typologies includes a physiological or biological dimension, as does Nietzsche's.

There is, however, an additional factor. One has to want to be what one is. In other words, to echo Kierkegaard, the imperative remains to "choose oneself." That act of choosing is the differentiating factor that bestows uniqueness because only the person who has certain characteristics can will to affirm or not to affirm them. For Kierkegaard, this choosing of oneself is an initiating act that activates an individual's potential and brings it to fruition. The capacity for choosing is itself a gift that we only realize when we put it to work. But where this action will lead is guided by a model or ideal – namely, for Kierkegaard, the life of Christ, toward which the individual is drawn in a futural and, for the individual, unprecedented direction.

Nietzsche, who rejects the idealization of the Christ figure, of the Christian path, or of any normative model of human purpose, moves in a radically different direction from Kierkegaard at this point because he wraps the individual inside the concept of the eternal recurrence.

OF WILL AND WILLING

Nietzsche understood and appreciated the emerging emphasis in 18th and early 19th century philosophy on the sovereignty of the individual but also felt that human self-legislation and originality were severely constrained by dubious universal norms. Moreover, he regarded as repressive all forms of morality based on religious authority or cultural and social conventions. These, he argued, impinged on individual creativity.

How then could people become aware of these socially influenced, self-imposed constraints? How could they liberate themselves in order to discover their self-evaluative worth and the powers of their unique creativity? This would require a courageous, daring and even dangerous independence of thought and character. Would conventional forms of the philosophical treatise be adequate to announce this wake-up call or would an entirely unique communicative style be needed? Since he made human liberation the task of his philosophical project, Nietzsche had to find new ways to address his readers. He focused on the philosophically critical idea of the Will.

The concept of the will is usually associated with human volition – the capacity to act and to make choices. Kant elevated the idea of the will to what would seem to have been its highest stature – the source and basis of human autonomy, the capacity to legislate for oneself nature's gift of irreducible dignity. Thinkers before Kant had the conviction that an intelligible and moral universe existed independent of human cognition and that it was an expression of the will of God. Through God-given powers of reason humans were able to discern this rule-based universe and to devise principles of morality that harmonized with the grand design. Where God's will had been, Kant introduced man's. Not through intellectual contemplation but through choice-making would the Good be discovered in the formation of the principles of action.

Kant argued that the human will is bound to follow the claims of reason to turn desire toward right action through obedience to principle of universalization. His "categorical imperative" decreed: "Act only according to that maxim whereby you can at the same time will that it should become a universal law." We should only will what we would want everyone else to likewise will, by putting our intended action in the form of a maxim we would then extend to all mankind. Such tested maxims, reformulated as principles, would serve as the underpinning of freedom for the individual and for society. To will or choose what you would not want others to choose and will would be contradictory to the integrity of the will. No one possessing a rational mind would make choices that were in contradiction to one's rational powers.

Take, for instance, cheating on one's annual tax bill. Perhaps a person has received some small amount of income that would be hard for the IRS to identify. Why not just make this one exception to practicing complete honesty, save yourself a few dollars, and probably avoid the risk of being discovered and hence incurring a penalty? If one subjected this choice to the categorical imperative, one would have to propose to oneself a maxim that, under similar circumstances, it is fine if everyone cheats a little on their taxes to save a little money, considering that it's likely they won't be found out. But this means, by implication, that the tax cheater endorses living in a society in which dishonesty is approved in matters of taxation.

Although this could have profoundly negative consequences (which it does), the possible outcome of the decision was not the basis of Kant's moral imperative. Rather, the principle of going contrary to one's own sense of duty by violating the rule of universality showed that the decision was in error. No rational being would want to live in a world in which everyone had a duty to cheat on his or her income tax.

The autonomy of the will, as opposed to its heteronomy – obedience to merely external constraints, rewards and conditions, e.g. the fear of being caught and penalized by the IRS – should be understood independent of any religious creeds or dogmas, revelations or beliefs. Kant offered the basis for a primarily secular society that saw the ascent of the individual over religion and government when these failed to honor the intrinsic value of the person, which is, namely his or her freedom. Government policies and religious edicts are subject to change. The natural sciences produce new ways to understand the laws of nature. So a principle of morality that could guide decision-making without succumbing to these fluctuating claims and conditions would provide a more stable and trustworthy basis for personal morality and contribute to the harmonious coexistence of rational wills that Kant termed the "kingdom of ends."

An entirely different, more encompassing, idea of the will was introduced by Arthur Schopenhauer (1788-1860), an interpreter and critic of Kantian thought. Schopenhauer argued that Kant had merely replaced God, the external master of morality, with a new form of domination, universal moral principles that constituted an inner tyrant-conscience.

Schopenhauer asserted there was a force of will operating throughout the cosmos – a blind, undifferentiated, ceaseless impulse to existence, to life, that preceded human willing, which was only one of its many manifestations. Indeed, the difficulty with human willing is that we are driven by a quest for happiness that brings many desirable "goods," such as fame, fortune and erotic love. But in seeking and attaining these goods, argued Schopenhauer, we find our satisfaction soon evaporating, leaving us to return to the search for an elusive happiness, a questing act that repeats itself over and over. Eventually, for those able to grasp the situation reflectively, we realize that all of life is vanity, desires are insatiable, and happiness an illusion.

Unlike other animals, asserted Schopenhauer, because humans have the capacity for memory and thus concept formation, humans can indulge in acts of deliberation. And in this lies their suffering, because they realize the futility of striving as they experience "dreadful thoughts." In what echoes certain Hindu beliefs, Schopenhauer placed the cause of suffering at the feet of the human being who wills, desires, is disappointed, and is plagued by the capacity to remember. Only the true mystic or saint, capable of snuffing out the force of desires past and present, can become detached from the obsessions of the will. Schopenhauer famously speculated that if an individual were completely honest and enlightened, given the choice on the death bed whether to live life over again, he or she would prefer "complete nonexistence" to another chance at life.

What then would make life tolerable while our hearts are still beating? Schopenhauer recommended an ascetic attitude toward life that called for renunciation, resignation, and a suppression of the will. This, in turn, would lead to greater composure and tranquility. Additionally, Schopenhauer argued that to achieve a more tranquil state of consciousness, the individual should focus on aesthetic perception. Through works of art, and especially music, we get carried away, losing ourselves in the rich sonority of the orchestra, the music evoking pleasurable emotions that conjoin us to what is universal – joy itself, sadness itself.

Schopenhauer believed that music, or at least certain kinds of classical music, tonally echoed the basic structure of the world. Organic and inorganic reverberate in the very range of musical tonalities. Great music, which for Schopenhauer is music that comes closest to expressing the purest idea of feelings, puts us in touch with the force of the omnipresent will, the very energy of the cosmos.

Richard Wagner, an admirer of Schopenhauer's ideas, sought to create the ideal of music to which the philosopher pointed. Schopenhauer believed that opera was the musical form that came closest to representing the power of the general will. Under his influence, Wagner set out to write his famous opera, *Tristan and Isolde*, a musical dramatization of the Medieval German poetic romance that premiered in 1865. The extremely emotional opera opens with the famous Tristan chord, a yearning, dissonant thematic introduction that then moves to a second dissonant chord, a device of harmonic suspension used throughout the opera to keep the listener in a state of emotional suspense, poised in expectation of a musical resolution only to be carried through a series of prolonged unfinished cadences that are not resolved until the finale of Act 3, the moment of Isolde's death.

While Nietzsche believed that Schopenhauer had grasped the most fundamental truth of human existence – that non-rational forces reside at the foundation of all creativity and of reality itself – he gradually became disenchanted with Schopenhauer's philosophy of dispassionate disengagement, repulsed by what he believed to be its life-denying negativity. Instead, through his scholarship he discerned a wild, amoral, instinctual "Dionysian" energy within pre-Socratic Greek culture, though the spirit of that culture had been weakened and submerged by the Apollonian forces of logical order and reflective seriousness and by the life-denying ethos of Christianity. Nietzsche believed that the life-giving vitality of the god of ecstasy and intoxication could still be recovered.

He challenged Schopenhauer's view with the idea of the eternal recurrence. In his *The Joyful Wisdom*, Nietzsche introduces the daemon who sets before the individual an hour glass that he offers to turn over and over again as the individual's life is perpetually relived, including the past that remains in memory. While Schopenhauer offered the enlightened one the compensation of being able to see life as a whole, a detached form of Stoic resignation, Nietzsche postulated that if among the myriad life experiences one had encountered there occurred "one tremendous moment," then this ecstatic instance could become the source of a "great affirmation" of life, The Joyful Wisdom – indeed, its redemption.

It was self-punishment in despair over an unmodifiable past that Nietzsche found unacceptable in Schopenhauer's philosophy. Instead, he proclaimed an affirmation of life that would eclipse moral doctrines that called for resignation. What sort of person would be capable of this life affirmation while starring directly into the vortex of nihilism? For Nietzsche, it was the Übermensch, the Overman, sometimes also called the Superman who would exhibit this capacity.

Only such a noble warrior of a creature could defy the degradation of the human spirit and its culture that Nietzsche saw in Schopenhauer as a reflection of the decadence of society that accompanied the end of the 19th century. This decadence was not a descent into degeneracy and vice or escapist hedonism but the failure of creative energy to reach its apogee in great works of art. Schopenhauer's philosophy was just one more sign that a negative spirit had been wearing away the vitality of life and the will to live as though without end. Only the Übermensch could bring about a "reevaluation of all values."

THE ARTIST AS OVERMAN

Who might we think of as an example of the Overman? One possibility is the larger than life, perpetually innovative artist, Pablo Picasso. He described his epoch-making, monumental 1907 painting of five nude female prostitutes, Les Demoiselles d'Avignon, his "first exorcism painting," inspired in part by Nietzsche. Picasso set his own rules both for his artistic work and for his life and many loves. Just as one new art movement, such as Cubism, would come to fruition through his creative genius, he would move on to yet another groundbreaking style such as surrealism and symbolism, while experimenting in collage, ceramics, stone and metal sculpture, printmaking and stage design. He was never satisfied with one artistic achievement or one lover.

Picasso was indifferent to conventional morality and propriety, he painted portraits of his various lovers, depicted scenes of death, illness, devouring monsters, the comic and tragic figures of jugglers, Gypsies (Roma) and jesters, of the life and death contest between matador and bull, in short the Schopenhauerian world of representations of the force of will for which he, as if responding to Nietzsche's calling, rose to the occasion as its uncompromising equal.

The influence of Nietzsche's view of attitudes towards history, when combined with the notion of artistic genius and self-overcoming, is reflected in Jaime Sabartes's account of his twenty year-old friend, Pablo. Picasso, says Sabartes, asserted "that the authentic artist must remain unaware of anything that culture kept one from seeing, put a brake on spontaneity, while the artist must be able to project directly on to the canvas what he wants to say" (quoted in Cabanne, 1977). Ironically, Picasso, whose father was an artist and art teacher, spent much of his youth studying art and making reproductions of famous works hanging in the Prado Museum in Madrid.

So it is not the case that Picasso was without influences, nor was he "unaware" of the history of art. What, in Sabarte's account, Picasso does to practice forgetfulness is learn from and then set aside what had already been accomplished in order to freshly observe his environment, respond to it, and express that response through the medium of the painted canvas or the drawing on paper. Also, Picasso became absorbed with so-called Primitive art, at first of Spanish origin and later of African, and found in these forms of tribal art the kind of direct expression "not bridled by theories," that he wanted to achieve in his visual images. Sabartes goes on to say that Picasso was sure that "a painter found his deepest sincerity in suffering."

Picasso is only one among a large number of avant-garde artists in Madrid and in other European capitals at the beginning of the 20th century who embraced a message they heard in Nietzsche's writings or in popularized versions of them, a message insisting that art should be a spontaneous act, unmediated by intellect, the uninhibited self-expression of genius. The artist must tap into the most elementary forces of nature and ego, which could sometimes mean setting aside the learned rules of artistic composition. And so these avant-garde artists began to study the works of tribal cultures, "primitive" masks, ritual figures, images that seemed to spring more directly from the subconscious. Artistic freedom would be linked to political freedom, and Picasso would cast his lot with the growing movement of anarchists who sought to liberate society from oppressive governments.

Did these artists truly understand Nietzsche or were they hearing only one or two themes in the Nietzschean opera of the Übermensch? With the exception of the Italian Futurists, they did not embrace Nietzsche's enthusiasm for the exhilarating effects of war and, if anything, were anti-militaristic. They turned Nietzsche's Dionysian occultism into the bohemian subculture of the smoky cafe, the glittering dance hall, and the rumpled bed but also into the ecstatic dance, such as *The Rite of Spring* (Stravinsky). We will return to this issue of what it might mean to become Nietzschean but for now continue with our exploration of the philosophical aspects of what it means to go beyond the ordinary human.

For this superior being, the Übermensch, to bravely navigate the uncharted, because irrational, waters of thought and feeling unsupported by a structure of pre-existing meaning, required advancing Kant's autonomous being as the new helmsman only now freed from the restrictions of a rational, duty-based morality and from the self-denying fears of a judging deity.

Nietzsche thus proclaimed both the "will to power" and the "death of god" as the dual banners of his enlightened warrior. And though he occasionally used the term "blond beast" to describe this figure – an unfortunate image that was later picked up by the Nazis – his Overman was not an Aryan supremacist but a self-affirming noble creator spirit. As such, the Übermensch is characterized as embodying the will to power, as spontaneous, aggressive, and ready to reinterpret the givens of life to assert new meanings, ready to give new form and shape to an unfolding future. The Overman has won a victory over religious piety and has now linked his fate to the god Dionysus. In short, he or she has learned the cosmic dance.

Nietzsche believed that Kant, among other philosophers, had already demonstrated the obsolescence and irrelevance of a revealed god and that the impressive advances of the natural sciences had further demonstrated that almost all natural forces could be explained by means of mathematics and physics, eclipsing the role of a supernatural god. Therefore, the god of the Christian culture had lost its credibility and was now revealed as a human projection that enabled the priestly class to dominate and subdue the masses or the "horde" by employing such concepts as sin, guilt, virtue, damnation, fallenness and so on.

Nietzsche's proclamation of the will to power brings the concept of the will to its most radical formulation. What drives the world and everything in it is an unconscious force that is neither good nor evil. Either one discovers, acknowledges and affirms this force or one avoids, denies or inadvertently succumbs to it. Nietzsche seems to have tapped into the unconscious mind, both collective and individual. Perhaps he believed he was doing a would-be elite class of noble warrior Übermensch a favor by trumpeting and prophesying their imminent arrival. Leaders of the Third Reich claimed to be just such an elite warrior class, though Nietzsche would have quickly disowned them.

One who also harkened to Nietzsche's proclamations was the Swiss psychiatrist Carl Jung. He found inspiration for his exploration of the collective unconscious in Nietzsche's identification of the Dionysian cultural force as an antidote to the one-sidedness of the rationalistic and scientific culture of the Western world, the Apollonian. Jung saw the ancient past, mythology in particular, as the gateway to the unconscious, which in turn was a point of access to the hidden powers and meanings of the universal Self.

Jung regarded the unconscious as a way to connect with a higher or deeper reality. This would be one of several reasons why Jung broke from the Freudian branch of psychoanalytic theory. We will return to this subject in the chapter on Jung.

BEING NIETZSCHE

As is the case in other philosophical autobiographies, we do not assume that the first-person narrative of the philosophers is necessarily different from their other philosophical expositions. Even though the autobiography often gives us a sense of the thinker's intentions and motives – a behind-the-scenes look, so to speak – this written work blends in or adds to, rather than standing above, the thinker's other works. Consequently, we as readers are still faced with the task of making sense and meaning out of what has been offered to us.

Nietzsche makes this challenge especially paradoxical because he takes what might seem to be two different stances. On the one hand he argues that every work of philosophy is a kind of confessional that reveals the thinker's own dilemmas and perplexities. Yet, at the outset of *Ecce Homo*, he insists: "Don't assume that what you read, even though I tell you it is about my life, is identical with who I am."

Can both these statements be simultaneously true? The answer is yes. But only if we remember that as readers we remain interpreters of meaning and that in the philosopher's autobiography, no matter how much he or she reveals an authorial intention, we still do not have direct access to the heart and soul of the writer but only a proximal encounter. We can grasp thinkers' points of view and try to reenter the circumstances, historically, both public and personal, of their lives in so far as they make them available to us in the mutually shared realm of the written word.

Few of us would choose to live a life such as Nietzsche's, though we may aspire to greatness, genius, unprecedented creativity, literary productivity, and posthumous fame. Who would be willing to pay the price? Still, if Nietzsche is correct, we share in his "crisis," as each of us is the battle-ground between the forces of the Dionysian and Apollonian. Moreover, we live in societies and cultures that are extensions of what Nietzsche saw coming and beyond anything he could have imagined.

The condition of the individual in Western post-industrial societies is paradoxically to have few conflicting moral imperatives or restraints, a great deal of encouragement to be unique and special, if not creative, and yet to live in mainly secular, highly bureaucratized, consumer-oriented, high-speed media-connected environments. In the Nietzschean way of looking at things, only an elite group of noble, self-creating warrior types could emulate his ideal of the Übermensch. We have seen such groups and such people from time to time. They might include the so-called merchant tycoons or robber barons of the industrializing West – the Carnegies, Fords and Vanderbilts. They include the Hitlers, Mussolinis, Stalins and (not to be chauvinistic) Richard Daleys and Huey Longs.

And what about the intellectual and artistic elites or the elite of the new cyber culture, Bill Gates, Steven Jobs and other techno-geniuses? How would Nietzsche differentiate among these Übermenschen? Would Nietzsche have lauded the benevolent dictator, the enlightened despot, and the power elite of post-industrial democracies who seek to control the masses?

Somehow, I think the answer is no. Just as he did with Schopenhauer and Wagner, he would find some fatal flaw, compromise of character, and betrayal of ideals in all of these individuals and their coteries, because that is Nietzsche's task, his destiny: to destroy idols. To be Nietzsche or Nietzschean is to subject oneself to living cheerfully without the support or consolation of a sense of meaning or purpose. Here again we have Tennyson's Ulysses who, after the long heroic journey and return to home and hearth, wills to venture forth once again "to seek a newer world," and with his fellow mariners, "to strive, to seek, to find, and not to yield."

To be a Nietzsche is to assign values and meanings as self-chosen, not passively received ideals, to plumb the depths of one's drives and instincts, and to be an interpreter rather than a follower of cultural norms that otherwise delimit the expression of individuality.

Speaking of expressions of individuality, Nietzsche claims he is the last disciple and initiate of Dionysus, the god of intoxication and sexuality. Yet erotic love plays a small role in his work. Most of his comments about women are disparaging, and all of his Übermenschen are Men. Though he uses metaphors of fecundity and pregnancy, those birthing creative new ideas and art works are always men.

This has led to some speculation that perhaps Nietzsche was gay or at least had homoerotic tendencies. A gender or feminist-oriented study of Nietzsche's work seems highly appropriate to more fully appreciate the complexity of his work and character.

FIELDWORK AND REFLECTIVE WRITING

Make a list of important moments in your life. If, as in the film *After Life*, you were given a number of days to reflect on these moments and then to choose one, which one would you choose? And if you could have this moment recreated and made into a short documentary-type video, who would you want to play the roles of the people in this remembered time? Would they be well-known actors, family members, friends or even voices behind animated characters?

Suppose this now timeless moment was meant to represent the essence of your life – your values, life purpose, and source of meaning. What then would be the title of this film and to whom would you want to give it for safekeeping? Perhaps even for viewing at a memorial event after your death or even to be shown annually on the commemoration of your birth or death?

Consider writing the script for this video documentary that would immortalize you.

READER'S GUIDE

Philosophers such as Nietzsche who aim to lure the reader up a steep mountain trail into rarified air and who address the reader in multifarious and enigmatic ways, shaking the reader's confidence by awakening and challenging his or her presuppositions about the very foundations of every-day life, are not for everyone. For those who do feel the pull of curiosity through the halo effect that radiates Nietzsche's fame, influence and reputation into intellectual, literary, artistic, philosophical, and political communities of interest, timing is crucial.

Much depends on the temperament of the reader and his or her open-ness to absorbing the words of a literary stylist and radically irreverent thinker such as Nietzsche. And a great deal may depend on the reader's prior knowledge and familiarity with the "idols" that Nietzsche seeks to topple. For someone with little religious training or attachment to a faith community, Nietzsche's relentless attacks on Judeo-Christian morality would have little impact except perhaps to reinforce fashionably assumed attitudes about the evils of "organized religion." Similarly, lack of familiar-ity with philosophical idealism ranging from Plato to Kant and Hegel, would leave most readers scratching their heads. And if you've never listened to or attended a Wagnerian opera, you might be clueless about the hullabaloo over the *Ring Cycle*.

There are two types of entry into the corpus of Nietzsche's work. One is to begin by reading *The Birth of Tragedy, On the Genealogy of Morals* and perhaps *Beyond Good and Evil*. These can be appreciated and studied with benefit by those who enjoy grappling with ideas, with critiques of scholarship and historical analysis, with issues in the history of ethics and political theory, and with a kind of pre-psychoanalytic probing of the human condition. For those who are more drawn to the lyrical and pro-phetic, *Thus Spoke Zarathustra* is a thrilling read even if you do not understand everything that is being said.

As for secondary sources, of which there are thousands, Steven E. Aschheim's *The Nietzsche Legacy in Germany 1890-1990* (1994) provides a fascinating way to see Nietzsche's life philosophy through the eyes of those who, reading the works in the original language, interpreted and made use of them for their own purposes. Along those lines, Pierre Cabanne's *Pablo Picasso: His Life and Times* (1977) is a compelling resource. In Walter Kaufmann's well-known and respected *Nietzsche: Philosopher, Psychologist, Anti-Christ* (fourth edition, 1975) the thinker is rescued from his detractors, misinterpreters, and those who see him as a predecessor to fascist National Übermensch-type Socialism.

7

Sartre and De Beauvoir
Under the Covers

Like Kierkegaard and Nietzsche, Jean-Paul Sartre and Simone de Beauvoir focused their attention on the role of the finite human being and the conditions of choice and self-determination. Following the Nietzschean tradition, they sought to critique cultural norms and systems of thought that impinged upon human freedom, especially conceptual frameworks that relied on arguments of determinism – whether biological, historical or religious. But unlike Nietzsche and Kierkegaard, Sartre and de Beauvoir were interested in what might constitute authentic human relations and social flourishing. Defiant of social norms and traditional values, they proclaimed: Human life is absurd! Should we wring our hands in despair? No, they insisted, we should celebrate the dissolution of preexistent meanings. Clearing away the inauthentic opens the way to the authentic.

This is one of the rallying cries of the existentialist movement. At the heart of their philosophy is a self with the freedom to invent its own meanings and purposes. If we understand that there is no preformed moral universe, only a socially constructed one we are born into and receive as a body of bourgeois values embedded in a culture shaped by the accidents of history such as the capitalist economy, class structure, Church doctrine, and cultural dogmas attributed to some type of laws of "nature," then we waken to the realization that we are under no obligation to accept these values. We are free to make our own. So the absurd life is really the opportune life if we realize that we are free to become ourselves. This, however, will turn out to require a fair amount of effort, as Sartre and de Beauvoir's philosophical autobiographies make clear. The story begins with some colorful names.

He favored her college nickname, *Castor* (Beaver), because her industrious, energetic and cheerful qualities reminded him of that sleek semi-aquatic creature. At times she called him Hedgehog because, when downcast over some turn of events, he had a tendency to hunch up in a defensive ball. We learn these terms of endearment from Simone de Beauvoir (1908-1985) who celebrates the flowering of her intellectual and amorous relationship with Jean Paul Sartre (1905-1980) in the second of four autobiographical volumes, *La Force de l'Age* (*The Prime of Life*), published in France in 1960 (English translation, 1962).

De Beauvoir traces parental, social and educational influences on her childhood in the first volume of her autobiography *Memoirs of a Dutiful Daughter* (1958/59). In the second she recounts her relationship with the youthful budding philosopher, Sartre, her first teaching experiences, the dawning of her writing career, the personally felt political tensions in Europe leading up to the Second World War, the German occupation and then the liberation of France. This sixteen-year period is for de Beauvoir as momentous and calamitous as for the millions of people across Europe and beyond.

By the time de Beauvoir turned fifty in 1958, when she first felt the urge to write autobiographically, she and Sartre were already internationally famous for their literary and philosophical achievements, notorious for their open relationship as unmarried lovers, and highly controversial for their eccentric version of left-wing politics. If other philosophers' private lives were hidden from view or deemed irrelevant to their published writing, there appeared to be a seamless connection between the call to freedom proclaimed in philosophical works such as Sartre's *Being and Nothingness* (1938/66) and de Beauvoir's *The Ethics of Ambiguity* (1947/48) and how they had chosen to lead their lives.

The daring couple, associated with the philosophical movement called Existentialism, had even been featured in a 1957 issue of that bastion of middle-class Americana, *Life* magazine. To the American public Sartre and de Beauvoir epitomized the generation of post-war radicals who occupied Left Bank cafes and smoke-filled cellar nightclubs dressed in black turtleneck sweaters with flowing skirts and ballerina slippers for the women and blue jeans for the men, drinking *le vin rouge* and smoking endless numbers of pungent Gauloises cigarettes, while espousing such intoxicating slogans as "existence precedes essence" or that to be human is to be "condemned to freedom." Sartre and de Beauvoir would embrace Kierkegaard's concept of despair but dismiss the existence of his God as of "no importance in our philosophy."

Sartre's modest 190-page account of his childhood, *Les Mots* (*The Words*, published in 1964 in both French and English) looks flimsy and inconsequential when compared to the thousands of pages of de Beauvoir's testimony to the philosophical stances she shared with him. *The Words* is a tale that does not mention de Beauvoir because its chronology ends a decade before he even meets her.

This first literary foray into the autobiographical realm is also Sartre's last. After his death de Beauvoir would publish his correspondence to her in the two-volume collection entitled *Witness to My Life: The Letters of*

Jean-Paul Sartre to Simone de Beauvoir (1983/92), and make other unpublished papers public including *Notebooks Toward a Moral System* and *War Diaries: Notebooks from a Phony War*. And while in interviews with magazine and newspaper reporters Sartre would acknowledge great love and admiration for de Beauvoir ("she thinks like a man"), there is an imbalance of literary reciprocity that at times creates the impression of unrequited love.

Sartre was a prolific writer, producing not only philosophical essays on a wide range of topics such as the function of emotions, the personality of the anti-Semite and the political role of literature, but also novels, plays, and Marxist-psychoanalytic-philosophical biographies such as his lengthy study of theatre of the absurd French playwright and former criminal, Jean Genet. His political flirtations with Marxism led to invited trips to Castro's Cuba and countries of Eastern Europe. Nominated for the Nobel Prize for literature in 1958, Sartre declined the award, saying this type of approval would distract from the integrity of his work.

Because de Beauvoir so completely aligns her views with Sartre's (they talked them through together) and periodically defends Sartre's ideas in her autobiographical writings, we can regard their philosophical views as compatible. However, we will see that de Beauvoir begins to find her own somewhat divergent perspective in *The Ethics of Ambiguity* (1948) and later in the book that helped to launch the modern feminist movement, *The Second Sex* (1949/53). Sartre, too, later in life veers off (from de Beauvoir's point of view) into strange new territory, practically repudiating his Existential phase as he tests the waters of Chinese leader Mao Zedong's brand of political theory. We will, therefore, want to pay attention to their differences.

CAFÉ LIFE

Recounting the period that was her self-described "prime of life," de Beauvoir presents numerous scenes and situations endowed with the attributes of dawning awareness and maturing self-realization. Readers are invited to follow de Beauvoir as she tests the strength of her convictions, relinquishes certain beliefs and assumptions and forges the determination that enabled her to write her first novels.

She simultaneously weaves in the way the political and social forces of national and international conflict – especially the rise of National Socialism (Nazism), the Russian Revolution and rise of the Stalinist regime, and the coming of World War II – swept over her life, casting her into collective situations not of her making, situations forcing her to become part of an overwhelmingly larger history. In this sense, the story of her personal liberation is intertwined with that of whole countries, social classes, minorities, and, in the post-war period, the struggle of colonial peoples (e.g. the Algerian War). All the life-changing events that de Beauvoir depicts over this sixteen-year period involve Sartre, her partner in liberation. The following event captures something of the tension and ambiguity of their lifelong relationship.

In the way de Beauvoir tells her story readers may sense an echoing of the 17th century author La Fontaine, whose animal fables revive the tradition of Aesop. She was barely twenty years old, and Sartre three years her senior, when the two awoke early one morning as their train reached the Austerlitz Station in Paris. Snuggled together on their hard third-class seats, the two friends were returning from three glorious days of tramping across the French countryside, where they had climbed the ramparts of medieval castles, peered into ancient cave dwellings and conversed with farmers, blacksmiths, inn keepers and all sorts of other interesting people. They enjoyed sleeping under the stars.

Now they were exhausted from their travels and famished, having eaten nothing for two days except "a prune flan in the train station at Tours." They made their way through the maze of the Jardin des Plantes and arrived at a favorite haunt, the Café Closerie des Lilas, which was just opening. But there they discovered they had not a *sou* – a penny – between them. Undeterred, they plopped themselves down at an outdoor table and called, "Garçon." In a matter of minutes they were eagerly sipping cups of hot chocolate and devouring piles of fresh baked croissants.

Wiping their lips and stretching their weary limbs, Beaver and Hedgehog were wonderfully contented. They looked at each other lovingly and smiled at their good fortune to have found such perfect partners. But now how would they pay? To be sure, they were the most honest and honorable of creatures and would never dream of slipping away and leaving the bill unpaid. Then Hedgehog said: "Listen, Beaver, wait here while I climb into a taxi and go wake up one of our friends who will surely lend us the money." Beaver agreed, though she didn't like the garçon's suspicious glances as she pretended to sip from a now empty cup. I've been left like a hostage, thought Beaver. It must have been at least an hour later when, at last, Hedgehog returned. "*Regarde,*" he exclaimed, and showed her a handful of shiny coins.

Such was the carefree life of the two friends, Beaver and Hedgehog, who relished their spontaneity, freedom and shared adventures. How brilliant their lives and how dazzling the ideas they entertained, for they loved to talk about literature, politics and philosophy into the middle of the night until they could hardly keep their eyes open.

Revisiting this time in *The Prime of Life*, de Beauvoir would write about that morning on the café terrace and about her relationship with Monsieur Hedgehog, exclaiming: "Our way of life was so exactly what we wanted that it was as though it had chosen us." Thinking back on the life that had once seemed destined to offer them everything for which they could possibly ask, a life based on certainties about such things as the progress of social justice for the peoples of the world and the promising role the twosome would play in helping to bring this about, Beaver confesses: "We were wrong about almost everything."

While she does not explain just yet how she reached this conclusion, her later revelations bring out how the coming of war, occupation under the Nazis, the murder of various friends, the Allied liberation, several bouts with serious illnesses, post-war political intrigues, even their literary success and fame had taken a toll on them. Moreover, it would turn out that Hedgehog had a tendency to run around with all sorts of other handsome creatures besides Beaver, and this did not please her.

It wasn't that Beaver regretted the past, only that she was determined to make a fair and honest account of what she had learned and how she had come to learn it. Is there a moral to this tale? Perhaps that life would be simpler though less interesting were it not for the existence of others.

If Kierkegaard's existential inner life is represented by imaginary walks within the walls of the patriarchal home, Sartre and de Beauvoir's dismissal of the interior life as an escape from social responsibility is expressed in frequent allusions to the scenes of café life. What more fitting place for the philosophers who lead their personal lives in public view and who, rather than condemning the "crowd" as an amorphous leveler of selfhood, see the world we share with others as the theater of personal identity? The café is the public living room where you can eat, drink, smoke, talk, see and be seen by others. For the Europeans the café was the preeminent public space and for de Beauvoir and Sartre, who both did a great deal of their reading, writing, flirting and smoking there, it was the main stage of the philosophical life.

Her depiction of the scene at the café evokes both the attraction of and tension in the lifelong collaboration between Castor and Jean-Paul. Both born of French middle-class families whose values and aspirations they rejected in their youth, they were nevertheless academic high achievers. Sartre received his degree in philosophy (the French *agrégation*, equivalent to the American doctorate) in the same year as de Beauvoir, the spring of

1929. Though three years older, he had failed the written exam the previous year because he insisted on parading the originality of his thought rather than proving his mastery of the western philosophical tradition. Chastised, the following year he placed first in the examination, while de Beauvoir placed a close second. Some say, had it not been Sartre's second time around and that he was the product of the elite École Normale Supérieure and she of the Sorbonne, she would have placed first. Their degrees qualified them to teach at the high school and college levels, which for a period of time they did.

But now, before the call of employment and Sartre's obligatory military service, the two enjoyed a precious time of endless walks in the Luxembourg Garden and outings into the countryside. And if their planning was poor and they did not have sufficient funds to cover a homecoming breakfast, so what? A quick taxi ride could remedy that.

Anyway, where else could two young lovers go to be together when they lacked a private room of their own? Simone was waiting for a lodger to move out of her grandmother's guest room and Jean-Paul still lived at home with his mother and grandparents. Their lovemaking would have to take place in a grassy field and their intellectual communion over croissants and hot chocolate in the public world of the café where it should be apparent to anyone that they were on the brink of great things. Still, there was the little annoyance. Simone was left on her own while Jean-Paul woke up friends. And what could have taken so long? Just how trustworthy was this man with his boundless ambition and countless opinions? And how often would she be stuck like that, keeping up a front that everything was fine while nervously awaiting his return? Who, after all, was Jean-Paul Sartre?

SELF-CREATION THROUGH WRITING

Sartre's autobiography dissects and catalogs the illusions fostered by a middle-class family childhood. Ironically, according to Sartre, these illusions helped to shape the disposition of the future imaginative writer and thinker. He recounts that his father died when Sartre was still a young child and that he went with his mother to live with her parents, Charles and Louise Schweitzer. The grandparents, especially the grandfather, spoiled the child, affectionately called little Poulou, and made him think he was the center of the universe. But one day Poulou overheard a critical remark that made him realize that the adults in his life were just pretending because they liked the way he adored Grandpa.

Little Poulou, who was something of a tyrant toward his mother, began to see his grandparents' and other adults' lives as just so much play-acting, a sham of self-deceptions and hollow truths. So he withdrew into his notebooks where he invented tales of adventure and bravery in which he became the genuine article, the hero. Then he saw that this too was only make-believe. But by then he had discovered two great truths – first, that no one is really anything but what they invent for themselves through word and deed; second, that people who fail to recognize this truth blame their shortcomings on either circumstances or unconscious forces.

For Jean-Paul, being a writer would be his way of inventing himself and changing other people's lives. He would sum up his great revelation in a simple, curiously circular, proposition of predestination: "I was born to fulfill the great need I had of myself." Grasping the power of creative self-invention, Sartre would proclaim: "I was born of writing."

De Beauvoir also traces the source of her literary career to a rebellious liberation from her childhood background and the search for a means to declare her individuality. As a young girl, Simone felt caught between parents holding different religious outlooks. Her father was a free thinker and her mother a strict Catholic. This confusing situation forced her, she says, to think for herself.

Simone was a bright and ambitious child who did well at school. Her father thought she should pay more attention to her appearance than to her books and studies because, after all, how would the latter help her to land a husband? But Simone did not want to marry and come under the dominance of a husband. Nor did she want to bear children or lead a respectable middle-class life. Instead, she longed to become a writer, an independent woman with an income of her own, and a champion of the working classes. In her adolescence she awoke to the possibility of another life, her own, and threw herself headlong into claiming it.

Having alluded to marriage as this "revolting fate" in her cultural critique of women's subjugation, *The Second Sex*, she goes on to challenge herself in *The Prime of Life* by asking the question: "Freedom I had – but freedom to do what?" As if in partial answer, she recounts the ecstatic days of autumn 1929 when, awaiting a teaching assignment, she sits in the Café Closerie des Lilas sharing bread and chocolate with the short, bespectacled Jean-Paul Sartre. Like most young middle-class people, the two of them have great expectations of what they will make of their lives. But unlike most young people, they achieve what they hope for, though their fame and unconventionality exact a heavy price. Still, de Beauvoir knows that she has gained her freedom to choose, for better or worse, her life with Sartre.

De Beauvoir prefaces this unplanned, sequel to *Memoirs of a Dutiful Daughter* by explaining her three purposes. First, she wants to set the record straight about the rumors and falsehoods that have obscured her and Sartre's purposes as intellectuals and social activists. Second, she feels compelled to respond to the many hundreds of would-be writers who have been clamoring for advice. And third, she is responding to a strange urgency that has made her dimly aware that her experiences form a "pattern which the future seems unlikely to modify very much." She has set herself the task of detecting "just what the pattern might reveal." Moreover, she feels she must do so "now or never." Since the manuscript must have already gone to her publisher, we assume that de Beauvoir was successful and that her autobiographical imperative is now also ours.

Anticipating the criticism of succumbing to bourgeois self-preoccupation, de Beauvoir insists that it isn't just her life she is writing about. She asserts that anyone who approaches an "autobiographical study" with candor and honesty cannot help "illuminating the lives of others." Since we are known to others and to ourselves through our actions, argues de Beauvoir, we therefore belong to others as they belong to us. A personal history is therefore not a private possession but a socially shared one.

De Beauvoir and Sartre rarely lived under the same roof, though their love affair spanned several decades. Perhaps, in contemporary parlance, they just needed their own space. There is another reason, which she recounts. Sartre considered theirs to be what he called "an essential" love. Such a love, he believed, was so strong, so fundamental, it might just leave a little room for the inessential, the "contingent" love affair, of which, it turns out, he had a great many.

De Beauvoir accepted this notion in part because she shared Sartre's conviction that freedom of choice is the hallmark of what it means to be a human being. However, her personal narrative also tells of her anguish over Sartre's short- and long-term affairs that were to draw them emotionally and geographically apart. Only after her death would subsequent biographers reveal another side of the story – her love affairs with both men and women, some of which she kept secret from Sartre. In *The Prime of Life* she does admit, "There are many things which I firmly intend to leave in obscurity."

In their opposition to social conventions of their day the couple shared the optimistic belief held by other members of the French Left that society could be reformed and mankind made over in a new image. While they believed that class differences should be abolished, they were more anarchists than Socialists. Ultimately, they believed that only the life of the individual was real because it was the true foundation of self-determination.

They also believed that colonialism, as seen in India and Indo-China, was about to be overthrown, and that capitalism about to succumb to the Socialist and Communist uprisings then sweeping the world. Like many of their political fellow travelers, de Beauvoir and Sartre dismissed the rising threat of Hitler and his political party in Germany and believed the Spanish Republicans would prevail against the Fascist leader, General Franco. These beliefs, as de Beauvoir would later point out, were to be proven false. And she would admit that the very structure of middle-class society which they opposed had bestowed upon them the privileges of a first-rate education, expectations of fame, if not fortune, and the social connections that could help make all this possible.

De Beauvoir argues that anyone reviewing his or her life is obligated to take a critical stance by acknowledging presuppositions and self-certainties that turn out to be erroneous. Her narrative is replete with the kind of self-criticism one reads about in those communal confessionals that gripped the Chinese villages during the period of the Cultural Revolution. Her commentary may remind us more of the soul-searching self-criticism of an Augustine than the defensive bravado of a Rousseau. There is something of the documentary style in de Beauvoir's memoirs. Selective, yes, in order to protect the identities of those still living. But with a prose tone of flat though often beautifully rendered factuality, especially about relationships.

What especially troubled her, says de Beauvoir, were other people. In this respect, she was not unlike Sartre who has a character in one of his plays exclaim: "Hell is other people." For de Beauvoir, "The existence of Otherness remained a danger for me, because I could be charmed, beguiled, and intrigued by the glittering surface appearance of things without asking myself what lay beneath." Aware that she could easily become lost in the gaze of the others, how did she imagine her relationship with Sartre? To de Beauvoir, Sartre was an "anomaly," since the two of them formed "a single entity, placed together at the world's center."

Sartre and de Beauvoir aspired to live a deeper truth than what they regarded as the petty moralisms and superficial conventions of middle-class society. Yet the goal of their conversation, she with her cigarette and he was his pipe, was not a spiritual epiphany, a momentary union with a divine being. They rejected any talk of "*la vie intérieure*," the interior life of the soul, arguing that it only provided people with excuses for their illusions and shortcomings. Instead, they favored the ideal of a personal merging of reason and will, the individual grasping his or her ineluctible capacity for self-improvement and self-invention. For their breed of "existentialist," a label that had been bestowed by a French journalist on an assortment of thinkers and writers, what must be overcome is self-deception, *mauvaise foi*, which was the greatest of failings, stemming from belief that we can excuse our misdeeds and failures to act by invoking the workings of an unconscious mind. Denying one's own radical capacity for freedom is the basic sin of mankind while salvation rests on the power to critique and overcome our own weaknesses.

In *The Words* Sartre portrays the process by which he began to find himself. "I was almost nothing, at most an activity without content, but that was all that was needed." At first little more than the fictitious invention of the adults who surround him, he begins to write his heroic adventure stories – "The liar was finding his truth in the elaboration of his lies." His own legitimacy as an independent being with intrinsic rights and purposes is as yet unspecified. He recounts how his grandfather would hold an annual celebration to mark the publication of a new yearbook for the society of German language teachers, members of his institute. And how, at one of these occasions, in the midst of the lively party, his grandfather cried out, "And where is Monsieur Simonnot?" The missing personage was in that moment placed on a pedestal in the eyes of little Poulou as the man more real and present than himself.

"How would it be if I," thought little Jean Paul, "were sought out in the middle of a large gathering, and grandfather would proclaim, 'Ah, but where is Sartre?'" In this child's mind, to be recognized as "among the missing" bestowed upon you the status of a presence to be reckoned with. You had your inalienable place in the universe so that should you be found missing, that empty place, that absence, would exert such a great force on the minds of others that their own full presence would be diminished. For in the case of M. Simonnot, an absence meant existence. And that is what little Poulou wanted more than anything in the universe: to exist.

How then did a person come to be a someone in the eyes of others? Wasn't it by first being oneself? If you did not establish yourself as a presence to be reckoned with, then why should others bother themselves about you? Well, they might because you were their child or grandchild. But that would only mean that you were someone-for-them. You couldn't control who you were for them, which might not be who you thought you should be for yourself. You really weren't anything yet for yourself until you were self-conscious. But to be self-conscious, you had to have intentions, desires and motives – projects that were yours to carry out.

The facts of your birth, your homeland, social class, hair color, disposition, the religion or absence of religion into which you happen to have been born, were pure contingency, simply accidental. True, many people felt they had a claim on these attributes just as people spoke of having *their* coffee and *their* croissant. They took possession of these things because somehow they already belonged to them, like something that was meant to be and assured you of who you were.

But no, says Sartre, such presumptions are acts of self-deception. We fool ourselves to think our lives are built up on the solid ground of the givens. The first authentic act of self-consciousness is to grasp oneself as a pure potentiality that is yet to be realized. We do not come into this world with a set of inherent values that lend a fullness of presence to our lives. We awaken, as it were, from the slumber of ignorance, our unfreedom, catching a sudden glimpse of the fact that we are nothing yet, that we are the creatures whose destiny is yet to be claimed. So of course we should feel some anxiety, some vertiginous sensation that the bottom of our universe has suddenly dropped out, the way if you ever go on one of those amusement park whirling rotors, the floor falls away and you find yourself pinned to the curved wall by centrifugal force. What is at first frightening is moments later exhilarating. Such weightlessness. Such freedom.

Yet this freedom to become holds a small terror because in apparent weightlessness we experience the infinitely heavy burden of the will. We make excuses; we squirm and struggle to escape the bright light that shines down upon us, showing us in all our nakedness. We may refuse this responsibility. We have been tricked, taken out into the middle of the ocean and told to swim when everyone knows we cannot and will drown. But what of faith and God, the creator of the universe and all the creatures therein? Another fiction, a supernatural person we invent in order to give ourselves the right to invent ourselves. Which is to say, a means by which we deny our freedom by attributing to another the rules of the game and the throw of the dice. We are as gods, Sartre implies, because we enact our own creative powers, the first of which is the power to deny, to cancel, to clear a space in the plentitude of the given universe and ask: But where is Sartre?

No one can take our nothingness from us. The power of the negative can subdue great armies, vast seas of opinion, fixed customs, rigid rules of what constitutes good art, powerful governments, old habits, established roles of what it means to be a man or a woman, and yes, even stale love affairs. Instead of proclaiming with Descartes, as the first principle of being, "I think, therefore I am," Sartre would have us proclaim, "I obliterate all else, therefore am I the nothingness, the not-yet and, therefore, the power whose being lies in the capacity to be." The true starting point of philosophy must be freedom, not mind. In Sartre's case, that starting was born of writing – "I existed only in order to write, and if I said I, that meant I who write."

Conflict, says Sartre, is our primary relationship to others, because we are always trying to wrestle free of the other person's possession of us. We are enslaved by the other, says Sartre, even the way the other looks at us shapes our bodies, renders us naked, sculptures us, sees us as we shall never see ourselves. The other holds a secret, says Sartre, the other holds us captive, has stolen our very being. True, I am responsible for how I appear to the other, but I am not the foundation of the other's gaze. I want to recover myself from the other, to stretch out my hand and grab hold of this being that is held up before me in the gaze of the other.

Sexual desire is one such mode of absorbing the other into myself and thus recovering the possession of myself. Thus, one body desires another, which, in turn, may desire back. Desire is the revelation of the bodies swirling in a vertigo of hunger to consume one another, the final state of which, says Sartre, is the "swoon." We caress the other to incarnate him or her and in doing so incarnate ourselves, turn ourselves into flesh. "Desire is expressed by the caress as thought is by language," says Sartre. He must know, because he invented himself through words. And because he is nothing more or less than a pile of words, he speaks hypnotically, like a spider to a fly.

Simone de Beauvoir differed from Sartre about the conditions of freedom. Sartre took the polemical view that even a person who is enslaved can construct a personal history in which he or she was a free being and can aim to restore that freedom. But de Beauvoir disagreed. "You cannot claim freedom while residing in a harem," she asserted. There are some conditions that almost completely eliminate the possibility of imagining one's freedom. This insight would later lead de Beauvoir to undertake her study of women's status in history and society. While *The Second Sex* would help establish the foundation for the women's liberation movement, de Beauvoir did not see it as a manifesto for collective action, since she still regarded the individual as capable of overcoming imposed social inequalities and prejudices, as she believed she had managed to do throughout her life. And while de Beauvoir insisted in *The Ethics of Ambiguity* that "to want to be free is also to want others free," since human liberty "cannot be accomplished except through others," the basis for collective action remained unclear and the implied social imperative unconvincing.

Dubious of the socialist and communist belief in the inevitable course of history, denying the philosophical positions of a Kant or Hegel who saw the universal human condition as a basis for deducing abstract principles of right and wrong, and rejecting the church's claim to knowledge of an independent order of moral truths revealed through the divine mind, Sartre and de Beauvoir stood in an ideological no-man's land. In their solidarity with the working class, they considered themselves communists, but the party disdained their philosophy, questioned their loyalty and rejected their membership. The church denounced them as atheists and immoralists. Even their views of literature as a mode of engagement to promote social justice were attacked by the literati as narrowly utilitarian. In short, Sartre and de Beauvoir drew criticism from all sides. Under such circumstances, possessing the protective attributes of a beaver or a hedgehog proved highly useful.

Not surprisingly, de Beauvoir and Sartre's lives were sharply delineated by their chosen vocation as writers. This is who they were and what they did though at times de Beauvoir will insist that she was as strongly attracted to "Life" in all its immediacy as to writing, which is a mediating and reflecting activity. They are among a rare breed of writers, in that they produced both works of fiction and non-fiction and, in the latter case, works of philosophy that required familiarity with the technical vocabulary of certain schools of thought.

THE WRITER'S LIFE

There are many language uses and language barriers in the literary and philosophical world of de Beauvoir and Sartre. First of all, there is the work in translation for non-French readers. While this may seem a merely technical matter of accuracy, it turns out to be political, especially in de Beauvoir's case with the politics of gender and sexuality. Her English language translators are most often men who, as feminist scholars point out, blunted de Beauvoir's graphic biological descriptions and references to lesbianism and other forms of sexuality as described in *The Second Sex*.

Second, Sartre adopts the terminology of German philosopher Edmund Husserl, the founder of Phenomenology, an important 20th century European philosophical movement. Phenomenology is based on the assumption that human consciousness as interrogated by the subject's own consciousness could provide the foundation for knowing about what Husserl called the "life world" (*Lebenswelt*), that is, the constructed reality of unfolding experience. Husserl developed a highly technical, inelegant if not arcane vocabulary for naming the conceptual tools needed to undertake the rigorous process of describing the journey of consciousness turned upon itself and then upon the consciousness possessed by other minds, a realm he identified as "intersubjectivity."

Third, because of their commitments to the theory of being (ontology) in Husserl, then modified by Sartre (and modified several times more later in his life and career), only certain ways of writing about experience were possible because they were the necessary requirements of what it meant to be authentically a self. Let us start from this third point.

Philosophers, especially Western philosophers, love to divide things in two and then worry about how to either get them back together in a unity or hold them apart without destroying their oppositional relationship. The duality embraced by Sartre was the Husserlian distinction between that which has consciousness and that which does not. What is critically unique to consciousness is that it is always consciousness of something. Husserl, taking over an idea from the psychologist Brentano, said that consciousness is always projecting an awareness or a form of "intentionality." Human consciousness is manifested through acts of intention such as perception or imagination, while all other beings are confined to themselves and unknowable to us because they are simply what they are in themselves as non-intentional beings. Sartre, using some Hegelian language, named this dualistic ontology of intentional and non-intentional beings, that which is "for-itself" (*pour soi*) and that which is "in-itself" (*en soi*).

One of the most vivid and dramatic accounts of what happens when a for-itself encounters an in-itself is the scene in Sartre's novel, *Nausea*, when his hero, Roquentin, stares at a tree in the Luxembourg Gardens and discovers that this object can never be fully incorporated into consciousness, because it can only be perceived through the filters of perception while it strenuously resists and even, or so the character imagines, insists upon its inscrutability. "*Les choses sont contre nous,*" says Sartre elsewhere – it seems as if "things are against us." They resist or deflect our penetrating gaze.

Sartre's ontology fits his apparent indifference to the beauty of nature, which he regarded as an alien and impenetrable realm, while de Beauvoir was a great lover of outdoor recreation (especially hiking), the natural world of plants, trees and flowers, and of landscape painting. Sartre's ontological outlook would certainly produce the sensation that to be a human consciousness was to be a stranger in a strange land, a lonely *pour-soi* in a vast realm of *en-soi*. Fortunately there were many other *pour-soi* beings with whom one could consort. But if human consciousness could figure out this fundamental duality, didn't that imply it could also find a way to unify intentional and non-intentional being? The answer for Husserl was yes. He called this unifying element the "transcendental ego." Not that consciousness could ever experience "tree consciousness," but consciousness could observe its own multiple acts of intending or going out of itself in fresh experiences that gathered new awareness (Husserl's "transcendence"), and out of that awareness posit a positional and enduring self – the indubitable "sum" (the "I am") of Descartes' "*Cogito ergo sum.*"

But Sartre would have nothing to do with this foreign intrusion into consciousness of things-in-themselves. At its core consciousness is devoid of anything except its process-like character of intending. The qualities of consciousness are emptiness, nothingness and spontaneity. Sartre did not deny that out of the acts of this radically free, because radically empty, consciousness an ego (*moi*) would form. But this ego would not be interior to consciousness like a behind the scenes voice or inner actor who can play the part of many personae, but that this ego was an intersubjective construct as dependent on others' intentional acts as upon its own. Sartre loved detective novels and American cowboy movies in part because the characters were often portrayed (at least in the 1920s and 30s when he first watched them) through their actions, not hidden motives or unconscious drives. This actor was Sartre's notion of the ego.

Accepting this position meant for the writer that the forms of literature created would need to conform to this dualistic ontology and to the duties and responsibilities inherent in the way a self is situated in a world with others. For one thing, it would mean there could be no omniscient narrator who stands above the characters and action like a god. There could only be points of view as gathered by individual consciousnesses, deflected or affirmed by other consciousnesses, and the whole drama ultimately about nothing else than freedom to be and that which stands in the way, such as the impenetrable in-itself otherness of a tree, the repressiveness of a dictator or colonizing nation, or acts of false consciousness.

This would also mean that if and when it came time to write about oneself, one's life, which after all is one of the acts of transcendence most favored by our Existentialists, then this act would require regarding one's own experiences as if they were those of some curious other with whom one had considerable familiarity despite a curious detachment. This double vision was due to the fact that the writer was recollecting the past actions of what de Beauvoir called a "probable object," one that would continue to possess the ability to surprise. In this sense, says de Beauvoir, "one can never know oneself, but only tell about oneself." And while there would assuredly be realizations about past false assumptions and self-deceptions, there would not and could not be regrets or remorse, only one's vow to do better next time.

There is no psychological back door in the lives of the existentialists, no excuses, and no forgiveness except insofar as one redeems oneself through the corrective laying bare of the facts of a life. The existential auto-biography is a clinical procedure requiring the scalpel of vigilant and rigorous honesty in how that life is described.

To the inattentive reader, *The Prime of Life* will seem like a straight-forward first-person narrative, a chronicle drawn directly from memory of a relationship retold against the background of French intellectual, artistic and political history. And though the dramatic momentum is periodically interrupted by summaries of Sartre's and de Beauvoir's own ideas, theories and beliefs, the book at first appears relatively formless and less obviously a philosophical autobiography than, say, Kierkegaard's *Point of View* or Rousseau's *Confessions*.

Because the content is varied and vast, we may easily overlook de Beauvoir's methodology. But in her prefatory comments about the rela-tionship of the writer to her public she presents us with one of the major tenets of Existentialism, that the choices we make (existence) determine (precede) who we are (essence) by creating values that we embody, and not the other way around. Almost every scene and character profile in her memoir is about freedom – freeing oneself from rules of social conduct, from family expectations, from the restrictions (both explicit and implicit) about what a woman could or should do, from political domination, from self-deception and self-imposed limitations. And her views of others are also about initiatives taken or not taken to forge one's own destiny. This is the narrative arc that holds the memoir together and keeps the reader's interest. And there is an added way in which she accomplishes this.

We are what we do and to and with whom we do it. Since we do and are many things with many people, including ourselves, the most authentic way of portraying one's life is through what might be likened to the Cubist painter's technique of constructing an image made up of multiple perspec-tives and profiles. Unlike the brilliant self-portraits of a Rembrandt that radiate a sense of a single, if conflicted, inner soul and draw the viewer's gaze towards the painter's eyes, the Cubist self-portrait is all planes and angular surfaces, reflecting multiple aspects of personality. Based on her conviction that there is no single inner self but instead the many selves we are to others, de Beauvoir approaches her autobiographical task as one of presenting multiple profiles of oneself and others.

THE PROBLEM OF TRANSPARENCY

Five years after de Beauvoir's death in 1985 Deirdre Bair's definitive biography appeared. And with it were revealed many of the omissions and perhaps deceptions that would raise critical questions about de Beauvoir's autobiographical standard of veracity. While other philosophers' stories about personal political quarrels, secret love affairs, love triangles, uses of drugs and alcohol, mental health and physical deterioration would constitute just so much trivial and irrelevant gossip, in the case of Sartre and de Beauvoir they qualify as admissible evidence in the trial of existential authenticity.

Since their lives were supposed to be emblematic of their philosophical positions, each fact that came to light would either support or confute an existential proposition. De Beauvoir knew this, since she provided Bair, through a long process of interviews in her Paris apartment, with the previously untold facts as she saw them. And so the probable object became a more definite, more comprehensible one in the mind and subsequent words of her biographer and her readers. When the language of autobiography is placed beside that of biography, critical issues of revealed and concealed identity are raised.

Probably the biggest issue for admirers and detractors of de Beauvoir was the distinct impression that she played a somewhat subservient, traditional female role in relation to Sartre, insisting he was the more brilliant of the two and that it was her main task in life to assist him in his various enterprises. Despite his infidelities (Sartre, from Bair's account, was an incredible womanizer well into his old age) she would remain the loyal Castor, sitting there at the café, dutifully waiting for him to come back. So the philosopher and novelist who helped to propel the women's movement was not the liberated ideal after all, critics cried. In addition, de Beauvoir also had numerous heterosexual and lesbian affairs about which she never told Sartre, thus breaking their pact of complete transparency. So it appears these liberated relationships are not what they seem, other critics chimed in.

De Beauvoir must have known these reactions would be forthcoming when she revealed a great many more facts in assisting Bair to further document both her life and Sartre's, as well as other individuals with whom they shared intimate friendships and sexual relationships. Perhaps she needed her biographer to help her transcend the limits of the autobiographical; she needed an accomplice. In this way she would be able to insure the enduring status of the "possible object" as an untethered subjectivity, now more available for public scrutiny than ever.

The appearance of Hazel Rowley's *Simone de Beauvoir and Jean-Paul Sartre: Tête-à-Tête* in 2005 drew upon previously unpublished journals and letters that Sartre and de Beauvoir left behind for posthumous publication. As Rowley points out, the two "have continued to divulge their tangled secrets from beyond the grave." And what a tangle they were. But what do we make of this time-capsule release of information? Does it justify Sartre's goal to be "transparent to posterity" or was it their way to insure they would remain the talk of the town for decades to come? More importantly, knowing this information about seductions, love triangles, intentional deceptions and manipulative intricacies would tarnish their reputation, what do they say about what it means to be an existentialist of the Sartrean/Beauvoirean ilk?

To some, these revelations only confirm the erroneous ways of a philosophy of self-invention. "This is what happens," we can hear them moralize, "when people make gods of themselves. They place themselves beyond good and evil. In their zeal for self-liberation, they loosen all bonds of propriety, lose track of the basic dignity of others, and violate their own convictions." To these individuals the biographical facts of Sartre and de Beauvoir's lives indicate not only a failure of decency and authenticity but also the failure of Existentialism as a guiding philosophy. Yet others will persist in their admiration for the couple as unique individuals and as social theorists. Rowley herself, perhaps ambivalently, praises them for "the courage and daring to flout convention... Maybe they strained at times against their own philosophy, but whatever their failures, few people have lived life more intensely." We will return to the issue of whether intensity justifies ontology in a discussion of identity.

Before we explore that complex issue, a word about translations. Luise Von Flotow in her essay "Translation Effects: How Beauvoir Talks Sex in English" (2000) provides scholarly evidence that de Beauvoir's original French language depictions of sexual encounters in her novels and of female sexual initiation in her groundbreaking *The Second Sex*, were frequently abridged or mistranslated. Translators, says Von Flotow, have to recontextualize from one language culture to another. Consequently, "the cultural and ideological context in which a translation is produced and marketed will have an effect on the way a text is prepared, consciously or unconsciously, for the new audience. Further, the translator's personality, identity, experience and background will feed into the new text, also affecting the translated version."

Von Flotow points to several kinds of distortions: a tendency to make female characters speak more crudely in English than in the original French, deletions of controversial sexual matters such as sections of *The*

Second Sex dealing with the practice of clitorectomy practiced in some Muslim countries, and censorship of sex scenes in novels such as *The Mandarins*. Considering the censorship laws still in effect in the United States in the 1950s, the suppression of sexual content in literature should come as no surprise. But the indirect consequence of translation distortions in matters such as female sexuality and eroticism is that some of the criticism directed against de Beauvoir's perceived "patriarchal" views on sexuality may derive in part from how her work has been rendered into English.

De Beauvoir does not produce erotic scenes in *The Prime of Life* or in any other volumes of the memoir, so censorship issues may be less critical. But she does discuss issues of sexuality and gender, and is well ahead of her time in recognizing that aspects of the erotic and exotic are culturally constructed rather than based on facts of nature. Taking her own emerging sexual passions as a case in point, de Beauvoir marches courageously into the public domain by discussing the body and the physical as philosophical ideas. One is not simply born but becomes a woman or a man, de Beauvoir argues, since sexual roles are culturally ingrained well before we acquire the ability to judge for ourselves. So even aspects of what had been regarded as involuntary and primal may turn out to be mutable and transformable under the existential banner of choice, the wellspring of identity.

IDENTITY AND DIFFERENCE

Sartre and de Beauvoir have been both admired and criticized for substituting the possibility of choice making where formerly the principle of necessity seemed to rule. They looked dispassionately upon every aspect of human experience in order to detect elements of the will, hints of self-deception, and the capacity for agency. They sought to counter where tradition suggested acceptance of normality, the immutability of personality, social hierarchy, and the purely biological or forces of historical inevitability. How far, then, can we extend the margins of freedom across the domain of the involuntary and the necessary? Can we envelop the entirety of our existence within the realm of freedom?

De Beauvoir and Sartre spent endless hours analyzing their friends' personalities and relationships, applying the latest psychoanalytic and Marxist theories, only to find fault with them at the point that these theories excused the individual from having conscious choice. In *The Prime of Life* de Beauvoir writes that also they carried their discussion into the realm of the relationship between "our rational and physical selves." And here they diverged.

*We were always trying to distinguish, both in our own
lives and those of others, between the built-in physical
characteristics and the freely willed act. I criticized Sartre
for regarding his body as a mere bundle of striated
muscles, and for having cut it out of his emotional world.
If you gave way to tears or nerves or seasickness, he said,
you were simply being weak. I, on the other hand, claimed
that stomach and tear ducts, indeed the head itself, were
all subject to irresistible forces on occasion.*

This distinction between what is "irresistible" and what is "freely willed" will become a critical tension between their ideas and in their relationship.

Launched upon the lifelong journey that was their relationship, de Beauvoir and Sartre strove to coordinate their political and literary activities. Sartre, already certain that literature was his calling, took the lead as a writer and de Beauvoir functioned as apprentice, critic and muse even after she had initiated her own literary career. Their occupation as writers was never merely a job, a profession, or even what one might call an artistic vocation. Writing was a mission to remake the world, and those who would undertake such a mission would have to make certain life-defining choices.

*Literature, I thought, was a way of justifying the world by
fashioning it anew in the pure context of imagination –
and, at the same time, of preserving its own existence
from oblivion. Childbearing, on the other hand, seemed no
more than a purposeless and unjustifiable increase in the
world's population.*

And she goes on to compare the writer's dedication to literature to the vows taken by a Carmelite nun. She did not, de Beauvoir insists, have anything against motherhood, except that her calling, her concept of the writer's life, precluded the obstacles that childbearing and child-rearing would present. The offspring that she and Sartre would deliver up were books intended to change the world. Literary productivity was the hallmark of Sartre and de Beauvoir's life and relationship. When, in the early phase of their relationship, de Beauvoir was not engaged in working on a novel, Sartre chided her that she was becoming like one of the heroines in the novels of George Meredith, who battle for independence up to a certain point and then lapse into accepting the role of domestic companion. This of course goaded de Beauvoir and she renewed her vows to become a writer lest she lose Sartre's respect and attention.

Having become sexually active with Sartre, de Beauvoir describes her struggle with physical desire.

I had emancipated myself just far enough from my
puritanical upbringing to be able to take unconstrained
pleasure in my own body, but not so far that I could allow
it to cause me any inconvenience.

Once initiated into the pleasures of sexuality, she discovered that the awakened "physical appetites were greater than I wanted them to be." The headstrong and willful Castor disliked not having complete control over her life in all its aspects. She willed to direct her energies into her projects – teaching, reading, writing, sharing with Sartre – and the emancipated life they enabled her to live.

When we conjure up an image of the philosopher, we might be inclined to picture a figure like Rodin's famous "The Thinker," that brawny giant with his massive head resting on a fist-supported chin puzzling over some ponderous secret of the universe. Associated with the activity of philosophy are words like contemplation, reasoning, speculation, analysis and introspection. But our Existentialists identify themselves first and foremost as writers, not thinkers. More than that, it is in choosing to be as writers that they give birth to themselves to fulfill what Heidegger would call their "own most possibilities." They remake the world as they find it in their imagination and place themselves within it as the characters they will themselves to become.

True, our Existentialists are not typical members of the philosophers' guild. In fact, most philosophers are excruciatingly obtuse writers who seem reluctant to embody their abstract ideas in the finite realm of language and who reach for inelegant and awkward terms and phrases whose sequences are controlled by the mechanics of logically required constructions. With the exception of a rare few such as Plato and Nietzsche, philosophers are not talented writers, though they must rely on writing and secondarily on speaking (their dutiful students sometimes then composing books issued in their teacher's name, as was the case with several works of Aristotle, Heidegger and others) to communicate their thoughts.

If, as de Beauvoir and Sartre believed, we are what we do or, even more precisely, what we are doing, since we cannot rely on what we have done, our past, as a substratum of selfhood, then to identify oneself as a writer is to make that activity identical with one's very being. It is writing that makes thinking possible, not the other way around. As de Beauvoir insisted in a series of articles on Existentialism published in *Les Temps Modernes* in 1946, the novelist writes as a means of self-discovery. In the process of fiction making, truths about the writer emerge. The novel is then a form of self-education.

However, there is a caveat. To create fictional characters, the novelist must allow these creatures of words to take on their own reality and to act, think, feel and speak, as they must. This means the writer follows after them, hurrying to catch up. "The novel must escape from its author," says de Beauvoir, and its characters must "impose their will upon him." A consequence is that the work of fiction may lead to impasses, unexpected and irresolvable dilemmas which may – if the author insists on complete honesty – require concluding inconclusively, thus leaving the reader hanging.

Manifestation of this philosophical position toward the role of the arts can be seen not only in de Beauvoir's novels but also in the "New Wave" of French cinema of the 1950s and 60s, whose work by directors such as Alain Resnais, Francois Truffaut and Jean-Luc Godard frequently end with the hero or heroine caught in an anguishing dilemma. One thinks of the last scene in Truffaut's 1959 film, *The Four Hundred Blows*, with the protagonist, a lonely, misunderstood young boy who has just fled a juvenile detention center, running across the sand to the edge of the sea until, freeze framed, his anguished face fills the screen and the movie ends. We find this same effect in more contemporary novels. The fictional character's superior awareness to that of his or her creator is played out in Philip Roth's quasi-autobiographical *The Facts*, in which his protagonist, Zuckerman, claims to be the real truth teller who has been educating Roth all along.

Writing tells us who we are and what we think and feel. One never stops, never retires from writing until one can no longer hold the pen upright (or make one's fingers dance upon the keyboard).

De Beauvoir's pursuit of the writing self led her into contextualizing the "possible object" in the universe of discourse of history, ideology, and political movements. These are not mere fabrications but powerful conditions, contingencies that force the writer-thinker into having to take a position. The writer finds him- or herself in "situations" that are not of his or her own making. The Nazis not only invaded France in 1940, they invaded the free movement of the possible object and relegated a huge number of life choices to the realm of the impossible. Thus situated, the writer still had choices – put away the pen, write harmless escapist literary works that would not offend the occupiers, become a spokesperson for the enemy in exchange for certain privileges, or write works of protest, though perhaps thinly veiled in the guise of mythology or fable.

Each of those various writers' possibilities was taken during the Occupation. Some paid for their choice with their lives or, in the case of collaborators, post-war imprisonment. Sartre chose protest literature, participating in underground newspapers and producing wartime works such as his play, *The Flies*, a retelling of Aeschylus' tragedy, *Orestes*, about the young prince who returns to the kingdom in which a usurper who has murdered his father, the former king, prevails over inhabitants who live in guilty collusion. The play is a parable of the Occupation, subtly hinting at the French Resistance call to overthrow the French collaborators and the Nazi oppressors. Unaware of the message dressed in the guise of Greek tragedy, the German authorities allowed the play to be staged.

In her memoirs de Beauvoir locates herself in a wide variety of scenes – the café, the street, train station, bedroom, classroom and countryside. As a writer she participates in the complex weave of social and political conflict. Sartre's *The Words* seems to place him, rather more godlike, above the field of battle. Sartre is the man who is completely transparent to himself. What to others such as Kierkegaard would constitute the mystery of self-creation is to Sartre no mystery at all since he can explain and describe the psychological, linguistic and political forces that conspired to produce his ironically circular destiny: "I was born to fulfill the great need I had of myself." Though she will make similar assertions, de Beauvoir seems much more connected to her physical, tangible reality, running a race to catch up with situations and passions that are beyond her control. It is tempting to compare our Existentialists with the sky god and the earth goddess. Still, as de Beauvoir insists, since Others have the power to appropriate authors, we readers will incorporate the existential duo into our own pattern of choices, actions and values.

Did Sartre regard de Beauvoir as a Thing, the second-class female creature who derives her justification for being from the male, or did they actualize the egalitarianism and mutual freedom of choice they proclaimed in their essays, novels, treatises and plays? We can begin to answer that question as de Beauvoir gives their lives a sense of place, the dwelling of the French existentialist.

L'EXISTENTIALISME

The work of the Existentialist is an ongoing struggle for self-liberation. First, you have to abandon a number of myths that may be so ingrained in your mind as to be unnoticeable. For one, you have no substantial self, no inner or core "I" that remains the same despite the changes brought with experience. In fact, if we were to imagine a core it would be empty, a place of nothing, because we are the being who is not-a-thing but rather an activity of consciousness. Sartre employs the term "nothingness," borrowed from Hegel's Logic, where it forms part of the triad of elementary consciousness: being, nothing, becoming. Sartre uses this concept to dramatize the erroneous assumption of an earlier metaphysics that posited an *a priori* and indubitable self.

Second, the only true "you" is the self that is engaged purposefully with others and only insofar as these purposes are acted upon. Even memories, then, are meaningful only to the extent that you put them into the service of future directed "projects." They have no intrinsic message. The sum total of your memories is not you, an aggregation; rather you are the being who continues to elucidate the meaning of these memories. In this sense, the self is always in the process of becoming. Indeed, it is this process.

Our Existentialists worked hard to shake off the chains of ignorance that shackled them to conformist moralities. They scrutinized self-deceptions that would have provided excuses for not embracing true human freedom and sought to overcome indifference to the suffering of others. They acknowledged that the Existential philosophy, if lived experientially, imposed huge responsibilities on each person, making you a god, the creator of yourself and everything around you. And since you were a god, you had no need of other gods. This godlike burden can then be summed up as de Beauvoir puts it in her essay "Pyrrhus and Cineas" (1944): "Man only exists in choosing himself; if he refuses to choose, he annihilates himself."

To be godlike might suggest lofty detachment. What about relationships with others? Well, a third task is to realize that we make them up too. Since we live lives through future-directed projections of purposeful activity, we need others; indeed, we value others and create a bond with them "so that our existence becomes established and necessary." In what may seem like a bit of a conceptual leap from self to other, we see that who we are, as well as who we are becoming, is an enterprise inseparable from the becoming of others. Our part in the play of life makes no sense if there are no other actors. We cannot do without each other. But that makes our existence highly contingent. We depend on others but cannot control how they see us, what they make of us, or how they act towards us. Our freedom is in this sense delimited by others. For example, if you fall in love with someone who does not reciprocate, your project – a love affair – will be deflected through the other's freedom to make independent choices. If you are a woman or an older person, you may experience stereotypic projections emanating from Others such as men and younger people that blatantly or subtly restrict your freedom of choice.

Sartre and de Beauvoir struggled with the so-called "problem" of the Other (our Existentialists frequently add this capitalization). Every philosophy worth its salt must do likewise, especially if it takes its starting point within the sphere of individual consciousness. That sphere can quickly become an impenetrable wall or hall of mirrors, what philosophers call the dilemma of solipsism. Then all that we can know are appearances or surfaces that we interpret through the filters of our idiosyncratic perceptions. The barriers of self-deception and denial limit even knowledge of ourselves, and for the existentialist that means the absence of any core self or "transcendental ego." If there is no way to account for the reality of other lives and if as a consciousness we are isolated inside a world of our own invention, then we cannot make any definite assertions, because we would have no more privileged access to ourselves than to others and, second, since assertions require the common parlance of a shared language, which is social, communication would be impossible.

Because of the great emphasis it places on the sovereignty and uniqueness of the individual, existentialism has frequently been accused of solipsism and an inability to establish any kind of moral imperatives or recommendations for ethical conduct. In short, no coherent social theory seems derivable from the premises of existential freedom. De Beauvoir makes a valiant effort to overcome this criticism (especially from her friends on the Left) by insisting in *The Ethics of Ambiguity* that "to will oneself free is also to will others free."

The problem of accounting for the freedom of others will challenge Sartre and de Beauvoir throughout their careers as social activists, writers and thinkers. Their radical position that freedom is a self-given gift will put them at odds with any ideology that would make freedom secondary to other values such as the good of the state or the preeminence of a creator god. While they will always identify with left-wing causes, Sartre and de Beauvoir will be regarded as too individualistic to qualify as loyal communists or socialists. The tension in resolving the self-other relationship will drive Sartre late in his career to adopt a quasi-Marxist position that de Beauvoir would regard as alien to the Sartre she knows. De Beauvoir, on the other hand, will use the theory of the Other to focus on the conditions of women and, in a later major study, *The Coming of Age* (1970/74), that of older people.

De Beauvoir's alertness to the social and political dimensions of life and the need to justify oneself in the eyes of the Other, leads her earlier and more critically than Sartre to issues of unfreedom in which people are repressively denied the opportunity to choose themselves. Among the classes of such individuals are those colonial people dominated by the

French such as the Algerians, the workers subjugated and exploited by their capitalist managers and owners of industry, people living under tyrannical regimes, and women, who have long been defined as the property of men and treated as objects – whether of adoration or execration.

As to the notion of the absurd that Sartre asserted, De Beauvoir takes a somewhat different approach. She sees that concept as overstated, perhaps even dogmatic. She prefers the term "ambiguity" to capture the uncertain and undefined quality of experience for a being that has no fixed essence and belongs to no universal nature. This "lack of being," says de Beauvoir, is freedom that can be taken either positively or negatively. Lack of being can, for the "nihilist," one of de Beauvoir's character archetypes, justify holding no values, while for another archetype, the "adventurer," it constitutes permission to, as the saying goes, "drain the cup of life." Neither position takes the reality of others into serious consideration, hence neither position acknowledges the crucial "me-other bond" without which we are not persons and take no ethical stance.

BEING CASTOR AND HEDGEHOG

Simone de Beauvoir died on April 14, 1986, just one day before the sixth anniversary of Sartre's death and of the same cause, pulmonary edema. Ironically, the ashes of one who had shunned marriage were interred in the same grave as those of Sartre, his name appearing on the tombstone above hers – a fact that many feminists condemned. While Sartre was the more famous of the duo during his and de Beauvoir's lifetime, it is Simone who garnered more attention after her death since the enormously productive field of feminist scholarship would return to her epoch-making contribution, *The Second Sex*, and her political crusades for women's rights in the decades after its publication, to both praise her for playing the pathfinder's role and condemn her for not going far enough into the newly liberated territory. In 2006, the French government even named a new pedestrian and cyclist bridge crossing the Seine in Paris in her honor.

While de Beauvoir says she wanted to "rescue from oblivion" the many episodes of her life that turned out to be important historical moments and the important actors in those moments, she had an additional purpose. "What I wanted," says de Beauvoir, "was to penetrate so deeply into other people's lives that when they heard my voice they would get the impression they were talking to themselves." If this statement brings Emerson to mind, what follows only reinforces that association. "If my words multiplied through millions of human hearts, it seemed to me that my existence, though reshaped and transfigured, would still, in a manner of speaking, survive."

"In a manner of speaking" de Beauvoir was not the only writer who sought literary immortality, nor is the hope of something that will outlive the self an expectation unique to writers. We all have it. In the case of figures like de Beauvoir and Sartre, however, they are forever subjects of analysis, reinterpretation and judgment, unable, from the grave, to defend themselves or explain themselves further. Only what they have written remains though that constitutes a formidable body of literature that still holds the power to affect the consciousness of the reader who will "reshape and transfigure" the ideas of the authors.

FIELDWORK AND REFLEXIVE WRITING

Is there a modern-day equivalent to the early and mid-20th century French café? The "commons," a culturally accepted social space where friends and strangers mingled and met, had practically disappeared from the American townscape by the middle of the twentieth century, but that has changed. We might consider the American-style shopping center "food court" with its cluster of fast food counters and table and chair arrangements, sometimes ornamented by fountains, palms and even sculpture. In most, however, you could not smoke or buy a beer or glass of wine. Moreover, there are often questionable characters hanging out in such places and, besides, most people are in a hurry to eat and get on with shopping – unless they are teenagers or the lonely elderly. In fact, the latter might be an ideal person with whom to engage in conversation about whether we are individually responsible for the shaping of our lives.

There are the neighborhood bars, bistros, bodegas and, though disappearing, delicatessens. These have something of the dual private-public atmosphere and, in most you can order a drink (though you probably cannot smoke). Omnipresent are the numerous coffee shops, the Starbucks and Caribous. And then there are the mega bookstore chain cafes such as one finds at Barnes & Noble and in some independent bookstores. Many of these bookstores host author readings and book signings. Some even have outside seating under trademark-embellished umbrellas. It is to the latter that I recommend my reader to go in search of existential experiences (though smoking and drinking, unless you're in Europe, will probably not be included).

For a single person to approach another single person in order to strike up a conversation about, say, the contemporary role of the artist or how the writer is today situated in a world of giant multimedia publishers looking at how best to invest their marketing dollars, might be awkward. Some could pull it off. Attending one of the author readings, especially if you actually admire the author and want to get hold of his or her book, might make this form of social engagement easier. For you will already be part of an affinity group, people who share at least one common interest, the author's writing. In this setting, it will not seem suspicious if one finds a new friend with whom to engage in discourse. You will need to plan a strategy in order to insure that your subsequent conversation is about weighty matters and not trivia. If the featured book has some social relevance, aesthetic value or historical or political importance, this would provide the basis for your investigations.

I suggest three possible writing assignments. The first is in emulation of Sartre's account of how reading and writing brought forth the self-creating genius of little Poulou. Consider yourself the fictional creation of your family of origin. How do you think that (consciously or unconsciously) they meant to shape your character? And how did exposure to books or movies, beginning with those of childhood and youth, influence your emergence into the person you have become?

Second, consider de Beauvoir's judgment about the assumption of her youth, upon which her middle-class French existence was based, and her subsequent admission of how wrong she and Sartre had been about so many of their beliefs about the world. Give your account of how you discovered the "myths" concerning society and history that stood as pillars of your earlier years, only to come tumbling down when either the world changed, you changed, or both.

Third, consider how historical events (e.g. hurricanes, assassinations, technological innovations, wars, economic up- and downturns) have influenced your life. Try to depict your felt response to one of these events.

READER'S GUIDE

For those willing to undergo the Malkovichian transformations there are many tunnels into the minds of the Beaver and the Hedgehog. For a succinct, though some will say too simplistic, introduction to Sartre and de Beauvoir's brand of non-theistic existentialism, Sartre's book-length essay (available for free online), *Existentialism is a Humanism*, is a good starting point, followed by the collection of Sartre's *No Exit* and *Three Other Plays* (which includes *The Flies*) and then the novel, *Nausea*.

Those with continued interest in Sartre's literary side may want to move next to *What is Literature?* – a highly polemical work that asserts the writer's moral obligation to be socially and politically committed to the causes of social justice and human improvement. Those who are ready or have the background to tackle Sartre philosophical ontology should head directly into *Being and Nothingness*, a long and dense work that requires a slow and careful reading. What makes that highly conceptual, phenomenologically influenced work enjoyable are the many examples and digression that help to locate ideas in their tangible reality. And certainly readers should not miss *The Words*, what one of my colleagues described as the "story of the man who knew too much about himself." Still, it is a delightful and provocative first-person narrative that will surely hold up a mirror to the reader.

For the Beauvoirean experience, I suggest starting where she starts in telling her life story, *Memoirs of a Dutiful Daughter*, a highly accessible coming-of-age account that captures the conservative attitudes and values of the French middle-class family and the social conditioning from which it would seem impossible to break free.

Next, consider de Beauvoir's *The Mandarins*, the novel she says she "wrote with the most passion," the tone of which "is the most committed of all my novels." In *The Mandarins* the reader will find de Beauvoir's trinity of ideas about love, friendship and politics. The world of *The Mandarins* is remarkably bohemian with lots of casual sex and open marriages, political intrigues and Freudian soul-searching. The narrative viewpoint switches quickly back and forth between a handful of key characters and produces the existential dilemma of the individual's freedom delimited by the projected interpretation of the other.

De Beauvoir practiced applied philosophy in ways that launched two liberationist movements. *The Second Sex* (1949) draws on scholarly research into the history of women's lives, spanning from nomadic societies to the granting of suffrage in France in 1947. In it she applies the frameworks of biology, psychoanalysis and historical materialism (Marxist political economic theory). Case studies based on conversations with women in France and the United States add to the book's documentary feel. Anticipating, and helping to create the movement of postmodernism, de Beauvoir shows that where previously one had accepted gender differences as based on immutable facts of nature, now one would see that arguments from nature were in fact culturally engendered myths from which women in society would now awake. At the time she wrote the book she still believed that once made aware of their conditions and conditioning, women could throw off the shackles of oppression individually. Only later did she recognize the need for a political movement based on women's solidarity. A more recent unabridged translation of the *Second*

Sex by Constance Borde and Sheila Malovany-Chevallier, was published by Knopf in 2010.

In 1970 de Beauvoir followed with another scholarly analysis, this time directed at prejudices against the elderly. In *The Coming of Age* she turns a masterful piece of historical and literary scholarship into a liberationist manifesto, urging older persons to reject the imposition of stereotypes and to claim and exercise the right to remain fully engaged citizens with hopes and dreams still to be realized. Returning once more to the de Beauvoir-Sartre theory of the tyranny of the Other, she describes how prejudicial attitudes are projected in the gaze (*le regard*) of a younger person toward an elder, a look that says "act your age" or patronizes the older person, rendering him or her impotent and irrelevant. Older people are themselves culpable, says de Beauvoir, because they internalize the gaze of the other and turn themselves in old people wearing drab clothes and abandoning their projects as they deny having a future, claiming the past as a refuge of selfhood. The latter tendency, from de Beauvoir's point of view, is another case of self-deception or "bad faith."

While readers are encouraged to get to know our philosophical auto-biographers through direct encounter with their works, they may find great value in Deirdre Bair's impressive biography, *Simone de Beauvoir*. Bair's study will enrich the reader's historical understanding of 20th century French political, artistic and philosophical currents while providing information about the many people for whom de Beauvoir and Sartre were the deities or demons of *L'Existentialisme*. For readers who wish to explore the duo's complex love life as more fully revealed after their deaths, Hazel Rowley's lucid, non-judgmental treatment in *Simone de Beauvoir and Jean-Paul Sartre: Tête-à-Tête* is a good read.

On the issue of sexuality and translation, Luise Von Flotow's essay, "Translation Effects: How Beauvoir Talks Sex in English," can be found in *Contingent Loves: Simone de Beauvoir and Sexuality*, edited by Melanie C. Hawthorne (2000).

8

JUNG'S SUBTERRANEAN THRONE

French existentialists Sartre and de Beauvoir had limited tolerance for the psychoanalytic concept of the unconscious. To them, the theory put a boundary around self-responsibility by positing an unfathomable region of the human mind over which individuals would seem to have minimal control. Also, the unconscious bore a striking kinship to what they regarded as an excuse for self-deceptions, *la vie intérieure*, an interior life replete with transcendent voices promising access to immortality and eternity.

Our next autobiographer argued that Sartre and de Beauvoir's views constituted a "comical philosophy" advanced by intellectuals who, employing little more than abstract concepts, naively believed that they could do something to aid the cause of human self-becoming "through the magical power of the word." Though they radically diverged on the fundamentals of human nature, the existentialist twosome and our next philosophical autobiographer shared a profound interest in Nietzsche and his idea of the union of opposites.

Swiss-born Carl Gustav Jung (1875-1961) was a well-read theorist of human psychology, Medieval theology, mythology and comparative religion, who conducted a four-year long seminar on Nietzsche for his inner circle of colleagues and produced a uniquely reflective and influential autobiography, the publication of which in 1961 (English translation) coincided with the emergence of an international youth counterculture eager to push back traditional boundaries and explore new avenues of mind and spirit.

Thousands of people the world over were drawn to the profession of psychology because of this book. Additionally, the autobiography had a profound impact on religious seekers from both traditional and esoteric spiritual paths. While he already had a small following since the 1930s, Jung became an icon to the generation coming of age in Europe and America in the 1950s and 60s. Such Jungian terms as the "paired opposites," "introverted and extraverted personalities," the "archetypes of the collective unconscious", and the notion of psychological "complexes" became part of the common vocabulary.

But how would a medical doctor renowned as the founder of a school of psychoanalytic theory and therapy, Analytic Psychology, qualify as a philosopher? First, psychoanalytic theory had its roots in the epistemological metaphysics of Kant and in the prominent 19th century philosophers Schopenhauer and Nietzsche, as well as in the emerging schools of neural and behavioral psychology. Second, until perhaps the 1920s, there remained an ambiguous line of demarcation between psychology and philosophy since both were concerned with and claimed authority over the science of the human mind. And third, Jung approached human behavior and cognitive functioning with questions traditionally asked by philosophers, namely why the mind worked in certain ways and how those ways of working gave meaning to life and to human understanding of the cosmos. In other words, Jung advanced a grand theory of human nature.

Jung possessed considerable familiarity with the traditions of European and Asian philosophy. While still in his teens, he gained in-depth knowledge of the major schools of philosophical thought and had an early infatuation with the writings of Schopenhauer, which led into a serious study of Kant's *Critique of Pure Reason*. Later, as a medical student and practicing physician, Jung became conversant with the myths and religions of peoples from many part of the world. His study of Medieval Alchemy (chemistry and mysticism rolled into one) drew him into research on the ancient Gnostic tradition, the writings of whose mystic seekers went largely unknown to the educated public until the early part of the 20th century.

Equally important, like Freud, Jung challenged beliefs in the supremacy and reliability of the rational mind and, like Nietzsche, theorized that unconscious drives exerted profound influences over how people experienced and understood and misunderstood their lives. Jung regarded phenomena of the unconscious such as dreams, visions and fantasies as forming a gateway to fruitful participation in universal truths of human and divine actions and intentions.

Unlike Freud's theory of libido, sexual energy, Jung embraced a view that the sex drive was only one manifestation of human participation in the force of will pervading the universe. His theory of personality types (known today in its popularized form as the Myers-Briggs Type Indicator or MBTI), archetypes of the collective unconscious, the individuation process, the potential for human purpose and creativity, non-causal overlapping events or "synchronicity," and numerous other theories posed a challenge to the philosophical tradition that had placed so much emphasis on autonomy and self-mastery, on the analytical mind as the vehicle of self-knowledge, and on the primacy of knowledge of the empirical world.

Adding to the challenges to philosophy, the theory of personality types, like other determinist theories, suggests that each person is predisposed from birth toward a certain orientation in the way each perceives him and herself and the world. Consequently, even given environmental circumstances affecting our development we would be drawn by temperament at a fairly unconscious level to certain outlooks, which with growing self-awareness and linguistic refinement would incline us towards a particular philosophical disposition. Of course, our acceptance or rejection of a disposition does not determine whether a philosophical outlook has intrinsic merit and validity.

If one's philosophical outlook is as predetermined as one's temperament, then justifications and rationales for particular related theories and postulates we hold would be, so to speak, after the fact. In a sense, we do not choose a certain philosophical outlook, rather, we are predisposed to it. We could still exercise free will in embracing or rejecting an outlook to which we were innately drawn but this form of rejection or denial would lead to a conflicted sense of self. The theory of personality types is valuable for understanding and appreciating human differences and forms of social contribution but it can also lead to a relativistic quandary, since every psychological type would seem to have its own integrity and validity.

Jung's theory of the primacy of the unconscious presents a serious challenge to traditional rationality-based philosophies. If human beings are from birth temperamentally predisposed to a philosophical worldview, and if some of the deepest human truths defy the powers of rationality, in what sense can we claim a privileged perspective by which to know these truths? If someone devoted a life to the study of what lies beyond or below consciousness, how would that person communicate any discoveries in such a way as to make them intelligible, yet faithful to the nature of the non-rational experiences? And if this person also made the effort to construct a first-person narrative, would that person be able to reveal the uniqueness of this pursuit? These are the challenges to which Jung responded, though how he did so requires some explanation.

Jung's autobiography, *Memories, Dreams, Reflections* (hereafter, MDR), is not solely the work of his own hand. Jung was past eighty when he eventually agreed to the project of sharing his life experiences with posterity – something he had until that time opposed, except among the inner circle of his followers. Initially he was to dictate his memoirs to a scribe-editor, his assistant, Aniela Jaffé. This approach, writes Jaffé in the introduction to the published autobiography, "determined the form of the book."

However, as readers soon learn, the project veered off in a somewhat different direction. As the process progressed and Jung read the typescript of his dictation, he became increasingly engaged in the autobiographical act as a personal discovery process and decided he would try to write some of the chapters himself rather than dictate them. Jung told Jaffé that he was beginning to remember, "long-submerged images of his childhood" that bore an important relationship to theoretical works he had written in his old age. Consequently, he wanted to see if he could grasp more clearly the connections between his scholarly, scientific work and his inner life. To do that, he needed to take up his own pen.

Jung explained to Jaffé that in his experience, "a book of mine is always a matter of fate. There is always something unpredictable about the process of writing, and I cannot prescribe for myself any predetermined course" (MDR, Introduction). He added that tackling this project had become a "necessity," because if he neglected to stay engaged in the process for even a single day "unpleasant physical symptoms" beset him. For the sake of his own health, then, Jung was compelled to see the project through but to do so in his own terms.

In this sense the book, as such, is a collaborative autobiography with Jung reviewing and approving several drafts and the final version. In fact, there was considerable controversy over the original German publication and even more over the English translation, published the year of Jung's death, as the heirs to Jung's estate exercised considerable control over what could or should be included. So despite Carl Jung's stated wishes, some chapters were excluded. This surrounding controversy, then, became an extended part of a narrative that others would seek to unravel decades later. Even in its incomplete form, Jung's autobiography, according to Jaffé, has the power to "transmit the atmosphere of his intellectual world and the experience of a man to whom the psyche was a profound reality." In what sense could this reality be communicated?

Jung insisted, "The way I am and the way I write are a unity." Jung's autobiography, seems less a unified whole and more, to use an analogy of "dwelling" that Jung himself invokes, like a peasant's rustic shelter to which have been added architecturally refined side and rear room extensions, a second floor with gabled windows and a turreted stone tower. Parts of the book/house are handcrafted by Jung specifically for the autobiographical project (the first three and the final chapters), others are the results of edited dictation, the use of previously unpublished manuscripts, and a couple are prefabricated, annex-like additions (e.g., a chapter based on segments from a previously published essay on Freud). A five-page "Retrospect" closes the story, followed by appendices containing selected correspondence (with his wife, Emma, with Freud, and with Richard Wilhelm, translator of the ancient Chinese prophetic fortune-telling book, the *I Ching*), and the previously unpublished lyrical-mystical piece, "Seven Sermons to the Dead," a work that might remind us of Nietzsche's prophetic styled *Thus Spoke Zarathustra*.

The house analogy is appropriate, as Jung and his patients frequently reported dreams of dwellings that within the Jungian interpretive framework could represent the depths of the unconscious (as basements, cellars, subbasements and other underground structures), emerging consciousness (mysterious corridors and unfinished rooms) and the heights of fantasy (attic spaces or high storied towers). "A house depicts a situation in life," said Jung who had a lifelong fascination with making both miniature and full-size stone buildings. Of an imagined house, said Jung, "One is in it as one is in a situation." If we read the autobiography with this analogy in mind, we find we are moving first into the subterranean and then up towards the towering heights.

In the last pages of his autobiography, Jung sums up his life's calling. He was, he says, marked out as a child by powerful dreams that awakened him to the inner world of the unconscious. He spent a lifetime trying to understand what these dreams were trying to tell him and figuring out how similar processes went on in other people's lives and in the great spiritual traditions of the world to which we are all connected though we may never acknowledge or be open to that connection.

Jung says he finds most people unaware of the significance of the dream world because their access has been cut off as a result of their rational, scientific education, narrow cultural upbringing and fear of the unknown. This disconnection may also be the result of conventional, rule-bound religious training. The consequence of paying careful attention to his unconscious mind was that Jung became something of a loner, a man devotedly attuned to a secret inner life. He shared that secret with some of his patients, people in whom the unconscious forced itself into prominence, as if symptoms were the signs of a spiritual calling rather than of just an illness.

Given this perspective, it is not surprising that the Prologue of his autobiography begins with these words: "My life is a story of the self-realization of the unconscious." While Jung strove, as scientist, doctor and healer to bring critical objectivity to his work, he felt he could not do the same in the case of his self-narrative because he could not "experience myself as a scientific problem." Science, argued Jung, makes use of concepts of averages and generalizations, and these cannot capture the "subjective variety of an individual life." What he must do, says Jung, is tell his "personal myth," and whether what he tells is, in some conventional sense, "true" is less important than that he tells his fable, his truth. He cannot "bring the language of science" to bear on this project.

We have heard other philosophical autobiographers make similar declarations – distinguishing between writing from the recollection of felt experience versus trying to adhere to a factual accounting. To Jung's notion of his personal myth, we should recall Kierkegaard's exhortation: "Only the truth that edifies is truth for you." Still, Jung dedicated his life to what he hoped would be a legitimate science of studying myths and fables, both personal ones and those of tribal cultures and ancient peoples. And he brings a lifetime of analytical skills based on a large number of experiences working with patients, conferring with other expert psychologists and reading their books and journal articles, and observing tribal peoples in different parts of the world. Why could he not, then, bring these insights to bear on his own autobiographical memories?

Like many other philosophical autobiographers, Jung addresses the epistemological problem of the self-narrative. The difficulty, says Jung, is that we have no standards, no "objective foundation, from which to judge ourselves." And sounding remarkably like his Swiss-born compatriot of an earlier century, Rousseau, he adds, "I know that in many things I am not like others, but I do not know what I really am like." He is, says Jung, echoing what we might understand as a reflection of the Gnostic tradition, "a splinter of the infinite deity."

Jung based his selection of what should be included in his story on times "when the imperishable world irrupted into the transitory one." Though the autobiography includes memories of travels, acquaintances and surroundings, these, Jung says, "have paled" besides those of more "interior happenings." Offering us a fascinating analogy, Jung says that our lives are like that of a plant that lives on its rhizome. The horizontal roots and shoots – components of a plant that are hidden below the soil – are the most important, while the parts that appears on the surface (e.g. leaves and flowers) last only a summer and then wither away.

The chief criterion of Jung's narrative is to communicate this bursting forth of the infinite or unchanging reality into the finite world of continual change. This requires capturing how certain aspects and messages of the unconscious made their way into his (and, indirectly, our) consciousness. Pursuing this type of quest is how, according to Jung, he was different from others who did not recognize the role of the infinite in their lives and the sources and moments in which the timeless asserted itself into the temporal.

Since we are not the authors of the timeless, but rather participants in it, and if this is the most essential truth of what it means to be a human being, then at the deepest level there can be no judging "I" who can give a detached account of a life. The status of the authorial voice would be in question. Yet, paradoxically, Jung is quoted in the introduction as saying, "All my ideas and all my endeavors are myself. Thus the 'autobiography' is merely the dot on the i." And Jaffé reports that as the process went along, Jung "moved further away from himself" until he was able to see himself and his life's work from a distance. To Jaffé, Jung achieved an impersonal or detached position regarding the value of his life and work while he saw himself as part of a perennial quest.

Clearly, readers are faced with a number of caveats and enigmatic statements as they begin exploring Jung's autobiography. They serve to alert the reader that following Jung's story is going to require not only an act of suspended disbelief but a willingness to participate with openness to one's own unconscious resonance with Jung's tale, if that is, indeed, something that one can will.

THRONE OF GOLD

It is highly appropriate that, as a psychiatrist, Jung would attribute to certain childhood reveries and dreams the transformative impetus that set him on his course to study the unconscious mind. These experiences, understood in retrospect, alerted Jung to his inner life and posed the challenge of how to reconcile powerful inward or private experiences with more outward, socially or publically shared ones. The tension between the inner and outer life forms the drama of MDR.

The inattentive reader may gloss over some of the ways Jung fulfills his guiding principle. For example, in the book's first chapter ("First Years"), through what sounds like a response to an interviewer's question Jung shares his earliest memories. Claiming that these come from the second or third year of life, he recalls certain physical and geographic places associated with the vicarage into which his parents moved in 1875. These memories are fragments, recounted as documentary-like snapshots – the garden, the laundry house, the church, the nearby castle and the falls. But then he tells us of awakening from a nap in his pram and seeing "golden sunlight darting through green leaves," and remembering "a sense of indescribable wellbeing."

We are not prepared to realize it yet, but this image of sunlight and foliage, of golden light and green leaves and blossoms of nearby bushes, will return repeatedly in the autobiography as Jung associates gold and green with a sense of blissful oneness. Like Medieval or Renaissance icono-graphy that prescribes which colors are to be associated with holy figures and natural elements (green with nature and fecundity, red with the Holy Ghost, brown with the Virgin Mary, gold with God and the kingdom of heaven), Jung's seemingly casual references to colors remembered in association with sensations of oneness and well-being lead the reader from one scene to another. Then the olfactory and auditory senses make their debut.

Jung remembers his first conscious experience of smell – milk he was spooning up with bits of broken bread in it. And of the Alps – he pictures them "in glowing sunset reds." He watches the waves on Lake Constance with "inconceivable pleasure." He remembers his father holding him and singing and recalls spending several months with a spinster aunt who looked after him while his mother was hospitalized for symptoms that Jung believes were connected to difficulties in his parents' marriage. Then there was a maid with black hair and olive complexion whose, to him, exotic warmth, provided the basis for "a component of my anima" (female soul aspect in the male psyche).

He remembers the roar of the Rhine Falls and the burial of people who drowned after being swept over the rocks. And he remembers a moment of terror when he saw a black-robed figure coming along the road who turned out to be a "Jesuit," a vaguely sinister apparition that he had heard his father, the Protestant minister, discussing with a colleague. These fleeting, long-preserved images of early childhood prepare us for the life-changing dream that "preoccupied him for the rest of his life," though he was only three or four years old when he first dreamt it.

In the dream, Jung says, he is in a meadow that stretches back from the sexton's farm near Laufen Castle, which we know by now is a real place. There he discovers a dark rectangular stone-lined hole in the ground with a stone stairway leading down. Fearfully and hesitantly, he descends to find a doorway with a rounded arch across which hangs a heavy, green embroidered curtain. Curious to know what lies behind it, he pushes the curtain aside and sees in the dim light a rectangular chamber about thirty feet long. The ceiling is arched and made of hewn stone. A red carpet runs across the flagstones from the entrance to a low platform on which stands an ornate golden throne. He moves nearer. Something occupies the throne. Not the human figure of a king or queen, rather something that at first appears more like a tree trunk twelve to fifteen feet high and one and a half to two feet in diameter. It reaches, says Jung, almost to the ceiling.

The tree trunk appears to be made not of wood but of living flesh and is crowned by a hairless, rounded head from which a single eye gazes upward toward a bright aura. Though this entity doesn't move, Jung says he feels that at any moment it might crawl off the throne like a gigantic worm and slither toward him. He is paralyzed with fear. Then he hears his mother's voice calling from outside and above: "Yes, just look at him. That is the man-eater!" Jung wakes up in a cold sweat.

The child Jung makes his way into the underworld of the unconscious. He has a life-altering experience that will take a lifetime to decipher, a task that will become his vocation. Appropriately, he writes about the dream as if it were ongoing. Since it can still be vividly recollected, the dream has remained with him throughout his life. Jung regards the dream as a kind of initiation or invitation into another reality. Much later in life, when he became knowledgeable of anthropological studies and had visited tribal peoples in America, Africa and Asia, he found the dream intelligible, though in the autobiography he only hints at the connection with fertility rituals, cannibalism, and the power of creativity. What is important about the dream in early childhood is that it opens an archway (if you will) behind a green curtain that draws the child's innocent mind down the red-carpeted path to the mysteries of the subterranean world, where light from above radiates down on a golden throne upon which rests the phallus of power and wisdom.

Since Jung believes that the symbolic elements of dreams have the power to orient us towards the future, we have to keep in mind the events and people that will play an important role in his subsequent story. Based on the precocious dreams and fantasies that awakened the younger Jung's discovery of what he regarded as "God's will," he quickly grows into the view that most of the adults in his life, including his father, have little grasp of the true nature of the divine power and authority. In fact, Jung disparages his father's version of Christianity and paints a sorrowful portrait of his father's life and early death. Later in his adulthood, it is the father figure of psychoanalysis, Freud, with whom he does professional battle and, in a sense, displaces from the throne of power. By not offering a definitive interpretation of the phallus on the throne dream, Jung leaves readers free to exercise their own active imagination.

The images of green and gold reappear several times in the auto-biography. For example, in the chapter "Confrontation with the Unconscious," Jung recounts a dream from 1912 in which he finds himself in a "magnificent Italian loggia with pillars, a marble floor, and a marble balustrade." He is sitting "on a gold Renaissance chair" in front of a beautiful table "made of green stone, like emerald." Jung figures out that the table is linked to "the alchemical legend of Hermes Trismegistus," the legendary ancient teacher of magical mysticism, who was supposed to have left behind "a table upon which the basic tenets of alchemical wisdom were engraved in Greek."

In a chapter discussing his research and publications ("The Work") Jung recounts that in 1939 while working on his book on *Psychology and Alchemy* he had a dream in which he saw the figure of Christ on the Cross. Christ's body was of "greenish gold." This vision was "marvelously beautiful," says Jung who then figures out the connection with his research: the greenish gold revealed "an essentially alchemical vision of Christ... the living quality which the alchemists saw not only in man but also in inorganic nature." For Jung the dream shows him that the spiritual is linked to the inorganic, embodied by the metallic skin character of the Christ figure.

One has to wonder at the coincidence of another image. Not long after the green table dream Jung tries to reconnect with his childhood by taking up a creative activity – building miniature villages out of stones gathered from the nearby lake shore. Among the village structures he has built a stone church but has yet to install the altar. Then, "by chance," his eyes alight on "a red stone, a four-sided pyramid about an inch and a half high." He knows immediately that this is the right choice. Once he has set the stone in the little church he makes the connection with the "underground phallus of my childhood dream," a connection that produces "a feeling of satisfaction."

It is possible that Jung read Nietzsche's *Ecce Homo* and, while he frequently mentions Nietzsche in the autobiography, he does not reveal any connection with Nietzsche's experience of transformation beside the pyramid-shaped boulder in the Upper Engadine. Perhaps this symbolic acquisition is one of those archetypal moments in which the timeless irrupts into the temporal, about which Jung theorizes.

Again Jung invites the reader to wonder: why would a pyramid-shaped red stone placed in a miniature church to represent an altar produce a sense of completeness related to the troubling enigma of the early childhood phallic throne dream? And why are red, gold and green such resonating colors of primal being? Certainly, the answer must exceed the bounds of rational thought and so we are brought to an impasse in our exploration. If, however, we return to Jung's own analogy of the dwelling as representing the person in both body and mind, we may gain further insight.

Jung's autobiography is a temporal miniaturization of his life, just as his miniature stone replica villages serve to externalize the unconscious mind, itself a microcosm of the larger cosmos. The phallus as image of authority is threatening, especially to a young boy, until he can picture himself occupying the golden throne. His whole life is a matter of drawing aside the green curtain of nature, walking down the red-carpeted primitive nave in an initiation rite, and arriving at the gold throne that is now empty and into which he may place himself. The four-sided pyramid, representing Jung's view of the sacred number four or the "quaternity" in religious symbology as exemplified in the mandala, a concentric design, usually of circles within squares, used in Buddhist and Hindu spiritual practices. This, to him, is the true power of the divine, the altar of sacrifice and redemption. This is what, according to this reader's speculations, Jung discovers in retrospect and interprets as foreshadowing his destiny.

Jung's autobiography gives the impression that with the exception of his parents and certain luminaries such as Freud, Adler and scholar Richard Wilhelm, people were, at most, secondary to the main currents of his life. Jung's road to salvation was at times painful, at other times ecstatic. For Jung, the road to salvation was a solitary one. He struggled to reconcile the outer worldly and the inner timeless self through manifesting the unconscious, that repository of the eternal.

By the time his autobiography was constructed, Jung had enjoyed a distinguished career, traveled widely, served as head of the Psychoanalytic Society, founded an Institute for teaching his brand of psychoanalysis, received numerous honorary degrees from universities all over the world, and published a large and widely read body of work that was translated into numerous languages. In old age he had suffered a major heart attack that brought him to the brink of death. So he may have thought that now only the inner essence of his story, rather than a full reckoning with the personal and historical past, was worth exploring.

Every autobiographer must exercise selectivity in what to include. Yet there is a surprising absence of the social world in Jung's autobiography or an expression of benign indifference to the world of appearances and mundane existence. His self-proclaimed "mythic" life expresses the quality of parable, as Jung depicts himself doing battle with the demons of the psyche. By reading other sources such as Deirdre Bair's extremely well researched biography, *Jung* (2003), we learn that Jung had several lovers, none of whom are mentioned in the autobiography.

His own decades-long relationship with Antonia (Toni) Wolff, which his wife barely tolerated, is not mentioned. Apparently, there is a whole chapter of the autobiography tucked away in a family archive about their relationship. But the family did not want this aspect of the patriarch's life included. One has to remember, Jung was both groundbreaking and highly unconventional as a practicing psychiatrist and psychoanalyst. Many of his contemporaries thought he was a spiritualist drawn to the occult and to parapsychology, not a real scientist. Clearly, editorial politics loom in the background of the autobiography.

Concerning relationships, Jung says he was present and accessible as long as the other person remained related to his inner world. But if that link were broken, Jung would have no further use for them. We might be startled to read Jung's narcissistic confession: "I had to learn painfully that people continued to exist even when they had nothing more to say to me." In Jung's autobiography, it seems that by the time of old age (and several years after the death of his wife), no one else existed but himself. And not even himself, for he concludes the book paradoxically: "That alienation which so long separated me from the world has become transferred into my own inner world, and has revealed to me an unexpected unfamiliarity with myself."

Jung, who from childhood presents himself as barely a finite historical person, vanishes at the end from his own narrative. It is in this moment it dawns on us: the phallus on the throne is a god who is no longer a threat to the one who learns not to fear this "man-eating" power. To the fearless one comes the gift of light from above – enlightenment and transcendence. In this way Jung concludes his mythic tale.

PSYCHIC HOUSEHOLDS

If, as Jung intimates at the very beginning of *Memories, Dreams, Reflections*, his book is a narrative myth spun with assistance from Aniela Jaffé, and if, as he asserts throughout the corpus of his work, myths function as overarching symbol systems that connect us to universal themes emerging from the archaic past, then the complex dwelling that is his autobiography should serve to bring readers home to their own psychic households.

It must have required considerable courage for the distinguished elderly Swiss psychiatrist to tell the world about a phallus on a throne in an underground sanctuary or about a fantasy state in which he pictured God on his heavenly throne defecating on the Basel Cathedral, with devastating effect to its impressive roof and to the sin-struck mind of the young child. He was sixty-five before he even told his wife about the underground throne dream. He must have been convinced that the world was ready to accept these secrets as not simply the strange workings of an eccentric mind but as what is fundamentally human.

The working presupposition of Jung's studies of myth was that despite their diversity they pointed to a non-rational, potentially unifying history of the human experience. Jung's periodic insertion of childhood and adulthood dreams and fantasies gives the autobiography a temporal structure like that of Augustine's *Confessions*. Augustine's narrative shifts back and forth between a linear or diachronic account of the events that make up his life story and a kind of God's eye view, omniscient narrator account that gives to certain moments in these events a timeless, transcendent quality and a sense of how, as Jung might put it, the eternal erupts into the temporal.

This perspectival shift may annoy some readers as it gives the autobiography a circular inner logic that is sometimes hard to follow. But Jung is aiming to evoke the unity or the wholeness of a human life that includes the tension between the unconscious and the conscious, what unfolds gradually and what comes upon us suddenly. For Jung, the remembered dream or fantasy, including ones that occurred long ago, are as if simultaneous with, though hidden from, the ordinary sequences of a life history.

In the autobiography Jung offers his life as a model of living in and through the mythological. He assumes that his stories can reach out to unknown readers and thus link their households to his. The work Jung undertook to awaken his connection to the mythical is the task he suggests to readers looking for a redeeming attachment to the socially repressed past. Jung takes a position with regard to the study of mythology that anticipates the work of Joseph Campbell and others for whom archaic myths are not just the colorful ways that pre-scientific people understood their world but repositories of permanent wisdom for understanding the working of a cosmos in which the human, the natural and the spiritual are interwoven. In this sense the mythical can be empowering and liberating.

It is hard to determine whether Jung was convinced that he could directly communicate his myths, dreams and fantasies to the reader even if they had their origins in a universal, primordial historical past. After all, myths, whether Greek or Persian, Hebraic, Christian or Islamic, are usually accompanied by rituals of participation such as a dramatic enactment, the singing of hymns and recitation of psalms, chanting of tales and incorporation of symbolic foods, the lighting of candles and incense, immersion in water, or sacrifice of a piece of skin (circumcision). These enactments bring myths to life. Perhaps MDR can serve as a literary invitation to such participation.

With the exception of the lyrically prophetic, Zarathustra-like, "Seven Sermons to the Dead," the last appendix of MDR, there is little of the emotionally evocative literary and novelistic artistry one finds in autobiographies such as those of Augustine, Rousseau, Sartre or de Beauvoir.

Jung's candid biographical accounts and his efforts to capture primal moments of childhood, communicating his passionate commitment to resolving the tension of the inner and outer self, do take the willing reader on a metaphorical journey of self-transformation. And towards the end of the autobiography the reader does have an impression of the narrator shedding his finite historical clothing as he prepares to transcend his mortal life, intimations Jung has already encountered in his reported near-death experience.

Jung avoids as the older person's syndrome of getting lost in personal reminiscences. He remains engaged with the powerful images (dreams, imaginings, fantasies) that constitute his myth. In this way Jung feels he has been able to "see the line which leads through my life into the world, and out of the world again." Just as we followed him from earliest childhood glimpses of color and reveries of bliss, we observe Jung slipping away in old age as he yearns for the "out of the world" ecstasy of detachment. Of what use then is the stuff of autobiography: the historical?

In the chapter on "Work" Jung insists: "Without history there can be no psychology, and certainly no psychology of the unconscious." His studies of neuroses due to blocked emotion led him to develop the theory of the unconscious mind. To prove that the phantasmagoria of dreams, fantasies and hallucinations that lay concealed within were not all caused by physiological changes or trauma-induced distortions of conscious life, he subjected his own dreams and emotional life to an intense analysis that led him to discover parallels in tales from mythology and ancient religions in both the eastern and western traditions. Freud had already done much the same, showing, for example, that the Greek dramas of Oedipus Rex and Antigone or the Biblical narrative of Moses and the Exodus were enactments of stages of the human unconscious. In this sense, all history, or at least the motives of those who enact it, is at bottom the expression of the psychological.

Freud's approach was to reduce history to the interplay of psychological forces. The most irrational human emotions and the loftiest spiritual and philosophical reflections were ultimately the byproducts of libidinal energy, i.e. sexual desires and related repressions and sublimations. Where Freud pried up the glossy veneer of civilization to expose its dark hidden substructure, Jung sought to reveal glowing, awe-inspiring stonework. Had Freud followed his insights another step, Jung argued, he would have broken through the crust of reductionist scientific understanding and discovered that the transpersonal subterranean world of the unconscious was the vast foundation of all human striving, not the biological bargain basement of repression and denial.

Consciousness, for Jung, was the distorting lens of the inner light of being unless, through critical self-reflection and psychoanalytic or spiritual guidance, the individual gained the ability to free him- or herself from anima and animus projections, repressed fantasies and societal blinders. The unconscious was that function of the human mind that served as a repository of archetypes, patterns of behavior, and godlike figures that represented principles such as the unity of opposites, the Great Mother, the Wise Old Man, the Hero, the Maiden, the Shadow, or the warfare of light and darkness that both surrounded and went on inside us.

Jung's collective unconscious reminds us of Plato's theory of forms – eternal and invisible objects, like mathematical equations, or, in Plato's case, ideas that were the true constituents of reality. Except Plato was vague about where the ideas dwelt, and in any case they were cool, emotionless and otherworldly. In contrast, Jung's archetypes are warm, even hot, certainly luminous. And he places them, like Augustine, in a realm underived from the powers of reason, but antecedent to and, as it were, undergirding individual emotion.

Unlike Augustine, Jung inverts Plato's hierarchy of knowledge that takes one from received opinion and sense perception (shadows) to the realm of pure ideas (the Good). He inverts even the Christian order of spiritual ascent so movingly portrayed in Augustine's moment in the interior garden. Unity with the divine lay, for him, not in moving upward through the sensuous, the emotional, the rational, to the Godhead, but in descending through emotion into the underworld where, one might encounter Cerberus, the three-headed dog of Hades, or the fallen angel, Satan, and a vast torture-chamber catacomb worthy of Dante. But no, for Jung it's the realm of the godly.

If archetypes, which seem ahistorical, play such an important role in the story of human nature, what could Jung have meant about history being necessary for psychology? Jung's historical investigations of Medieval alchemy, a subject regarded by most modern scholars as misguided chemistry stirred into a pseudo-mysticism, provided him with what he considered evidence of earlier attempts to decipher the unconscious mind. And alchemy, in turn, led him to retrace the roots of Gnosticism as a similar direct pursuit of the invisible, noumenal world within the human psyche. So his own inquiry, he claimed, was not without historical precedence. Finding that others have earlier trod the same path does not prove the path is worth pursuing. It may lead to the same dead end. Jung must have meant something else.

Jung used history as a canvas on which to paint dramatic scenes from other eras – for example, the Medieval alchemists with their complex pictures of arcane symbols and figures of people, animals, fire, and chemical equations which, to Jung, spoke of inner psychological states. He pointed to the Gnostics with their Mary Magdalene, their Thomas and Jesus, Martha, and Mary the Mother of God, who dwell somewhere intermediately between the status of gods and real people. In this way they reflect our position in the world, our possibilities for stepping into the inner life. "Here," Jung seems to be saying, "are historical precedents for my investigation of the psychology of the unconscious. From earlier periods you see people working on the same problems and quests. It's not just something I've made up. There's a long tradition of such seeking. Mine is like theirs. We are fellow travelers and you, my reader, can become one of us."

Ultimately, Jung's claim is that these quests are temporally equidistant from some central destination, since every quest for the eternal is only a moment, an instant, away from its goal. In *The Meaning of Psychology for Modern Man* (1933) Jung asserted, "The true historical event lies deeply buried, experienced by all and observed by none," that it is only in the life of the individual "that the whole history of the world, ultimately springs."

For Jung, history is psychohistory. Economic domination, border disputes, religious crusades, wars of ideology, these are the symptoms of unconscious projections that arise in the individual and gather into the group mentality of the myth of the Folk, the race or national destiny. Unless we understand this, claims Jung, we will be the agents of the dark forces of history. Whether as a collective people we have a choice in this matter remains unclear. But concerning individuals, Jung is more optimistic.

History as external chronology is just what Jung wants to transcend, just as the Gnostics wanted to experience direct knowledge of God through their own means rather than through the hierarchy of the priesthood or the codified and approved pathways already established by the church fathers. Superficial history is the burden, the accumulation of falsehoods, and the sediment through which Jung wants to break.

This is why he spends so much time telling us about his father's inability to find joy or religious exultation in his mainstream Protestant ministerial duties and beliefs. Whereas he, the child pregnant with the man he will become, already at the age of four or five has been directly tested by divine powers, has been offered dreams and the choice to suppress or follow their lead. Jung had gained a deep inner conviction of the richness, the gifts that were there for the taking, though it would take decades of searching and study to ready himself for the revelations through which he could be transformed.

IDENTITY AND THE GUIDING IMAGES OF WHOLENESS

Jung's personal life and professional career are interwoven developments devoted to achieving the integration of what Kierkegaard would have called the finite and the infinite. Beyond the mask-like persona we learn to exhibit through the roles we play in everyday life (the finite) there is a deeper, potentially more authentic Self (the infinite) that includes the personal unconscious with its drives and instincts, the collective unconscious with its timeless archetypes that connect us to ancient mythology and to our ancestral past that strives to live on through us, the male or female soul projection (animus or anima, depending on our gender), and the shadow or undeveloped, usually shunned or denied aspects of ourselves.

The quest of what Jung called "individuation," to which each person is called, involves integration of the finite and infinite, the reconciliation of apparent opposites, conquest over distorting projections (attraction to idealized others, the will to dominate others, the pursuit of imagined happiness-producing fame and fortune), and surrender to one's true destiny bestowed by divine intentionality that operates throughout the created universe.

From a young age, Jung tells us in MDR, he experienced dual personalities and corresponding inner voices. Personality No. 1 was the ordinary dutiful Swiss child who strove to succeed in life while personality No. 2 was an authoritative adult from the 18th century who was wiser, more skeptical, and more visionary about life and the ways of the world than No. 1. Jung believed that each person had a set of dual personalities and that learning how to reconcile them was a lifelong task. For example, he sensed in his own mother a second and rather uncanny personality. While frequently ill and withdrawn into her private life as the No. 1 personality, she had the capacity as personality No. 2 to utter premonitions and prophetic truth, though she seemed unaware of doing so.

A person, from this Jungian perspective, is a mysterious creature whose narrow, socialized ego identity, which enables him or her to function "normally" in society and the world, is a surface over the depths and richness of a more complex being. If Jung's autobiography is allegorical of what is essentially true for all, then each of us is a destiny on the way to becoming itself through integration of the inner and outer, the dualistic personas, the dominant and shadow characters. Each of us is the contemporary improviser who is free to invent him- or herself and, simul-taneously, the generational inheritor of both familial karma and ancient mythical forces.

In a famous essay, "The Soul and Death" from 1934, Jung describes identity as developmental by comparing a person's life to a parabola of ascent and decent with age thirty-five as the bisecting midpoint. In the first half of life (the ascent), says Jung, we are preoccupied with the outer life of education, family, career and the quest for independence. But in the second (descending side of the parabola), post-thirty-five age half we become more attuned to our "inner culture" and less concerned with outward material gains. In this half we become more consciously challenged by the seeming opposites of life that require resolution if we are to attain an integrated wholeness.

Not surprisingly, Jung's own life is testimony to this shift of attention. He undertook to immerse himself in the waters of his own unconscious mind at about the age of thirty-five and came close to a psychotic break-down through trying to discover the inner mythology of his being.

JUNG IN PHILOSOPHICAL CONTEXT

Jung was born into the late 19th century European culture of pietistic Protestant Christianity. His father and many of his uncles were ministers. Consequently he was exposed at an early age to the rituals and liturgy of the Protestant church with its funerals and burials, weddings and baptisms, and annual cycle of religious celebrations. From childhood Jung would also eavesdrop on theological discussions among his uncles and family friends. He began to receive instruction in Latin at the age of six from his father, who was trained in classical philology and Middle Eastern languages, which accounts in part for the son's extensive knowledge of Roman authors and Medieval theologians who wrote in Latin and became sources for quotations and phrases that appear throughout the body of his work.

We learn from Jung's autobiography and published letters that this reli-gious milieu lacked the joyful, uplifting, spiritual quality that would have witnessed to the presence of a living god. Instead he experienced a form of Christianity that was hollow, rule-bound, dreary and vacuous. His lively imagination, vivid and sometimes terrifying dream encounters, and his questioning mind produced a sharp dichotomy between unexplained emotional quandaries about the nature of God, Jesus and the presence of evil in the world and what struck him as a disengaged, abstract and even anti-intellectual theological milieu that he experienced in his home and in the churches he frequented.

As Jung matured, he came to realize that what must have exerted a profound impact on his father and other mainstream clergy was the pervasive influence of contemporary scientific attitudes that cast serious doubts on any non-materialistic, non-empirical forms of knowledge. Known as positivist science, its insistence on observable, measurable physical phenomena had come to dominate European intellectual life, making traditional forms of religious observance seem antiquated or irrelevant. Jung would himself be trained in the scientific tradition of the new discoveries in physiology, psychology, neurology, anatomy and Lamarckian (the now-defunct theory that characteristics can be inherited from one generation to the next) and Darwinian-influenced biology. Yet, from an early age, he had profound experiences of what he took to be transcendent and transformational "irruptions" of the eternal into his mental life.

Neither materialistic science nor the available teachings of theology offered Jung the insight he sought to reconcile the inner and outer worlds of experience. Jung believed his father's unwillingness to discuss these matters with his maturing teenage son reflected the sadness and spiritual emptiness of his father's life and premature death. And it indicated the declining vitality of mainstream Christianity. We can almost hear the teenager's voice in the mature Carl Jung admonishing his father when he writes in an introduction to an essay on "The Psychology of the Trinity" (1942): "People who merely believe and don't think always forget that they continually expose themselves to their own worst enemy: doubt."

Like Nietzsche, Jung perceived that the God of conventional Christianity was moribund. But unlike Nietzsche, Jung believed that from a very early age he had had direct experiences of the divine through dreams and unbeckoned fantasies. The traditional Christian God may have succumbed to the forces of modern life, but not so the interior God that manifested itself in dreams and fantasies. Whenever he spoke as a youth about this divinity and its powers, he drew incredulous stares from schoolmates and raised eyebrows from adults. He learned it was better to remain silent.

By the time of his confirmation in the church, Jung had given up hope for the institution of traditional Christianity. Yet he continued to search for ways to deepen and to express his feelings of inner spirituality. Later in life when he subjected church doctrine, such as the idea of the Trinity and rituals such as the Mass, to his theory of archetypes of the collective unconscious, he sought to assign profound psychological value to these doctrines and rituals for human wellbeing.

Though he claimed he was neither a philosophical empiricist nor an idealist metaphysician, but rather a medically-trained doctor and healer, Jung in his writings revealed that he was a serious student of late 19th and early 20th century philosophy and current schools of psychology. The dilemmas he inherited and understood stemmed from the battle between the camps of objectivist thinkers and scientific experimenters who developed theories based on empirical data and those holding a more subjectivist and spiritual orientation. In short, Jung belongs to a line of reflective individuals who saw their task as one of reconciling science and religion.

Three European thinkers are particularly important in the development of Jung's psychological theories: Kant, Schopenhauer and Nietzsche.

From Kant Jung gleaned two central insights about the richness of subjectivity. First, that knowledge resided in each person who could use the innate categories of perception to process sense experience, though always within the limits of the human power of reason. By means of the Kantian "schemata," an individual projected a map of intelligibility onto both the outer world of things sensed and the inner or immaterial world of ideas and concepts. Examples of the latter would range from concepts in mathematics and physics to those of morality and beauty. They did not depend exclusively on the experience of the senses.

Second, as applied to how one conducted one's life, each person had an innate sense of the morally good, but this capacity needed awakening and developing through the power of reason and the recognition of the superiority of universal principles over mere idiosyncratic inclinations or revelatory claims. Whether this innate sense of the morally good was a sign of the presence of an omniscient and benevolent deity could neither be proved nor disproved, said Kant. But to Jung, the "fact" that such an inward sentiment existed provided the basis for valuing the idea of an inner deity.

Kant's work fed Jung's growing interest in how the mind might possess a unity of knowledge that preceded sense experience. Reading Kant must have confirmed the importance and validity of inner states such as dreams and fantasies, though Kant was more focused on categories related to cognition and perception. And other thinkers who studied Kant drew far different conclusions than Jung. In their view Kant had demonstrated the limits of human knowledge as essentially subjective and therefore relative to the knower. For them the human mind was irredeemably cut off from having direct experiences of anything unfiltered through the human mind itself.

Kant's infamous *Ding an sich*, the thing-in-itself, a hypothesized reality separate from the schemata of the would-be knower, lay outside the bounds of intelligibility. This would hold true not only for objects of sense perception but for all objects the knower sought to understand – including God, nature and even the mind itself. If there was no humanly accessible independent reality, then no set of universal moral values could ever be derived from studying the cosmos. This is where Schopenhauer and Nietzsche come into the picture.

Schopenhauer took this Kantian "critical" theory and turned it into a form of skepticism, making it the basis of his philosophy of stoic withdrawal from the world and from the quest for happiness. Others, following Nietzsche, felt that the entire edifice of metaphysical speculation and rational system formation had collapsed and could never, and need never, be rebuilt.

It is perhaps difficult for us to appreciate the impact of Schopenhauer (whose writings are rarely considered in college philosophy classes) and Nietzsche (whose reputation has waxed and waned several times over the past century) on a wide range of intellectuals, political leaders, scientists, theologians and artists. What we need to keep in mind is the way their writings and theories reflected a profound belief in the idea of all-pervasive energy that operated throughout the macrocosm of the universe and was mirrored in the microcosm of the individual's life.

For Schopenhauer this energy or driving force, which he called the Will, was arbitrary rather than purposive. For Nietzsche it was a resource of strength and creativity for those who had the courage and knew how to tap into it. When this way of thinking intersected with a theory such as Darwinian evolution, it reinforced the idea of a unified cosmic process while challenging scientists, philosophers and other thinkers as to whether the facts offered proof of a guiding intelligence or only confirmed the existence of an accidental and often capricious process. This same debate continues to this day, as does the quest for a unifying theory of both the natural and the human world.

Jung, reviving the ancient Greek term *psyche* (which has often been translated as soul), put the realm of the unconscious in the place of Schopenhauer's idea of the Will as the presence of an encompassing cosmic force that manifested itself in all forms of life. The uniqueness of the human being was that the human unconscious mind could reveal the meeting place in the universe where the temporal and the eternal intersected. This meant that unconscious phenomena like dreams, fantasies, and the universal symbolic manifestation of what Jung would call the collective unconscious, were all indicative of how human beings continued to participate in the world's creative process. In making this leap of interpretation, Jung pushed psychoanalytic theory toward the religious and immaterial domain. So to him, symptoms of mental illness were signs of both unresolved conflict and also spiritual callings as yet unrecognized.

It was the nature of the psyche, while its content might be timeless, its manifestation was oriented to realization in the future life of the person. Hence, Jung's whole epistemology was teleological. The essence of the psyche was to fulfill an inherent attraction to union with the divine as its ultimate *telos* or goal. This conviction encouraged Jung to see the patient as the source for his or her own cure, since the patient held the key to inner health, although the therapist could assist in unlocking that door. This would require the therapist's sympathetic participation in the process. So a therapist had to go through psychoanalysis training in order to qualify as a competent guide who had personal familiarity with the workings of the unconscious.

We have to keep in mind that the general field of psychology had traditionally come under the purview of philosophy, while the medical science of psychiatry focused more narrowly on diseases of the mind. As cognitive, experimental and neurological psychologies began to develop in the late 19th century, psychology became an empirical science that shed most of the vestiges of speculative metaphysics. Still, the history of science shows that it is difficult to resist the urge to both pose and answer questions about the how and why of empirical findings and restrict oneself to pure description – the what. Yet values and predispositions toward certain kinds of meanings have a way of creeping into even the most objective-seeming observations and theories. And this brings us to Freud's work and its impact on Jung and the future of the science of the mind.

Freud came to announce the new science of the unconscious mind with the biologically-based theory of drives and instincts, and with the tripartite concept of the mind as id (realm of the innate sexual and aggressive impulses that are the source of energy for all mental activity), superego (the mental agency of self-observation and censorship), and the ego (that which mediates between the conflicting demands of the id and the superego and employs defense mechanisms that allow expressions of the id compatible with the external world as judged by the superego).

When Jung first began to read Freud's work (e.g. *The Interpretation of Dreams*), he was enthralled. Here was an empirically-oriented medical researcher with bona fide credentials who could document the existence of the inner world, now understood as the unconscious, as a powerful resource. Depending on the patient's ability and the skill of the analyst, unconscious thoughts could be brought to consciousness, freeing the patient from their domination. This study of psychopathology, Freud argued, could also throw light on the psychology of the "normal" person's psychological makeup.

Then a young practicing psychiatrist tending patients in a mental hospital in Zurich where he worked under Eugene Bleuler, a leading expert on schizophrenia, Jung thought that Freud had established the possibility of beneficial talk, rather than mainly restraint and drug-based, therapy, for the anguished mind. Psychiatry at the time, says Jung, consisted mainly in making diagnoses, medically classifying and then warehousing the unfortunate mentally ill in institutions with scant hope of positive outcomes from treatment. Moreover, there was little interest in the particulars of the patient's life history, since mental illness was generally considered an organic disease of the brain or nervous system. Freud and Jung paid increasing attention to patients' life histories, dreams and fantasies as a method in a search for ways to heal the sufferers.

When they first met for an appointment, so the legend goes, Freud changed his schedule for the day and he and Jung talked for thirteen hours straight – truly a meeting of minds. The twin difficulties that would gradually emerge were that Jung did not believe sexual instincts provided a sufficient and exclusive source of psychic motivation to account for all mental phenomena, and he increasingly saw the unconscious mind as a gateway to knowledge that could not be attained through reason alone.

Here was the path to the religious experience, to the eternal that resided within the temporal. But Freud would have nothing to do with what he regarded as wishful or magical thinking, especially at a time when the new science of mind had not yet gained attention or legitimacy. He regarded himself as an empirical scientist describing the human psyche from a biological and mechanistic viewpoint, not as a pastor, metaphysician or mystic.

Jung pursued his ideas through his psychiatric and psychoanalytic practice, his studies of religious thinkers and the mythologies of tribal peoples. Taking this direction, he would disappoint Freud, who had seen Jung as his eventual successor. The two theorists parted company, and Jung, who consequently lost all standing in the Vienna-based Freudian circle, launched a separate Swiss-based association of analysts more attuned to his theoretical standpoint.

Each person, thought Jung (drawing on the Gnostic tradition), was a splintering off or a spark of the divine light with which the psyche sought reunification. This theory of the human soul was almost the opposite of that of the Freudians, who tended to regard the activities of the human mind as grounded in the biology of human neurology and as having evolved to promote the survival of the species. For the Freudians the psyche was not so much future-directed as it was driven by the past, by the antecedents of species development and the traumas of childhood.

Libido, sexual energy, was for Freud the most powerful motive of human inclination. Human progress, if one could put it that way, was a matter of individuals and societies growing up by mastering the irrational instincts and demands of the primitive part of human experience through the power of reasoning. But to Jung the rational was only part of the wealth of the human mind. Too much emphasis on the rational had led to feelings of depravity of the soul and futility of human existence as reflected in mechanical religious rituals, escapist and conformist cultural tendencies, and rampant materialism reflected in both preoccupation with acquisition of worldly goods and scientific knowledge that excluded everything other than what could be sensed, measured and observed.

Still, Jung was not exactly a mystic, nor did he seek to launch a new religion or become a religious prophet (though he would appear very much the prophet to others). He was determined to find empirical proof for the constitution of the psyche and, in so doing, validate his own experiences from childhood while contributing to the world's understanding of the purpose and value of human life. For Jung direct experience, not just observation, was the key to "empirical" knowledge.

Probably Jung's most famous – or infamous – contribution to psychological theory was his notion of the collective unconscious. Like his peers in the field of psychoanalysis, Jung worked with the hypothesis that the unconscious mind revealed itself in the form of drives and instincts. The sexual urges in all animals guaranteed the perpetuation of the species. Related to the procreative urges, the instinct to make nests was again not learned behavior but instinctual. Complexes such as the Oedipal with its repressed incestuous desires were viewed as universal aspects of the unconscious.

Regarded from a Schopenhauer-type framework, evidence of the unconscious would confirm how little we know about the forces that control our lives, the hidden sources of our motives, or our place in the larger scheme of things. True, we might gain a richer and healthier understanding of our needs, wishes, urges, conflicts and impulses. We might gain greater tolerance and acceptance of human diversity and find more humane ways of dealing with mental illness. But early Freudian psychoanalytic theory with its clinical vocabulary seemed to communicate a diminution of human dignity and value, a reduction of cultural ideals and accomplishments to baser purposes, such as animal survival, procreation and the drive to dominate. Jung, who wanted to save a place in the modern world for the human dream of eternal life and a sense of ultimate meaning, sought to move the field in another direction.

Below the superficial level of the unconscious with its drives and instincts, argued Jung, is a deeper realm. An archaic or primordial process that has taken eons to form is revealed in the human capacity for symbol formation. Whether expressed in dream images or mythical stories and rituals, this process is how we encounter general characteristics or "archetypes" by which we participate in a universal or collective unconscious. For Jung the collective unconscious is not a matter of metaphysical speculation but an empirical fact of experience. Dream images, ancient myths, the religious narratives and images of world religions all bear testimony to forms of knowledge of life and the universe that cannot be accounted for by culturally transmitted or consciously derived processes. Yet they make themselves known among peoples in a multiplicity of geographical places and in the limited range of volitional human behaviors.

Jung uses the term "archetypes" in a variety of ways that include the infant's smile response to the mother's face as well as the Madonna's smile as depicted in countless iconographic paintings from the Renaissance. In this sense archetypes are closely linked to instincts and unlearned behavior patterns that are found in all animals and to primordial forms that are somehow inherited from one generation to another. Jung sometimes drew on the theories of inherited cultural attributes proposed by Lamarck and his followers. In his early work Jung described the archetypes as images that had been "laid down in the brain" (1928, *The Psychology of the Unconscious*). But later (e.g. the fifth edition of the same work) he sought to avoid equating activities of the soul with the physiology of the brain. Jung was not a mind-body dualist, far from it. But he vacillated when considering whether the richness of the human psyche lent itself to materialist descriptions.

If human beings had not learned to distrust, fear, doubt or deny the rich bounty of the unconscious mind, they would find immense beauty and sustainable happiness through accessing the depths of their own souls. That this inner exploration might be fraught with difficulty and anxiety

Jung himself would not deny. After all, he risked plummeting into madness in order to study the workings of the inner mind before there was anything like the proverbial thread of Ariadne to guide one out of the labyrinth.

The ultimate goal of Jung's theory of psychological development was full individuation understood as union or alignment with the transcendent Self. And the Self, for Jung, was the center of one's being – an inner activity that lay, metaphorically, somewhere midway between the conscious and unconscious, taking both into consideration, drawing on both sources. As he states in his 1935 commentary on Richard Wilhelm's *The Secret of the Golden Flower: A Chinese Book of Life*, the Self functions as "the center of gravity of the total personality." The Self is the ultimate archetype in that it can serve to regulate and integrate all other archetypes. Jung's personal narrative evokes just this process.

BEING JUNG

The mere fact that we have the term "Jungian" suggests that Jung's theoretical construction of a science of the mind has garnered considerable attention and identification. Being like Jung or wanting to emulate Jung's life would pose many challenges, not the least of which is to undergo self-analysis and to use play as a way to externalize a lengthy soul-searching process that could at times be deeply disturbing and anxiety provoking.

To be Jung-like would mean being open to one's dreams and fantasies and to believe (and experience) one's interconnectedness with all things both organic and inorganic. The Jungian questing person would have a foot in two worlds, the world of the perennial archetypes and the world of everyday existence. To dwell only in the former would be to suffer a psychosis since the person would lack a grounded existence. To dwell only in the latter would be to live a mechanical, humdrum existence.

As for spiritual involvement, it's unlikely that one would follow a conventional theistic course, since Jung, though remaining a Protestant, disparaged traditional Christianity and dogmatic faith traditions in general. Would he have approved of New Age spirituality? Jung was open to ideas that became important New Age influences, such as parapsychology, various occult traditions, Buddhism, yoga (he was a practitioner) and the esoteric tradition that included Gnosticism and Kabbalistic interpretations. He longed for a sense of attachment to ancient origins and would probably have been suspicious of beliefs that smacked of egoism or personality cultishness, or had faddish and simplistic formulas for happiness and enlightenment, or lacked significant historical roots.

In an era of persistently male-dominated scientific careers, many of Jung's early students were women, including women physicians. Consequently a large body of feminist Jungian theory has emerged since the 1930s with several important feminist authors finding a large popular audience in the feminist movement that began in the 1970s. This would suggest that embracing a Jung-like existence would not belong to a strictly male provenance.

FIELDWORK AND REFLECTIVE WRITING

Jung grew up in a period influenced by a three-stage picture of human history that went back to the Italian philosopher, historian and autobiographer, Giambattista Vico (1668-1744) and had been embraced by many 19th century thinkers and philosophers of history. There are three phases in the evolution of human consciousness: magic, religion and modern empirical science.

Jung seems to have taken that model and turned it on its head. In his version of scientific research (based in part on direct experience), religion and magic (as myth and alchemy) persist in the contemporary unconscious. Through his study of the sources of unconscious images, Jung sought to take possession of (and risk being possessed by) his own mythical inner world. Short of Jungian psychotherapy, how might one undertake a similar exploration?

The works of so-called "new-age" authors are replete with techniques to tap into the unconscious as are the "image work" methods of workshops on psychodrama, visual art therapy, various forms of meditation, and the revival of occult practices such as numerology, astrology and alchemy. Many readers may already be engaged in one or more of these practices. I want to suggest something more down to earth.

Many people surround themselves with figures of animals such as chickens, frogs, cats, dogs, lions and bears. These figures occupy mantels, breakfronts, desks, walls, gardens, mailboxes and even bathtubs. Children's books, another source of animal images, often feature talking, thinking and feeling goats, hippos, bears, crows, snakes, geese (as in Mother Goose), elephants (Babar) and foxes. Animated films are another vast repertory of talking (and dancing and singing) animals. Images of animals connect us to primary and elemental emotions and dimensions of experience. They are also represented in most of the symbols of the astrological zodiac.

Do you have such a "totem" (symbolic or emblematic) animal? Look around your home and you may discover the presence of animal images. Or perhaps you collect such figures. I have a friend who seeks out rhinos in ceramic, in photos, in paintings and in literature. She places these objects in strategic places in her home. To understand the mythical aspect of these images, one can go online to websites that direct searchers to museum collections, scholarly studies of animal totems, and a vast literature on how to understand the subconscious significance of the animal figure as an energizing, protective or guiding, symbol. Next we go to the writing assignment.

In Chapter VI of MDR, entitled "Confrontations with the Unconscious," Jung describes his decision to give himself over to images coming from the unconscious. Until this time in his life he has hesitated to plunge into the uncharted waters of the unconscious except as a professional mental health diagnostician trying to understand his patients' accounts of their troubling and disorienting dreams and hallucinations. Now, he vows to engage in self-analysis in order to find out whether he can discover a deep-seated mythical orientation such as those he has found in the cultures of various peoples. He will do so through dream analysis, reflection on fantasies and through an intriguing process he calls "active imagination."

He realizes that by opening himself to the exploration he may "run into the same psychic materials which is the stuff of psychosis and is found in the insane." He knows these unconscious images have the power to "fatally confuse the mental patient." Yet he is willing to undertake this experiment because he seeks to enter "the matrix of mythopoeic imagination which has vanished from our rational age." But how will he, the psychiatrist, not succumb to the plight of many of his patients – incapacitation and even institutionalization? Worried, Jung thinks of Nietzsche, whom he believes to be a forerunner in this process of opening oneself to unconscious images and who "lost the ground under his feet because he possessed nothing more than the inner world of his thoughts."

Unlike the wandering and detached Nietzsche, Jung's psychic ballast, he surmises, will be his medical and psychiatric training, the grounding attachments of his "normal" and routine family life, engaging in playful activities such as stone and woodcarving, making miniature stone villages, and through a process of recording and drawing unconscious images.

As to conjuring up unconscious images, Jung recorded conversations with fantasized personages in small leather notebooks with black covers (which become known as the Black Books), from which he would later transcribe these writings into handsome Gothic style calligraphy embellished with illustrations. This transcription from the period 1914 to 1930 will become *The Red Book*, a folio volume bound in red leather and resembling a medieval manuscript. *The Red Book* remained inaccessible for sixty years and was only made public in 2009 through a special publishing venture allowed by Jung's heirs.

While the precise method Jung used to engage in active imagination remains unknown, from his close associates' accounts it appears similar to the technique used by many writers of fiction who put themselves into a meditative, receptive state in order to conjure up known and sometimes completely unknown characters – based on real or imagined people, animals, Biblical figures, heroes from ancient sagas, and so on.

As these figures become manifest – whether as voices in the mind, visual apparitions, or in other ways – the writer listens and watches before responding with questions or comments. As these virtual relationships become established, the writer may turn to these same figures for continued dialogue. Eventually the writer who wishes to create a tangible product from these experiences must give the material a shape by transitioning to the more rational process of organizing the content into an intelligible narrative through the writer's consciously employed craft. Writers of fiction frequently comment that their characters took on a life of their own when this process was followed.

In a similar way Jung found himself in intense conversation with a host of characters, such as Salome, a guru-like figure named Philemon, the Biblical prophet Elijah and numerous mythical creatures from Egyptian and other mythologies. In many ways these virtual unconscious images became Jung's guides and teachers. In researching the sources of many of these image characters, the editor of *The Red Book*, Sonu Shamdassani, found that most could be traced to the pages of books that were in Jung's library and with which he was familiar. But Jung breathed life into them and allowed them to take control – at least temporarily.

While I would not be so bold as to recommend that readers descend into the unconscious part of the psyche like Jung, I think the method of active imagination can be productive within certain boundaries. If you have not tried this technique before, it may be beneficial to gain some practice with less daunting "images" than that of, for instance, a parent, a patriarch or matriarch from a religious tradition, or a deceased loved one.

I recommend perhaps beginning with a long lost friend, a former teacher, or a fictional character from a favorite novel. The keys to this process include putting oneself in a safe and quiet place, accepting the figure that comes to you, letting the figure initiate contact and take the lead, avoiding putting words in the character's mouth, tolerating what may at first seem foolish or even disgusting, and allowing the process to run its course – at which point the actively imagined figure may grow faint or you may sense that your conscious mind is taking control.

Some people will engage in this process by writing down the conversation as it unfolds. If you are facile on the keyboard or with pen and paper, this method may work well. Otherwise, it might be best to wait until you awaken from the semi-conscious process before trying to record the conversation, the setting and other pertinent elements of the experience. Adding an illustration can also be further illuminating.

READER'S GUIDE

Jung's autobiography, *Memories, Dreams, Reflections*, is an excellent starting point for making one's way into the Jungian worldview. While it presupposes some familiarity with Jung's earlier works, the autobiography provides a general understanding of major concepts and how they emerged from both the personal and intellectual-spiritual backgrounds of Jung's life and thought. The autobiography also contains a glossary explaining some of Jung's key concepts.

Many of Jung's mature ideas are communicated through anthologies such as the often-cited *Modern Man in Search of a Soul* (published originally in 1933 and reprinted multiple times up to the present). *Modern Man* provides an overview of various themes of Jung's life work such as the aims of psychotherapy, the theory of types, the stages of life, the relationship between psychology and spirituality, and Jung's embrace and subsequent rejection of Freud.

Deirdre Bair's exhaustive history, *Jung: A Biography* (2003) is lengthy but well researched and written. Jung admirers will learn more about Jung's life, his family, lovers, friends and enemies, health and travel, than they may have wanted to know.

For a probing and hostile critique of Jungian theory and the Jung circle, readers might consider Richard Noll's two books, *The Jung Cult: Origins of a Charismatic Movement* (1994) and *The Aryan Christ: The Secret Life of Carl Jung* (1997). A powerful refutation of Noll and other detractors' arguments is found in Sanu Shamdassani's *Cult Fictions* (1998), a book that recounts the formation of the Jungian movement, organization of the Zurich Psychology Club and other Jungian associations.

Shamdassani, as mentioned, has edited and written an introduction to *The Red Book,* which, while rather expensive to buy, can be borrowed from a library and is worth careful consideration for understanding this momentous period in Jung's life. An important exploration of the mainly 19th century philosophical influences on the formation of Jung's ideas is found in *Philosophical Issues in the Psychology of C.G. Jung* (1991) by Jungian analyst Marilyn Nagy. Nagy holds a Ph.D. in philosophy, so is at home in both domains.

On the side of feminist Jungian scholarship, the works of M. Esther Harding should not be missed. Her *Woman's Mysteries, Ancient and Modern* (originally published in 1935 but still in print with a revised updated 2001 edition) and *The Way of All Woman* (1933 and still in print, 1990) are highly readable and influential Jungian contributions to contemporary feminism.

9

BUBER'S HOUR ON THE BALCONY

Like a sage out of the pages of the Hebrew Bible, a handsome, white-bearded Viennese-born Jewish philosopher made his appearance at the annual gathering of therapists, artists, writers, theologians and other members of the intelligentsia drawn to the Jungian school of analytic psychology. At the time of the Eranos Conference held in Ascona, Switzerland in 1934, Martin Buber, then in his early fifties, was well-known for his compilations and interpretations of Hasidic tales that he had rescued from relative obscurity and translated from Hebrew and spoken Yiddish into modern German, from which they would eventually be retranslated into other languages.

In addition to highlighting the often paradoxical wisdom, religious zeal and story-telling skills of enigmatic Talmudic scholars and eccentric seer rabbis living in small, mainly Jewish, villages and towns of Eastern Europe, Buber had written an influential book of philosophy, *Ich und Du* – translated in 1937 into English as *I and Thou* – exploring the triadic personal encounter and true presence of one individual to another that served as an opening to the divine. A spiritual humanist, Buber rejected a theology of separation between the sacred and the profane. In a speech given in 1930 to an institute of Protestant German Christians, he offered this life-affirming Hasidic Jewish perspective: "There is no true human share of holiness without the hallowing of the everyday."

Buber belonged to a small group of Jewish intellectuals educated at European universities but deeply immersed in Judaic thought through traditional family upbringing and Jewish parochial training. They sought to stem the tide of assimilation and conversion that came with the new rights and freedoms bestowed on Jews in the aftermath of the 18th century Enlightenment, the 19th century emancipation of Jews, and rise of the relatively more secular European state.

He served as a colleague of progressive Jewish educators participating in the Free Jewish House of Learning (*Freies Judisches Lehrhaus*), a continuing education academy founded in Frankfurt, Germany, in 1920 by the Jewish philosopher Franz Rosenzweig. Buber was by that time an outspoken Zionist promoting immigration to Palestine and espousing the controversial viewpoint that should a Jewish homeland be established, it should be shared equitably with the existing Arab population.

Buber was drawn to the Eranos Conference because he had been impressed by Carl Jung's writings on religion and the way he pointed to the transpersonal and awe-inspiring nature of the spiritual quest. After all, Jung's theory of the collective unconscious not only linked each person to a transcendent and primal past that was shared by all mankind, but also suggested that through participation in these universal symbols and myths, each of us is connected to everyone else on an intimate if not always acknowledged level. Jung implied that spiritual seeking and devotional practices were natural and essential human impulses common to all cultures and religions.

When appropriately pursued – free of fanaticism, hostile dogmatism and victimizing projections – these links to the life-guiding, soul-enriching archetypes provided a bond between people who shared a mythical consciousness. For example, though the archetype of the Hero may show itself differently in hundreds of myths and legends, having, as it were, "a thousand faces," each could be understood across the breadth of mankind.

Through the various lectures and papers delivered at the conference, Buber recognized that Jung's work encouraged a healthy ecumenical attitude while lauding the positive benefits of religious practices. The popularity of the Jungian approaches to comparative religion and mythology would later be exemplified in the well-received works of such followers as Erich Neumann (e.g. *The Origins and History of Consciousness*) and Esther Harding (*Woman's Mysteries: Ancient and Modern*). Their contributions are testimony to the way the Jungian perspective has given freshness and vitality to the spiritual quest and affirmed a common bond between people of diverse faith communities, as it did for Buber.

Seventeen historically calamitous years after the Eranos Conference, in an essay "Religion and Modern Thinking," Buber continued to call Jung "the leading psychologist of our day." Reading with approving nods, the Jungians regarded Buber as a kindred spirit. Many were followers of the ideas of both men. So it came as a great shock to adherents in Europe, America and Israel when, in this 1951 essay, a long-simmering controversy between the two men burst into the open. After praising Jung, Buber criticized him sharply for contributing to what Buber called the "eclipse of God." Jung, argued Buber, had overstepped the bounds of psychology and ventured into the realm of religious metaphysics. Jung had made the individual psyche the only true portal to deeply penetrating knowledge of the divine presence. The consequence of this viewpoint, to Buber, was that God seemed entrapped in, if not a projection of, human psychology.

Buber did not regard Jung as a religious naturalist – one who postulates that religiosity is simply the human need to project ideals, super human powers and deified qualities in order to pursue lofty personal goals and establish rules for human relationships. But Buber claims Jung's psychology of religion did come close to picturing the human encounter with the divine mysteries as more accessible through self-knowledge gained through delving into the unconscious than through acts of faith.

This type of Gnosticism, according to Buber, would make God dependent on the human psyche, would make what Rudolf Otto called the "numinous" quality of the divine Other immanent within humans, resident in the psyche waiting to be discovered by descending the Jungian stairway into the unconscious. For Buber, echoing the orthodox Jewish tradition, God is wholly transcendent of the human mind, addresses the human in an awakening call, as when the God of Genesis cries out to Abraham: "Where are you?" To which the patriarch responds with his famous Hineni, "Here am I." For Buber the intimate relationship, the trusting dialogue of faith between the human and the divine, is overshadowed ("eclipsed") in the Jungian soul-searching quest.

While Buber had hoped to participate in the 1935 Eranos conference, the rise of the National Socialist movement in Hitler's Germany precluded his travel. A few years later, on the brink of the Holocaust and the European destruction of the Jewish people, Buber and his wife, the novelist Paula Winkler, fled to Palestine with their two children. There a position was found for him as a professor at Hebrew University in Jerusalem.

By the time of his death in 1965 Buber had become a world-renowned author, religious thinker and prophetic voice of the world's desperate need for authentic dialogue and true meeting between people and between the individual and God. Buber became famous for what he called the "dialogical principle," which he applied to matters of faith, community building, political mediations, education, art, psychology and other arenas of life. Buber would attribute the origin of his pursuit of the "interhuman" to a moment in childhood when, standing on a balcony overlooking the inner courtyard of his grandparents' farm in Galicia (then part of the Austrian Empire), he experienced a sense of primal aloneness.

THE BALCONY

When he was just a child of three, Buber's mother left him and her husband. Though he does not offer details, biographers report that she ran off with another man. Buber would not see her again for twenty years. At the age of four in 1882 he was sent from Vienna to live with his paternal grandparents on their country estate near the town of Lvov (now Lemberg). In the first vignette of his slender autobiography, *Meetings*, he pictures himself leaning against a second-floor balcony railing, gazing into the "great rectangular inner courtyard" of the house while in the care of the daughter of a neighbor. Out of nowhere, says Buber, the older girl volunteered an answer to an unasked question, "No, she will never come back." Buber says these words "cleaved evermore to my heart."

Over the years Buber would revisit this moment, each time finding added meaning and significance. Ten years later he perceived that the condition of his private loss applied to mankind as a whole. Everyone existed in a state of separation, charged with feelings of abandonment. Some years later he says he coined the term *vergegnung*, "mismeeting" or "misencounter," to capture this sense of absence or disconnection. The first vignette ends with the ambiguous pronouncement: "I suspect that all that I have learned about the genuine meeting in the course of my life had its origin in that hour on the balcony."

What did he mean? That he bore the wound of maternal separation, which is the fate of every child, a condition that sets into motion the quest for reconnection with a mother substitute? No, that would be too narrowly and reductively Freudian for this Jewish religious thinker. Is this scene, reminiscent like a photographic negative of Augustine and Monica gazing down into their inner courtyard, a deeply painful acknowledgment of the distant beloved that sets in motion a quest for spiritual reunion? What about the older child who feels compelled to utter the words that confirm the four-year-old's greatest fear? Is she the messenger or prophetess of misencounters?

Buber intimates that his whole philosophy – how the divine presence makes itself known through genuine interpersonal encounters – is rooted in this decisive experience, a touchstone moment of loss and absence, of bereavement, so unlike the four-year-old Jung's dream of fear, power and awe, which would haunt him and set him on his lifelong quest.

One could speculate endlessly on this story of primal separation and perhaps that is what Buber intends. For parallels to this suggestive brevity, we might think of the many famous Biblical stories that we may feel we know in great detail – e.g. Jacob wrestling with an angel, Moses and the burning bush – only to find, when we return to the text, that little more than a single line or two is used to tell the story and that we have only the wider narrative context to interpret it. Similarly, many of the fragments Buber offers us trigger a wealth of possible personal meanings though they do not explain themselves. Intrigued but lacking explanation, the reader is drawn into their depths.

The circumstances of how Buber's personal narrative came about reveal much about the man. Like Jung, Buber had mostly avoided writing about himself throughout his career. Perhaps, like Jung, he believed that everything he had written as a scholar already revealed the passions and concerns of the author and that the particulars of his personal life were, at most, of secondary importance.

Fortuitously Paul Arthur Schilpp, the editor of an important series of tomes, the *Library of Living Philosophers*, chose Buber as the figure for the twelfth volume published in 1967. Each volume consists of some twenty to thirty essays written by critically friendly and unfriendly scholars addressing the intellectual contribution of the chosen philosopher. Then the spotlighted scholar writes a response to these criticisms and interpretations. Schilpp would also ask for an intellectual autobiography that would be set at the beginning of the volume. Many of these autobiographies turned out to be quite lengthy, over one hundred and in some cases more than two hundred pages. Buber's, by contrast, was brief – less than fifty.

Like Jung's autobiography, the construction of Buber's was done collaboratively with the co-editor of the Schilpp's volume, Maurice Friedman, the chief translator and scholarly exponent of Buber's work in English. Together author and editor chose personal anecdotes from Buber's previously published work, pieced together with thoughts and recollections freshly written for the Schilpp volume where the piece would bear the prosaic title, "Autobiographical Fragments."

According to Friedman, who wrote in the Introduction to what then became a separately published book now entitled *Meetings: Autobiographical Fragments*, the fragments were "ordered according to chronology, significance, and their place in the body of the text or the appendix." Friedman, who later wrote a three-volume biography, *Martin Buber: Life and Work*, and the philosopher himself, seemed to be on an I-Thou or genuine dialogue level of collaboration, as Buber placed great trust in Friedman's suggestions. This means the overall form of the autobiography derived from two minds, not one – appropriate, perhaps, for a philosopher who emphasized the principle of dialogue and the primacy of the relational.

Friedman writes that despite the fragmentary nature of the small volume and the presence of a second guiding hand, the "events and meetings" described in this book offer the reader "the most real teaching that Martin Buber has left us." This is a remarkable claim about a man famous for the dialogical principle who once proclaimed "all real living is meeting." Do we not "meet" Buber in his other books?

Friedman quotes Buber as saying: "I am no philosopher, prophet or theologian, but a man who has seen something and who goes to a window and points to what he has seen." Those who expect to be taught by him, says Buber, will be disappointed when they find out that all he does is point. Perhaps what Friedman is alluding to is the way Buber chooses to speak to his readers and listeners by means of the legendary anecdotes of the Hasidim, his translation of the Bible into German, and his various often poetic works of philosophy.

Now, through these shared fragments of Buber's encounters with people and situations, extracted moments from a lifetime of experience, Friedman wants us to have the "genuine dialogue" that has been his personal experience with Buber. He knows that these vignettes are more self-revealing than most of Buber's other writings. Friedman also knows that "pointing" is another way of saying that a person has experienced the ineffable – that which cannot be communicated directly but only hinted at.

Following a disclaimer that this first-person narrative will not provide remembered details of his past, Buber, like Jung, narrows the scope to "rendering an account of some moments that my backward glance lets rise to the surface, moments that have exercised a decisive influence on the nature and direction of my thinking."

Without preliminaries, Buber launches into the work of "rendering," offering us twenty numbered accounts of scenes, situations and portraits, the first of which, described above, is entitled, simply, "My Mother." If the reader has any prior knowledge of Buber's theory of the interhuman and dialogical principle, that we are fundamental relational beings, then he or she should not be surprised at this starting point – the co-presence of mother and child. In this instance, the tale Buber has to tell is almost the complete opposite of what we might be expecting, for this is a story about separation and absence.

Image two is a cameo profile of Buber's grandmother. Adele. It was she who managed the couple's extensive business dealings so that her husband, a self-taught philologist, could carry out the production of a critical edition of the *Midrashim* – a mixture of Biblical interpretations, rabbinical wisdom and sagas. Despite the fact that "except for edifying popular books," reading of secular literature was generally forbidden to Jewish girls, Grandmother Adele had managed, from her youth, to secretly collect and read many of the classics of 18th and early 19th century German literature in periodicals and books. When she married at age seventeen, she brought this storehouse of literature and her habit of concentrated reading into her new home, where she immersed her two sons in that tradition.

Buber describes how he would watch her work over her account books and then pause to whisperingly recite an important passage from some book she was reading, and copy some snippet into her ledger along with her own reflections. From his Grandmother Adele Buber learned to have dialogues with the characters and authors, thus breathing life into inanimate books. Buber says that for his grandmother, "experiencing and reflecting on experience were not two stages but, as it were, two sides of the same process." His Grandfather, says Buber, demonstrated the philologist to be a "true lover of the word," but his grandmother was even more influential as his role model for the "love for the genuine word."

A great deal is compacted into Buber's portrait of his grandmother. Take, for example, Buber's assertion that his grandmother both had experiences and reflected on them simultaneously. Is this something we all do or is it a rare capability? Think of a highly engaging conversation in which you are fully present. You do not listen to the other person and only afterwards think of what you want to say in response. When your turn comes, you simply speak your mind, often not knowing what you are going to say until you hear yourself saying it. Somehow reflection and comprehension are happening as a response is forming. In other words, the conversation's give and take is spontaneous while, hopefully, remaining thoughtful and sensitive to the other person. This is what Grandmother Adele modeled for Buber in the way she read, spoke to others, and even sat in silent meditation as she gazed out a window. Reflection did not distance her from what she addressed or let address her, it corresponded with the word of the other.

By the time we read this second vignette, we sense that these brief stories do constitute a kind of teaching by pointing. They embody Buber's essential philosophy and its critical issues. In the first, absence points dramatically to the search for presence – something that otherwise might simply be taken for granted. In the second, reading is recounted not as a passive process but as a matter of allowing oneself to feel addressed by the voice, or voices, of a book and to simultaneously address these voices as having the capacity to anticipate the reader. In other words, reading is a dialogue that takes place "between" reader and book and creates the reality of the "between." In contrast, there is something different going on with Buber's scholarly grandfather; something we do not quite understand yet, though clarity will come in one of the book's subsequent vignettes.

In vignette number 11, "The Horse," we learn that when Buber was eleven years old, he began spending the summers on his grandparents' country estate, where he was especially fond of visiting the stable. His favorite horse, a broad dapple-gray, was his darling. He loved to stroke the horse's neck. Whether smooth-combed or wild, the horse's mighty mane yielded to the young Buber a revelation of the presence of the Other. The unspoken dialogue consisted of Buber's caressing hand and the complying, inviting massive thereness of the animal, whose vitality was palpable to the child's touch. A thou to a thou, each a participant in a conspiratorially silent relationship of intimacy. But when young Martin became self-conscious of the pleasure he experiences by touching the horse, the magical bond dissolved. After that, while the scene appears identical, something in the horse's gaze and demeanor is different. Boy and horse have passed over into what Buber in his philosophical writings would call an I-It relationship – a phenomenon to which we will return.

Buber reports in another vignette that at around the age of fourteen he became overwrought with attempts to understand the nature of time. If time was finite, as geology and our mortal life would suggest, then how might one grasp its beginning or its end? And if time was infinite, which Nietzsche's "eternal recurrence" assertion suggests, then we must picture a boundless realm with neither beginning nor ending. The young Buber found this dualism of time perplexing and disorienting. Perhaps it fore-shadowed his struggles with the religious and secular conceptions of time, the sacred and the profane.

Buber says he pondered obsessively whether time had a boundary at each end, or was, metaphorically speaking, edgeless. He tried to imagine himself at either end of time but if posed at the beginning, he would "take a blow to the back of his neck" that sent him reeling forward, and if at the end, he would feel "the rap of a stick against his forehead, flinging him backward." And if time had no boundaries, then he'd go flying off into space and grow so dizzy he had to fling himself to the floor.

Then, one day, someone put a copy of Kant's *Prolegomena* in his hand and his perplexity was resolved. Time does not exist independent of us, asserted Kant, rather we constitute our perceptions and concepts of time (as well as space and causality) out of the equipment of our minds. From this insight Buber concluded that time is not external but internal and that whatever trouble we have with it is a difficulty of our own making.

He made a further leap. If we perceive through the frameworks of space and time, then as sources of these creations, are human beings not also positionally somewhere and sometime else? Could we not be said to dwell in eternity, which Buber described as "that which sends forth time out of itself." He associates this concept of a time-creating timelessness with a conception of a deity that "sets us in that relationship to it that we call existence."

In vignette 15, "A Conversion," Buber explains that in the earlier years of his adult life he saw himself as "religious." He gives us a beautiful account of how even some familiar object could become "unexpectedly mysterious and uncanny." Suddenly, it seems, "time could be torn apart" and he could be "delivered to fullness" in a supra-mundane state of "illumination and ecstasy and rapture held without time or sequence." The finite and the infinite spheres of life remained disconnected for Buber at this time. There was always a transition, the moment of crossing over from one to the other. Though deeply drawn to the otherworldly, Buber experienced an incident and a judgment.

One early afternoon he received a visit from a young man. Many people came to talk with the person they perceived as sagely. Buber was attentive and listened but he failed "to guess the questions" that the young man did not put forth. Later Buber learned that the young man had not come for a chat but to make a major decision. What sort of decision – marriage, suicide, joining the military, converting – we do not find out, only that the young man came in a state of despair and Buber, who believes he should have met this young man in such a way as to affirm a sense of meaning, failed him and failed himself.

What dawns on Buber is that separating life into two spheres – the mundane and the sacred, the time-bound and the time-unlimited – breaks the wholeness of life. Better to make all of life "religious" than to segregate it into a separate sphere. And he concludes: "You are not swallowed up in a fullness without obligation, you are willed for the life of communion."

The vignettes do not contain overt criticism of religious or philosophical outlooks. However, fragment 15 is a warning against indulging in forms of mysticism that lead to indifference toward the world shared with one's fellow beings, including the conflicts and differences we encounter with others in everyday life. Buber first dazzles us with his description of what deeply inward religious life can be like, and then throws cold water in our face. For we, like him, may have turned away from someone in his or her hour of need because we were preoccupied with something that seemed loftier, more transcendent or more pressing.

Most of the vignettes have a way of drawing us back to the "between" and away from either the strictly subjective or objective, from the superiority of "being right" to the humility of "being with." We are cautioned against seeking what Jung called the *mysterium tremendum* in our inner being if that quest means forsaking our responsibility to others. The message here is that an ontology that cannot accommodate an ethical standpoint within its compass fails as a description of the Being of human being.

At the very end of his autobiography, in Vignette 20 Buber takes up the subject of "Books and Men." He says that earlier in his life books had been more important than human contact. But after years of intense exchanges with all kinds of people, including many bad experiences with the evils of the Nazis and painful conflicts with the British who controlled Palestine and with the Arab population opposed to the immigration of Jews, these encounters had, says Buber, "nourished the meadow of my life as the noblest book could not do." And good experiences, he adds, have made the earth "a garden." Buber is full of these paradoxical statements. How can such disappointing encounters "nourish the meadow" of a person's life? Is he speaking metaphorically? Do they produce tears of anguish that force him to recognize life's deeper truths? Buber says books take him into a "paradise of great spirits," but that he can't live there.

And he poses a peculiar dichotomy. The world of spirit, God's world, the inner life, makes certain demands, while the human world, full of conflicts and "mismeetings," makes others. Unlike the mystic and the scholars who prefer the cloistered life with books, pens and paper, Buber chooses and is nourished by the tough "brown bread" of personal struggles with his fellow man.

Buber assigns genders to the two worlds. The spirit is masculine while the world is feminine. The masculine spirit bestows speech that turns into books, the feminine, "the human world," is capable of producing "a word-less smile," a silence of greater value than books and spirit. Men, says Buber, are made up of "prattle and silence." It is in the silence that you can hear the spirit as soul, which he calls "the beloved." We are born without books and will die without them, concludes Buber. But, if we are fortunate, we will die with another's hand in our own.

Throughout his adult life, Buber wrote books about relationships and silences. In the beginning was the mother who abandoned him and whose absence taught him a profound lesson about separation and longing, fundamentals of the human condition. Toward the end, three years before his death, he wrote about closing the door of his study to immerse himself in books, only to reopen that door to see a human being looking at him. Buber was fundamentally a religious humanist. God's presence was not exclusively manifest in books, not even in the sacred Torah, nor in the private recesses of the mind but through "meetings" and the yearning triggered by "mismeetings." This is why Buber both honors and circumscribes the devoted work of his grandfather. One can easily get lost in the labyrinthine twists and turns of Talmudic interpretations and in the minutia of *Halakhah*, Jewish law, and forget that the most important sphere is the proving ground of human interaction.

Going back chronologically to vignette number 18, "Beginnings," we find Buber providing a bibliographical sketch in which he recounts the process of collecting, interpreting, retelling and publishing Hasidic tales and legends. He says that when he wrote the introduction to *The Legend of the Baal-Shem* (1908) his comments represented a first articulation of what would eventually become the "dialogical principle." The principle occurred to him as he was drawing a "radical distinction" between myths and legends. The latter, exemplified in the kind of ethically and mystically pointing stories uttered by Jewish sages to awaken the heart and enlighten the mind of their followers. For Buber legends possess as their essential characteristic a "calling" to the listener who, in turn, is put in the position of responding.

Ancient myths, argues Buber, feature a type of god who "does not call, he begets; he sends forth the begotten, the hero." In contrast, one might think of the Biblical "legend" of Abraham who is called by his God and responds. Abraham even argues with this God about the fate of the people of Sodom and Gomorra. Moses, too, has conversations with the God of the Exodus and the revealed God of Sinai. The rabbis and sages associated with the mystical Hasidic movements in Eastern Europe and Palestine continued this tradition of communicating through legends. Having lived in some of these communities, Buber had first-hand experience.

The seeds of the dialogical principle, having been planted, would slowly germinate, breaking the soil in Buber's introduction to his 1922 book, *The Great Maggid and His Followers,* where he presents his formulation of the "two-directional relation of the human I and Thou." Then Buber devotes two years to working on his magnum opus, *I and Thou.* Concerning preparation for writing this book, Buber reveals something both puzzling and telling.

So Buber explains that he read almost no other works except Hasidic material during the two years devoted to a book that would address not just Jewish sources and audiences but would venture into the wider realm of European philosophy and offer something relevant to the non-Jewish reader. Buber acknowledges there were other influences from his previous studies, such as Kierkegaard and the German philosopher and anthropologist, Ludwig Feuerbach (1804-1872), whose writings contained hints that the capacity for relating was at the heart of the human experience. And, though he does not mention Nietzsche in this context, we know how the Zarathustra legend beguiled Buber in his youth. Buber mentions that he did choose one other book to ponder during these two highly solitary years – Descartes' *Discourse on Method*. Perhaps this is another one of those "pointing" gestures that Buber alludes to, since he gives absolutely no explanation as to us why he made this choice or, for that matter, why he bothered to mention it.

Following Buber's finger, we step away from the balcony of sorrow and out of the immediate framework of *Meetings* in search of the famous Frenchman with whom Buber will have a bone to chew. To assuage impatience with what may seem a circuitous academic exercise, let me assure the reader that there is light at the end of the tunnel and that the intellectual excursion will have its payoff. For Buber Descartes represents what is wrong with modern philosophy and its abstracted thinker.

THE PROBLEM OF THE OTHER

When Descartes, in his 1637 groundbreaking little book, *Discourse on Method*, demonstrated the process of rigorous doubt and rational analysis that led him to his famous *"Cogito ergo sum,"* "I think, therefore I am," he aimed to accomplish three things: first, to show that the thinking subject was the indubitable foundation for knowledge; second, that the clear and distinct or self-evident character of this foundational moment should serve as a criterion for all valid propositions; and third, that the existence of the subject would depend on its continuing engagement in thinking.

Descartes' little exercise has often been described as the beginning of modern philosophy in that Descartes gave the thinker philosophical primacy; a position that, in the Scholastic philosophy of the middle ages, had been assigned to God, Nature, Being, the abstract logic of numbers, or to the deduction of innate ideas. The primary existence of the thinking subject was Descartes' Archimedean principle of leverage: "one firm and immovable point... that is certain and unshakable." And to further prove the merits of his method, Descartes included with the *Discourse* three essays on scientific subjects – optics, meteorology and geometry, to which, using analytical reasoning, he had contributed important research results.

One difficulty that Descartes would face, if he did not want to be condemned for eliminating the exalted place of a divine being in his system of thought, was how to justify belief in the existence of an infinite and perfect God of creation. A second related difficulty was to show how to move logically from the mind of the finite subject to an intelligible world that included other thinking subjects. Descartes manages this great leap by claiming that he has a concept of perfection in his mind, a conception that he cannot account for based on information he has acquired through his senses. He finds the correlate to perfection only in the idea of God and proceeds to demonstrate, by means of an "ontological proof," the logical certainty of God's existence.

Some scholars have speculated that this leap from the finite, existing thinker to the irrefutable stature of the divine was Descartes' way of heading off a possible conflict with the Catholic Church, since in his scientific writings he favored the Copernican heliocentric model of the universe which, at that time, had precipitated Galileo's imprisonment, as directed by an edict of the ecclesiastical authorities. Others regard the ontological proof as Descartes' solution to avoiding ending up in the dead end of solipsism.

Starting with the subject, the "I" of the "I think," and having made it the center of the intelligible universe, the great problematic legacy that Descartes bequeathed to subsequent thinkers, including Buber, was the problem of enabling this existing thinker both know of and belong to the world of others. Descartes does this but only by drawing a sharp distinction between the human body and its mind – the first having extension (i.e. occupying space), the latter being not occupying space. Applying principles of analytical geometry to the workings of the universe, Descartes gives it a mechanical-like quality. The natural world then becomes wholly different from the human. Perhaps Buber saw this as the beginning of making the natural world an I-It realm, perceived as ready to be used by man for his benefit but at the cost of an alienation from nature.

There have been many challenges over the centuries to Descartes' formulation. For example, more than three hundred years later Kierkegaard aimed to refute Descartes' conclusion by arguing that to claim "I think" as the primary survivor of all-consuming doubt is to ignore that one presupposes the existence of the "I" and to merely have shown that an "I" that exists thinks. For Kierkegaard this is not a logical argument but a psychological one, since it is difficult for us to embrace the proposition "I do not exist." More importantly (and Buber knew this), for Kierkegaard the true starting point of philosophy is the situated existence of the individual as a creature conscious of living in the condition of finite time. This precognitive primacy of existence, not an abstract thinking-subject, is where philosophy must begin. But again, though we may gain the reality of the existing self, how do we reach out to the presence of the other -- which for Kierkegaard is not only to the other person, the neighbor, the beloved, but also to God?

A good deal of philosophical work from the middle of the 19th century to the present has concerned the relationship between self and other – what philosophers call the problem of intersubjectivity. And with this problem there has persisted the parallel problem, also inherited from Descartes, the choice of method – coming up with the way that one could not only prove the possibility of intersubjectivity but also demonstrate it. One important approach has been the assumption that, like Descartes, we are capable of interrogating our own minds and penetrating so deeply into the nature of subjectivity that we discover that the Other is, in some sense, already present and was never absent. One of the most important figures in this tradition is Edmund Husserl (1859-1938), the founder of the phenomenological school of philosophy in whose 1931 book, *The Cartesian Meditations*, a case for intersubjectivity is set forth.

Husserl's book is "Cartesian" because like Descartes he starts (and, some would say, ends) with the subject as first-person point of view – i.e. with consciousness. The book is based on lectures that Husserl, who was born and raised in Moravia, then part of the Austrian Empire, gave in Paris, so that is another reason the published lectures were linked to Descartes. Like Descartes, Husserl realized that if one bases a philosophical system on the first-person perspective, it is going to be difficult to escape from solipsism. Husserl's approach to grounding philosophy in first-person consciousness is daring, because he aimed to show that the thinking subject could take a position of reflection that would enable him or her to set aside (Husserl calls it "bracket") actions of the conscious mind that are so deeply embedded that ordinarily we are unaware of them. He called this state the "natural attitude").

While the natural attitude reflects an "unconscious" condition, it is not meant in the Freudian or Jungian sense because that use denotes almost complete inaccessibility to impulses and drives that only appear to consciousness as images (e.g. in dreams and fantasies). By unconscious is meant that which one had been previously unaware of – aspects of perception that are so immediate in operation as generally to remain undetected. For Husserl, by interrogating consciousness to discover how this unconscious mind constructs the reality of everyday life, all the unconscious beliefs that make rational thought possible would be uncovered. Because Husserl believed that human consciousness possessed the capacity to give intelligible structure to reality, he called this process "transcendental subjectivity." Transcendental here means that the conscious mind in a sense goes beyond itself by generating structures of consciousness that are constitutive of (i.e. help build up) the world of the conscious subject.

By taking what he called the "phenomenological attitude," this reflective position of delving beneath the taken-for-granted experience of consciousness, Husserl aimed to describe not only the way the individual conscious person constitutes his or her world, but how the reality of the other person and the shared (or socially constructed) world gets established. Husserl proposed several ways.

First, he recognized that in ordinary life, we possess the capacity for empathy – we are able to put ourselves in other people's shoes and imagine what they might be thinking or feeling. But Husserl wants us to "bracket" this "natural attitude" in order to see how it is that we hold a belief in empathy. Phenomenologists like to use phrases like "lay bare the rational structure underlying" this or that aspect of consciousness. So in "laying bare" empathy, Husserl argues that within individual consciousness (but, at first, only at the unconscious level), we find a belief that because we perceive other subjects as displaying traits more or less like ourselves, having bodies like ourselves, we ascribe to them an "egocentric" positioning in the world akin to our own. We do this not by conscious derivation or by conscious analogy, but in the immediacy of perception.

This notion of immediacy is crucial to understanding phenomenology as a method for describing how consciousness builds up its reality and the shared reality of the world of others. Husserl wants us to believe that an incredibly elaborate and subtle series of mental processes occurs in ordinary consciousness that enable us not only to constitute ourselves as a psycho-physical creature operating in a spatiotemporal order, but to experience other people as also occupying similar standpoints. Taken collectively, we perceive a commonly shared (though uniquely experienced) "life world" which becomes for us the objective realm that we inhabit with others. What is terribly important for Husserl is to convince us that this complex operation is not mediated by learned behavior, conditioning, ideas or any other type of intervening steps. There has to be a kind of unconscious all-at-once activity going on that is all part of how consciousness "intends" or directs itself and constitutes itself and by extension perceives the larger world as independent of my consciousness and is, in that sense, "transcendent."

Our credibility is certainly challenged by this notion that we are capable of examining how consciousness works, as in a slow motion movie. And then to proclaim that, while there seem to be many complex steps of this building-up of consciousness, we do it automatically and effortlessly. And even more importantly, that we can actually stand, so to speak, beside ourselves in such a way that while the movie is playing at super-fast speed we can actively slow it down by learning to practice the phenomenology attitude and figure this all out, or better, "uncover it."

Holding our credulity in suspension for now, all we need to know is that Husserl's descriptive study of human consciousness had a profound impact on many other European thinkers, including those variously classified as existentialist, phenomenologist, or postmodernist, most notably Martin Heidegger, who was one of Husserl's students, Jean-Paul Sartre, who was for a short time a student of Heidegger's and who attended some of Husserl's lectures, and other notables – e.g., Max Scheler, Merleau-Ponty, Emmanuel Levinas, Alfred Schutz, Jacques Derrida and Paul Ricoeur. Each, in his own way, took Husserl's theories and methods in a fresh direction. But each struggled with the problem of moving from the construction of individual consciousness to that of the other, and to a world they might share in common. Each had to deal with the challenge of moving from an ontology and/or epistemology rooted in subjectivity to the formulation of how a world shared in common should work – an ethics of the socially good, the morally correct, and the right.

In its more popular and sociological form, phenomenology eventually became a rallying cry in fields as diverse as anthropology, pedagogy, psychology and even aesthetics. Researchers and practitioners were encouraged to enter into and value the experiential dimension of their subjects and to restrain themselves from projecting categories and concepts that could distort their understanding of the Other.

FROM HUSSERL BACK TO BUBER

In 1928, when he was already fifty years old and well established, primarily within the circle of European Jewish intellectual life, Martin Buber attended a lecture given by Husserl. Buber was already immersed in the thought of those thinkers profoundly influenced by Husserl and his attempt to establish a science of consciousness and intersubjectivity. When introduced in the lecture hall where Husserl was about to speak, Husserl exclaimed, "The real Buber? Why, he is a legend."

The "legendary" Martin Buber's approach to intersubjectivity has as its starting point the theory that there are two ways of engaging the world of people and things: through "the speaking of" an I-It or an I-Thou word or relationship. Buber does not mean that we say these hyphen-linked words aloud. Rather they signify dispositions or evaluative attitudes of consciousness. We will see that why Buber refers to "speaking" I-it and I-thou will turn out to form a crucial difference from the approach taken by Husserl.

An I-It attitude meant you viewed people and objects as means to other ends. Friendships might serve as links to power and influence. The natural world of plants and animals might be thought of as existing to be exploited as food, raw materials or for aesthetic appreciation. By contrast, an I-Thou relationship is qualitatively different. You would experience the other, whether person or thing, as not only an end in itself but also as an intimate, though still separate, part of your very being. The presence of the other would call forth your presence. You would be fully there, fully aware, experiencing the other through a framework of mutuality, not use.

Buber asserts you could feel the other as if you were in their skin, feel their skin feeling your skin. Or if it was a tree, then you might feel the organic living quality of the thing as something in-itself, not a future pile of lumber or even a place to grab a bit of shade. Buber argued the I-Thou wasn't some kind of unification experience like in Zen, where distinctions between subject and object, here and there, are abolished and you lose all sense of difference. He insisted the "over-thereness" of the object had to remain intact and inviolate. There had to be a "between," otherwise all relationships would collapse in a huge vacuum of nothingness or into a solipsism in which the other was nothing but a figment of your imagination.

Buber's radically different approach was to claim that the primary human experience is first intersubjective and only then, secondly, subjective. That the dawn of human consciousness is already relational rather than that the relational or intersubjective is derived or constituted out of the working of the phenomenological self, the transcendental ego. The person is born into a world in which they are already addressed by the presence of, in a concrete sense, the mother, father, things, world and the Thou of all creation. But it is as if we had forgotten these original experiences, lost track of them, and cannot rediscover the primary conversation because of the cacophony of distracting noises that contribute to isolating the individual.

The Thou is an *a priori* structure of our very being and forms the condition that makes possible the encounter – or, as Buber likes to call it, the "meeting" of one Thou with another in mutual communion. Everything depends on how the person "comports" him or herself – whether in the mode of I-It or I-Thou. But while comporting is similar to Husserl's "intending," the possibility of authentic meeting is already given in the very primacy of consciousness. That is why Buber can declare in *I and Thou* that before all else, "In the beginning is the relation: as a category of being, as readiness, forming form, model of the soul; the a priori of the relation: the innate Thou."

Immediacy, reciprocity of the partners, and a common origin out of the realm of the "between" are the three main characteristics of the I-Thou relationship. The triadic character of the I-Thou is made apparent to us in certain revealing moments. The surge of affection, care, protectiveness and awe that may arise on the occasion of the birth of one's infant child is an instance in which the I-Thou relationship comes to the fore. While the infant is completely dependent on us as parents and is the result of our own generativity and love, the infant is utterly its own reality and yet belongs to us intimately, is a gift of the power of that which is already bestowed through our creative nature. While the infant is not yet ready to choose to comport itself, the infant immediately responds to its environment and instinctively reaches into the relational bond of nursing.

Similarly, in laboring to write a poem or solve a mathematical problem, we may experience a world coming to meet us as an inspirational metaphor or image, numerological realization, or even an internal voice surprising us with the gift of abundance that exceeds what we could only hope for but not force into being. In such moments it is as if time stands still and the shell of our separateness dissolves, not eliminating our individuality but transforming it from the state of needing and doing to one of belonging and being.

Unlike Husserl and his followers, Buber does not arrive at intersubjectivity, the realm of the between, by putting sense perception into slow motion, but by attending to what he calls the "basic words," the "spoken" I-Thou and I-It. Put slightly differently, the I-It relationship evokes a "speaking about," while the I-Thou infers a "speaking to." With a little reflection, we probably all know the difference that Buber is identifying. Language, rather than perception, only makes sense as a common medium even in situations when language is limited to gestures and grunts, as when we are trying to communicate with strangers in a foreign language of which we know only a few words. Frequently, we hear or may ourselves have experienced, an occasion of genuine fellowship in a brief encounter with a shopkeeper, taxi driver or hotel clerk in which a glance expressing care and concern sparked the I-Thou word.

Turning to an even more familiar context to illustrate Buber's conceptions, how many of us have sat in a classroom or lecture hall in which an otherwise brilliant professor holds forth, monologue-style, talking "about" a subject in which he may have a passionate interest, but not "talking to" us, the students, his Others? And then suddenly, as if awakening from a trance, the teacher looks up and says: "Do you understand why this is so important?" Everything changes. We are addressed, acknowledged, invited to dialogue, drawn into mutuality. But only if the question is authentic, not merely rhetorical and, therefore, not expecting a response. When the professor's question is authentic, when he or she takes the chance of being surprised by the indeterminacy of the response – which is the freedom and independence of we, the students – only then does the classroom become dialogical and the I-Thou form of comportment encompassing of the situation.

At the moment of switching from speaking about to speaking to, the professor does several things: the professor puts him- or herself in the position of the students in order to understand what it is like to be the listener and perhaps to return to an earlier experience as a student struggling to understand; second, the professor acknowledges and honors the presence of the students as not only autonomous beings but as his or her students; third, the professor releases the singular possession of the subject matter into the shared space and time of the situation as available for personal appropriation, not just as the transfer of knowledge from one mind to another; and fourth, the professor and students may feel, in that moment, the true meeting of persons as an awe-inspiring coming into presence of the transcendent spirit, as when we sometimes say of a highly charged shared emotional moment: "And then an angel passed through the room." For Buber, this metaphorical angel is the "between."

Our hypothetical professor cannot help but switch back to an I-It modality when giving tests and assigning grades. Moreover, as in many situations, the possibility of mutuality is here asymmetrical since power and authority are shared unequally between teacher and student. In an essay on education, Buber remarks on this and warns of the temptations that may arise if and when the teacher oversteps the bounds of the relationship, turning the intimacy of the bond of learning into an erotic encounter. It is not unusual for a professor who has the capability of "speaking to" his or her students to gain disciples and even a lover or two. It is also possible that, fearing the danger of losing a position of authority when made vulnerable through the I-Thou attitude, a professor will dwell in the mode of "speaking about." Strangely enough, this may have been true of Buber himself, as we shall see.

Based on this philosophy of discourse, we can now understand what drew Buber to the tales of the Hassidim. It was the story-telling tradition of the rabbis, the question and attempted answer method used traditionally in the study of Torah and its interpretations (the Talmud). These discourse-based communal activities opened the possibility for a "speaking to" one another. Perhaps not surprisingly, Buber is likelier to take us into the rabbinical study, the classroom, the Israeli agricultural collective (kibbutz or moshav) than the synagogue sanctuary to observe how the divine presence, the holy Thou, comes into being.

SO WHY DESCARTES?

If one were to read *I and Thou* concurrently with the *Discourse on Method*, one would likely conclude that they had little in common except one thing – both speak about the capacity and situation of the "I." And although Buber's work proclaims the dialogical principle, that without a Thou there is no I, and that philosophy must begin with the concreteness of the human experience, he aims to accomplish this without abstractions such as a disembodied cogito. Ironically Descartes' *Discourse* is in many ways the more personal, reader-friendly and dialogue-provoking of the two books.

For despite Buber's extensive knowledge of and intimate involvement with the Hasidic legends as a method of teaching, little of that background informs the style of *I and Thou*. Rather the work is from beginning to end a long series of pronouncements, uninterrupted by stories and rarely by illustrative examples. Yet it is here that Buber proclaims the dialogical principle, aims to establish the foundation of intersubjectivity, announces the "twofold attitude" of mankind as consisting in the "primary words," I-Thou and I-It. So was Buber's reading of Descartes just a way of passing time when he was not working on his big manuscript? The answer, I believe, turns on the issue of discourse and Buber's philosophy of language.

Descartes' *Discourse* has simultaneously the character of reflection and speech. He writes as though he were sharing his inner thoughts with his reader. He recounts the assets and limitations of his Jesuit schooling and his various wanderings around central Europe to observe humankind and see what wisdom he could derive. Descartes uses himself as a role model; he invites us to follow along as he brings his readers into an overheated room where he spent the winter. There, on a certain day, he figured out a series of mental steps that constitute his "method," one that would guide readers through a process of systematic doubt. Anything that did not pass the test of possible deception, distortion or falsity is rejected as a starting point of thinking. Only that which is clear, distinct and certain would qualify.

Buber criticizes Descartes' method in his essay, "Religion and Philosophy" (1951). "When we hear him talk in the first person," says Buber of Descartes, "we feel as if we were hearing the voice of direct personal experience. But it is not so." Rather, argues Buber, like so many other philosophers, at a crucial moment in the process, Descartes looks away from the concrete situation of the "living, body-soul person," refocusing in abstraction to claim the achievement of attaining, doubt-free, a thinking consciousness that he identifies with the ego, "I am," of the *ego cogito*.

Buber wants to halt the methodical Descartes before he turns away from his bodily, finite existence, and bring him back to the lived reality of a being that is already situated in a world with others who dwell with him and without whom there would not be a consciousness or an "I." Buber asserts that Descartes' effort to "capture the concrete starting point as knowledge" was "in vain." That it is "only through genuine intercourse with a Thou can the I of the living person be experienced as existing." In other words, genuine, non-abstract "discourse" should, as a form of communication, reflect the primacy of how humans are situated – as being-in-relationship, being-in-the-world, and being-addressed. Instead of infinitude and an unlimited deity as innate ideas, Buber asserts a pre-conceptual, quasi-linguistic contact with the God who calls to the individual as a Thou.

To establish his primary truth of the I-Thou relationship, Buber has to subdue Descartes' entrancing voice, as it leads us towards disembodied abstract speech, to turn him back to the concrete situation of the person. In *I and Thou*, Buber's mode of discourse is less a logical demonstration of conceptual points than a sermonic testimony to the discovery of hidden truths.

In short, Buber's discourse is normative in "pointing" through the window of the text toward how we should conduct our relationships with others. Unlike Descartes, Buber does not offer the reader a process or pathway to reach his picture of the world. For this reason, and because he chooses to invent his own vocabulary, Buber's position remained at the margins of the history of philosophy, though his poetic style and ethical message brought him considerable fame and prestige in the disciplines of theology, religious studies and psychology.

After all that hard work, we deserve a break.

TIME FOR A MOVIE

We may find a beautiful illustration of Buber's philosophy of dialogue and the primacy of the interhuman in the 2000 film, *Cast Away*. Tom Hanks plays the role of Chuck, a time-obsessed FedEx systems analyst who winds up stranded on an uninhabited island in the South Pacific after the cargo plane in which he was a passenger goes down in a violent storm. Chuck goes through the usual litany of figuring out how to spear fish, make a fire without matches, find shelter from sun and storm, and prepare signal fires should a ship appear on the horizon.

His ordeal drags on for months. Without human contact he finds himself becoming disoriented and discouraged. Suddenly, in a moment of illumination, he takes a volleyball that has washed up on the beach and, using his own blood from a hand wound, paints a face on it. The ball already bears a brand name, so he begins to address the anthropomorphized "head" as "Wilson," his newfound friend.

By having conversations and debates with Wilson, finding a Thou to address, Chuck reestablishes his sense of self. Wilson provides Chuck with "someone" to (pun intended) bounce off ideas and feelings. Moreover, it is with and through Wilson that Chuck realizes that relationships with family, friends and his longtime girlfriend were the bedrock of his life – a life that he put on hold (left suspended as if it were an abstraction) because of his commitment to the job of ensuring speedy delivery of packages (the world of utility, of "its").

By turning something that ordinarily would be considered an "It," an inanimate physical object used in a sport, into a Thou by means of dialogue, Chuck finds reason to go on and eventually to make a desperate attempt to float himself on a raft back into the world of others. During the raft journey he loses Wilson in a storm and, distraught and forlorn, abandons hope. Luckily, he is rescued but when he rejoins his family and friends, all of whom assumed after four years that he was dead, he finds his girlfriend has married and become a mother. Still, the film has a suggestively happy ending, pointing to Chuck's reappraisal of his life values.

The plot of *Cast Away* is among many tales derived from the classic story about shipwrecked isolation and exile, Daniel Defoe's *Robinson Crusoe*. However, the protagonist Robinson's equivalent of a Wilson is an escaped aboriginal slave whom he dubs Friday. Robinson decides to teach Friday to speak English and to educate and convert him to Christianity. Besides the oblique reference to the stigmata (Chuck's face-painting use of blood from his hand wound), *Cast Away's* exile is, by contrast, a secular fellow, though he begins to invent little rituals involving Wilson. Is Wilson a surrogate god?

Chuck never becomes mystically united with Wilson's totemic aura. Rather, it's through the conversations and even disagreements with Wilson that Chuck upholds his side of the relationship, thereby affirming that what lies between him and Wilson is precious if not essential to his survival. The credibility of this relationship is what makes the film successful. Audience members identify with Chuck's situation of isolation and loneliness. They, too, become attached to Wilson – at least for the duration of the film. Perhaps the scriptwriters of *Cast Away* were influenced by Buber when they chose for the frenetic Chuck the last name Noland (No-Land) and assigned salvation to Noland's co-star, a volley-ball used in the net game of address (serve) and response (return).

Chuck Noland's four-year experience of what it might have been like to live before the advent of metal tools and civilized discourse was a life-changing lesson in human anthropology. Buber was also interested in what he called a "philosophical anthropology."

BUBER'S ANTHROPOLOGY

Like Rousseau's speculations about prehistory, Buber sees arising "in the spiritual history of primitive man" the distinction between the "two primary words," I-It and I-Thou. Buber's aboriginal beings display a naturalistic I-Thouness as they experience an "original unity" with their surroundings. Objectification, in which self and other are perceived as distinct and separate, has not yet occurred. To support this hypothesis Buber cites examples of aboriginal speech such as the Zulu equivalent of (in English) "far away" as (in the Zulu language) "There where someone cries out: 'O mother, I am lost'."

Buber's choice of this example conveys an eerie echoing of his own maternal separation. Gradually, this kind of holistic language and concurrent consciousness with its undifferentiated subject-object relation gives way to consciousness of one's body as separate from others, and eventually to the use of objects as tools. The primary relational character of the undifferentiated "I" turns into the duality of the attitude toward others as "over against" oneself, or object-like. That which is over against me – that is, separate but belonging to my awareness – can then be treated as either an "it" or a "thou."

For Buber, in the development of language and consciousness, something has been gained and something tragically lost. He calls "That melancholy of our Fate" the loss of unitary innocence – when a thing like a tree was not yet regarded as something useful for making fires or shelters, an It, but as an organic part of one's intimate being – when trees spoke to human of their common bond, their partnership. Today's reader cannot help but think of the characterization, whether accurate or idealized, of Native American and other tribal peoples' beliefs and practices in their relationship to the natural. People, animals, clouds, wind and rock are all imbued with the power to speak and to be addressed.

Buber quickly shifts from the shaky ground of speculating on primitive man to his own directly experienced understanding of the life of the child.

Buber quotes a "mythical saying of the Jews" that "in the mother's body man knows the universe, in birth he forgets it." Here is a bit of the Platonic theory of anamnesis, the soul's loss of knowledge of immutable ideas upon entering corporeal existence. For Buber it is not knowledge that is at stake but a sense of being, of presence, which is why Buber alludes to the yearning for reunification with the mother as the desire for "cosmic connexion" with its "true Thou." As if tipping his hat to Jung, Buber says it is not just this specific mother that one abides in but also "the womb of the great mother, the undivided primal world that precedes form."

The gradual process of fetal development and then the laboring of birth ease the process of separation from the mother so that the infant experiences a transition from the spiritual primacy of union to the natural intimacy of the mother-child relationship. Then the infant begins to discover herself through seeing, hearing, touching and shaping her world. Buber says the infant is not a blank slate upon which sensations write the perceptions that will eventually turn into recognizable objects. Rather, it is as if an object – the red carpet, a Teddy bear – "rises up to meet the grasping senses."

Sounding like a voice from Rilke's "angelic orders," Buber describes the infant's actions as readiness to receive the gifts of the things of the world. In this way, the infant makes of each thing a Thou of relationship. And in the midst of this Thou-making of things comes sound as the pre-linguistic utterance through which the infant begins to make conversation; prattling to something as unlikely a Thou as a "simmering kettle." Imagine what Buber would have made of Chuck Noland's "Wilson"?

The behavioral psychologist would cringe to hear Buber postulate that an infant's encounters with the things of perception are not matters of stimuli to which the infant responds as a "reflex." Buber rejects the notion that a child first perceives an object and subsequently puts himself in relationship with it. It is, Buber insists, the relationship that comes first, as the primacy of perception originates in a meeting between the infant and its world. Presumably, Buber is delivering his own version of phenomenology, one in which the real does not come about through the actions of the transcendental ego or some other Cartesian starting point grounded in subjectivity. Rather, he starts with the primacy of the relational as what makes possible the later development of the subject-object dichotomy and the corresponding grammatical constructions of articulated language. Buber summarizes his ontology of human being as "meeting" in a way that many readers will find more mystical than empirical.

> *In the beginning is relation – as category of being,*
> *readiness, grasping form, mold for the soul; it is the* a
> priori *of relation, the inborn Thou.*

To regard the development of the soul in narrower and more confining ways, says Buber, is not just mistaken but injurious if the "cosmic and metacosmic origin" is ignored or denied. Buber is perfectly aware that at some early point in development the infant does differentiate as a separate consciousness and does learn to handle and conceptualize objects as things of use and misuse. He is also perfectly aware that language too becomes more a tool of communication and manipulation than a medium of meeting. But he wants us to understand that within the depths of human consciousness an inviolable calling remains, as the deepest human need is to dwell in relatedness to others. This is why, for Buber, child rearing and education must be attuned to the human ontology of the relational and why, not only as subject matter, but also as pedagogy, education should be conducted in ways harmonious with the dialogical principle.

We now understand why Buber uses the term "spoken word" for both the I-Thou and the I-It relationships. Simply put, Buber sees in both audible and silent communication the primary ways in which we encounter others – whether in the human, the natural or the divine spheres. Buber had great facility with languages from a young age and mastered Latin, Greek, German, English, French, Italian, Polish, Hebrew and Yiddish, while he read in several others. In his youth Buber would fascinate himself by translating words back and forth between languages to try to figure out how meanings compared. However, Buber was not a linguist preoccupied with the rules of grammar and syntax or with notions of the priority of language to experience. Language, for Buber, was the medium of the relational.

From this account we may begin to wonder whether the divine Thou, the God who comes into presence and to whom we seek to make ourselves present is a humanistic concept. A version of religious naturalism honoring the primacy of the relational as awe-inspiring, and the "between" as transcendent, almost grounds the religious experience in human projection. To do so does not necessarily reduce the Holy to the human but it does make the Holy a humanly projected idealization of what is greater than and beyond the human.

Buber's experiential account of the spirituality of the relational makes it attractive to a wide spectrum of seekers but also runs close to a version of religious humanism. Buber has come under considerable criticism from the Orthodox Jewish rabbinic and scholarly community for this apparent flirtation with humanism, a flirtation that would seem to bring the divine down to the level of the human. This possible interpretation of the I-Thou relations and the awesomeness of the "between," combined with the fact that Buber was not an especially observant Jew, subjected Buber to sometimes vicious attacks, especially after the Bubers moved from the suburbs of Berlin to Israel in 1939. Many observant Jews were shocked that the famous exponent of a highly personalized and quasi-mystical Judaism seemed to be more of a secular European than a pious Hasid.

Yet, running counter to religious naturalism, Buber insists that God is not knowable but is approachable; that we cannot speak truthfully about God but we can speak to God. And in the second edition of *I and Thou*, published in English in 1957, he added a Postscript. In that section he defends his characterization of God as a person – "eternal" but nevertheless a "Thou." He dismisses other conceptions that make of God a "principle" or an "idea," insisting that God's "infinitely many attributes" are threefold: spiritual being, natural being and personal being.

Buber understands that God can be thought of as ineffable (the *mysterium tremendum*), as omnipresent in the natural world and cosmic order, and as approachable in human-like ways. God, however, cannot be too much like a human for that would be to risk the kinds of anthropomorphisms of which Maimonides warns us – a kind of childish religiosity. For Buber, God is the Absolute Person, unlimited and not restricted to the interhuman, but present in it. Buber says that in our conversations with God – which has been the subject of most of his writing – he has tried to show "God's speech to men" as "instruction, message, demand." For Buber, this personalistic relationship to God reveals itself both biographically and historically. Elsewhere, Buber talks about "hallowing" this world and our relationships within it. The temporal is then not divided between the mundane and the extramundane or sacred, rather reverence, mystery, awe and communion belong everywhere and always, but most especially in the moment in which the I-Thou is spoken.

IDENTITY

For Buber individual identity is inseparable from relationships to others. There is no primal separate self or private inwardness that holds the treasure of one's unique being. If, as Augustine proclaims, "truth lies in the inner man," then for Buber that inner man contains a conversation with the divine and with the human. Buber's conception of authentic identity as relational being is in part rooted in his experiences with Hasidic communities and the legacy they offer to "modern man."

From the age of four to fourteen, when Buber lived with his paternal grandparents, he would spend the summers on his father's estate in Bukovina. His father would occasionally take young Martin to visit a nearby Hasidic community in the village of Sadagora. In an autobiographical essay, "My Way to Hasidism" (first published in 1918 and translated and reprinted forty years later in the anthology, *Hasidism and Modern Man*), Buber relates how as a child he saw the dirt, poverty and lingering Medieval character of the people and their Rebbe. But he also saw and, more importantly, felt the Rebbe's spiritual leadership and the joyful sense of community that derived from embracing and feeling embraced by a common spiritual heritage. This produced, Buber later reflected, a quality of Judaism in which the sacred and secular were not separate realms; rather there was "one kingdom, one spirit, one reality." As he grew up and received a formal secular education, Buber drifted away from Judaism and became caught up in matters of the higher intellect. This attitude led him to look down upon these Hasidic communities, as he puts it, "from the heights of a rational man."

Buber was drawn back to Judaism through the Zionist movement. He became passionately involved in verbal and literary debates over the nature of a Jewish homeland. For the Jewish people Buber wanted a spiritual renewal commensurate with a restored sense of dignity and pride. Buber believed this homeland must be guided by and embody Jewish spiritual values including the love of one's neighbor. By contrast, the Jewish state advocated by the Polish journalist and Zionist leader Theodore Hertzl was primarily a political and ideological one, a secular state in which Jews would be free to practice their religion but where the society and its state apparatus would be strictly secular. Tired of the fractious atmosphere of his modernist life, Buber sought solace by immersing himself for five years in Hasidic lore and legend and spending time in various Hasidic communities. Now the adult and educated Buber became open to the teachings of the *zaddikim* and what they might offer their modernized co-religionists, the "enlightened" Jewish population of Western Europe.

Buber crafted a unique view of personhood by bringing together his background in modern philosophy, especially his awareness of attempts to ground knowledge and ethics in subjectivity and consciousness, with the Hasidic spirit and its elements of Jewish mysticism that pervaded everyday life. The core of Buber's personalistic ontology, combined with this profound experience of community, led Buber to the view that the individual was never an isolated entity as a creature whose fundamental disposition was "being with others" or, to use his German neologism, "*mitsein*."

Identity for Buber involves confirmation and mutuality. In a famous on-stage conversation in 1957 with the eminent psychotherapist Carl Rogers, Buber drew a distinction between the therapist "affirming" the whole person of the client with all his or her bright and dark areas of personality and the therapist "confirming" the client by bringing his whole being into presence to demonstrate his willingness to accompany the client on his journey toward what, as Buber phrased it, "he is meant to become." This mentor role of the therapist echoed the role of the sage Rebbe who realized that he was responsible for helping his congregants, not by standing above them, but with them in confirming a shared sense of meaning.

When it came to issues of identity, Buber was highly aware that decep-tion and deceit were ever present. He drew attention to the difference between the dispositions of "being" and "seeming." Anticipating Irving Goffman's theories in *Presentations of Self in Everyday Life*, Buber recog-nized that we all have a tendency to prepare a face to meet the face of others so as to gain approval and acceptance. But "seeming" to be something that we are not inhibits the possibility of mutuality and openness that characterize the I-Thou relationship. Freeing ourselves from "seeming" requires courage. We have to shed the protective armor of titles, status, self-certainty, superiority and inviolability. It is easier to dwell in the I-It relationship than the I-Thou.

BEING MARTIN BUBER

Buber characterized his philosophical position as occupying a "narrow ridge." He trod this precarious pathway between traditional orthodox beliefs and a more humanistic and anthropological estimation of the human condition. He cherished Judaism and Jewish values but he placed individual choice of spiritual practice above religious dogma – which meant above the powers of the religious authorities. Indeed, Buber seems to have taken a most difficult and precarious position in both life and thought because he risked appearing self-contradictory in his complex philosophy, ethical stance and social engagement.

For example, while he brought Hasidism and its oral and written legacy out of the darkness of the impoverished and backward *shtetl* of Eastern Europe, in his early published works he did not limit himself to producing a near-literal translation of these tales. Rather, he absorbed their meanings and retold them in such a way as to make them more intelligible, and perhaps more palatable, to a modernist Jewish reader and to a wider non-Jewish audience.

Later, Buber would be criticized for falsifying Hasidism by editing out what he believed were corrupting overlays that stories might have acquired when being passed from generation to generation. He may have edited them to express edifying messages that came from his own more rational and intellectual values and education. Buber defended himself by arguing that he had become so immersed in the Hasidic spirit that he could differentiate the gold from the dross to bring out the most authentic and original versions of the tales.

Buber was also caught in an apparent contradiction in his ontology of the I-Thou and the human being's relationship to the Eternal Thou. Buber retained a personalist quality to his conception of deity because he wanted to emphasize God's presence in the world and to humankind. This led many scholars and lay readers to assume that Buber was propounding some type of mysticism, or direct experience of the divine through human actions. But Buber disavowed mysticism, claiming that the spirituality of his young adulthood distanced him from the intimacy and responsibility of human encounters. Moreover, Buber argued that one could not pursue revelation and religious ecstasy but only readiness through faith and selfless actions. God does the choosing – mystics are people who have received an unsolicited gift and burden. Consequently, to some Buber is mystically obscure and to others, too worldly.

Buber's position on the Jewish state and Judaism's relationship to the wider world also reflect his "narrow ridge." He wanted the newly formed state of Israel to embody the best of Jewish values and ethics and yet not be a theocratic "Jewish state." Fleeing to Palestine from the Nazi rule engulfing one country after another, Buber championed a return to the homeland of the Jewish people but, ever the idealist, he envisioned a country shared equitably with Arab neighbors. Ironically, he would live most of his life in Israel in the home of a former Arab Christian family that fled from Israel during the War of Independence. Moreover, Buber's Judaism seemed more humanistic than pietistic, more based on principles than dogmas and prescribed observances, such as following the kosher laws and obeying the Sabbath restrictions on working, driving or using electricity.

Buber was such an iconic figure that his almost mythical stature led to both curiosity and scrutiny as to whether the actual person embodied and lived up to his own ideals. This led to the 1988 book by Chaim Gordon, *The Other Martin Buber*, a collection of edited interviews conducted by the author in Israel in Hebrew of people who had worked with or studied under Buber or were members of his family. The result was a "revisioning of Buber's image," in which the author revealed that Buber had not been "the great master of dialogue that some of his admirers and idolizers strove to present."

Reviewing the twenty-seven interviews with non-family members, Gordon concludes that while Buber was an attentive listener in one-on-one conversation, he maintained his distance, and while he was an eloquent and charming speaker, he was not an engaging teacher, nor did he have close friends. Rather, he was surrounded by "an almost impenetrable circle of loneliness."

FIELDWORK AND REFLECTIVE WRITING

Buber's approach to intersubjectivity has had profound influence on contemporary approaches to disciplines as diverse as education, theology, nurse training, anthropological fieldwork, "humanistic geography" (qualitative study of how people relate to nature, place and space) and family therapy. In most instances, it is his emphasis on the ideal space of relationships – the possibilities of authentic communication and community – that has attracted the most attention.

Reflecting the interrelationship of the I-it orientation to the I-thou, Buber's contemplation of a tree in *I and Thou* suggests the qualitative differences between the two frameworks of perception. First he sees the tree simply (though eloquently) as a picture: "a rigid pillar in a flood of light, or splashes of green traversed by the gentleness of the blue silver ground." He moves on to seeing the tree as movement of nutrients and photosynthesis, as a classifiable species, as exemplifying certain laws of nature, as a number or "pure relation between numbers," and so on. Finally, he says, "but it can also happen, if will and grace are joined, that as I contemplate the tree I am drawn into a relation, and the tree ceases to be an it."

Buber insists that all the previous ways of looking at the tree have value and validity and that they are not abrogated by the non-instrumental form of uninterpreted relating. Rather, this appreciation of the tree for what it is in and of itself, rather than in projected categorical terms, complements these previous approaches, surrounding them with a halo of sacredness. Nor are subject and object fused into a unity of undifferentiated oneness.

I invite the reader to conduct a similar experiment by choosing to contemplate an object in the natural world, an artifact of human construction, or a person. One approach that is both enjoyable and often quite astonishing is to visit a museum and pick out a painting or sculpture and look at it for at least half an hour. You may need to take a couple of short breaks. Be sure to look all around the artwork including the edges or, if sculpture, every side. Use a notebook to record what you see at five-minute intervals. How does your perception change? Museum-goers often expect that an object that may have taken its maker weeks, months or even years to create should reveal itself in a matter of a few seconds. But this is to treat the object as an It, not a Thou.

Buber's autobiography, *Meetings*, consists of twenty vignettes that produce an intimate montage-like picture of salient scenes from his life. Each tale points toward larger meanings that can be traced to aspects of Buber's philosophy of encounter, the "between," and the dialogical principle. Readers might try their own hand at making a list of relationship scenes; doing so first, spontaneously, by just jotting down one or two sentences to be used as placeholders. Then, like Buber, write a two or three-page description of one or two of these scenes. Choose ones that attract your attention in the moment. Give each scene a title. If this approach works for you, continue to expand all the other scenes and give them titles.

Next, using a technique from Ira Progoff's journal-writing approach (http://intensivejournal.org/index.php), choose one detail – an object, image, person, in one scene – and write a dialogue with this entity, giving the selected detail a voice. Let this object initiate the conversation. When the conversation loses energy, stop. Reread the dialogue and give it a title. Compare the title of the first vignette with the title of the dialogue. What do you find?

READER'S GUIDE

Buber's small volume, *Paths in Utopia* (English translation, 1939), though perhaps hard to come by, is especially valuable because it shows how Buber puts theory into practice. The work offers Buber's views as a social thinker, a communitarian Socialist who warns of centralized Soviet Federalism, a proponent of the kibbutz and moshav movement in Israel, and an advocate for the mutuality of community. The book offers a profound critique of the use of collectivization as a means to other ends – the victory of the proletariat and the establishment of state dominated community life. A recent anthology edited by Asher Biemann, *The Martin Buber Reader* (2002), provides an excellent historical and topical selection of Buber's work. Maurice Friedman's *Encounter on the Narrow Ridge: A Life of Martin Buber* (1991) is a highly readable shorter version of his exhaustive three-volume biography, *Martin Buber: Life and Work,* and contains an excellent annotated bibliography of Buber's most important works.

There are several anthologies of Hasidic tales that are worth reading but *Tales of the Hasidim: Early Masters and the Later Masters* (now in a single volume, 1991) is an especially enjoyable and valuable book that expresses the mature Buber's interpretation of this mystical and communal movement. For those ready for the experience and who have the time and patience, *I and Thou* is certainly worth the effort for understanding the heart and soul of Buber's most famous ideas.

10

GANDHI'S CELL

In 1939 Martin Buber, having fled from Nazi Germany to Palestine, wrote a letter to a highly esteemed world leader pleading a case for the right of the Jewish people to a homeland. Addressing him in the letter as "Mahatma," an honorific Sanskrit term that had become linked with this leader's name, Buber sought to persuade the "great soul" that objections to Jewish settlement in the Arab-dominated British-controlled land of Biblical peoples was based on an inappropriate comparison between the plight of Indians straining under the yoke of the British Raj and Jews being rounded up and shipped off to concentration camps under the Nazi regimes wielding power in Europe.

Buber was an author and professor. He was writing to a political and spiritual leader whose views were followed by millions of people. Despite his lack of official political power, the Mahatma, Buber knew, had tremendous moral authority, and his opinion could be an important factor in gaining support for the liberation of the Jews of Europe as they secured rights to citizenship in Palestine.

There may be other reasons why Buber appealed to Gandhi. By the time of this letter Gandhi had spent decades of his life preaching, teaching and attempting to demonstrate the "truth-force" (*Satyagraha*) bound up with combining principles of spirituality and political self-determination and forging a moral link between a life of contemplation and participation in the secular world of economic and political realities. This, Gandhi believed, must be the basis for establishing a nation whose citizens would be inspired and guided by moral values of religious tolerance, social inclusion, equality and spiritual harmony.

Buber had similar aspirations for his new homeland – that while con-figured as a secular nation, it would be guided by the highest Jewish moral principles at all levels. Unfortunately, Gandhi did not grasp that the situation of the Jews of Europe was far different from that of the Indians of his native country and of the Indian minority of South Africa where he conducted his first civil disobedience campaigns in order to secure equal rights. He was convinced that the kind of civil disobedience that Indians were conducting, namely non-violence (*ahimsa*), could work anywhere.

It would take eight more years for Gandhi to lead his people to gain self-rule from the colonizing British government. The British Empire had dominated Indian life for over a hundred and fifty years. For what started out as the seemingly insignificant presence of the British East India Company gaining the right to conduct trade in the early 1600s turned into the quasi-governmental private company of powerful merchants having its own army to control vast swaths of India by the late 1700s.

In 1857, following an ill-fated Indian Rebellion, also called the Indian Mutiny since it involved an uprising among Indian troops serving in the colonizers' army, the British government dissolved the East India Company and took full control of the country. The new administration, hoping to pacify the native population, conducted reforms that included increased tolerance of religion and the recruitment of Indians into the civil service. A Viceroy was appointed to rule India. In 1876, as an intended token of recognition of the country's importance to the British crown, Queen Victoria was declared Empress of India.

The then nine year-old Mohandas Karamchand Gandhi, a native of Porbandar, a fishing and sea-trading town on the Arabian Sea coast of the peninsula of Kathiawar, today part of the Gujarat state of India, was probably not impressed by the Queen's new status in the life of his country.

If there was ever a young person whose background, early educational performance, temperament, physique and lack of social access to privilege and power ruled out any possibility of a rise to political, spiritual and philosophical influence, it was this child, who in almost every way could be described as a nonentity. Even when he did manage to undertake legal studies and pass the bar examination, he lost his first case because he was too shy to cross-examine the defendant.

But obviously something did change. Something remarkable developed in this shy provincial youth from a middle-caste family with limited financial resources, already burdened with a marriage when he was barely in his teens. Some rare quality enabled Gandhi to become not only a brilliant political tactician, leading some of the world's most famous mass-participation liberation campaigns, but also a major interpreter and translator (into his native Gujarati) of sacred Hindu scriptures such as the *Bhagavad-Gita*. He also became a commentator on Christian theology, a correspondent of the Russian novelist-philosopher Leo Tolstoy and an exponent of English art critic and social philosopher John Ruskin's ideas about aesthetics and community. Gandhi was also a student of the American transcendentalists, Thoreau and Emerson, and shared their enthusiasm for the natural world. In fact, Gandhi would become an inspiration to the 1970s "deep ecology" environmental movement.

Gandhi's collected writings comprise some ninety volumes. Though he was not a systematic thinker in the sense of presenting a well-organized and integrated body of theories and ideas, he provided the material for others to gather into a profound philosophical statement. Of Gandhi's interpretation of the Indian theory of the "four aims of life" (*parusharthas*), University of Calgary Emeritus Professor of Political Science Anthony J. Parel avers that "with its focus on the need to bring a working harmony between the political, economic, ethical, aesthetic and spiritual values, [it] was meant to remedy what he [Gandhi] saw as the malaise of modern secularism" (2006).

Columbia University philosophy professor and noted author Akeel Bilgrami would likewise affirm that Gandhi's ideas and political strategies "flowed from the most abstract epistemological and methodological commitments" (2001). Gandhi's principles of personal and societal liberation through a commitment to non-violence have had profound influence on other civil rights leaders, most notably Martin Luther King, Jr. How amazing, then, that Gandhi's contributions to the history of thought and political action could spring from such intimate personal matters as a conflict between sexual passion and filial piety, personal honor and a commitment to social justice, extreme modesty and soaring political expectations, a silk chimney-pot hat and a turban.

THE PRISON

Gandhi's autobiography, subtitled "The Story of My Experiment with Truth," was written in his native provincial language, Gujarati, mainly while he was incarcerated in the Yeravda prison near Bombay (now Mumbai) during the years 1922-1924. Not the first but one of the longest of Gandhi's jail terms, it followed an intense period of civil disobedience that spread from his home state in southern India and mobilized the wide socioeconomic and religious diversity of the entire subcontinent.

At his trial in March of 1922, Gandhi pleaded guilty to the charge of inciting disaffection toward the government. He appealed to the English judge that the accused should receive the severest penalty for this offense unless, like Gandhi, he believed that British rule over India was an unsupportable evil, in which case the judge should instead resign his post. Gandhi received a sentence of six years. He was released after two following an emergency appendectomy.

In his prison cell Gandhi maintained his usual routine. He awoke at 4:00 a.m. to pray, using hymns and prayers of an eclectic nature that spanned Hinduism, Islam and Christianity. He then worked from 6:30 a.m. to 7:00

p.m. at writing letters, magazine articles, and a history of the non-violent civil disobedience movement he had helped to lead in South Africa (*Satayagraha in South Africa*) as well as his autobiography. He also studied voraciously, acquainting himself with the sacred writings of the major religions (Hinduism, Islam, Zoroastrianism, Sikhism, Buddhism and Christianity), improving his knowledge of Sanskrit, Urdu and Tamil. As no artificial light was allowed, after another period of prayer and meditation Gandhi went to bed at 8:00 p.m. (Brown, 1989).

He also devoted four hours each day to the spinning and carding of cotton fiber for making *khadi* cloth, part of the *Swadeshi* (freedom) movement Gandhi had helped to inaugurate across India as he encouraged the rural poor (and, indeed, whatever their station in life, all his compatriots) to refuse to purchase imported British goods and learn to make their own fabric and clothing.

While his autobiography does not contain a physical description of the prison, his contemporaries would easily picture him in his austere cell with its pallet bed and a few personal objects including the spinning wheel, typewriter and some books. They knew that every word of his story issued from within the space of his incarceration. What more revealing context could he have chosen to symbolize the harsh realities of colonialism and of the imprisonment of the Indian spirit, whose demise had caused millions of people to accept and tolerate the foreign rule that should have been unacceptable and intolerable? Yet from Gandhi's point of view all human beings are metaphorically imprisoned by false beliefs, prejudices, impulsiveness, greed and other behaviors that inhibited spiritual perfection. In this sense we are all in jail. The prison cell is, for Gandhi, a metaphorical architecture of the soul. It frames the entire contents of the autobiography.

Gandhi's personal narrative recounts the period from his birth in 1869 to the year 1921. Composed of five "parts" and a total of 162, two- or three-page chapters, the life story was serialized in the weekly Gujarati magazine *Nivjivan* from 1925 to 1928 before being translated into English and other languages. On the surface, the autobiography does exactly what Gandhi implies by the subtitle – he shares with readers an account of his attempts to discover the best principles for leading his life and the consequences of putting these principles to the test of real life experience. While there is nothing remarkable about the personal narrative of someone trying to live up to his convictions, in the case of Gandhi the plight of countless millions of people depended on how the experiments would turn out.

The deeper level of the autobiography requires a more nuanced reading. Gandhi repeatedly insists that his experiments and findings are not necessarily applicable to everyone else's situation. He claims no authority for his advice and encourages his readers to "carry on [their] own experiments according to [their] own inclinations and capacity." However, by the time Gandhi wrote the autobiography he was already a revered leader and controversial personage. He knew that what he put down on paper could have a profound effect on his fellow countrymen and on the Indian independence movement.

He had devised and led mass demonstrations of civil disobedience that involved work stoppage, strikes, tax-paying refusals and other forms of non-violent protests in agitating for Indian self-rule against the British Raj. And he had seen his most cherished hopes dashed by the outbreak of violence against Europeans, between Moslem and Hindu, and on the part of the British-controlled police and military, leading Gandhi to realize that his strategy was premature. He had already founded several spiritual communities or ashrams where his principles concerning agricultural self-subsistence, diet, work, religious tolerance, education and rules of interpersonal behavior were virtually the law. One might speculate that Gandhi hoped to turn all of India into a country of village ashrams following similar practices. His autobiography was, therefore, intended as a guide to moral virtue.

It would be difficult for us to put ourselves in the shoes, sandals or bare feet of his contemporary readers, but we need to read with metaphorical bifocals or, even better, trifocals. Gandhi can appear to be engaged in an innocent recollection of events that he simply enjoys calling to mind. Those close to him in space and time would have been familiar with the conditions he describes of family, tradition, housing, village and town life, modes of transportation, and general attitudes that derived from accommodating to generations of British dominance. They would have been able to read between the lines. I suspect that even the most unself-conscious story in the autobiography has a political and spiritual message for those both within the Gujarati language sphere, which was about ten percent of the Indian population, and those in far-off Indian states.

Gandhi is a sly fox and, whether consciously or unconsciously, he plays the visionary leader and the role model not only for the emancipated India but also for the emancipated Indian. That is why his story was so widely followed by his contemporaries, by his British detractors and supporters and by people in Europe and the Americas (Gandhi was chosen as Man of the Year by *Time* magazine in 1930).

The autobiography tells us that Gandhi was the youngest of four children born to Putlibai, his father Karamchand Gandhi's fourth and last wife (his previous wives were deceased). His mother, Gandhi reports, was a pious woman who with an iron will would adhere to vows such as fasting and prayer even when afflicted by serious illness. Gandhi claims that he was an indifferent student but that there was one thing to which he was adamantly committed – telling the truth. During an examiner's visit to their school, five pupils, including Gandhi, were to write the correct spelling of words on the chalkboard. Only Gandhi had misspelled one word. When his teacher tried to signal him to observe the other boys' spelling and correct his own, he refused since he believed that "copying" was forbidden. By his own account, Gandhi remembers himself as shy, withdrawn and inflexible when it came to telling the truth.

In Part 1, Chapter III, Gandhi sorrowfully recounts his child-age marriage to Kasturbai, a preteen who would continue to live with her parents several months of the year. She was more like a playmate, says Gandhi, than a wife, though gradually he found himself playing the jealous and controlling husband.

Chapters VI and VII describe one of Gandhi's first experiments – meat eating. Mohandas was persuaded by a friend, Mehta that one thing that enabled the British to dominate India was that they ate meat and, hence, were bigger and stronger than most Indians. He tempted Gandhi, who eventually succumbed and participated in what was presented as a "reform" of the prescribed Hindu adherence to vegetarianism. The same friend, he says, inflamed his jealous suspicions about his wife's activities and continued to mislead him for about a year. Other rebellious acts of Gandhi's youth included smoking cigarettes, stealing a small amount of gold from his brother and visiting a brothel (but not having intercourse). Eventually, Gandhi would admit the theft of gold to his father whose single tear says Gandhi, "cleansed my heart, and washed my sin away."

These sins of commission reminiscent of Augustine's *Confessions* build up to the momentous "double shame" of Chapter IX. Gandhi is now 16 and performing care-giving duties for his ailing father. His wife is expecting their first child. While massaging his bed-ridden father's aching legs, he would be fantasizing about having sex with Kasturbai, despite her late stage pregnancy. He completes his duties to his father one night and goes to his bedroom where he disturbs his sleeping wife in order to fulfill his erotic needs. Just then comes a knock at the door and a servant announces, "Father is no more." Gandhi is overwhelmed by shame. Sadly, a few days later his wife suffered a miscarriage.

This brief tale helps Gandhi to convey several moral principles: childhood marriages should be abolished because children are not yet ready to handle the responsibilities of matrimony and because they distract from the young person's need to focus on education; young people need to learn self-control and self-discipline and not engage in erotic self-indulgence; duty to one's parents must come before all other obligations and certainly before the pleasures of the body. Gandhi did not spell out these tenets in the autobiography but he wrote about them elsewhere and spoke about them in hundreds of talks he gave all over India.

These introductory accounts must have been extremely familiar to his readers. They help to establish Gandhi as having had an ordinary youth, tempted by the usual pleasures, lacking in self-control, indifferent to study but having one overriding trait – unadorned honesty.

> *If anything that I write in these pages should strike the reader as being touched with pride, then he must take it that there is something wrong with my quest, and that my glimpses are no more than mirage.*

His stories presage the struggles that are yet to come – adherence to the voice of conscience even when the call of that voice will mean denying pleasures, passions and urges. In this way the reader is invited to put himself (and possible herself) in Gandhi's position and to see personal weakness and the temptations of everyday life as momentous character-building rites of passage rather than as trivial episodes of little consequence to adult life.

The chapters recounting Gandhi's youthful struggles and his eventual travel to London, where he studied for the bar, are animated by the tension between aiming to succeed in the world of the colonizers and being true to one's homeland and people. Gandhi is fully aware that for his literate reader, whether in Gujarati or English, the temptation and fascination with all things English is part of the liberation struggle. He reports that during his time in London, he had himself fitted out in a stylish evening suit hand-tailored in Bond Street, wore a double watch-chain of gold, and doffed a then-stylish chimney-pot hat. Gradually he learned to castigate his efforts at conformist imitation. Still, he needed to find an honest and dignified way of living as a minority person in English society.

Gandhi's solution is to find friends among the English who will promote his maturation and development without requiring that he change himself into a little Englishman. To that end he locates a vegetarian restaurant in London and he finds his way into a society of vegetarians who elect him to a board post. Vegetarianism, exotic for turn-of-the-century England, brought Gandhi into contact with Theosophists, Buddhists and other spiritual seekers including various Christians who abhor foods obtained from the killing of animals. Some of his new friends want him to teach them about his own faith tradition, Hinduism, but Gandhi admits he is unfamiliar with the literature of his Hindu background. With their encouragement, he begins a study of the important Hindu text, the *Bhagavad-Gita*.

All along Gandhi anticipates a job in India as a barrister. His kinfolk expect him to earn enough income to join his elder brother in supporting the extended family, which has been left with meager means following the death of Gandhi's father. Little in what Gandhi says about himself would suggest a political reformer working within. Rather, Gandhi presents himself as more of a stumblebum. He is impressed with the material achievements of Western civilization but dubious as to how they contribute to a morally righteous life. Instead, what he sees around him is preoccupation with wealth, status and possessions. He notes the pervasiveness of class differences, indifference to the spiritual life or, if in pursuit of a spiritual life, then that life distorted by exclusion and condemnation of followers of other faiths.

Gandhi is like Rousseau in faulting Western "enlightenment" for not offering its benefactors a sense of meaning, tranquility or even good health in the crowded and polluted cities. Industrialization has led to many evils, observers Gandhi, such as child labor, environmental degradation, poverty, loss of self-reliance and corruption of values. By implication, he seems to be asking himself and his readers why would India, even if freed from British rule, want to become like industrialized Britain? Is there another pathway besides the modernist economic and cultural life of industrial societies? We still do not see the coming reformer in these chapters but do sense the seeker after truth whose determination is being tested on all sides.

Part 2, Chapter IV, of the autobiography stands out as a turning point. Gandhi is working in the law office of his brother's business partner when he is asked by his brother to intercede on the partner's behalf with the local Political Agent over a legal matter. Gandhi knows the Agent from his time in England and is on friendly terms. But now the setting is India, not England. Gandhi is reluctant to intercede and use his friendship (a "trifling acquaintance") as leverage but he cannot refuse his brother. He meets with the Political Agent and is at once cut off by the angry British officer who chastises Gandhi for abusing his acquaintance and when Gandhi persists in trying to make his case, the Agent calls for an underling who throws him out of the office. Seeking advice from a respected and more experienced Indian barrister, he is told to get used to this treatment and to "pocket the insult." Gandhi licks the wounds to his self-esteem, vows never again to place himself in a "false position" or to exploit a friendship, and concludes: "This shock changed the course of my life."

The shock is Gandhi's rude awakening to the facts of life under the British Raj and the intoxication of power indulged in by British officers who hold little respect for their subjugated charges. While he is advised by friends to accept these conditions and learn ways to work around them, Gandhi realizes that his run-in with the Political Officer has jeopardized his future in the local courts of law. Moreover, he is disinclined to accept the status quo. At the same time he is also learning about the "petty politics of the country," the intrigues among the British officers who have control of the Indian states and their strategy of playing the Indian princes off against each other.

As if awakening from a pleasant dream, Gandhi gains direct experience of the impact of foreign rule and of the degraded state of Indian society. Summarizing his situation, he says: "This atmosphere appeared to me to be poisonous, and how to remain unscathed was a perpetual problem for me." Here is the emerging voice of conscience and the will to lead a virtuously pure life that is so remarkable about Gandhi. Here is the mirror he holds up to his fellow countrymen who, reading his account, can only shake their heads. But here also is the streak of stubbornness, pride and determination and resistance to injustice that Gandhi wants to evoke in his reader.

The consequence of the foregoing episode is that when an opportunity to travel to South Africa for a one-year legal position comes to him, Gandhi sees it as the only way out of a dead-end situation for earning a living. It is in South Africa where the fledgling reformer comes up against race prejudice and the color bar imposed against Indians who have come to work in Natal, a British colony that would later become incorporated as a province in the Union of South Africa in 1910 and the Republic of South Africa in 1961. Part II of Gandhi's autobiography recounts his numerous experiences of discrimination, including being asked in court at Durban to remove his turban, being thrown off a train at Pietermaritzburg in the Transvaal colony after refusing to move from the first class to a third class coach despite holding a valid first class ticket, then being forced to ride atop a stagecoach instead of inside where his ticket allowed, and so on.

Gandhi becomes familiar with the plight of both the indentured unskilled workers and the literate traders who have migrated to South

Africa seeking economic betterment. When the Natal Legislative Assembly passes a bill to impose an annual tax on indentured servants who, if they cannot or will not pay it, must return to India and seek readmission to South Africa, Gandhi organizes a protest. He succeeds in gaining the trust of fellow Indians from all walks of life and religious affiliations to found the Natal Indian Congress in 1894, with himself as the Secretary. He uses this organization to mold the Indian community into a homogeneous political force, publishing reports detailing Indian grievances and evidence of British discrimination in South Africa.

In 1896 Gandhi goes to India to fetch his wife and children. On his return to South Africa a white mob attacks them and almost manages to lynch him, though later he refuses to press charges against any of the mob members, stating that it is his principle not to seek redress for a personal wrong in a court of law.

In South Africa, following passage of a law requiring Indians to register with the government and obtain an identity card, Gandhi formulates his principle of non-violent civil disobedience under the banner of the newly minted term "Satyagraha" (*satya* = truth, *graha* = devotion). And so begins a seven-year struggle in which thousands of Indians are jailed (including Gandhi), flogged or even shot for striking, refusing to register, burning their registration cards or engaging in other forms of non-violent resistance, until a compromise is negotiated between Gandhi and South African Colonial Secretary General Jan Christiaan Smuts.

GANDHI AS PHILOSOPHER IN ACTION

In Part 2, Chapter XXII, Gandhi captures the emerging clarity of his life's purpose. He articulates his philosophy of "self-realization," stating that he "had made the religion of service" his own, since "God could be realized only through service," which in his case was the service to his fellow Indians. Readers can only marvel that a person who is neither a swami nor other type of authorized holy man can take it upon himself to assert that it is possible – or even necessary – when pursuing the most deeply inward path to knowing God, that this path should involve forming organizations, staging protest, going to prison, cleaning latrines, nursing the sick, and in myriad other ways advocating for the rights of the disenfranchised. As role model, Gandhi goes completely against the grain of Indian hierarchical tradition. He demonstrates how it is possible for an ordinary person to find personal meaning in a sacred tradition through acts of authentic appropriation.

Gandhi fuses vegetarianism (and later fruitarianism) with non-violence, and the two taken together with truth seeking and political and spiritual emancipation. This combined form of emancipation that Gandhi has in mind will be reflected in the pamphlet-length book he writes during a voyage back to South Africa from India in November of 1909, *Hind Swaraj*, Indian Self-Rule.

Gandhi is calling for a new way of life in India, one that entails responsibility and self-control, elimination of the caste system, introduction of gender equality, and the appropriate use of technology rather than centralization and mass production. He will advocate rural agrarian communities of self-subsistence and mutual aid and moderation in all things. He will recommend the practice of chastity after the desired number of children has been reached, as part of freeing oneself from the life of the passions. He will recommend an ascetic life of indifference to the pleasures of consuming spicy foods, possessing fine clothing and jewelry, and having servants do so-called menial chores.

If his fellow Indians begin to embrace these qualities, which Gandhi associates with living a pure, morally virtuous life, they will be better prepared when self-rule becomes a reality. Otherwise Indian independence will simply mean life continuing as it has been, only now under the spiritually dissipating conditions of modernity. Gandhi despaired to picture a future free India perpetuating gender inequality, the caste system with its Untouchables, urban crowding, preoccupation with material gain and intolerance, if not violence, between Hindu and Moslem. He wanted to show by the way he led his own life that conditions of society could be happily different.

Almost every chapter of the autobiography offers a practical moral lesson concerning the qualities and virtues of Gandhi's version of the new Indian life. For example, in discussing "cultivating purity" through proper diet (Part 3, Chapter XXVII), Gandhi reports on his experiments with fasting and going to a fruit diet. Soon, he realizes, the consequence of the dietary experiments is that his appetite is increasing and it dawns on him "that fasting could be made as powerful a weapon of indulgence as of restraint." He has to learn by trial and error not to dwell on the "relish of food." He comes to the realization that the goal is to "just keep the body going," mastering diet so that it serves not only the body but also the soul until the body "begins to function in the way nature intended it to do."

Part V of the autobiography covers a period from about 1915 to 1922. During this time Gandhi has returned from South Africa to India, where he is still a relative outsider to the party politics of his native land. The end of this period is marked by his two-year incarceration following his rise to national fame as leader of the non-cooperation movement. By then Gandhi is a middle-aged man on the verge of what in traditional Indian society would be considered readiness for the third stage of life, retirement, or even the fourth stage, *sannyasa*, the life of the ascetic who withdraws from society and devotes himself to seeking *moksha*, that is, release from *samsara*, the cycle of birth, death and rebirth. But Gandhi has, in a sense, been a *sannyasin* from early adulthood. Moreover, he has redefined the pursuit of *moksha* as both a religious and political duty. He demonstrates this in several ways.

During this seven-year period Gandhi establishes the Sabarmati Ashram or spiritual community in Ahmedabad, applies the principles of satyagraha to settle the grievances of indigo plantation workers in the Champaran district of Bihar (a state in eastern India), helps to settle a textile workers' strike in Ahmedabad and a peasants' protest in Kheda, attempts to recruit volunteers for the Indian army to fight in support of the British in World War I, leads a huge national protest against the 1919 Rowlatt Act (which gave the imperial government the power to imprison and take to trial without jury suspected terrorists, including political agitators), takes a leading role in the Indian National Congress (a non-governmental Indian quasi-advisory body), supports his Muslim country-men in their efforts related to the Khilafat Movement (which concerned the status of the Sultan of Turkey following World War I), takes over the running of two political weeklies, and throughout this period continues his experiments with diet, fasting, prayer and educating children, his own and that of other families living in the ashrams.

Gandhi's numerous experiments come into intense internal conflict as reflected in the last sixteen chapters of the autobiography. First, he contracts dysentery during the extremely strenuous process of going, often on foot, from one village to another, exhorting his younger countrymen that by volunteering to enlist in the Indian army to support the British in World War I, they will demonstrate their loyalty to the Crown and thereby show their readiness to assume greater control over their own destinies when India becomes a self-governing dominion within the Commonwealth.

Refusing medicine, milk and beef tea as going against his dietary vows, Gandhi's condition deteriorates until he believes he is "Near Death's Door" (Chapter XXVIII). His wife and doctor argue that taking goat's milk, as opposed to the milk of cows (which are considered sacred animals and which Gandhi believes are widely mistreated), should not contradict his self-imposed dietary restrictions. He does not agree, because he believes in adhering to the spirit of a vow, not just to its letter. However, if he wants to recover and devote himself to protesting the pending Rowlatt Act, he must do something for his health, even if it offends his sense of moral purity. Gandhi relents, begins consuming goat milk, undergoes an operation for fissures of the bowel, and survives.

Meanwhile, the Rowlatt bill becomes an act, despite strong objection by the Indian National Congress. Gandhi then conceives of a radically new type of protest. He convinces his political associates to call a nationwide *hartal*, a work-stoppage day during which millions of people go to bathe in sacred rivers or the sea, engaging in fasting and prayer, as they demonstrate unprecedented unity against the tyranny of the Raj.

The day of civil disobedience is an impressive success. However, violence breaks out in several major cities, either because of the interdiction of the police and military or because the crowds become inflamed and break out in a destructive rage. At first enthralled by the success of the *hartal*, Gandhi is disheartened and depressed when he hears about the violence that erupted from what was supposed to be a well-controlled enactment of *satyagraha* and *ahimsa*. He comes to the conclusion that he has made a huge miscalculation.

In Part 5, Chapter XXXIII, he explains his mistake. "Before one can be fit for the practice of civil disobedience one must have rendered a willing and respectful obedience to the state laws," Gandhi writes. With considerable psychological insight into the process of moral development, he realizes that for the uneducated masses obedience to laws is not a matter of intelligence and free will but simply due to fear of punishment. If people have little sense of their "sacred duty," then when called upon to engage in civil disobedience, it's as if they have been given permission to express their anger through any means they choose. Gandhi sadly concludes: "I had called on people to launch upon civil disobedience before they qualified themselves for it, and this mistake seemed to me of Himalayan magnitude."

Following the Rowlatt *satyagraha*, Gandhi vows to discontinue the movement of non-violent civil disobedience and to explore other means of protest. One of the first he hits upon is the *khadi* movement – teaching people how to spin, card and make their own cloth. He throws himself into using his weekly publications to better educate the literate public, and through them the poorest and most illiterate, about the spiritual meanings and importance of preparing themselves for self-rule through developing their own capacity for personal self-rule, what we would call moral autonomy.

Gradually, Gandhi realizes that at this stage of his life, having come close to death several times and still feeling exhausted and frail, he needs to devote himself to a period of self-reflection. But now he is besieged on all sides by people who seek the blessings of a holy man (*darshan*) or advice about everything from marital conflicts to labor disputes.

Gandhi cannot see his way forward. He grows doubtful about his ability to mediate growing conflicts between Hindu and Moslem, as well as between the political moderates and the more extreme groups that favor the forceful overthrow of the British, no matter the cost in lives. It is just at this moment that he is arrested and sentenced to a term in prison. The final unnumbered chapter, "Farewell," does not mention his incarceration, since the autobiography establishes this context in the Introduction. Rather Gandhi asks his reader to "join with me in prayer to the God of Truth that He may grant me the boon of Ahimsa in mind, word and deed."

Gandhi needs the support of his countrymen if further steps toward liberating India from British rule and preparing for the establishment of a morally enlightened country are to be accomplished. The challenges ahead are huge: the eradication of the caste system, peace between Hindus and Moslems, and economic self-sufficiency through the development of appropriate technology such as the spinning wheel – which would later be symbolized on the flag of India.

GANDHI'S USE OF AUTOBIOGRAPHY

Acting as a servant to one's community by embracing a set of hypothetical truths, and then seeking to discover whether these truths can withstand insults, physical abuse, incarceration, legal battles, betrayals, matrimonial strife, racism, hunger, illness and the temptations of fame, is not for the faint of heart. In his effort to teach by example and to reveal personal weakness, moments of despair and ignoble actions – as well as by bearing witness to the benefits of right living – Gandhi makes himself a kind of Indian Socrates, at least the Socrates we encounter in Plato's early *Dialogues*, such as the Apology, Meno and Phaedo. Like Socrates, he is brought to trial (more than once) and accused of misleading not only the youth of India but also fomenting rebellion among its adults. And, like Socrates, he uses the courtroom to both justify the purity of his intentions (which, for Gandhi, were to improve the moral conditions of both colonizer and colonized) while insisting that, if found guilty, he should be given the maximum punishment.

Gandhi's admissions of failure to live up to his own moral convictions, and his attribution to a divine power of escape from close encounters with infidelity, dishonesty, self-deception and near-death experiences, place Gandhi in the Augustinian tradition of the confessional autobiographer. Both write about childhood pranks, stealing, temptations of the flesh and other moral transgressions. Augustine practically invented the self-revealing personal narrative. We know Socrates' speeches and life-history reflections through others, especially his most famous student, Plato, who makes Socrates the main character of his *Dialogues*. Both Socrates and Augustine stand at the font of the Western autobiographical tradition – a tradition to which the Easterner Gandhi does not belong.

In the Introduction to his autobiography, Gandhi acknowledges sharp criticism from "God-fearing friends" that writing an autobiography "is a practice peculiar to the West." They did not think it was a good idea, especially because Gandhi might appear to have come too much under Western influences – precisely the Western self-aggrandizing way of looking at the world, a kind of despotic egoism that has had such unfortunate consequences for Indians and other Asian peoples.

Gandhi counters this concern by assuring these friends (and his millions of readers) that he is not writing a "real autobiography," but rather recounting his experiments, which are what his inner life has been all about. His story, Gandhi implies, is only of value to others insofar as it exemplifies certain principles of right living. Moreover, he is not going to focus on his experiments in the "political field," which are already well known, but on his experiments in the "spiritual field," which are known only to himself, even though they have been the source of his powers in the political arena. His use of the autobiographical form will then not reflect self-praise (by implication, the tendency exhibited in the Westerners' autobiographies) but humility, since through this writing he will discover and reveal both his hopes and his limitations.

The overarching theme of the autobiography, says Gandhi, is what he has been "striving and pining to achieve these thirty years," which is "self-realization, to see God face to face, to attain Moksha," understood as release from the cycle of birth and death. For most Hindu believers, dedication to attaining Moksha would have implied a world-renouncing life lived in prayer and meditation, completely free of such secular concerns as activities in the courts of law, political congresses or parliamentary chambers.

But Gandhi strove to exemplify a different approach to Moksha by aiming, through the political and legal process, to improve the lot of his countrymen as well as of humankind in general, while renouncing hatred, anger, envy, pride and self-degradation. Through the brief and simple stories of his autobiography, Gandhi does nothing less than attempt a fundamental reinterpretation and transformation of the Indian spiritual tradition. He does this by giving new meanings (though, he would argue, recovering original ones) to ancient beliefs, tenets, sacred texts and traditions. He attempts this without seeming to judge and certainly not belittle them, but rather to present himself as their most obedient follower.

By positioning himself in the autobiography as the humble narrator of the events in the life of a truth-seeking public servant, Gandhi is able to communicate his life lessons. These include diet (vegetarian and fruitarian), self-control (including celibacy beyond reproduction, *brahmachharya*), universal love (non-violence or *ahimsa*), the evils and irrationality of the caste system, personal hygiene, pretentiousness and lack of self-esteem as reflected by inauthenticity in dress, simplicity of lifestyle, non-attachment to things such as clothing, jewelry and money, adherence to spiritual practice (meditation, yoga, prayers, recitation of sacred hymns and poems). Other lessons include faithfulness to one's conscience, loyalty to that which deserves it, scrupulous honesty, respect for authority (even when conducting civil disobedience), politeness, the making and upholding of vows, and many other guiding principles that were part of his truth experiments. He says directly what other philosophical autobiographers infer: "What is possible for one is possible for all."

Curiously, Gandhi comes back to the issue of adopting the Westerner's autobiographical form in Part 4, Chapter XI, more than midway through the work, where he addresses the subject of "Intimate European Contacts."

At least a year has passed since he began writing the weekly portions of the autobiography, when suddenly Gandhi feels the need to return to justifying the purpose of his project. He reiterates that the order and logic of the autobiography were not planned and that all along he has been guided by the way "the Spirit" moves him in the moment. That "Spirit," says Gandhi, is "the world's faith in God" as he has experienced it. And although he has not yet "known Him," that has been his purpose, as reflected by the experiments described in the autobiography.

Gandhi adds, "Writing it [the autobiography] is itself one of the experiments with truth." Gandhi even raises the possibility that maybe he should halt this project, reminding readers that it was not his idea in the first place. He insists that he was encouraged by other *Satyagraha* (co-leaders in the "truth-force" movement) to "provide some comfort and food for reflection for my co-workers." So really, if he has made a mistake, "they must share the blame." Still, since he has not heard any "prohibition from the voice within," he must continue with what he has started "unless it is proved to be morally wrong."

Gandhi repeats all these qualifications as he acknowledges that his narrative cannot possibly serve as a history of the times, since he has needed to be selective in what to include or exclude. Who knows, he asks, when in the midst of something momentous, what for later generations will be judged significant and what minor or irrelevant? Gandhi will just have to take his chances and do the best he can. Again, this entire discussion precedes Gandhi's account of how he took various Englishmen into his trust and even into his household, some proving themselves faithful friends and others disappointing ones.

GANDHI AND HUMAN DEVELOPMENT

Gandhi's realization, reported at the end of his autobiography, was that the vast majority of his countrymen had not reached a necessary stage of moral reasoning to responsibly exercise civil disobedience because of their lack of education and spiritual readiness, their decades of passivity toward political life under foreign rule, and because of superstitions and certain religious and cultural traditions that discouraged them from thinking for themselves. Of his countrymen, Gandhi says they were "like children in political matters," children who "do not understand the principle that the public good is also one's own good" (CW, V, 313).

Reframing Gandhi's assessment in more contemporary psychological terms, we draw on the work of psychologist Jean Piaget on stages of intellectual development and that of Lawrence Kohlberg on moral development, By Gandhi's own characterization, the vast majority of Indian peoples tended to approach cognitive and moral issues on the basis of concrete terms, rather than grasping situations and issues through a framework of more abstract conceptual understanding.

In Kohlberg's theory of the stages of moral development, what Gandhi observes would be equivalent to the obedience- and punishment-driven "pre-conventional level" of moral reasoning, which is egocentric in lacking recognition that others' points of view are different and possibly as valid as one's own. In this mind frame people are more likely to pay deference to superior power and prestige rather than a principle of moral values. Others of his countrymen may have attained stage two of this pre-conventional level, which reflects a "what's in it for me" position of self-interest. It's only in Kohlberg's Level 2, "conventional" moral reasoning, that individuals grasp the importance of interpersonal social norms and acknowledge the intrinsic importance of law and order as necessary for maintaining societal functioning.

If Gandhi was going to mobilize millions of Indian people in order to bring the British domination to an end, he had to rethink his approach. Otherwise, mass civil disobedience could quickly turn into murder and mayhem. He would, however, have a completely different idea of the ultimate goal of moral development from that of Western developmental psychologists who put a high premium on autonomy – learning to think for oneself using rational principles.

Thanks to his upbringing, which included considerable contact with adults from diverse social and religious backgrounds, and his education, including the three years of preparation for the bar in London, and owing also to his seemingly innate disposition as a person rigorously committed to speaking the truth, Gandhi exhibits Kohlberg's highest stage of reasoning, the "post-conventional." One who attain this developmental level is able to grasp universal ethical principles as internal to one's conscience, even when the individual's perspective may conflict with established social views. Kohlberg frequently cited Gandhi as among those admirable famous individuals (e.g., Jesus, Buddha, Rev. Martin Luther King Jr., Dag Hammarskjöld) who consistently demonstrated stage six moral reasoning.

Though Gandhi would exhibit qualities of post-conventional moral autonomy, his aim was closer to a hypothetical stage Kohlberg alluded to late in his career – an additional, though difficult to document, stage seven that Kohlberg described as a "morality of cosmic orientation." Here Kohlberg comes closer to Gandhi's way of thinking. Kohlberg allowed the possibility that a post-conventional moral thinker might ask the meta-ethical question, "But why should one be moral?" This type of question goes beyond the concern, "What should one do? How should one act?" The individual is now able to ask about the very foundations of ethical evaluation, such as where the distinction between good and evil comes from. Kohlberg wanted to consider the impact of religiosity on moral development and observed that among some highly evolved individuals who had attained stage six there was still a movement toward what he called "cosmic belonging." Accordingly, the individual, having attained a high degree of moral autonomy, nevertheless seeks to discover his or her place in the larger cosmos of nature, history and the transcendently divine. All along, this seems to have been the goal to which Gandhi aspired.

As a corollary, Gandhi's reading of ancient Hindu religious text is both non-literal and non-dogmatic. He believed that sacred poems like the *Mahabharata* (of which the Gita was one small part) were not intended as historical narratives but served as allegories pointing to certain truths about life. Sacred Hindu texts may reflect corrupting influences over time, may contain context-limiting edicts and prohibitions that contradict more contemporary values and ideas of morality. Gandhi takes it upon himself to pick and choose what he finds valuable and what seems harmful and immoral. He asserts it is the individual's responsibility to test the credibility of religious revelations "on the anvil of truth with the hammer of compassion" (CW, 24:320).

Gandhi has already brilliantly understood the need and importance of bringing the campaign for sovereignty to the common people if India is to become a democracy governed through mass public participation rather than a modernized state ruled by a tiny educated and privileged elite. He was able to discover the means of taking some of the most common and familiar acts of everyday Indian life, such as prayer, ritual purification, fasting, spinning (though this had become a lost art that had to be relearned), simplification of diet and possessions, and humility and modesty in manners, and to reframe these acts so that they symbolized through tangible behaviors the process of both self- and national liberation.

Given this context and the timing of the autobiography in the independence struggle, it's not surprising that Gandhi's personal narrative would contain not only an account of his spiritual yearnings and practices – placed before the reader in an attempt to exemplify one path to a virtuous life – but accounts that describe tangible experiences and events, for the most part unadorned by abstract, conceptual philosophical reflections. Gandhi is well aware of the gap between his life philosophy and outlook and that of the vast majority of his countrymen. He aims to close that gap. Therefore, his teachings must, like his choice of symbolic protests, speak in concrete terms.

In a few years, following publication of the autobiography, Gandhi will lead the famous 240-mile long "salt march" in which his followers, each carrying a copy of the Gita, will arrive at the sea shore and begin to harvest salt in protest over and in direct violation of the government-imposed salt tax. This brilliant choice of a simple and yet profoundly symbolic act would represent the great depth of Gandhi's religious and philosophical understanding of human affairs under his concept that truth is identical to divinely given laws. The more theoretical and philosophical commentaries and testimony to widespread literary and religious influences can be found in Gandhi's other writings, especially in *Hind Swaraj*, the 1910 manifesto of the independence movement. The key to understanding how Gandhi valued but diverged from the ideals of moral autonomy as the apex of human development lies in his distinction between duties and rights, body-centered versus spirit- or soul-centered ethics, and modern versus ancient societies.

THE NATURE OF DUTY

Gandhi was well aware that *dharma*, the Hindu sense of duty, was the foundation of classical Indian social philosophy. The two social institutions that depended on *dharma* were the four social castes (*varna*) – brahmin, kshatria, vaisya and shudra – and the four stages of life (*ashramas*) – student, householder, retiree and renouncer. Both the *Rig Veda* and the *Bhagavad-Gita* identified and approved of the caste system. Social position, occupation, obligations, and age-appropriate behavior were intimately connected with caste and life stage.

These ancient categories had the benefit of sustaining a harmonious social order as, in a sense, each caste and life-stage had its part and purpose in the make-up of the whole. But over time, as Gandhi was well aware, caste and life-stage differences led to sharply defined social distinctions and injustices – especially with regard to the caste of the Untouchables. Gandhi took several different positions regarding *varna*. Around the time of writing the autobiography (1922-24) he still attempted to interpret the caste system as emphasizing the harmony-in-diversity ideal of classes that suggested each had its place and importance that one was not better than another.

However, by 1935, he had reached a different conclusion. Searching to establish principles of egalitarianism, Gandhi argued that, as the title of one of his articles asserted, "Caste Has to Go." Gandhi argued that the caste system simply no longer fit into an age of individual rights and freedoms. Traditional prohibitions concerning inter-caste marriage, inter-caste dining, and limited choice of labor were antiquated and obsolete and conflicted with moral reasoning. Rather than doing away with caste entirely, ironically and paradoxically Gandhi proposed that the four be reduced to one.

Gandhi knew that not all duties derived from caste and life stage. General duties that transcended caste included non-violence, truthfulness, honesty (e.g. refraining from theft) and temperance, or control over one's senses. Gandhi championed these more universal duties and asserted that they were a natural part of the "quality of the soul," to be found in all human beings (CW, 32: 11). Gandhi hoped that the virtues would be imbued in civic nationalism and would replace the caste system of duties. The ethic of caste would be replaced by the ethic of rights.

From the very beginning of his public life, Gandhi was an advocate of human rights, first in South Africa in defending the Indian immigrants against laws prohibiting shared use of public spaces (such as sidewalks), the right to acquire, keep and dispose of private property, to vote in local elections, to travel without special passes and curfews, and to contract valid marriages in accordance with the rites of the Hindu, Muslim and Zoroastrian religions. In India he continued his campaign for civil rights on behalf of various worker and peasant organizations in locales across India and then broader freedom of speech rights infringed on by the Rowlatt Act.

It would seem, then, that for Gandhi rights would replace, or at least supplement, duties in the emerging independent Indian state. This, however, turned out not to be the case. Rights might replace duties dictated by caste and life stage, but not natural duties. Gandhi was well aware of Western sources for the theory of rights. He had read Hobbes, according to whom human beings were essentially possessive individualists who existed in a state of conflict with one another (the infamous "war of all against all"). So the securing of rights became the foundation for the establishment of the state. Duty, for Hobbes, was secondary and consisted of the individual's obligation to obey the laws of the state.

Gandhi rejected this account of human nature and of the primacy of rights as first and foremost self-protective. Instead, he argued that "natural dharma," that is a sense of duty that is an intrinsic part of the soul, not the dharma that derives from caste and life stage, contains the germ of moral growth. Just as one is duty-bound to act non-violently, truthfully, honestly and temperately, so individuals have the right not to be attacked, deceived, cheated or abused. In Gandhi's schema, dharma precedes rights.

Pointing to the British Reform Act of 1832, the American War of Independence and the French revolution, Gandhi asserted that the Western tradition included numerous examples of the use of violence to promote social change and the securing of rights. However, Gandhi insisted that rights secured by violence would always require additional acts of violence to sustain or extend them. And as long as societies were based on the ideal of individual acquisition of wealth and property, as long as greed was only restrained by rights (duties remaining weakly developed), a society would remain a battleground of contested wills and special interest groups.

Had he lived long enough, an example that Gandhi might have pointed to was the African-American civil rights movement. Though led in part by M.L. King Jr., who aimed to follow Gandhian principles of non-violent resistance, the civil rights movement nevertheless turned into race rebellions (so-called "riots"), street battles, assassinations, lynching and other forms of violence before major changes in federal and state laws brought equal freedoms (at least on paper) to the black minority. Though *satyagraha*, the soul-force of non-violent disobedience, brought India to the brink of national independence, that independence was also marked by the partition of India into Hindu and Muslim states, which resulted in an extremely violent upheaval that led to the slaughter of an estimated one million people.

Gandhi's concept of the relationship between duties and rights and his notion of the Indian tradition as distinct from that of Western nations, of modern societies versus ancient ones, grew out of his ontological theory of human being. The West, Gandhi asserted, was body-centered and materialistic, while the East was spirit-centered and non-materialistic. The underlying basis of law in so-called Western civilizations was the separate individualism and wants-driven character of a flawed view of human nature derived from the perception of the body as a self-contained, self-preserving physical unit. The physicality of the body became, by analogy, the private spatiality of the individual. Such an ontological basis for establishing human rights tended to direct a spiritual orientation into a quest for knowledge, which, in turn, evolved as a form of power useful as an instrument of control over nature and other individuals.

Hence, Western civilization was propelled by greed, which led to an economy that promoted limitless wants so that an endless stream of products could be pumped into the marketplace. Lacking the duty of self-discipline, Western civilization advanced a commoditized life style of acquisition, self-aggrandizement, possessive individualism and jaded appetites. It utilized the industrial and bureaucratic means of ever more rapid and efficient mass production. To Gandhi it was therefore not surprising that Western civilization – of which, at that time, the British Empire seemed to stand at the pinnacle – generated the kind of colonial imperialism that by violent means subdued and exploited other peoples and lands.

AN ALTERNATIVE FUTURE

The future, progress, speed and dynamic movement that are the hallmarks of Western civilization were in sharp contrast to what Gandhi viewed as the essence of traditional India: first, *satya*, truth in the sense of reverence for the eternal and unchanging in the midst of change, and respect for the natural world and all its creatures as well as inorganic complexity; second, *swadeshi,* not exactly nationalism but the sense of belonging to one's unique cultural and historical community and to the larger amalgam of such communities that made up the Indian civilization; and third, *ahimsa,* the non-violent relationship to all things including observance of animal rights, about which Gandhi had strong views.

If contemporary readers detect harbingers of the ideology of the modern ecology movement with its themes of biodiversity, human kinship with rather than superiority over nature, environmental protection, and so on, they would not be off the mark. Gandhi's ontological view of the universe was just such an orientation and value structure, based as it was not on a hierarchical image of man at the apex of a pyramid with the organic natural world below and the inorganic below that. Rather, Gandhi viewed the cosmos as a complex series of overlapping spheres. The cosmic spirit informed and structured the universe, therefore all creation was divine, an interdependent system that formed a coherent whole since it shared a common spiritual essence.

Norwegian philosopher Arne Naess (1912-2009) drew from Gandhi's moral and ontological insights to found in 1973 what he first termed "deep ecology" to distinguish it from what he believed was a shallow ecological movement based narrowly on environmental protection efforts and coexisting with the established structure of a consumer-driven economy and urbanized, centralized society. Echoing Gandhi, Naess argued what was needed was a reform of basic human relations with nature. In his landmark book, *Ecology, Community and Lifestyle* (1976/1989), Naess latched onto Gandhi's concept of *sarvodaya,* "to the best for all," a social policy that "emphasized the importance of decentralized industrial life and extensive self-sufficiency in India's five hundred thousand villages."

Gandhi was a role model for Naess, who quit teaching philosophy after thirty years at the University of Oslo to become an ecological activist. With other environmentalists, he chained himself to rocks in front of the Mardal waterfall, successfully lobbying the Norwegian government to abandon plans for a dam on the fjord that feeds the falls.

TIME AND MEMORY

Gandhi's autobiography is written in an uncomplicated, almost conversational style. The narrative is untroubled by issues of the status of the remembered past, the power of language to communicate certain inner truths, or of the mysteries of time that may emerge when a person tries to see him or herself in the context of nature and the cosmos. Gandhi, however, knows that his readers have grown up with cultural and religious beliefs about the four-stage cycle of life and what is appropriate at different stages. Some would also be familiar with the Hindu mythology of the cycle of time and know that they were living in the "black age" or *kali juga*, the violence and ego-led worst segment in the 4,320,000-year cycle of time, of which it occupies about one-tenth.

With his acute sensitivity to injustice and his personal commitment to leading a life of moral purity in order to attain *moksha*, Gandhi had what might seem to be a paradoxical concept and experience of time and memory. Like his interpretation of the messages of the *Bhagavad-Gita* ("Song of the Blessed Lord") as legendary tales of guidance, his own "song" was intended to serve as a similar way-finding tale of trial and error, vow and temptation, passion and purge. Though influenced by his studies of Christianity and particularly moved by the Sermon on the Mount, Gandhi accepted neither the exclusive redemption path of Christianity nor belief in Jesus as the sole "son of God." He therefore could not have accepted Christianity's eschatology of the "second coming" and "end of days" idea of the culmination of time and history. Rather, Gandhi was oriented to the notion of endlessly repeating cycles of time coupled with the possibility that an individual could pursue a morally perfected life that might free him or her from the cycle of reincarnation.

Gandhi, like the *Gita*'s Prince Arjuna, is a player in a vast cosmic myth whose temporalized and localized context is 20th century India under the oppressive rule of foreign invaders. Unlike other Indian independence leaders, Gandhi's goal is not to see his country head in the direction of other former colonial societies – becoming highly centralized and industrialized. He abhorred seeing his country turn into a culture in which individual freedom becomes the quest for material acquisition and wealth. And he rejected what he considers an illusion of progress. Instead, Gandhi champions a free, democratic India, tapping into the vast creativity and spiritual character of its people and inviting their participation at all levels, in making the country a healthier, more humane, morally righteous, village-based society with respectful treatment of the natural environment. Gandhi advocates for a country whose citizens are attuned to timeless spiritual truths that, freely chosen and adapted, call for religious and caste tolerance, non-violence as part of a complete lifestyle, universal education of all children, equality of the sexes and pride in one's ancient legacy.

Some of these goals, especially in the area of human rights, were accomplished in the post-Gandhi period of Indian history. But, quite dramatically, not others such as caste discrimination, conflict between Hindus and Muslims, poverty and government corruption (for more on this topic, see Ramachandra Guha's 2007 book, *India After Gandhi: The History of the World's Largest Democracy*.)

WHAT WOULD GANDHI DO?

Many aspects of Gandhi's chosen way of life resonate in postmodern secular societies like the United States. Concern for both a virtuous and a healthy way of eating is reflected in the growing ranks of vegetarians, vegans and followers of macrobiotic diets. The revival of the local farm, small-scale organic farming and food coops, as well as arrangements for buying directly from farmers, all echo Gandhi's belief in the wholesomeness of the rural way of life and a decentralized economy that can adapt to modern conditions. Spiritual communities, many of them based on Buddhist and Hindu precepts, have sprung up across the country. While there are communitarian groups that aim to retain traditional non-mechanized tools and equipment, such as the Amish and the Mennonites, the rising popularity of handmade clothing, fabrics, utensils, kitchenware, toys, furniture and other items that had only been available through industrialized mass production, also echoes the Gandhian faith in the dignity and character of manual labor.

It is hard to imagine popular pursuit of some of Gandhi's other tenets such as the renouncing of sexual pleasures, culinary delights and leisure activities, and the intensive practice of yoga, meditation, fasting, prayer and devoted service to others carried out with the greatest of humility and free of the covert intent of converting others to one's religious faith.

FIELDWORK AND REFLECTIVE WRITING

Consider fasting one day a week if you are in sufficiently good health. Try this for one month. Be sure to keep yourself well hydrated. Keep a simple log of your experience, noting changes in your feeling of hunger over the course of the day. To what extent does this act of self-deprivation affect your sense of awareness, physical desires, attention span, sensitivity towards others and use of time? You may want to take the dollar equivalent of savings in purchase of food from a grocery store or restaurant and make this a gift to a favorite charity (including your local food bank). Avoid breaking your fast with the consumption of a large meal. Rather, take some light refreshments first and gradually move toward a more typical meal.

Making vows is one of the ways that Gandhi disciplined his mind, body and spirit. He made vows to uphold family and caste traditions. For example, he vowed to his mother that he would follow the precepts of Hinduism regarding diet (e.g. abstaining from eating meat or consuming alcohol). Some vows were about what should and should not be eaten, others concerned abstinence from pleasures of sexuality and sensuality, and yet others related to fasting, prayer and honest conduct in business.

Historically, vows have been a serious matter, as reflected in the Jewish Day of Atonement prayer, the *Kol Nidre*, in which the congregants recite together a prayer to release them from vows made to other people (not God) in the previous year that are no longer appropriate or binding. Couples of many faith traditions recite wedding vows that are either pre-scribed by the standard marriage liturgy or are crafted by the partners to suit their particular values and situation. What other occasions call for vows? Vows and values seem to go hand in hand. Make a list of your most important values. Next, formulate these values as if they had originated as self-guiding vows. Describe how you have attempted to live up to the requirement of these vows as well as to determining that certain vows were no longer meaningful or beneficial.

READER'S GUIDE

Most readers, even if unfamiliar with the history of modern India, will enjoy Gandhi's *Autobiography: the Story of My Experiments with Truth*, which is widely available in paperback and available online at http://www.mkgandhi.org/autobio/autobio.htm. But an equally good starting point is his 1910 manifesto-like essay, *Hind Swaraj*, Indian Home Rule (accessible at http://www.mkgandhi.org/swarajya/coverpage.htm) that offers readers Gandhi's analysis of the factors that led to the British domination of India and of the injustices practiced in both South Africa and on the Indian subcontinent against people of color. Anthony J. Parel's 1997 edited version, which also contains an introductory essay and supplementary writings such as the Gandhi-Tolstoy correspondence, is the best English language version available (2002).

Raja Rao's 1938 novel, *Kanthapura*, beautifully and powerfully depicts the effects of the civil disobedience movement in a small village in south India. Among biographies in English, Judith M. Brown's *Gandhi: Prisoner of Hope* (1989) is accessible, well researched and insightful. Readers who want to go deeper into Gandhi's philosophical and theological influences will enjoy Anthony J. Parel's *Gandhi's Philosophy and the Quest for Harmony* (2009). A more recent work that details some of Gandhi's weak-nesses and foibles as well as assessing how well or poorly post-colonial India absorbed Gandhi's philosophy is Joseph Lelyveld's *Great Soul, Mahatma Gandhi and His Struggle with India* (2011).

For readers interested in understanding Arne Naess' discovery and application of Gandhi's ontology as relevant to the environmental movement, see his *Ecology, Community and Lifestyle* (translated by David Rothenberg, 1989).

11

UNITING CONTRARIES

The 19th century American poet, orator and philosopher, Ralph Waldo Emerson, speaking about the individual thinker's unique challenge, articulated a daring assumption, one that also underlies the fundamental premise of the philosophical autobiography. In his 1837 speech, "The American Scholar," Emerson praised thinkers, poets and artists who have the courage to "go down into the secrets" of their own minds, for in doing so they are the most able to "descend into the secrets of all minds." Pushing this truth-in-subjectivity proposition even further, Emerson exclaimed that when this soul-searcher "dives into his privatest, secretest presentiments, to his wonder he finds, this is the most acceptable, most public and universally true." As if to test his hypothesis, Emerson projects himself across the podium into the minds of his Phi Beta Kappa Society audience. Is not the truth of one's inner life, true for all? And he hears the audience members' affirming response: "This is my music; this is myself."

Readers of autobiographies as divergent in form and content as those of Augustine, John Stuart Mill and Simone de Beauvoir may or may not affirm of each or perhaps of any, "this is myself." Few of us have had conversations with our mothers concerning the taste of eternity and the structure of memory, not many have chatted with their fathers about the merits of a teleologically-based ethics, and even fewer have carried on discussions long into the night with a lover about whether gender should be factored into considerations of ontology.

But as for "this is my music," these same readers may discover in philosophical autobiographies themes that evoke or articulate their own engagements with philosophical issues, ideas and outlooks and with parallel experiences that have played a decisive role in their lives. This is because philosophical autobiographers tap their unique life experiences to offer a conceptual framework that aims toward more general truths captured in a theory of human nature, an epistemology, an ethical system, and in some cases a theology. We connect with them also because they engage in the deeply philosophical issues of everyday life.

In inviting readers to consider the plausibility of their philosophical positions – by describing the path they took to get there – philosophical autobiographers open portals through which we are invited to follow. Like the Malkovichian transformation with which we began this exploration, philosophical autobiographies beckon us into the life narrative of a particular theorist and thereby into the personal and social world conjured up by the author.

Descending into the secrets of one's mind could mean uncovering hidden motives, encountering disturbing doubts, or searching to recover lost or repressed memories. What Emerson doesn't say is that this "going down" is a lifelong process not a singular event. What is "privatest" and "secretest" in one period may be superseded in another. There is not one but, as Kierkegaard put it, many "stages on life's way." The inclination and ability to make sense of the content of these stages does not usually occur until the second half of life. The motives for a life review process leading to taking up the pen or, today, word processor may vary.

The influential 19th century philosopher, Schopenhauer, speculating on what he believed were universal stages of human life, presented a number of compelling analogies. Schopenhauer said the first half of one's life is like the contents of a book, the second half, the footnotes; the first half like the front side of a quilt, the second, the reverse, showing how the pieces are assembled into a whole. In the first half of life we yearn to have exciting experiences, but in the second half we long to understand them. What the second half of life teaches us, said Schopenhauer, is that the quest for happiness is an illusory one that only leads to suffering and disappointment. However, if we have the strength to detach ourselves from this quest, said the stoical philosopher, we may gain something in return – a contemplative state that allows us to "see life as a whole."

That is what Simone de Beauvoir alludes to when she explains her motivation to write autobiographically at age fifty. As mentioned in Chapter 7, she hopes to find in her life story a "pattern which the future seems unlikely to modify very much." And to detect "just what the pattern might reveal." No stoic, she is not about to relinquish pursuing political causes, love affairs, or research and writing projects. For however much suffering these "projects" may cause, they also bring her joy and a sense of meaning and purpose. But she is determined to see the unifying pattern, her life as a whole, even if, as she admits, it turns out to be a history filled with mistakes and illusions. That is what the second half of life offers us – a chance to glimpse larger and more persistent meanings in the pattern of the whole. And while de Beauvoir was a great champion for individual self-becoming and personal initiative, she affirmed Emerson's claim. What was revealed in her unifying pattern could "illuminate" the lives of others.

Given the necessary perspective, the philosophers who wrote the autobiographies we have considered did so when they reached life's second half, though that midpoint has shifted over the centuries. Jung assumed, optimistically and biblically, a 70-year life expectancy (it was actually 59 in Switzerland in the 1930s). In an article entitled "The Soul and Death," published in 1934, he marked age 35 as the midpoint of what he called the "parabola of life." Around the transition to midlife, claimed Jung, we begin to shift from focus on the external or outward aspects of life (e.g. pursuits of education, career, marriage, childrearing) to ones that are more inward (e.g. sense of meaning and purpose, of one's place in the context of history, culture and cosmos).

Jung's reference point, "the secret hour of life's midday," is more qualitative than quantitative, more attitudinal than chronological. For many of our autobiographers, the threshold to the second half would have come much earlier than it does today when average life expectancy at birth in post-industrial societies is close to eighty. Nietzsche and Kierkegaard died in their early forties but wrote their major autobiographical works close to the ends of their lives. Nietzsche, ever the exception, began writing autobiographically when he was fourteen and produced several youthful narratives. This shows that the inclination to review one's life on paper does not necessarily come at midlife or old age though the purpose of reflecting on one's experiences may be quite different in youth than decades later. And it is not uncommon for autobiographers to request that their written life stories not be made public until after their deaths, as was the case with J.S. Mill, Kierkegaard and Jung.

Still, to have the perspective and the skill to write a moving account of one's life and ideas and to do so with the intent of involving the reader in the process of discovery that requires a considerable degree of acquired literary skill, self-knowledge and detachment that may come with age and experience.

Anyone who has undertaken to write autobiographically knows that the process can be exciting, daunting and perplexing. The philosophically minded authors we have explored in this book certainly express all three characteristics. They remind us that the intentionally remembered past can be like a newly discovered box of old photos. Sorting through the pictures, we realize there is so much that we have forgotten. We may discover causes and connections that had earlier eluded us, and recognize the influences of historical events, social trends, and even fads and fashions in which we had, wittingly or unwittingly, participated. Looking at the photos, we may sometimes wonders: was I fully awake "back then" or did I inhabit some kind of semi-conscious dream state?

The reflective autobiographer discovers additional challenges: How to distinguish between what we remember of the past and what we imagine to have taken place, what the original experiences meant to us when we first had them and how, in retrospect, those meanings become amended, and how the developmental stages in our lives (with their psycho-physical challenges and different life tasks) influence our earlier and then subsequent interpretations.

To illustrate this latter point, consider a simple exercise. Recall how you felt about your mother and/or father when you were, say, five, twelve, seventeen, twenty-five, and so on. The child's point of view is likely far different from that of the subsequent young adult parent or even grandparent because, at advancing ages, we have different life experiences and reference points from which to understand our parents and the influences that helped to shape their lives. When we start seeing how their parents and even grandparents influenced our parents, we have arrived at a radically different perspective than that of our teenage self. And when we take in historical and cultural influences, we gain even greater perspective.

Those who enjoy writing as a means of reentering past situations know that the writing process can often overtake conscious thinking, producing many surprising insights when long neglected or suppressed memories are recovered. We may find ourselves writing furiously about what had formerly seemed incidental details – a book one happened to read as a student, a teacher's comment on a term paper, a fleeting infatuation, a moment at a funeral, a melody at a wedding, some chance words of encouragement from a boss or mentor. These now take on heightened meaning.

We may also harbor the assumption that by courageously seeking to plumb the depths of memory, daring ourselves to be ruthlessly honest in our explorations of the remembered past, that we will finally, as it were, get to the bottom of things. What were our motives in certain conflictive situations? Did we do right by Friend X or Cousin Y? There is, I suspect, no such bottom or ultimate interpretation, rather the pursuit, metaphorically speaking, is like a spiral. While we may expand our understanding of the personal past (which includes the life we share with others), gaining fresh insights on scenes we have probably come around to more than once before (hence, the widening curve), we can never escape the way in which our consciousness is situated in some contextual present. So, unless we are fixated on beating the same interpretative drum over and over (the flat circular path), there will always be new insights and revised meanings. Which is all to the good since a crucial part of wisdom in later life is flexibility.

In addition, the tools we consciously and unconsciously apply to the task of writing our way through our recollections are very likely ones we have come to prefer. Our orientation may be influenced by academic training, personal attraction to a mode of interpretative discourse (e.g., a psychoanalytic framework, a religious perspective, a political or ideological viewpoint), or through the influence of other autobiographical frameworks (e.g., feminist, mystic, postmodernist). So here we come full circle to the Malkovichian challenge of attempting to break free of the limits of the self's interpreting of the self. In the movie, John Malkovich insists on taking a turn plummeting through his own mind tunnel, only to discover the shock of solipsism – that everyone he meets looks and acts like a little Malkovich; everyone and everything is a projection of the Malkovichian personality.

Many of these issues have been touched upon in earlier chapters as we explored how each philosophical autobiographer both encountered and sought to work through epistemological, metaphysical and ethical questions triggered by the process of engaging in the self-narrating discourse. Under the metaphorical theme "places in the mind," spaces of self-change have been our major focus. We have been particularly attentive to how each philosopher finds a way to account for and characterize his or her self-transformative experience. The indirectly implied value of reading philosophers' autobiographies is that we can capture something from the philosopher's paradigm of self-change to apply to our own lives. This, however, presupposes that we feel impelled to seek some kind of self-change.

We can always be better persons. So goes the culturally pervasive theme of American transcendentalism with its emphasis on moral perfection as an ongoing process. Sometimes being a better person requires owning up to past mistakes and shortcomings. Enter the confessional autobiography. But not every philosophical autobiography is confessional, nor is self-improvement the obvious motivating factor in every case. Other motives for self-change include the desire or need to be truer or more honest with oneself, the aim of overcoming self-imposed limitations, resolving a feeling of disharmony or conflict between our inner and outer, private and public persona. It seems there must always be some kind of irritant or destabilizing condition – whether cognitive, emotional or both – that calls for self-change. Philosophical autobiographies report and evoke self-change as a completed transformation while describing life and thought before and after the process of self-change. Of course the old refrain, "It's never over till it's over," applies to the autobiographical project – until serious disability or death there's always more going on, and every summing up triggers new thoughts and feelings.

Now, by placing these paradigms of self-change side by side, like the pieces of Schopenhauer's quilt, we have an opportunity to discover both their differences and the threads of continuity that bind them together. In part, this is a useful exercise for identifying a powerful motive that seems to pervade the genre. In part, this is important intellectual challenge to the reader, and possibly the writer, of philosophical autobiographies.

REVIEWING THE PARADIGMS

A fully articulated paradigm of self-change is likely to have the following elements: a motivating factor (a need, fear, anxiety, physical change, bout of confusion, state of disequilibrium), perception of impasse, reluctance to change, a ray of hope or vision of fresh possibilities, a mechanism of transformation or a transformative power or an enabling capacity (coming, metaphorically, from within, without, above or below), awareness of differences between the before and after of self-change, awareness of the possible impact on others.

As a written narrative, autobiography entails a particular use of language to fashion a story for oneself and to communicate self-change to others. Self-change also entails certain notions about identity, memory, history, and a value assessment concerning whether a step has been taken forward or backward. Keeping these elements in mind, we survey our dramatis personae.

Think of Augustine and his mother, Monica, gazing into an interior courtyard. This is one of the extremely rare depictions of parallel self-transformation. Though we do not have Monica's version of the experience, we do have Augustine's claim that they communed silently with their God and with one another. Here, for Augustine, the Platonic tradition of philosophical contemplation of things eternal, invisible and immutable turns into the Christian seeker's ecstatic experience of divine love – his Sophia of wisdom becoming the Virgin Mary of redemption. For Monica, whose convictions of faith and life of piety already bespeak a conversion experience earlier in her life, experience of the noumenal only confirms her faith and completes her earthly journey.

Augustine portrays himself as a questing soul who longs for some bed-rock of truth that he has not found even though he has achieved many of the benchmarks of worldly accomplishment for someone of his social class. Something (besides his mother) nags at his mind that a better life must be possible. He suspects that what would satisfy him is a form of cosmic intelligibility that is unitive rather than fragmentary or dualistic. A unitive system of principles would bring harmony and tranquility to the knower and would produce an experience of consonance in which oneness with the universe would also be oneness with the self. He does not find a way to complete this contemplative journey, though his study of the Neo-Platonist philosophers takes him a long way toward that goal. Somehow the limited powers of one's mind do not seem adequate to completing the task.

It's not that he isn't bright enough to grasp both the logical analysis and the contemplative vision of the Platonic school. It's that he has to change not only his thought process but also his way of life if he wants to reach the state of being to which his condition of restlessness seems to urge him. The more he learns about his seeking mind, the more daunting his task becomes. He deeply admires some of the Catholic Christians he knows because they exhibit a kind of serenity while they participate in a loving community. He recognizes that a similar unitive quality underlies Christian theology, with its basis in monotheism, as well as the metaphysics he finds in Neo-Platonism. But he understands that unlike the philosopher's quest, which is a highly intellectual one, the quest of the Catholic Christian is different because it requires not the victory of the mind in discovering immutable truths but the mind's surrender in acknowledging the limits of its powers.

For Augustine, self-change must come as a gift from a power greater than yet internal to oneself. And why internal? Because, as Augustine discovered, God is in no place or space, though we can find Him through the portal of our minds and in the palace of memory, which are not physically contained by our bodies or the temporal, finite world. In the scene at Ostia, Augustine metaphorically ingests the God through the Eucharist, which parallels the tasting of Manna as the food given to the Hebrews in the desert, which, in turn, takes him full circle to the infant suckling at its mother's breast.

He, the seeker, had to do his part, endure his suffering, make a colossal effort. Otherwise, there could be no surrender worthy of the name. A single surrender is not enough for leading a life of surrender through self-discipline and self-denial. Augustine, if we can believe him, would have been perfectly happy to lead the life of a simple contemplative monk, maybe writing a few treatises on the side. Instead, he had the role of bishop foisted on him and became a figure of authority responsible for the survival of the Catholic Church in North Africa.

Augustine's conversion in the garden narrative remains an enduring inspiration for the religious seeker, particularly in the West. His narrative of the "vision at Ostia" marks the shift from the Greek religious mystery tradition, which Plato transformed into philosophical contemplation of timeless Ideas, to the Christian internalization of the God within.

The desire to gain a foothold in the eternal while still dwelling in the temporal, to be touched by the grace of God, to conform one's life to a spiritual discipline (prayer, chastity, contemplation), these and other attributes of commitment to a new life of the soul have beckoned thousands if not millions – countless numbers of whom have read (and taken up pen to emulate) Augustine's *Confessions*. We note, for example, T. S. Eliot's quasi-autobiographical *Four Quartets*. Eliot's lyrical meditation on the threefold character of time is thoroughly infused with Augustinian emotion and theology, as Eliot seeks "the still point of the turning world."

Almost 1400 years after Augustine invited them to witness his conversion in a garden and his epiphany in an interior courtyard, readers were beckoned to join Jean-Jacques Rousseau on a sultry summer day's trek along a woodland path from Paris to Vincennes. In his *Confessions* Rousseau tells how he stopped to rest under a tree in order to jot down notes for an essay contest he felt sure he would win. That, says Rousseau, was the life-changing moment that transformed a little-known itinerant music teacher into a heralded cultural critic and social provocateur.

Rousseau's self-characterization as the rural "solitary walker" points toward the ideal with which he imbued nature and the natural person. Rousseau's social critique, beginning with The First Discourse, launches simultaneously a therapeutic self-analysis that is eventually expressed in several autobiographical writings.

One can think of countless accounts by naturalists of their solitary hikes into the natural world where they could commune with nature and escape from the distractions of society. Though there is little evidence that H.D. Thoreau read Rousseau, the American self-described "moss-trooper" was influenced by the Romantic Movement's association of nature with innocence and authenticity, in part a legacy of Rousseau's writing.

Since Rousseau rejects the dogma of original sin, he finds he does not need an intermediary to enable him to recover his original and natural innocence, he only needs the conviction of sincerity and the courage to tell the truth or at least a close, though sometimes fabled version, of the truth. Rousseau muses that had he been raised in some idyllic rural village free of social pretenses, false ideals and distorted emotions about love and honor, he would never have had to write any of his troublesome books. Instead he might have conducted himself as a botanist, finding and classifying the wonders of nature as he led a simple life among people who spoke the truth and accepted differences of beliefs, the main thing being that they were all free citizens. Alas, this is not the life into which he was thrown by the accidents of parentage, childbirth, social class or historical epoch. When Rousseau gets the inspiration to write his contrarian essay on how the arts and sciences have failed to improve the moral character of his fellow citizens, his status as a minor celebrity – as a contributor to the new encyclopedia and as a somewhat successful opera composer – catapults him into fame with consequent public scrutiny and the envy of those who were supposed to be his friends.

Though Rousseau would write a whole book on the ideal education of a young person (*Emile*) that would produce an unaffected, unpretentious, plain-speaking, harmonious whole person, his own condition was too far-gone. Only his love of botanizing and habit of solitary trekking quieted his heart and tamed his obsession with denouncing his enemies and trying to convince his readers of the authenticity and sincerity of his intentions.

If both Augustine and in his secular way, Rousseau, present their lives as guided by a force of destiny, J.S. Mill and Harriet Taylor are of an entirely different mindset. For them, neither the idea of God nor nature offers a sacrosanct script that teaches true morality. Instead it is by possessing the dignity bestowed on one through free participation in society, ideally via the democratic process, that self-identity and self-worth are achieved. And that goes equally for men and women.

Mill's struggle with self-becoming was caused by a mechanical and emotion-deprived form of upbringing and education imposed upon him by his father, James Mill. But he admires and respects his father and is grateful to James Mill for the gift of a remarkable education that has given him many advantages. Consequently, John Stuart has to reeducate himself in cultivating the life of feeling which takes him away from the strict Utili-tarian outlook of his youth and more toward the burgeoning Romantic movement of his contemporaries, the English Lake Poets. This, in turn, prepares him to find love and intellectual friendship with Harriet Taylor. Mrs. Taylor is already of a sufficiently independent temperament to defy Victorian era social mores in choosing to make public her close bond with John Stuart. Together they form an intellectual and political activist partnership that anticipates Sartre and de Beauvoir.

Mill, wrestling with how to account for self-change, is haunted by his commitment to a deterministic view of nature and history. A metaphorical incubus sits on his chest. But he throws off the nightmarish creature with his insight that every event has multiple causes and, therefore, as one who must choose among them, his role as interpreter and willful agent remains intact. Clearly, for Mill the reading of the right book at the right time can produce profound self-change. That the book he "accidentally" chose was a memoir and an account of someone else's family situation, which he compares to his own, reveals Mill's capacity for self-transformation.

Like Rousseau, Mill connects his personal unhappiness with societal ills. In diagnosing the causes of his depression, he discovers serious flaws in English family life. He has to recover the life of feeling in himself while advocating for the importance of poetry in the education of youth.

Having a formidable father with an intensely active mind is a commonality between the Englishman, Mill, and the Dane, Kierkegaard. Like Mill, Kierkegaard went for walks with his father during which they would hold serious conversations. Kierkegaard's descriptions of taking walks as a child with his melancholic father inside their Nytorv home beside the Copenhagen city hall prepare us for the bounty and diversity of his literary works – excursions through what Kierkegaard called "the stages on life's way." Unlike Augustine, Rousseau and Mill, Kierkegaard has both a full-scale theory of individual development and of self-change. He took this into account in developing the strategy of his authorship as he sought to address his reader in both terms and tones that would invite receptivity. Ironically, by his own admission or claim he is an exception to his own theory.

Kierkegaard insists that from the early stages of his authorship, after he had written his dissertation on Socratic irony and as he set out to write *Either/Or*, he was already fully committed to Christianity, was already in what he described as the religious stage of life. At the age of twenty-three, Kierkegaard vows to pursue "what the deity really wants me to do." He will seek to embrace his own destiny: "To find a truth which is truth for me." Perhaps he had quickly and precociously passed through the earlier stages since they were not tied to chronological age.

Passages from his personal journals suggest that Kierkegaard regarded his vocational role as running contrary to the age in which he lived. Instead of trying to make Christianity easier to understand and practice, he would make it more difficult – which is to say, more personal, more intense, and more experiential. In this sense, to "choose oneself," a frequent exhortation from Judge Wilhelm in *Either/Or*, Volume II, is to choose one's path. But to choose one's path is no easy matter, rather it is fraught with risk, since one does not have any certainty of the outcome and one has to be prepared to pay the price of the leap of faith. Not that it calls for a life of irrationality but it may require renouncing the comforts and conventions of middle-class life and accepting the tensions bound up in one's own singularity.

Despair, the presentiment of hopelessness, is the primary symptom and impetus of the restless, because divided, self. Hopelessness stems from knowing that you cannot reconcile the simultaneous demands of the empirical, temporal life with those of your psycho-spiritual calling. You could spend your life evading despair rather than accepting it as the opening onto the path of the Christian life. Kierkegaard made it his vocation to point the individual back toward that "narrow way."

Despite Kierkegaard's pronouncement of the "indescribable bliss" that he found in serving God through the work of his authorship, expressions of joy are rare in Kierkegaard's philosophical writings; rather irony is the predominant tone. But in his religious discourses, written under his own name, we find the balm of reconciliation in the conviction that one has been found deserving of God's love. Kierkegaard's explicit public declaration of the strategy of his authorship did not deprive it of its effectiveness as a form of indirect communication. Perhaps he could have done without the use of pseudonyms in the first place. In *The Point of View for My Work as an Author* Kierkegaard turns the terrible burden of guilt, sadness and melancholy imposed on him by his father into a providential calling. This fits the famous Kierkegaardian theme of the wounded warrior who becomes the Knight of Faith.

Like Kierkegaard, Nietzsche recognizes duality and the challenges of uniting opposites as the underlying impetus to self-change. Unlike Kierkegaard, Nietzsche finds the authentic expression of conflicting opposites among the pre-Christian Greeks, in whom the Apollonian (characterized by restraint, form, beauty and illusion) and Dionysian (characterized by the chaotic, ecstatic and intoxicated) temperaments are manifested in rites, rituals and especially the dramas of the tragedians.

Foreshadowing the work of Freud and Jung, on whom he exerted considerable influence, Nietzsche recognized the power of the unconscious as the individual's most direct connection to the organic force of nature, one which would produce "the urge to unity" while maintaining the utmost tension of the contradictions inherent in the human condition. This effort to embrace the whole self in the union of opposites can only be accomplished (if at all) by the most extraordinary of individuals, the self-overcoming Superman. Nietzsche's paradigm of self-attainment is anti-Christian as it is anti-metaphysical. The only individual he can identify who comes close to resembling the ideal of the paradigm is the poet and dramatist Goethe.

However ephemeral Nietzsche's fully realized god-like being was, his descriptions of the creatively suffering, value-making, charismatic, noble warrior, the Übermensch, had a profound influence on how, in the early part of the 20th century, untold numbers of young people regarded their potential, whether as artists, composers or captains of industry.

A historically subsequent "discovery" of Nietzsche's paradigm came in the 1960s in the United States and Europe with the rise of the counter-culture. Nietzsche's books became enormously popular with a new younger generation. It would not be excessively speculative to see popular music such as rock and roll turning into the frenzied tempo of a whole range of musical groups who played at wildly expressive dance events, in which erotic energies were combined with light shows to create a modern-day version of the Bacchanalian ritual. Only now, instead of a mystical rite, the liturgical context was multiform, often influenced by psychotropic drugs and the importation of various forms of Eastern religion.

And one could point to any number of representative figures such as Harvard professors Richard Alpert and Timothy Leary who, coming from a traditional Apollonian background and middle-class respectability, began to experiment with the psychotropic drug, LSD, and entered the Dionysian realm, utterly changing their lives. For example, Alpert, after his spiritual awakening, became the noted guru, lecturer and author known as Baba Ram Dass (Servant of God).

Our café habitués, Sartre and Simone de Beauvoir would completely reject the Augustinian and Kierkegaardian ideas of providence or destiny, as they would reject the very idea of the inner life. To them, *la vie intérieure* was just so much escapism. Following Nietzsche, they insisted on the radical freedom to chart one's own path. They did recognize that conditions of poverty, social inequality, colonial domination, gender and, later for de Beauvoir, old age, imposed restriction on one's freedom to choose one's own values and live by them. They were often involved in political activism to right these wrongs though they tended to remain independent anarchists rather than party ideologues. Their own effort at self-emancipation, as depicted in their autobiographical writings and philosophical social critiques, inspired an international generation of exis-tentialist-oriented youths.

We might think of the internationally widespread women's conscious-ness-raising groups of the 1970s as exemplifying the secular existentialist emphasis on using critical analysis to debunk cultural myths about gender, motherhood, romance, marriage, career roles and attitudes toward the female body. Where the law-like character of "nature" had for centuries served as the favored defense for preserving the status quo, the existentialist exposed "culture" as the socially constructed and, therefore, malleable force of conditioning. Enabling women to see that they had internalized certain fixed choices that had been imposed upon them was a first step in helping them become aware that there were viable alternative.

This kind of personal empowerment was crucial to consciousness-raising groups, since it helped participants move from a passive or victim role to that of a self-liberating actor. While de Beauvoir did not call for collective action, feminists such as Betty Freidan and adult life transition expert Gail Sheehy did organize groups to encourage women to break free of the "feminine mystique." Twenty years after *The Second Sex*, de Beauvoir applied the same type of analysis to the socially imposed stereotypes of old age, producing *The Coming of Age*. Following in the wake of de Beauvoir, linking women's liberation to the emerging "senior power" movement, Maggie Kuhn, founded the political activist organization, the Gray Panthers.

The term "choosing oneself" had, with Sartre and de Beauvoir, a somewhat different meaning than it had had with the religious Kierke-gaard, for whom it meant choosing despair as the recognized condition of unfreedom. For them it meant recognizing and owning up to what might have been a state of culturally and socially ingrained ignorance, a condition of passively assumed values, with subconscious avoidance of the fact that one's finite life constituted a being-toward-death.

A compelling example of the awakening of the individual as a self-choosing actor can be found in the important work of Paulo Freire. The Brazilian educator who, following principles of liberation theology (influenced by Sartre), designed a highly successful literacy campaign for the uneducated poor. Through introducing the malleability of language, Freire enabled his students not only to learn to read but to recognize that their situation was neither fated by social class nor destined by some divine plan (see his *Pedagogy of the Oppressed*).

A liberator of another sort of consciousness, Carl Jung retained memories of his childhood dream of the penis on the golden throne. Over a lifetime of investigation, he would come to realize how the dream functioned to unlock the mysteries and powers of the unconscious. He would make it his life's work to understand the role that the unconscious could and should play in the life of the conscious individual. Like Rousseau, Jung regarded the Western European Enlightenment emphasis on reason and, later, the materialistic and highly instrumental scientific attitude toward knowledge and control of the natural world, as a distorting one-sided investment that would instead lead to the degradation of the natural world and horrifying wars of death and destruction, the results of dehumanization.

Jung set out to become the healing physician of the soul. He would, like Nietzsche, identify the oppositional character of the human condition in terms of not only the conscious versus unconscious polarities, but the oppositional structure of the personality types (introvert versus extravert), the male and female archetypes (animus and anima), and ultimately the opposition between the ego or finite persona and the all-inclusive Self, the archetype of wholeness. Psychological growth would require coming to terms with these opposing powers, not through favoring the dominance of one over the other or through some kind of synthesis. Rather, through a union that might be symbolized of yin and yang, the cross (vertical and horizontal), the star of David (overlapping, upward and downward pointing triangles), and the Tantric couples.

Jung would insist that unconscious symbols must complement the domain of conscious concepts if the whole of the human experience was to be unified. Consequently, his work in comparative mythology, where he traced the archetypes of the collective unconscious through the ancient history of the world, led to widespread fascination with mythology as a powerful human resource with just as much value as scientific reason.

While Jung's autobiography includes a brief account of marital tensions in the home of his childhood, Martin Buber opens his personal narrative by evoking a young boy's feeling of maternal loss. Buber's description of the scene from the interior courtyard of his grandparents' country estate is reminiscent of Augustine's depiction of him and his mother, Monica, sixteen hundred years earlier, looking down into the courtyard of the villa at Ostia. Buber's initiation into his quest to discover the primacy of the relational I-Thou attitude is triggered by a sense of absence – his mother's desertion of father and son and his awakening realization that she is gone forever. Buber is four years old when he experienced this primal separation whereas Augustine was thirty-three when he united with his mother in a shared glimpse of the eternal life. Soon thereafter, Monica dies and Augustine, memorializing her in the *Confessions*, becomes the witness to her life. Buber's mother remains a shadow, a missing person, the vanishing Thou. His search for the absent Other takes him into the tight-knit communities of the Hasidim gathered around their rabbinic leader where he hears stories about the Sabbath bride, the female aspect of the divine, a presence that brings the sacred into the temporal.

Buber channels his quest into the philosophical problem of inter-subjectivity, a legacy of his secular education, the insights from which he refocuses on the way the divine becomes present in Biblical stories. These, in turn, lead him to the safe haven of the Jewish people, Israel. But again, in the Holy Land becoming a quasi-secular state, he must confront the political dilemma of the Palestinian as Other.

Buber's primary words, I-Thou and I-It, are not oppositional categories. Buber points out that there are appropriate times for perceiving and dealing with things as useful objects or instrumental realities. So the binary pairs would seem to be complementary except when they come into conflict – as when a person is treated inappropriately as a thing to be manipulated, not as an autonomous Thou. And the sacred and profane, in Buber's formulation, are also not mutually exclusive domains, but rather, given a certain perspective, the sacred can be discovered in the ordinariness of everyday experience (what Buber calls "hallowing"). If anything, Buber's insistence on the underived reality of the intersubjective and the primacy of the relational, experienced as "the between," would seem to run counter to my hypothesis that all the paradigms of self-change reveal the encounter with and tension of opposites.

Perhaps it is in the realm of presence and absence, dialogue and mono-logue, isolation and community that we find polarity in Buber's work. Surely, Buber's life was transformed by absence but he found his way to presence through demonstration of the living faith of his coreligionist in the Hasidic communities. However, when the Holocaust befell the Jewish people, Buber's confidence in God's mutuality and ongoing dialogue with human beings took a serious blow. And though he tried to sustain this faith, despite having to acknowledge God's "hiddenness" or silence in the presence of historically unprecedented evil, Buber's writing on this subject (see "The Dialogue between Heaven and Earth" in *On Judaism* (1972), pp. 214–225) remains unconvincing.

Gandhi's is a life story told from within the literal and metaphorical framework of incarceration. In one sense, this was the unfortunate condi-tion of punishment wrought by the British colonizers, but in another sense a fortunate opportunity for Gandhi. He needed some time to recover from physical and mental exhaustion, to enjoy a reprieve from throngs of followers, to devote himself to study, meditation and prayer, and to rethink the premises of his campaign of non-violent civil disobedience that had lately gone awry.

In his prison-written autobiography, Gandhi reports several life-changing experiences, each echoing themes of humiliation and shame from injustices suffered or, especially toward his wife and children, rendered. Gandhi describes a life of vows and renunciations as he strives to lead a morally pure life. Key Hindu principles of non-violence, truth-seeking, sexual abstinence, purification through fasting, and devotional prayer shape his demeanor and sustain his remarkable sense of humility coupled with dignity.

Gandhi's adherence to and unshakable trust in an inner voice of conscience enables him to overcome moments of self-doubt, temporary setbacks in the campaign to free India from the British crown, and the criticism and judgment of numerous others, both well-meaning friends and arch foes.

OVERCOMING OPPOSITES, EMBRACING CONTRARIES

A thread of continuity wends its way through the otherwise diverse paradigms of self-change that our philosophical autobiographers exhibit. What they have in common is a confrontation with oppositional powers and forces. In every instance, the scenes of self-change express the sufferings of the philosopher who has heretofore sustained the tension of contrary impulses or the dissociation of the inner and outer person or simply despaired over the chasm between how one sees oneself and how one would like to be. In other words, they cannot, for the moment, see how to move forward. Some fresh power, divine messenger, or unanticipated catalytic agent must enter the picture to liberate the action.

The key scenes can be thought of as "compositions of place," a form of spiritual exercise recommended by Saint Ignatius Loyola (founder of the Order of Jesuits). Ignatius instructed his followers as part of their daily devotions to picture scenes from Scripture in order to intensify their prayers and meditations. Analogously, the philosophical autobiographer's use of the symbolic scene helps to convey an experience that might, in reality, have occurred more gradually, as if it were a stunningly vivid moment. Ideas and concepts whose deeper meanings are difficult to communicate abstractly, come to life in the hands of our autobiographers.

The greatest contraries Augustine faces are those of the temporal and eternal. The sighs, tears and pleadings that precede the two garden epiphanies enable him to regard his earlier life as an inner parable leading to salvation with the mundane events of earthly life taking on symbolic meanings that point toward the self-transformation that the human-divine God of Christianity makes possible. Augustine has searched for a radically different framework within which to understand and lead his life. He experiences a monumental gap between his outwardly successful life and the turmoil he finds within himself. Relinquishing his secular earthly life, he gains not just a more tranquil existence but is like a smitten lover, awash in adoring emotion and gratitude. And this feeling of abundance carries over from Book IX, the last chapter of the autobiographical portion of *The Confessions*, to the following four chapters that serve as meditative commentaries on memory, time and creation.

Autobiographical works by other religious thinkers such as Kierkegaard, Buber and Gandhi, we might speculate, are likely to exhibit a similar motif to that of Augustine. Kierkegaard's entire authorship is focused on the duality of the self as both finite and infinite – a mirror of the paradox of the god-man, Jesus. Kierkegaard's personal travails, only alluded to in *The Point of View* (but sending the reader to his eventually published journals and diaries for further elaboration) concerned the impossibility of marriage to his beloved Regina, the yoke of inherited paternal melancholy from which he could never release himself, his publically misunderstood intentions as a writer and thinker, and his tortuous isolation due to his secretive inner life. Only by placing his powerful imagination, literary skills and philosophical gifts at the service of Providence – that is, at the service of his God – could Kierkegaard surmount these impasses.

But Kierkegaard, unlike Augustine, is not so optimistic about the benefits of the life of celibate contemplation. He entices his reader to follow him through such exercises as comparing Socrates and Christ (in the *Philosophical Fragments*) only to sever the link between Greek reflection and Christian redemption. He is wary of the uses of doctrine as a path to salvation. Ultimately, his own life is testimony to singularity, not community; to faith as supra-rational, incompatible with the Platonic world of rational ideas. So while Augustine's sighs, tears, renunciations and pleadings paid off because God answered him in the voice of a child, Kierkegaard's leaves the reader much less certain that such striving will necessarily culminate in a garden song. Indeed, insists the Kierkegaard who dwells in "fear and trembling," we must continually assume that it might not.

Buber, too, as reported in his autobiography, has his youthful struggle with the finite and the infinite. And only by discovering, via Kant, that time is a function of the workings of human consciousness does he regain peace of mind. From Kant he learns that the phenomenal order perceivable by the mind remains a gateway to the noumenal (Kant's thing-in-itself) realm though the latter can only be taken on faith and not through the evidence of the rational mind. Still, this formulation of temporality opens the way for Buber to see that the intimacy and mutuality of an I-Thou relationship, which is concrete and self-altering, attunes each member of the dyadic relationship to an awareness of an added dimension or quality that conjoins them despite their differences, conflicts or distrust. As a member of the Jewish people, Buber would have ample reason to include an expression of suffering in his formulation of the intersubjective reality but he does not make that explicit. Certainly, personal vulnerability is a required risk of openness to the other.

There is plenty of suffering in Gandhi's story. Some of it is physical, as Gandhi describes his homeopathic and folk medicine methods for treating his own serious illnesses and those of his wife and children. He recounts the dreadful cholera epidemic that took a heavy toll on the Indian population in South Africa. Gandhi also saw a great deal of physical suffering when he led an ambulance corps for the British during the Boer War.

Mainly, though, he focuses attention on another type of pain, such as the dehumanizing effects of colonization on both the subjected population and on the moral character of the colonizers. Dedicating his life to eradicating this injustice, Gandhi is faced by the apparent sharp, if not contradictory, alternative between leading the life of a political reformer (life in the finite sphere) with pursuing the spiritual quest for inner enlightenment (the infinite realm). Gandhi's life-changing encounters with injustice – experienced as humiliation, powerlessness, discrimination, physical abuse and imprisonment – rather than diminishing him, strengthen his sense of dignity and his conviction that overcoming social injustice and overcoming the personal demands of the ego are interrelated and can be pursued concurrently. A whole country, Gandhi believed, could express outwardly what its spiritual aspiration sought to nurture inwardly.

Gandhi's inclination to universalize tenets of Hinduism, Christianity and other religions, and to see them as inherent qualities of common humanity, reminds us of Kierkegaard's attempt to take the life and teachings of Jesus away from the official state Lutheran church and place them in the hands and hearts of ordinary individuals and Buber's attempt to make all people village Hasids regardless of their religion. Unlike Gandhi, Kierkegaard could not free himself from subscribing to the exclusivity of the Christian message and the vital and unique role of its redeemer, while Buber, more a product of modernity and infinitely more an advocate for authentic community life, saw no limitations to Judaism understood in terms of universal life-affirming values.

Having clustered, in order to compare, our four explicitly religious autobiographers, we now turn to Nietzsche, who attempted to eviscerate any form of religious piety, and Jung who strove to embrace the union of contraries but took religion, at its deepest, as exemplifying openness to the unruly energies of the unconscious.

The Apollonian-Dionysian dichotomy is one version of Nietzsche's articulation of the oppositional character of human experience. And since Nietzsche insists that all philosophy is but thinly veiled autobiography ("a confession on the part of its author"), it would not be a great leap of interpretation to see Nietzsche's owns life as the struggle to hold opposites together and to draw inspiration and insight from the tension of these contrary forces. After all, he was a university-trained scholar equipped with extensive knowledge of the history of civilizations both West and East, a fine analytical mind conversant with classical as well as modern languages. He was also, like Mill, an improvisational pianist, an admirer of opera, and something of a European traveler. He knew how to conduct himself in polite society and had a reputation as a witty and engaging conversationalist. There we have Nietzsche the Apollonian.

Then there is Nietzsche the would-be Dionysian. On this side we have the artist, the prophet, the wanderer, the man who wills to celebrate chaos, the man dancing naked in his boardinghouse room, the author of some of the strangest and most eccentric books in the history of both literature and philosophy, a person who places himself one step above Jesus, Socrates, and the God of monotheism but on the same mountain top level as Goethe and Heraclitus.

True, Nietzsche did not participate in anything more Bacchanalian than attending Wagnerian operas and visiting a prostitute, nor does he seem to have torn live animals apart with his teeth during a frenzied mystical rite celebrating the Eleusinian mysteries. Perhaps he would have been better off if he had done these things. Instead, Nietzsche's heroic venture was to open himself to the vision of the Dionysian and to welcome the frightening and exhilarating powers of the irrational side of the human experience, the side closest to the natural world. This dark side is not perceived in aesthetic and instrumental terms, but as an overshadowing presence that threatens human consciousness.

Nietzsche does not offer us a program for self-development or self-change, though his message to embrace a life of extreme creative tension does call up the rebellious inner demon that is also part of who we are. Whether we can withstand the powerful blast of uncivilized nature and hold it in creative tension with its civilized opposite, is uncertain and requires an act of daring that is probably irreversible. Nietzsche never meant this as a recommendation for the masses, but rather for a tiny elite that would be prepared to take on the life of the Overman. You have to wonder what he would have thought if he could see paperback editions of his work sitting on bookshelves in shopping center mega-size bookstores or being downloaded onto e-readers off the internet.

Jung's version of the Nietzschean tension of opposites can be summed up by his famous statement: "Too much of the animal distorts the civilized man, too much civilization makes sick animals." Jung approaches the Nietzschean dichotomy as a diagnosing physician of the psyche. He recognizes the profound truths that Nietzsche has uncovered which, to Jung, is the story of the play of the unconscious in the history of human evolution. Like Nietzsche, Jung believes the power of the unconscious has been repressed by a life-denying or stultifying imbalance that is the result of overemphasis on rationality and secular modernity understood as optimistic commitment to the uses of scientific knowledge and bureaucratic organization as the acme of civilized life. Deny or repress the unconscious, argued Jung, and you wind up with compensation – a pressure cooker of violent energies that clamor for release. The "sick animal" would, according to Jung who foresaw it in a dream, break out of its cage and rage across the countryside reeking death and destruction on a scale never seen before – World War I.

Jung multiplied the number of opposites by finding them at all levels of the psyche: as personality types (introvert vs. extravert), shadow versus ego, archetypes of male and female unconscious energies, anima and animus, and finally the archetype of the whole self which is the union of conscious and unconscious powers. Is this a quest that the average person can undertake? Is it a prescription for mankind to heal a soul starved by too much rationality and too little of the beast?

Jung, in his midlife period of deciding to venture into the unconscious and to experiment with the extent to which he could reach the bottom of the human mind – i.e. the depths of the unconscious psyche, practiced what he called "active imagination." He would sit in his study in the evening, having led an otherwise routine family and work life during the day, and would mentally summon up whatever figures might come to him, often related to creatures from world mythology and from Christian and Eastern religious sources. He would then engage in dialogue with these mentors, guides, seers and spiritual seducers (who night lure him into dangerous waters).

Jung would record these apparitions in what he called the "black books," notebooks with black covers that served him as journals. He then transferred these imagistic encounters into a large-format portfolio book in which he used Gothic script and his considerable calligraphic skills to record his explorations, illustrating some of the scenes of his encounters by painting symbolic scenes and mandalas or other spiritual representations. This he called the "Red Book." It was made public some seventy years after its completion.

Today, we might consider Jung's approach a forerunner to art therapy, an image-making process, usually guided by an art therapist, used to overcome resistances to subconscious or unconscious content. Jung used other forms of externalizing his inward process such as stone-carving, making miniature stone villages, wood carving and so on. In other words, to give form to embracing the oppositional tensions of the psyche, Jung hit upon the idea of an artistic externalization.

At its most abstract, the oppositional in Sartre and de Beauvoir is the pair of terms taken from ancient ontological writing, being and nothing. The non-theistic French existential philosophers inherited this dyad from Hegel who based his study of logic on the primary triad, being-nothing-becoming. Hegel's abstract treatise on *The Science of Logic* (1812-1816), which like Kant's efforts in the *Critique of Pure Reason*, aims to elaborate the fundamental non-empirical concepts or categories that make thinking possible, is foreshadowed in his *Phenomenology of Mind*, where Hegel describes the workings of consciousness that precede and underlie thinking.

Sartre writes his own treatise on *Being and Nothingness* to demonstrate that the human condition is one of inhabiting the third position of the conceptual triad, becoming. In other words we are creatures of change who are not yet what we will be and are, at every moment, no longer what we were.

The crucial twist is that we have the reflective ability to realize our ontological condition and to discover ourselves as agents of self-change. As such, we can neither cling to the past nor dwell in some wishful state about the future. To borrow a term from Heidegger, we are perpetually in a state of "thrownness," as futurally-oriented consciousnesses who, at every moment, cannot help but to define ourselves by what we choose to do and not do. Everything then boils down to making choices and acting upon them. Wanting to be the author of the world's meanings was the way de Beauvoir described this orientation in her *Ethics of Ambiguity* (1947).

Simone de Beauvoir's important contribution to the Sartrean picture of the way becoming integrates being and nothing within it is her notion that consciousness is fundamentally "ambiguous" since becoming is an open stance toward life, values, meanings and choices. Attempts to put closure on becoming by making claims to possess closed ethical systems or knowledge of absolutes constitute denials of becoming, ones that lead to static and inflexible ideologies, totalitarian regimes of government or church, and modes of self-repression and self-deception. As children, we come into a world of ready-made values and established authorities, which generally we are taught to respect and accept. But with the dawning of self-consciousness comes our awareness of the multiple possibilities of meanings, values and choices and of our need to make choices for ourselves.

Simone de Beauvoir is more cognizant than Sartre that many conditions may prevail against our self-conscious awareness that we have choices. Among these are fears of daring to think for ourselves, the mind-controlling powers of a tyrannical regime, and repressive cultural messages about gender and age expectations. However, even under dire circumstances, freedom erupts into consciousness in the guise of anxiety. We experience angst because we feel the tension between the given of social reality and the possibility of the negation of the given, as when we doubt, question, disobey, or in other ways suspend our obedience to authority and the authorized. Suspension of allegiance to imposed rules, values and meanings leads to the realization of responsibility, though this may appear as what Sartre calls "dreadful freedom." Can we really accept responsibility for inventing the world and all that is both right and wrong within it?

John Stuart Mill did attempt to take such responsibility by making the happiness of mankind his goal in life and his own happiness a byproduct of his efforts. As an empiricist, Mill would have chuckled over terms like being and nothingness or transcendental categories of thought. He would have been far less likely to engage in an analysis of oppositional terms, though his own life is testimony to embracing contraries. Mill discovered that he was himself a counter-example to what turned out to be a one-sided system of education that aimed to cultivate only the analytic skills of a child's mind to the detriment of imagination and feeling.

But Mill did not regard the cognitive and the affective as opposing capacities, but rather as complementary. They only seemed opposing because the orientation in which his father, James Mill, based his pedagogy was hostile to the unruly qualities of emotion, feeling and fancy that, he believed, led the majority of people into superstition, prejudice and an incapacity for independent thinking. From a Sartrean point of view, John Stuart Mill might have interpreted his depression as angst stemming from rebellious thoughts that sought to overthrow a rigid system of imposed meanings. However, John Stuart did not have the temperament of a Jean-Paul; instead he had a real-life father who cared a great deal about how John Stuart would turn out, while Jean-Paul had no father, only a compliant mother and a magisterial grandfather.

Nevertheless, John Stuart managed to figure out a way to liberate himself by going to the works of the English Romantic Lake Poets. And then he found Mrs. Taylor, a figure that might be considered Mill's archetype of the anima (i.e., the female aspect of the psyche).

The powerful opposites in Mill's thinking would have to be freedom and necessity, another classical pair of dichotomous terms. Mill would never have "fallen back" on Augustine's free-will-granting God or Kierkegaard's "providence," or the Existentialists' self-becoming, because he espoused a logical commitment to a materialist theory of causality. But he had, somehow, to get the terrible weight of the incubus of necessity off of his chest in order to breathe new life into himself and, being Mill, he had to do that by means of analysis.

He might have taken a tip from de Beauvoir in determining that causality always included an element of ambiguity. Human consciousness can never discover every possible factor of cause behind any given state of results or eventfulness. And even if all possible antecedent causes could be discovered, there would be no ironclad way to determine which one was the single effective cause or even to rule out that there might not be multiple causes. Therefore, a willful agent must make hypothetical formulations, which entails ascribing meanings. A person does this within the orbit of his or her own life experiences, realized Mill, breaking open the closed system of his logic of the social sciences.

In a similar way, Mrs. Mill helped her husband John to see that unexamined social conditioning, not biological determinism, were holding back women's development. With his powerfully analytical mind and her empirical knowledge of the restrictive conditions imposed upon her sex, this dynamic Utilitarian duo set out to advocate for women's enfranchisement. The Mills challenged arguments based on principles of necessity derived from absolutist systems. They demanded new freedoms, which in turn helped men and women to create new lives.

Another philosopher seeking personal and social liberation, Rousseau is pulled in two opposing directions. He wants to be at one with nature – as transparent as flowing water – yet he also seeks to be self-sufficient, utilizing his own powers to redeem himself. While Rousseau sought to live in the immediacy and simplicity of the natural world, he devoted considerable time and effort to revisiting and reliving the past in order to free himself from its ensnaring complexity. Rousseau wrote in his *Emile*: "I would rather be a man of paradoxes than a man of prejudices." In this he succeeded.

Rousseau's discourses are filled with contrast between simplicity and complexity. Examples abound: the simplicity of nature and the complexity of society, the simplicity of the rustic life and the complexity of the aristocratic court and urbanity, the simplicity of sincerity and the complexity of mannered eloquence and elocution. His paradoxicality has baffled readers who find in him a bounty of apparent contradictions – e.g. the man of highly cultured refinement who decries the debilitating effects of the arts and sciences on human development, the thinker who uses subtle analysis and argument to exhort his readers to abandon cultural sophistication to recapture a state of lost naturalness, and so on.

While we are tempted to see Rousseau pointing us in one direction – to the simplicity of nature – he is more profoundly aiming to embrace the contraries of the natural and the social, rural and urban, plain or rustic and the complex and refined. Moreover, it is not just in his philosophical discourses that Rousseau embodies the paradoxical conjunction of opposites, but also in his well-received and frequently performed short opera, *Le Devin du Village*, the Village Soothsayer. In that work, as musicologist Edward Green points out:

> *The story praises artlessness, yet also implies the value,*
> *even perhaps the necessity, of 'urban smarts.' The opera is*
> *celebratory but asserts throughout the emotion of regret.*
> *The setting is entirely rural, yet its language is redolent of*
> *the court.*

So even in this operatic rustic love story of shepherd and shepherdess, Rousseau entertains simplicity and complexity through an aesthetic union of opposites.

In the pivotal scene on the road to Vincennes, Rousseau celebrates the moment in which inspiration divulged the full text of what later became the First Discourse, the award-winning essay that completely changed his life. Yet he claims to regret this because of the sorrows and disappointments that ensued from his newfound fame and notoriety. Even as he relates this tale, exhorting us to prefer the simple and solitary life close to nature, his means for telling us is anything but simple and natural.

MALKOVICHIAN TRANSFORMATIONS REVISITED

When viewing the movie Being John Malkovich, sophisticated film goers would understand that the title's namesake character is not identical to the off-screen actor. And when viewers see Malkovich in a well-furnished apartment talking on the phone or welcoming guests, they do not assume that this setting is his actual abode.

The "real" John Malkovich is inaccessible and unknowable except through our imagination. That is consistent with the film's theme – that imagining yourself in someone else's mind and body gives you a brief glimpse of timelessness. Why timelessness? Because for just that interval when you are "being John Malkovich" you have stepped out of yourself, transcended the limits of your own persona. You are, metaphorically speaking, suspended above the time and space of your life.

Yes, one might counter, but this is only in imagination, not reality. Besides, the time-space travelers in the film, after, so to speak, returning to themselves, do have memories of their experience being "inside" John Malkovich. So this sense of eternity, of being out of one's own lifetime, is an illusion, akin to literary fiction's goal, "the suspension of disbelief." When we come to the end of *Crime and Punishment*, *War and Peace*, or *Franny and Zooey*, our disbelief returns. These are just stories. We have to go on with our lives. Yet scenes and characters stay with us. We can no longer look at an axe in quite the same way, or hear the name Napoleon, or fail to associate the name Bloomberg with a certain cat. Good literature is like sexual initiation – "tasting it," we're never the same again.

Likewise, some philosophical autobiographies are infectious because, no matter how particular, distant, quirky, filled with foreign phrases and discomforting ways of looking at life and the world they are, there is something that touches us. Few of us have had conversations with our mothers like the one Augustine has with Monica, few have collapsed under a tree as a whole essay dumps into their heads, not many have had parents who believed their children were capable of learning Greek and Latin before the age of kindergarten, and few, even if they have been incarcerated, compiled a record of their struggle to right social wrongs or enumerate their vows as part of a spiritual quest while they sat in a cell. Still, we enjoy imagining what it would have been like to have these experiences. Moreover, they have the power to teach us – at first, while in a state of belief, then, back on the familiar ground of disbelief.

Each philosophical autobiographer brings us, perhaps more than once, to an impasse in his or her life. We feel the tension of their immobility. If, like John Stuart Mill, you have been raised to think a certain way – think and analyze rather than feel and imagine – and if this otherwise amazing educational background leaves you in a state of despair, because you feel like an empty shell, and if you cannot communicate your distress to anyone else for a whole host of reasons, then what do you do?

Well, we know how this story progresses (recovery), know the punch lines ("the flaw in my education was also a flaw in society"), the messengers (Marmontel, Coleridge, Wordsworth), and the consequences (falling in love with Harriet Taylor, writing *On Liberty*). Equally important, we know the ideas woven into the plot and how the narrative is as much about ideas as about the people who hold and sometimes have to let go of them.

The closing scene of *Being John Malkovich* is of a little girl gliding beneath the surface of a sun-dappled swimming pool in a country club setting. The viewer's perspective is from under water and the girl is swimming towards us. She is Maxine's daughter Emily, conceived through a convoluted tangle of portal travelers (Craig's wife Lotte Schwartz channeled through John Malkovich's body which impregnates Maxine).

Meanwhile, John Malkovich, having served his purpose as a surrogate, seems to have gone on to another place. Little Emily looks completely at home in this underwater medium. She will have quite a story to tell someday. No doubt, one that "raises all sorts of philosophical questions about the nature of the self, about the existence of the soul."

REFLECTIVE WRITING: WHICH PARADIGM FOR YOUR PHILOSOPHICAL AUTOBIOGRAPHY?

If you were to choose to model your own philosophical autobiography on one of the first-person narratives we have been considering, which one would it be? The broad range includes the spiritual quest and redemption motif (Augustine), the novelistic recreation of remembered events and people (Rousseau and de Beauvoir), the series of loosely connected personal vignettes (Buber), the phenomenological critique of the formation of one's childhood identity (Sartre), the intellectual authorship (or artistic career) account (Kierkegaard and Nietzsche), and so on.

In making this choice, you might also be choosing not only a style and tone but an organizational structure and a methodology for retrieving the past that is consistent with the author's philosophical outlook. Today's autobiographer has the advantage of building upon literary models that were genre-defining in their day.

Augustine's *Confessions*, with its theologically and metaphysically framed intimate details, was a new kind of quest narrative. Rousseau's *Confessions* reflects the 18th century novel and perhaps some aspects of the period's pornographic literature. De Beauvoir's use of the memoir already had numerous precedents, though her candor and critical self-scrutiny concerning mistaken assumptions in cultural and political matters adds a fresh nuance. Sartre's analysis of the formation of his literary self is also unprecedented. He uses this same methodology in biographical studies of other writers, such as the poet Baudelaire (1947), playwright Jean Genet (1952), and Flaubert (1971). Kierkegaard and

Nietzsche's accounts of their authorships, framed by information about fathers and upbringing, are also daring ventures into the genre of intellectual autobiography.

In addition to the conceptual framework, there is the issue of content – what aspects of a life the autobiographer seeks to focus on. Sartre writes only about the formation of his identity in childhood, de Beauvoir recounts episodes of her life from birth to just beyond age sixty. Some autobiographers examine certain periods of their lives, leaving other periods out of the picture. Buber portrays his relationship to a few family members and friends and to certain events and influences on the development of his philosophy. Jung, likewise, chooses to write about just a few influential people and mainly about episodes of his inner life. Gandhi shows us the inner (spiritual seeker) and outer (social activist) aspects of his life and how they are interrelated. Mill writes thematically about his unbalanced education and upbringing, making a private matter a public one. Other autobiographies we have been considering also exchange the microscope of self-scrutiny for the binoculars trained on the larger social landscape.

The philosophical autobiography could be thought of as the history of one's consciousness, including the development of one's values, sense of purpose and meaning, identity, beliefs and doubts, and major influences such as certain key people, events, theories, books, films, musical compositions, works of the visual arts, travel, and so on.

As a story-teller, bringing oneself to life as a literary character, the writer's task requires double reflectivity. Not only does one reflect on the remembered past but also observes and explores how it is possible to gain insight and knowledge through the autobiographical process. Many will find this kind of double reflectivity daunting, if not paralyzing. But for those of a reflective nature the philosophical autobiography will prove a fruitful enterprise.

RECOMMENDED READINGS

Philosophical works with an autobiographical inflection.

Carse, James P. (1998). *Breakfast at the Victory: The Mysticism of Ordinary Experience.* San Francisco, CA: Harper. A professor of religion connects the philosophy of (mainly) Sufism to daily experiences and situations.

Gaarder, Jostein (1994 translation from Norwegian). *Sophie's World.* New York: Farrar, Straus and Giroux. An informative and entertaining novelistic approach to the history of (mainly Western) philosophy.

Kaplan, Laura Duhan (1998). *Family Snapshots: A Philosopher Explores the Familiar.* Chicago: Open Court. A philosophy professor discovers the interplay of philosophical texts and family situations.

Magee, Bryan (1997). *Confessions of a Philosopher.* London: Weidenfeld and Nicholson. Follows the course of the Oxford and Yale-trained British philosopher (and BBC producer) exploring his encounters with philosophers and ideas ranging from the Pre-Socratics to Wittgenstein.

Manheimer, Ronald J. (1999). *A Map to the End of Time: Wayfarings with Friends and Philosophers.* New York: Norton. Philosophical themes and thinkers discovered in the midst of teaching philosophy to older adults.

HELPFUL HOW-TO BOOKS FOR REFLECTIVE WRITING

Cameron, Julia (1997). *Vein of Gold: A Journey to Your Creative Heart.* New York: Tarcher/Putnam.

Progroff, Ira (1992). *At A Journal Workshop: Writing to Access the Power of the Unconscious and Evoke Creative Ability.* New York: Putnam.

INDEX

www.ingramcontent.com/pod-product-compliance
Lightning Source LLC
Chambersburg PA
CBHW060025030426
42334CB00019B/2187